Dictionary of Painters

from A to Z

Stefano Zuffi

Dictionary of Painters
from A to Z

BARNES & NOBLE BOOKS
NEW YORK

Opposite
Albrecht Dürer
Self-Portrait, 1500
Alte Pinakothek, Munich

Graphic Design
Dario Tagliabue

Page Layout
Claudia Brambilla

Editorial Coordinator
Caterina Giavotto

Editing
Paola Noé

Technical Coordinator
Mario Farè

Quality Control
Giancarlo Berti

Translations
Elizabeth Clegg, Mark
Eaton, Christopher Huw
Evans, Felicity Lutz, Paul
Metcalfe for Scriptum,
Rome, Jay Hyams

© This edition published by Barnes & Noble
Publishing, Inc., by arrangement with
Mondadori Electa S.p.A., Milan
All rights reserved

2005 Barnes & Noble Books

M 10 9 8 7 6 5 4 3 2 1

ISBN 0-7607-7427-7

© 2004 by Mondadori Electa S.p.A., Milan

Pieter Aertsen

Amsterdam, c. 1507–1575

Although he was born and died
in Amsterdam, Aertsen worked mainly
in Antwerp, where he is documented
as having lived between 1535 and
1560, and where he set up a school,
from which his nephew, Joachim
Beuckelaer, emerged to follow in
Aertsen's footsteps. Aertsen did not
conform to the prevailing "Romanist"
taste, but introduced less formal topics
and such solid convincing realism that
he is considered a major forerunner
of Pieter Bruegel, and a pioneer in the
field of still life. Aertsen took his initial
inspiration from traditional subjects
in the Bible, such as *Ecce Homo*, Jesus'
meeting with the adulterous woman,
and Christ's visit to the house of
Martha and Mary. Gradually, the size
and compositional importance of the
narrative scene was reduced as it was
moved into the background and the
sidelines at the edges of the canvas.
Stalls richly laden with market
produce or well-equipped kitchens
began to take over the foreground.
The references to characters and
scenes from the Bible rapidly started
to disappear, but not to the extent
that they were no longer used for
similar narrative reasons in scenes
of daily life, as occurred in the studio
of the young Velázquez and even
in Vermeer's early work. Markets
and kitchens were on the verge of
becoming independent subjects
of the painting in their own right.
And so the foundations for the birth
of genre paintings were laid between
the end of the Renaissance and the
dawn of the Baroque period. They
enjoyed immediate success in royal
collections throughout Europe.
Around 1560 Aertsen decided
to return to Amsterdam, contributing
an element of solid realism
to the local school.

Pieter Aertsen
The Cook
1550
canvas, 28 × 33½ in.
(71 × 85 cm)
Palazzo Bianco, Genoa

Aertsen's compositions
were enormously
popular with collectors
throughout Europe.
In the specific case
of Genoese painting
(which was always
very open to new ideas
from Flanders), this work
is clearly the original on
which Bernardo Strozzi
based his painting
of the same name.

Pieter Aertsen
*Adoration of the
Shepherds*
fragment
c. 1560
oil on wood, 35½ × 23¾
in. (90 × 60 cm)
Historisch Museum,
Amsterdam

The tranquil head
of the ox and the partial
but expressive figures
of two shepherds are
all that remain
of the *Adoration
of the Shepherds*, a large
altarpiece painted by
Aertsen for the Nieuwe
Kerk in Amsterdam,
and destroyed in 1566
during a violent
iconoclastic campaign
launched by the most
outspoken radical
Calvinist preachers. It is,
however, no accident
that this expressive
fragment has been kept,
first in the town hall,
then handed over
to the Rijksmuseum,
and finally hung
in the recently restored
Historisch Museum
in Amsterdam. These
figures are so intense
and real that they truly
deserve to be described
as the precursors
of Dutch painting
in the "golden age."

Francesco Albani
Venus at Her Toilet
1618-1622
canvas, diam. 70 in.
(180 cm)
Galleria Borghese, Rome

This is one of a group
of four tondi
on mythological
subjects.

Francesco Albani

Bologna, 1578-1660

Albani studied in Bologna with the Mannerist Denijs Calvaert before joining the Carracci Academy where he was an enthusiastic pupil. Like so many other artists from Bologna, he moved to Rome to study classical art which he then applied with zeal to his own work. Albani's classicism can be seen in the altarpieces he painted after returning to Bologna. Among them is *The Baptism of Christ* now in the Bologna Pinacoteca Nazionale. His love of classical antiquity is still more evident in the cycles he painted on mythological subjects, a genre of painting he practically established. He used mythology in *Dance of the Amorini* or the allegorical tradition (elements, seasons) as the pretext to paint smiling idylls to which he added nymphs, goddesses, and happy little putti all set against luminous ideal landscapes. In this way he created an appetite for light-hearted, pleasant works which lasted throughout the seventeenth century. It did, however, tend at times to decline into insipidity. His favorite format for this type of composition was the tondo or oval.

7

Albrecht Altdorfer

Regensburg or Altdorf,
c. 1480-Regensburg, 1538

Son of the painter Ulrich Altdorfer, Albrecht trained under his father and acquired an almost miniaturistic interest in detail. He may have traveled to northern Italy in his youth and come into contact with Pacher. In 1505 he moved to Regensburg and soon became a public figure, employed in local administration. In 1509 he began to execute his most complex work, the altarpiece for the Austrian Abbey of St. Florian, completed in 1516 and later dismembered. Gradually his style developed from the minute miniaturistic detailing of his youth to a more monumental representation. A typical feature of his work is a great love for nature that led him to produce the first "pure" landscapes, freed from any iconographic pretext. Thus Altdorfer became the leading painter of the Danube School, the movement in the south of Germany that was characterized by an impassioned rendering of nature. In 1513 he was summoned to Innsbruck by Maximilian of Hapsburg, to become court painter. After acquiring considerable wealth and social status, Altdorfer entered politics, first becoming a city councillor and then city architect of Regensburg; in 1528 he was appointed burgomaster. During the 1520s, when religious, moral, and practical problems arose as a result of the Reformation, Altdorfer worked mostly on projects for public buildings and his pictorial output declined. The paintings of this period are particularly concerned with the perspective system and architectural setting. He executed the *Battle of Alexander* for Duke William of Bavaria in 1528. In the following years, as the German artistic scene emptied due to the death or departure of its leading figures, Altdorfer painted works that display his anxiety, his wavering between the Catholic tradition and Lutheran renewal. His last works are the tempera wall paintings in the Kaiserbad at Regensburg that were semi-destroyed by fire; only fragments remain.

Albrecht Altdorfer
Holy Family at the Fountain
1510
oil on wood, 22½ × 15 in.
(57 × 38 cm)
Gamäldegalerie, Berlin

Fra Angelico

Fra Giovanni da Fiesole, real name
Guido di Pietro
Vicchio di Mugello (Florence),
c. 1395-Rome, 1455

Actually regarded as "blessed" by the
Church, though not officially beatified,
this Dominican monk spent virtually
his whole life in the monasteries of his
order. Though some of his best-known
works—especially those in the
enchanting Convento di San Marco
museum in Florence—give the
impression of mystic, poetic isolation,
Fra Angelico was actually a pivotal
figure deeply involved in the cultural
and artistic debate of his day. He was
a leading artist in Florence during the
difficult decade that followed the
untimely death of Masaccio, and later,
at an advanced age, one of the first
great masters summoned to work in
the Vatican palaces. Trained as a
painter and miniaturist in the Florence

of the 1420s, still influenced by the late
Gothic style of Gentile da Fabriano,
Fra Angelico was to favor gold, pure
color, precious detail, and graceful
gestures and sentiments all his life.
He soon entered into contact with the
most advanced artists of the day and
he collaborated with the sculptor
Lorenzo Ghiberti on the splendid
Linaiuoli Altarpiece (1433, Museo
di San Marco, Florence). Fra Angelico
concentrated on a few subjects, for
example the enthroned Madonna
surrounded by saints or the
Annunciation, for various churches
in Florence and other cities,
independently developing a series of
"variations" on a theme through the
studied placement of the figures within
a deftly arranged framework of settings
seen in perspective. During the 1430s
Fra Angelico was certainly an "avant-
garde" artist who attracted the
attention of the young Piero della
Francesca, then just embarking on his

career. The vast series of frescoes for
the Convento di San Marco dates from
the period between 1439 and 1442.
Assisted by a school of painters in
which Benozzo Gozzoli was rising to
fame, Fra Angelico frescoed the chapter
house, the cloister, the corridors, and
the cells of his fellow monks. In 1446
he was in Rome, summoned by
Nicholas V to fresco the chapel
of St. Stephen and St. Lawrence in the
Vatican and execute other works that
have since been lost. The following
year he started work on the chapel
of St. Brizio in Orvieto cathedral, but
only painted a section of the ceiling.
The frescoes were to be completed fifty
years later by Luca Signorelli. He
returned to Florence and was still
occupied with various works for the
Convento di San Marco around the
year 1450. He was once again
summoned to Rome in 1453, where
he died in 1455, and was buried in the
Church of Santa Maria sopra Minerva.

Fra Angelico
Annunciation
c. 1441
fresco, 90½ × 126½ in.
(230 × 321 cm)
Convento di San Marco,
Florence

The Annunciation is one
of Fra Angelico's favorite
subjects. This version is
on the second floor of the
Convento di San Marco
beside the stairs leading
up to the monks' cells.
This position accounts
for the perspective
scheme of the scene, with
a portico extending along
the front and the left side.
The angel's iridescent
wings enliven the
subdued colors and the
details allude to the
Virgin's humility.

Antonello da Messina

Messina, c. 1430-1479

The painter who epitomizes and develops the characteristics of European painting in the mid-fifteenth century, Antonello da Messina succeeded in achieving a balance between the meticulously detailed Flemish approach and the solemn monumentality of Italian painting, between the application of Humanist rules of perspective and the atmospheric sense of light and color, between vivid backgrounds and animated figures. This is the result of a dynamic career that led Antonello to visit important artistic centers and to display a ready capacity to assimilate all the artistic innovations in the cities he visited, but at the same time he offered his own important contributions. The painter trained under Colantonio in Naples around 1450, and familiarized himself with the royal collections of Flemish and Provençal painting. Antonello had the opportunity to study the style and technique of the van Eycks: there were works by Jan in the Angevin collections and Barthélemy, also known as the Master of the Aix Annunciation, visited Naples in person. Antonello's interest soon came to focus on two subjects: the Crucifixion and the half-length male portrait against a dark ground. The dialog between Antonello and northern painters, especially Petrus Christus and Hans Memling, continued during the different stages of the master's life. He alternated periods in Sicily, where he produced many works—some of which were still traditional, others innovative—with journeys north through the peninsula. The oil-painting technique enabled Antonello to superimpose layers of color and create atmospheric, transparent effects of unprecedented sweetness. He had the opportunity to make a study of Piero della Francesca's works in Tuscany and the Marches, and acquire a powerful monumentality in his grouping of figures and a style of composition based on the geometric rules of perspective. His stay in Venice (1474–1476) was even more important, since it was crucial for the development of Venetian painting. In Venice he painted his most imposing works, including the San Cassiano Altarpiece, the surviving sections of which are now in Vienna, and the St. Sebastian now in Dresden. Alongside the already established features of his style, during the time spent in Venice, Antonello developed a greater interest in color and light, thus preparing the way for Giovanni Bellini's tonal approach.

Antonello da Messina
Crucifixion
1475
oil on wood, 20¾ × 16¾ in. (52.5 × 42.5 cm)
Musée des Beaux-Arts, Antwerp

Antonello produced different interpretations of the subject of the Crucifixion during the course of his career and they mark its main stages. The Antwerp version, painted during his stay in Venice, is the most complex and articulated. He sharply defines the line of a distant horizon where the landscape of water and countryside ends, thus dividing the scene into two distinct parts. Above, the drama of the three crosses, with the powerful contrast between Christ's restrained suffering and the tragic, contorted poses of the two thieves, is set against a boundless, pale blue sky. Below, the figures of Mary and John—their poses expressing two different human reactions to the ordeal of the Crucifixion—are placed in an earthly setting so crammed with details, symbols, and animals that it truly rivals the finest meticulous Flemish painting.

Antonello da Messina
St. Jerome in His Study
c. 1475
oil on wood, 18 × 14½
in. (46 × 36.5 cm)
National Gallery,
London

Formerly attributed to
Hans Memling, this
painting is an
extraordinary blend of
the Italian and Flemish
styles. In accordance
with Leon Battista
Alberti's precept, the
painting presents itself
as a "window," a precise
viewpoint on a scene.
Dressed as a cardinal,
St. Jerome sits engrossed
in his book in a
comfortable study,
whose simple, severely
functional elements,
combined with a
subdued elegance,
reflect the personality
and tastes of this
learned Humanist. This
room, however, is set in
a much larger area with
a splendid tiled floor, an
arched gallery, and five
different windows that
open onto a landscape
flooded in dazzling light
and a sky with soaring
swallows. Pots of
aromatic herbs and still
animals (a partridge and
a peacock on the
threshold, and a
symbolic lion in the
shadows on the right)
in no way disturb the
saint's concentration.
Despite the precise
rendering of each and
every detail, however,
the painting has a
monumental breadth
that is the most
characteristic feature of
fifteenth-century Italian
figurative art; it
transcends the
limitations of its small
format to become a
universal symbol of the
supremacy of the mind,
of intelligence, and of
education that is
enlightened by wisdom
and a love of nature.

Giuseppe Arcimboldo
Milan, 1527-1593

In the middle of the sixteenth century Arcimboldo made a normal debut with youthful works including designs for windows and tapestries respectively in Milan and Monza cathedrals and frescoes for the cathedral of Como. None of these gave any inkling of the bizarre originality he would soon develop. In 1562 he was summoned to the Imperial court in Prague and almost immediately his original and grotesque fantasy was unleashed. He composed portraits and allegories by superimposing a variety of objects. Arcimboldo's style has been so often imitated over the centuries that it is sometimes difficult to make exact attributions. He has been seen by some as the forerunner of Surrealism in the last century, but, more to the point, he should be seen in his own context at the end of the Renaissance. This was a time when people (collectors and scientists alike) were beginning to pay more attention to nature. Arcimboldo really created the fantastic image of the court in Prague, creating costumes, set designs, and decorations. Emperor Rudolf II set him the task of researching and buying works of art and natural curiosities, as well as giving him countless commissions for paintings. In 1587 Arcimboldo went back to Milan but stayed in contact with the Emperor. Towards the end of his life, he sent the Emperor the idiosyncratic portrait of him in the guise of the Greek god Vortumnus.

Giuseppe Arcimboldo
Winter
1563
canvas, 26 × 20 in.
(66.5 × 50.5 cm)
Kunsthistorisches
Museum, Vienna

The painting is part of a cycle dedicated to the four seasons. Each one is symbolically represented by a startling and evocative juxtaposition of fruits and objects typical of that time of the year. Arcimboldo found this subject particularly congenial and often painted groups of pictures on themes like the four elements (Earth, Air, Water, Fire).

RETABLO DE LA CAPILLA
LLAMADA DEL PAPA.LEVAN
TADA POR CALIXTO III EN
EL SOLAR DE LA NAVE
CONTIGUA.DISPERSOS SUS
ELEMENTOS POR LUENGOS
AÑOS.REUNIERONSE EN 1924
PARA PERPETUA MEMORIA

Jaume Baço
Tríptico de los Borja
(Altarpiece of St. Anne)
c. 1447
panel
Collegiate Church, Játiva
(Valencia)

Painted during his stay
in Italy, this triptych was
commissioned by the
Catalan cardinal Alfonso
Borgia, then in the
service of Alfonso of
Aragon, who later
became Pope Callixtus
III (1455-1458).
The central panels show
St. Anne and the
Madonna with Joachim
and the Archangel
Gabriel, and the side
panels depict St.
Augustine with St.
Monica and St.
Ildefonso with the
commissioner. Except
for the classicizing
architecture of St.
Ildefonso's throne, the
only Italian note that
contrasts with the rest of
the composition, this
work is evidently
influenced by Flemish
painting and
particularly by van Eyck,
through the art of
Petrus Christus.

Jaume Baço
Jacomart
Valencia, 1410-1461

The favorite painter of King Alfonso V
of Aragon, who called him "el nostro
leal maestro Jacomart," he was active
in Valencia until 1442 when he left for
Naples, where he executed various
works and exerted a considerable
influence on the painters of the time,
including Colantonio. In 1445 he was
back in Valencia, but in 1446 he was
once again summoned by the king and

returned to Italy, this time to Rome.
Despite Italian influence, his
background remained Flemish. In fact,
economic prosperity in Valencia had
favored the rapid spread of the
northern style of painting that was
immediately adopted in a form that
was more in keeping with local taste.
His only documented work is the
Altarpiece of Cati, commissioned
in 1460, a year before his death, and
executed mainly with the assistance of
his follower Joan Rexach; other works
were attributed to him, including the

Altarpiece of St. Anne in the collegiate
church in Játiva, and the panels in
Valencia Cathedral depicting St.
Benedict and St. Ildefonso that reveal
a fine sensibility and a very personal
interpretation of the Flemish style.
Rexach's contribution to them is
evident in the elaborate decorative
motifs and the abundant use of gold.

Hans Baldung Grien

Schwäbig Gmünd, 1484/85-Strasbourg, 1545

Having moved to Strasbourg when he was a child, Baldung Grien trained in this city on the Rhine that was to remain his favorite place of residence. In 1503 he went to Nuremberg to become acquainted with Dürer. The young Hans soon became the great master's most faithful pupil and one of his best friends, so much so that when Dürer left for Venice he entrusted his workshop to the talented eighteen-year-old. Baldung Grien took full advantage of this wonderful opportunity and adopted the style and mindset of the greatest genius of the German Renaissance. He mastered, as no other contemporary did, the varied techniques, the different atmospheres, the truly universal vision, and the extremely delicate balance, destined to last for a few precious years, between the legendary, light, and courtly

legacy of the German "Gothic" and the controlled monumentality, bathed in the light of classicism, that derived from Italian Humanism. When Dürer returned to Nuremberg, he found his pupil had become an already brilliant and independent painter, ready to take the big step; in fact, Baldung Grien returned to Strasbourg as a master. He consolidated his success by working ceaselessly and was surprisingly eclectic. He produced religious illustrations for treatises on the Madonna, painted nude maidens looking in the mirror, threatened by the figure of Death, fairy-tale knights galloping through the woods; and Christs in the tomb. In 1510 he began to devote himself to themes connected with the image of the female body, which ranged from monstrous yet seductive witches to allegorical figures. In 1512, when Grünewald was working at nearby Isenheim, Baldung Grien began to execute his most important work, the polyptych for the high altar in

Freiburg Cathedral. It is a large altarpiece with side wings whose central wall depicts the *Coronation of the Virgin* flanked by two panels with the *Apostles*; on the side wings, four *Episodes from the Life of the Virgin*; behind, a large *Crucifixion*; and below, the *Portraits of the Four Commissioners Worshiping the Virgin*. For four years, until 1516, Baldung Grien moved to Freiburg and devoted himself to this masterpiece, which became one of the major works of the German Renaissance. The year after he completed the polyptych, Baldung Grien returned to Strasbourg. The climate had changed and there were disturbing rumors of the Reformation. The painter who had just celebrated the glory of the Virgin Mary was one of the first followers of Luther. From then on and for almost thirty years (he died in 1545), he executed only a few small religious works and mostly painted allegories and moralizing subjects, illustrated books, and produced works on his favorite theme of witches.

Hans Baldung Grien
Altar of St. Sebastian
From the Collegiate Church in Halle
1507
oil on wood, central panel, 47¾ × 31 in. (121.2 × 78.6 cm)
side panels, 48 × 12½ in. (121.5 × 32 cm)
Germanisches Nationalmuseum, Nuremberg

Giacomo Balla

Turin, 1871-Rome, 1958

The oldest but also the most long-lived and consistent of the Futurists began his career as a painter in Rome, where he moved in 1895. He soon came under the sway of Divisionism, painting remarkable pictures inspired by social realism and the industrial suburbs. In 1909 he became a committed member of the new Futurist movement, founded in Milan by the writer Filippo Tommaso Marinetti. Balla's activity, in the brief period of early Futurism, was prolific and enthusiastic. While Boccioni was chiefly interested in the problem of the dynamic breakdown of forms, Balla preferred to investigate light and color, through such studies as *Iridescent Interpenetrations*. The painting that sums up Balla's early Futurist phase is the *Little Girl Running on a Balcony* (1911-1912), where the color is split up into individual touches, producing an effective sense of movement.
In 1915 he drew up the program of "Futurist Reconstruction of the Universe" with Depero, and after the end of the war his activity extended into a variety of fields, including cinema, interior decoration, design and textiles. Later Balla went into isolation, showing a distinct tendency toward abstract art.

Giacomo Balla
Little Girl Running on a Balcony
1911-1912
oil on canvas
49¼ × 49¼ in.
(125 × 125 cm)
Galleria d'Arte
Moderna, Milan

Federico Barocci

Urbino, 1535-1612

It is not only his dates that make Federico Barocci a suitable candidate with which to close any history of Italian Renaissance painting. Born in the Marches, Barocci acted as the linchpin that joined the great masters of the sixteenth century with the new art, from Carracci to Rubens, that was to emerge in the next century. Barocci trained in his native Urbino with its incredible artistic legacy. He seems to have been particularly conscious of Raphael's contribution to his own style. From his earliest work he incorporated Correggio's sunny grace enriched with his personal and warm taste for Venetian color. After an unhappy stay in Rome he returned to Urbino for good (1565). The fact that he was not in the center of the cultural world did not stop Barocci from wielding decisive influence, thanks also to the way that he stuck exactly to the Counter-Reformation's tenets on religious art drawn up at the Council of Trent. His compositions had a simple and direct fluidity and included touching details from everyday life. This did not, however, stop him from attempting more ambitious compositions from time to time, such as *The Deposition* in Perugia cathedral, 1569; *The Virgin of the People* (Uffizi, Florence, 1576-1579); *The Martyrdom of St. Vitale* (Brera, Milan, 1583). In these paintings we can see how he gradually tried to introduce a feeling of wider space. In his later works, Barocci's spirituality and contemplative nature emerged more clearly, pointing decisively toward the beginnings of the Baroque.

Federico Barocci
Annunciation
1592-1596
canvas, 97¾ × 65½ in.
(248 × 170 cm)
Santa Maria degli Angeli, Coli-Pontani chapel, Perugia

Barocci's altarpieces reveal his precise and rapid response to the instructions issued by the Council of Trent on religious art. The Mannerists may have had a refined intellectual quality but they were too often abstruse. Mannerism was now definitely swept aside. In its place came simple images with an obvious flow to them, free of mysteries or complications. Sacred episodes were set in the context of everyday reality. This can be seen from the way Barocci includes the Ducal Palace at Urbino in the background and fills the picture with descriptive detail, including the sleeping cat in the foreground. The figures' sweetness of expression is a direct reference to Correggio.

Jean-Michel Basquiat
New York, 1960-1988

A young man in search of success and fame, Basquiat came into full awareness of his artistic vocation only following an unexpected encounter with the deity of pop art, Andy Warhol. The son of a Haitian father and a Puerto Rican mother, Basquiat worked out a pictorial language that incorporates primitive African art, totems, and masks, all in keeping with the multiethnic spirit that pervades New York's outer boroughs. In his paintings, poetry, phrases, or words—expressions of the subculture of the street—together with human figures summarily sketched in, stand out against backgrounds rendered with lively, bright brushstrokes that follow the modalities of abstract expressionism. In 1983 Basquiat and Warhol began an intense collaborative effort, turning out more than one hundred paintings in which the contribution of each is recognizable and setting up a group show whose poster eloquently presents the two artists as contenders in a boxing match. A year after Warhol's death, Basquiat died of a drug overdose at the age of twenty-seven.

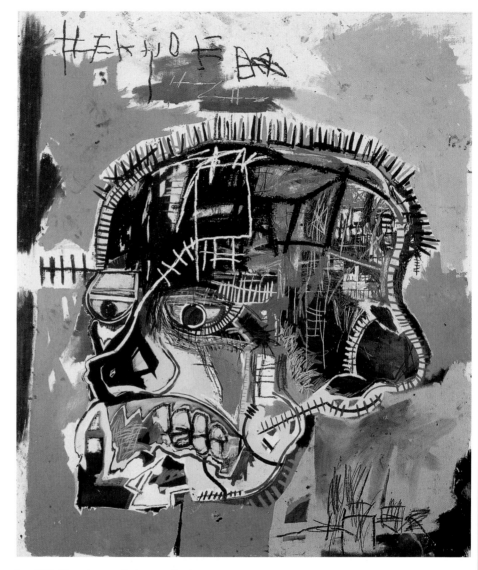

Jean-Michel Basquiat
Untitled "Skull"
1981
mixed media on canvas
81½ × 69 in.
(207 × 176 cm)
Eli Broad Family Foundation, Santa Monica, California

An iconographic element that dates back to the seventeenth century as a symbol of death, the human skull is here the protagonist of the work, but covered with scars and stitching that locate it somewhere between cartoon character and clinical case.

Max Beckmann

Leipzig, 1884-New York, 1950

An independent and intense personality, Beckmann's life and career are exemplary of the condition of the artist in the troubled decades between the two wars. After an initial training at the Weimar Academy, Beckmann spent time in Paris and Geneva. In 1904, following the success of a one-man show, he moved to Berlin. Over this period his style changed several times, passing from late Impressionism to Realism. Like Dix, however, Beckmann discovered the roots of German Expressionism during the First World War, finding in them an effective means of expressing his dismay at the agony it caused, at the physical, moral, and social devastation. The tragic cruelty of a painting like *The Night* (1918-1919) made Beckmann one of the greatest interpreters of the terrible conditions in defeated Germany. Yet in Beckmann's work, unlike that of Dix and Grosz, it is possible to detect the influence of other, contemporary European movements, such as Cubism and, in the twenties, the call for a "return to order." Alternating his activity as principal of the school of fine arts in Frankfurt with journeys to Paris, Beckmann gradually transformed his graphic style of Expressionism into scenes and figures with simplified, monumental volumes, which also showed a renewed taste for color. In 1937 he was forced to leave Germany following persecution by the Nazis and spent the war years in Amsterdam, painting pictures on a large scale. In 1947 he moved to the United States, where he taught at Washington University in St. Louis, Missouri, before settling in New York.

Max Beckmann
Self-Portrait in Tuxedo
1927
oil on canvas
55½ × 37¾ in.
(141 × 96 cm)
Fogg Art Museum,
Cambridge, Mass.

The stern features of the face, the volume sharply defined in black and white, and the graphic emphasis on outline place Beckmann within the current of German Expressionism.

The choice of dress, however, shows that Beckmann was also a refined and ironic interpreter of Berlin society.

Giovanni Bellini

Venice, c. 1430-1516

Giovanni Bellini's successful career encompasses all the stages of development in Venetian painting from the late Gothic style to the tonal and atmospheric approach of the early sixteenth century. Born into a family of painters, Giovanni learned his craft in the workshop of his father, Jacopo. Until the age of thirty, Giovanni diligently assisted his father in producing works in a delicate, precious, precise style. Some echoes of Humanist innovations—also as regards the anatomical handling of figures— entered his painting after the marriage of his sister Nicolosia to Andrea Mantegna (1451), but Giovanni differs from his brother-in-law in his greater attention to color rather than draftsmanship. Starting with his first independent works in the 1460s, he characteristically focused on exploring ways of rendering the natural atmosphere, through the color and luminosity of the landscape backgrounds. The monumental Pesaro *Coronation of the Virgin* (1471-1474) is far closer to Piero della Francesca's geometric and architectural schemes. Bellini had become the major figure in the Venetian School, and this role was confirmed by his rapid, independent interpretation of the innovations suggested by Antonello da Messina, who arrived in Venice in 1474. The works produced over the following years, for example, *the Enthroned Madonna from San Giobbe* (Accademia) and the triptych in the Church of the Frari, herald the advent of a new period in Venetian art, in which a complete mastery of the rules of perspective blends harmoniously with a far softer and warmer handling of light than in contemporary works produced in central Italy. In 1483 he was appointed official painter to the Venetian Republic, a post he was to hold for thirty-three years. He ran an important workshop: two generations of Venetian painters received their training there, including Lotto, Giorgione, and Titian. Even in the early years of the sixteenth century, he continued his quest for a broader atmospheric vision that he also applied to imposing altarpieces. The final surprise is the execution of paintings on secular subjects like the *Feast of the Gods* (1514), formerly in Ferrara, now in Washington, and the *Lady at Her Toilet* (1515), in Vienna. On his death, his position as official painter was taken over by Titian, who held it for sixty years.

Giovanni Bellini
Enthroned Madonna from the Church of San Giobbe
c. 1487
oil on wood, 185½ × 101½ in. (471 × 258 cm)
Gallerie dell'Accademia, Venice

This majestic composition is Giovanni Bellini's response to Antonello da Messina's *San Cassiano Altarpiece.* The general organization follows the traditional arrangement of a group of figures symmetrically placed in an interior seen in perspective, which is emphasized by the group of three angel musicians at the foot of the throne. The most innovative aspect is the all-enveloping light that seems to play on the gold mosaic in the conch of the apse.

Following page
Giovanni Bellini
Coronation of the Virgin (Pesaro Altarpiece)
1471-1474
oil on wood, central panel, 103 × 94½ in. (262 × 240 cm)
Museo Civico, Pesaro

This brilliant work, formerly in the Church of San Francesco in Pesaro, marks the abandonment of all remaining elements of the late Gothic style and the adoption of the monumentality and the geometric rigor of Humanist art. Following the example of Piero della Francesca, Bellini also achieved a "perspectival synthesis of form and color," but added a new interest in light and landscape. The hills of Montefeltro appear in the background, in the marble frame of the throne. The episodes depicted in the predella and the figures of the saints on the side columns evidence the artist's delicate tonal sensitivity.

19

**Gentile
and Giovanni Bellini**
*St. Mark Preaching in
Alexandria*
1504-1507
oil on canvas, 136½ × 303
in. (347 × 770 cm)
Pinacoteca di Brera, Milan

This vast scene was begun
by Gentile Bellini in 1504
and completed after
his death (1506) by his
brother Giovanni.
Giovanni gave the
buildings at the sides
a simpler and more
monumental aspect
to achieve a perfect
orientation of light and
accentuate the figure of
the Evangelist preaching to
the people of Alexandria.
This canvas is reminiscent
of a theater stage: a crowd
of figures, with a group
of veiled Arab women
in white in the center,
is gathered to hear
the words of St. Mark.
Despite the profusion of
exotic detail, this superb
setting inevitably reminds
the spectator of Piazza
San Marco, though the
noble composure of the
oriental dignitaries
suggests an involuntary
acknowledgment of
Ottoman power.

**Giovanni Bellini
and Titian**
Feast of the Gods
1514
oil on canvas, 67 × 74 in.
(170 × 188 cm)
National Gallery of Art,
Washington, D.C.

This moving masterpiece
of Giovanni Bellini's old
age was painted when
the master was in his
eighties for the study of
Duke Alfonso d'Este in
Ferrara, known as the
"camerino d'alabastro"
or alabaster room.
The group of gods has
gathered on a summer
afternoon, as though
for a meal in the open
air. The varying colors
enhanced by
atmospheric light suggest
contacts with Dürer.
The landscape,
especially the dense
foliage of the trees, was
painted over by Titian
to bring the painting
into closer harmony
with the other works
decorating the duke's
exquisite study.

21

Bernardo Bellotto
*The Kreuzkirche
in Dresden*
between 1747 and 1756
oil on canvas
77½ × 73½ in.
(197 × 187 cm)
Hermitage, St. Petersburg

A few years later, during
his second stay in
Saxony, Bellotto was to
paint the demolition of
the Gothic church,
which had been
bombarded and was
rebuilt in Rococo style.

Opposite, top
Bernardo Bellotto
*View of Vienna
from the Belvedere*
1759-1760
oil on canvas,
53¼ × 83¾ in.
(135 × 213 cm)
Kunsthistorisches
Museum, Vienna

Commissioned by
Empress Maria Theresa
of Austria, this
masterpiece shows
Vienna's hills in the
background and the
monuments rising
above the historic
center. The view is seen
from the terrace of the
Belvedere, the villa built
just outside the city
gates by Eugene of
Savoy. Bellotto has
chosen to portray the
parade of splendid
though somewhat bored
figures of the local
nobility in the warm
afternoon light.

Bernardo Bellotto
Venice, 1721-Warsaw, 1780

Bernardo Bellotto, Canaletto's nephew on his mother's side, was a great traveler. He made only rare, brief stays in Venice (and hence plays a very minor role in Venetian painting), but spent far more important periods in the capitals of eighteenth-century Europe. Endowed with exceptional talent, Bellotto studied with his uncle and displayed a truly precocious flair for the small figures used to animate views. At the age of seventeen, he was already a registered member of the guild of Venetian painters, but left soon afterward for his first long journey. His route took him to Rome, but by way of many other Italian cities. Even in the early years of his career, Bellotto displayed a great ability to capture the architectural, environmental, and even atmospheric features of the places he visited. Even more meticulous and precise than his uncle, Canaletto, Bellotto loved variety. Only in very special circumstances would he repeat views already painted, since he always preferred to seek out new ones. Above all, his work is dominated by light. Wherever he was, Bellotto waited for the finest days and clear, fresh skies to observe the panorama with absolute precision and perfect clarity. On his return to Venice after his travels in Italy (which took him to Rome, Florence, Turin, Milan, the lakes of Lombardy, and Verona), in 1747, at the age of only twenty-six, he accepted the invitation of Augustus III, the prince-elector of Saxony, and moved to Dresden. His first stay in Saxony produced two series of splendid canvases depicting the "Florence of the Elbe," painted for the prince and for his prime minister, Count Brühl, who was also a patron of Giambattista Tiepolo. In 1758, Empress Maria Theresa summoned Bellotto to Vienna, where he produced views of the capital of the Hapsburg Empire. The prince-elector of Bavaria then invited Bellotto to Munich, where his stay was prolonged for five years. There followed another stay in Dresden and then his final years were spent in the service of Stanislaw II of Poland in Warsaw, which he depicted with loving care in views that later served as models for reconstruction work after the devastation of World War II.

Bernardo Bellotto
*The Kaunitz Palace
and Gardens in Vienna*
1759-1760
oil on canvas
52¾ × 93 ¼ in.
(134 × 237 cm)
Museum of Fine Arts,
Budapest

George Bellows
Columbus, Ohio, 1882-New York, 1925

In 1904, at just twenty-two years of age, George Wesley Bellows moved to New York and began studying with Robert Henri. Soon he became Henri's favorite student, particularly because of his efforts to establish a style capable of fully expressing the American experience, but also because of the vitality and energetic passion he showed for painting, supported by extraordinary technical skills. Among his preferred themes were the daily life of the middle class and the streets and squares of New York. He made landscapes of Maine and Rhode Island, along with several portraits, but the works that earned him an outstanding place in the panorama of American painting at the beginning of the century were his intense presentations of boxing matches. In 1909 Bellows entered the National Academy of Design, and was in fact its youngest artist; the next year he began teaching at the Art Students League in New York. The 1913 Armory Show introduced him to European painting, and exposure to the works of Matisse and the Fauvist painters had a large impact on his palette and lent greater vigor to his brushstrokes. In 1917 Bellows, along with other members of The Eight opposed to academic painting, was among the promoters of the Society of Independent Artists. Bellows's painting was also influenced by the simplicity and the rarefied atmospheres of the works of another of Henri's students: Edward Hopper. Bellows's career and life were short; he died of peritonitis at forty-three.

George Bellows
Stag at Sharkey's
1909
oil on canvas
36 × 48 in.
(92 × 122.6 cm)
Cleveland Museum of
Art, Cleveland, Ohio

The entangled fighters, muscles tense and bodies twisting under the force of the blows, the press of the crowd, the referee leaning to one side as he observes the match, along with the vigorous brushstrokes, give this image a sense of action and dramatic, vital energy. A clear parallel is Luks's painting *The Wrestlers*, famous for its powerful and effective style made more dramatic by the use of bright illumination against a dark background. Between 1900 and 1911 organized boxing matches were against the law in New York, but in private arenas like Tom Sharkey's club those who could afford the steep admission price could witness clandestine matches. This painting could serve as a poster for urban realism at the beginning of the century.

Bartolomé Bermejo
Cordoba c. 1440-Barcelona c. 1500

A brilliant and disturbing painter, Bermejo trained in the Netherlands and traveled throughout the kingdom of Aragon. Between 1474 and 1476 he lived in Daroca, where he painted the *Altarpiece of St. Dominic of Silos*, the artist's first documented work, which was begun in 1474 and completed in 1477 by his follower Martín Bernat, and the *Altarpiece of Holy Grace*, now dismembered. The *Crucifixion* in the collegiate church of Daroca is one of his most beautiful panels. Bermejo then moved to Saragossa, where he lived from 1477 to 1481, without, however, leaving any documented work from this period, and

subsequently he resided in Valencia until 1486. He may also have spent some time in Italy, which would explain the presence of his work, the *Altarpiece of the Virgin of Montserrat*, in the cathedral of Acqui. In the end he arrived in Barcelona, probably the final destination of his ceaseless wandering, where he executed one of the most important works in Spanish painting, the *Pietà*, commissioned by Canon Desplá in 1490, which is modeled on van Eyck's painting, though the influence of Venetian tonal painting and the grand scale of Lombard art is also evident. No further information on his career exists after 1498.

Bartolomé Bermejo
Altarpiece of the Virgin of Montserrat
c. 1485
panel
Cathedral, Acqui Terme

Commissioned by a merchant from the town of Acqui, Francesco della Chiesa, who is portrayed on the central

panel kneeling beside the Virgin, this triptych is uneven in style, since the central panel, where the Virgin and Child are set in a vast landscape, was painted by Bermejo himself, while the side panels were designed by the artist but executed by Rodrigo de Osona.

Gian Lorenzo Bernini

Naples, 1598–Rome, 1680

Bernini was by far the most important Baroque sculptor and architect of seventeenth-century Europe and one of the key creators of the whole Baroque era. But he worked initially as a painter. His work reveals a sure and brilliant hand, free from any trace of pedantry. He studied in Rome under his own father, Pietro, and soon proved one of the most precocious infant prodigies in the history of art. His work was immediately sought after by the major collectors. He was little more than an adolescent when Cardinal Scipione Borghese commissioned him to sculpt a monumental cycle of four large marble groups, among which was his defining masterpiece *Apollo and Daphne,* which can still be seen in the Borghese Gallery in Rome. When Pope Urban VIII was elected (1623), Bernini became the focus of a colossal Baroque-style modernization program in the Vatican. Using his talents as a sculptor, architect, and town planner, Bernini reshaped St. Peter's and the huge square outside it, starting with the installation of the bronze canopy over the high altar. Then with extraordinary vigor Bernini embarked on a series of sculptures and buildings that literally changed the face of Rome. We need only mention his stupendous fountains (like the River Fountain in Piazza Navona), his huge marble group *The Ecstasy of St. Theresa* that is installed like a theatrical set in the transept of Santa Maria della Vittoria, or his lifelike portrait-busts. It is these busts that we can compare to his rare and precious paintings. In this context, however there is still much study to be done.

Gian Lorenzo Bernini
Self-Portrait as a Young Man
c. 1620, canvas,
15¼ × 12 in. (39 × 31 cm)
Galleria Borghese, Rome

This painting is of paramount importance to reconstruction of his young œuvre of paintings. The nervous rapidity of the brushstrokes and the quick flash of his eyes reveal his desire to capture expression in an instant, as Bernini did systematically in his sculpted portraits.

Left
Pedro Berruguete
*Federico da Montefeltro
with His Son, Guidobaldo*
1474-1477
panel, 25½ × 29¾ in.
(64.5 × 75.5 cm)
Palazzo Ducale, Urbino

When he was engaged in
executing the *Portraits
of Illustrious Men* in the
Palazzo Ducale in Urbino,
designed and painted in
part by Giusto of Ghent,
his figures became
immediately distinguished
from the descriptive
rendering of the Flemish
master. The perspective
and compositional
function of the planes
accentuate the
monumentality of the
half-length figures with
their individualized
faces, enveloped in
flowing drapery, while in
the extraordinary full-
length portrait of the
duke, northern realism
blends with the
monumentality of
Melozzo da Forlì and the
rigor of Piero
della Francesca.

Pedro Berruguete
*St. Dominic Raising
a Child*
c. 1495
tempera and oil
on wood
48 × 32¾ in.
(122 × 83 cm)
Prado, Madrid

Pedro Berruguete
Paredes de Nava, Palencia
c. 1450-Avila, c. 1504

Berruguete trained in Fernando
Gallego's circle, but his earliest works
are clearly influenced by Flemish
painting, especially that of van Eyck.
In 1474 he was in Urbino in Italy,
where he worked with Giusto of Ghent
on the decoration of Duke Federico
da Montefeltro's palace, particularly
the study and the library. The duke
himself, a great humanist, was certainly
responsible for the general scheme of
the project. The upper portion of the
study was decorated with a series
of half-length portraits of illustrious
personages, both past and present,
while a magnificent full-length portrait
of the duke in profile, seated at a
lectern with his son, Guidobaldo,
presided over the group. The library
had the figures of the liberal arts, seated
on sumptuous thrones decorated with
precious stones, and Federico da
Montefeltro with his son Guidobaldo
and the court listening to a lecture. On
his return to Spain in 1483, Berruguete
forgot what he had learned in Italy and
went back to rich gold grounds and
a decorative style taken to the extreme,
motifs that can be found in works like
the altarpiece in the church of St.
Eulalia, executed between 1490 and
1500, and dedicated to the life of the
Virgin. His last commission was the
high altar in Avila Cathedral, an
unfinished work that was completed
by Juan de Borgoña, where the interest
in perspective and light is reminiscent
of Italian art.

George Caleb Bingham

Augusta County, Virginia, 1811-
Kansas City, Missouri, 1879

One of the greatest interpreters
of the American myth, Bingham
created a series of images that are
both cogent and easily approachable.
He grew up in rural Franklin County,
Missouri, where his father owned a
farm, and he turned to painting early
in the 1830s, earning a modest name
for himself as a portraitist. Initially
self-taught, he soon felt the need for
formal artistic training, going first to
Philadelphia, where he studied on his
own at the Pennsylvania Academy of
Fine Arts in 1838, and then to New
York, where he came in contact with
William Sidney Mount. In the next
decade Bingham discovered his true
calling as a painter of daily life and
painted the well-known series of
bargemen with which he achieved
national fame. In 1845 the American
Art-Union purchased four of his
works, including *Fur Traders
Descending the Missouri*, one of his
most famous paintings. In this, as in
other works dedicated to scenes of life
on the river, Bingham emphasizes
the positive aspects of the presence of
human civilization in wilderness areas.
His fur traders are frontier heroes; by
blazing the first trails, they opened the
way for commerce, thus contributing
to the advance of civilization. For
Bingham, active in Missouri politics,
his scenes of life along the river are
documentary images recording the
social and political types of his times.
From the end of the 1840s on,
Bingham expressed his strong passion
for politics in a series of paintings of
elections (such as *The Verdict of the
People*); what he was most interested
in is the spirit of popular
participation, as evident in the
contrasts and variety of expressions.
Bingham sailed to Europe in 1856 and
spent the next three years studying
painting, most of all in Düsseldorf.
The changes in his style that resulted
from this experience did not please
everyone: his line grew more incisive,
his colors more metallic. When he
returned to America he continued his
active involvement in politics,
primarily in the small frontier towns
along the Missouri.

George Caleb Bingham
*Fur Traders Descending
the Missouri*
1845
oil on canvas,
29 × 36½ in.
(73.7 × 92.7 cm)
Metropolitan Museum
of Art, New York

In his scenes of daily life
along the Missouri
River, Bingham
constructed an
iconographic repertoire
composed of simple
myths and the small
events of daily life on
the frontier. In this
painting, one of many
pairs of traders travels
the river, bringing a load
of furs to market in the
city. The cold light
of early day embraces
the two traders; their
immobile shadow
spreading across
the surface of the river
suggests an unreal
atmosphere, a
metaphysical dimension.

William Blake
London, 1757-1827

Unquestionably the outstanding figure in a contradictory and stimulating period, the artist and poet Blake is not easy to understand. In his pictures and writings a taste for the fantastic and the medieval is blended with mysticism and the ferments of a precious Romanticism. Alternating literary and theoretical work with his activities as a painter and engraver, Blake was trained at the Royal Academy of Arts and went on to give expression, along with Füssli and Flaxman, to the controversial impulses of an era of transition. Particularly interesting are his illustrations of stories and poems, with their extremely close relationship between text and image, as in the ambitious and incomplete series of watercolors for Dante's *Divine Comedy*. While Blake's themes are rooted in imagination, mystery, biblical visions, and even hallucinations and the Gothic novel, the technique used for their expression is an innovative one: Blake has to be considered a pioneer of experimentation in the fields of color engraving and the printed miniature.

William Blake
Pity
1827
watercolor
16½ × 21¼ in.
(42 × 54 cm)
Tate Gallery, London

William Blake
The Good and Evil Angels
1795-1805
watercolor
17½ × 23½ in.
(44.5 × 59.4 cm)
Tate Gallery, London

Umberto Boccioni

Reggio Calabria, 1882-Verona, 1916

Futurism was probably the most important artistic movement to emerge in Italy during the twentieth century, and Boccioni was its founder and most committed and significant exponent. For a brief period (cut short by the First World War, in which Boccioni lost his life following a fall from a horse) the group of painters, writers, and musicians led by Boccioni and Marinetti was one of the most active and interesting avant-garde movements in Europe. The phase of his formation, during the first decade of the century, saw Boccioni pass from Balla's studio to Rome and then set off on a series of long journeys (to Venice, Russia, and Paris), which allowed the painter to compare the technique of Divisionism with the principal expressions of contemporary art. Settling in Milan in 1907, he was attracted by the social themes of the Lombard painters of the late nineteenth century and watched with curiosity the growth of the new working-class districts on the industrial outskirts. The encounter between Boccioni and Marinetti, a brilliant and eccentric writer, marked the birth of Futurism: a lively and energetic affirmation of the world, a rejection of the past, and a love for anything in movement, for action, noise, and dynamism. Boccioni wrote the basic manifestoes of Futurist painting, as well as theoretical texts on the motivations and aspirations of the avant-garde. In the same years as Cubism emerged, Boccioni sought to represent things simultaneously from different viewpoints, in his rare but fascinating sculptures as well as in his paintings. His vivid colors, forceful brushwork, and themes chosen with an evident symbolic and demonstrative intent are manifestations of a positive approach to creativity, open to influences from technology, sport, and progress. The outbreak of the First World War (in which Boccioni took part as a volunteer) marked a turning point in his style, which grew more thoughtful and less frantic. All too soon his death interrupted any possible further development.

Umberto Boccioni
Brawl in the Gallery
1910
oil on canvas
30 × 25¼ in.
(76 × 64 cm)
Pinacoteca di Brera, Milan

With an amused eye, Boccioni depicts the small crowd that gathers around two scuffling women. The freedom from the traditional schemes of painting is apparent in the abbreviated forms and blazing colors, which create the effect of a vortex of movement.

Umberto Boccioni
Matter
1912
oil on canvas
88½ × 59 in.
(225 × 150 cm)
Mattioli Collection, Milan

This is actually a portrait of the artist's mother. A subject that Boccioni returned to repeatedly, it is here tackled on a monumental scale, in a painting of very great significance. As Boccioni himself wrote in an explanatory text, the artist is seeking a complementarity between the figure and its surroundings. Through an enveloping movement, his mother "enters" the armchair, forming a single piece of "matter" with it.

31

Arnold Böcklin

Basel, 1827-San Domenico di Fiesole, 1901

Trained at the Düsseldorf Academy, the young Böcklin traveled to Brussels, Antwerp, and Paris for the purposes of study, and then moved to Rome in 1848. Here the impact of the ancient world served as a powerful stimulus to his imagination, as is apparent from paintings like *Roman Landscape* (1851) and *Centaur and Nymph* (1855). In 1860 he was appointed to the chair of painting at the Weimar Academy, but in 1862 he was back in Rome, going on to visit Naples and Pompeii. The experience was to have a decisive influence on his later work. In 1866 he returned to Basel and then spent the years from 1871 to 1874 in Munich. Finally, he went to Florence, staying there for a decade (1874–84) and eventually returning to spend the last years of his life in Fiesole. The course of his artistic development was a singular one, distinguished by a Symbolism that owed nothing to the morbid and uneasy climate of the French movement, but stemmed from a mixture of myth and reality, past and present, in the ambiguous atmosphere of an allusive use of symbols that recalls the Wagnerian synthesis of the arts. According to Böcklin, every picture had to tell a story, to make the observer think as if it were a poem and to leave the impression of a piece of music.

Arnold Böcklin
Anacreon's Muse
1873
oil on canvas
31 × 23½ in.
(79 × 60 cm)
Aargauer Kunsthaus,
Aarau

Painted during the years of intense creativity that he spent in Munich, from 1871 to 1874, the work is a homage to music and poetry, as embodied by the Greek lyric poet Anacreon. The female figure of the muse is depicted with realism and academic precision, showing how Böcklin's painting represents a quite unique aspect of the fantastic art of the end of the century, shunning the suggestive effect of the vague and indistinct.

Pierre Bonnard
Fontenay-aux-Roses, 1867-
Le Cannet, 1947

After playing a leading role in the
debate over developments in Post-
Impressionism and promoting
a significant reexamination of the
questions of color and drawing,
Bonnard made a conscious decision
not to proceed along the road of the
avant-garde, choosing instead to
pursue his own investigation of
poetics. Abandoning his legal studies
to enter the Ecole des Beaux-Arts,
Bonnard was decisively influenced by
his contact with the Nabis group,
which centered around the figures of
Gauguin and Maurice Denis. Bonnard
fully shared the movement's artistic

ideals but did not let himself get
caught up in its exaggerated
mysticism, limiting his participation
to the purely pictorial aspects. A
regular contributor to the influential
Revue Blanche, during the last decade
of the century he defined the areas of
color on his figures and descriptive
elements with great intellectual rigor,
abandoning chiaroscuro and the soft
play of shadows dear to the
Impressionists. His tranquil images
of an intimate and affectionate way
of life are profoundly different from
the lively pictures of popular dances
and houses of prostitution produced
by Toulouse-Lautrec over the same
period. Along with Vuillard, Bonnard
painted bourgeois interiors, lingering
over the hidden corners of everyday

life: his use of a soft and sinuous line
made him a forerunner of Art
Nouveau. After a period of reflection
on Impressionism during the first few
years of the twentieth century, when
Bonnard returned to themes of city
life, the rapid emergence of the avant-
garde movements drove him into a
sort of voluntary exile, seeking the
bright colors and light of the
Mediterranean. Moving to Le Cannet,
Bonnard concentrated on just a few
subjects (conversations in the garden,
the body of his companion, modestly
laid tables, simple landscapes,
domestic interiors like the bathroom
or kitchen). Right up until his death
he went on conjuring up the colorful
mystery that is concealed in the folds
of daily life.

Pierre Bonnard
The Open Window
1912
oil on canvas
29¼ × 44½ in.
(74 × 113 cm)
Musée des Beaux-Arts,
Nice

This charming picture
sums up many of the
characteristics of
Bonnard's painting: his
ability to capture a vast
amount of light, the
silent and shady
interiors of houses,
the flowering of gardens
in the summer.

33

Hieronymus Bosch

Jeroen van Aken 's-Hertogenbosch,
c. 1440-1516

Little is known of Bosch's life and
career; much is left to conjecture
and the experts are not always in
agreement. However, the extremely
individual style of his paintings, and
research into the collections in which
the main works were found has
permitted the works to be catalogued,
though the dating of them is doubtful.
Hieronymus Bosch is a pseudonym
the artist adopted to sign some of his
paintings and it is the Latin version of
his first name Jeroen (Jerome) and a
short form of the name of the town
where he was born, 's-Hertogenbosch
(Bois-le-Duc), in the south of
Holland. His real surname was van
Aken, which would indicate that his
family came from Aachen. His
grandfather and father were both quite
famous painters, so the young
Hieronymus trained in the family
workshop. His earliest independent
works, with satirical scenes depicting
man's stupidity and vices, can be dated
to the 1470s. In 1480, an independent
artist, he bought the panels of an
altarpiece that his father had left
unfinished. This was his first contact with
the Confraternity of Our Lady, attached
to the cathedral in 's-Hertogenbosch,
which he joined in 1486-1487. His
membership in this confraternity has
been connected with particular cults
and traditions that might be at the basis
of the possible esoteric or heretic
doctrines underpinning certain
paintings. Some of his most famous
works date from the last decades of the
fifteenth century, like the large triptychs
of the *Hay Wain* and the *Garden of
Earthly Delights*. For a number of years
his presence in his hometown is not
documented. It is very likely that
during this period, between 1500 and
1503, he traveled to Venice, where
he left important paintings, recorded in
Cardinal Grimani's collection in 1521.

His contact with Italian painting
and Dürer (who was also in Venice)
resulted in a mutual exchange of
influences. Bosch's style remained
extremely original, but it became
enriched by a new awareness of
composition, of vast landscapes, and
new chromatic effects. The *Temptation
of St. Anthony* in Lisbon is an
exceptional demonstration of this; it
was to be followed by the *Adoration of
the Magi*, in the Prado, Madrid, which
displays a further development in his
pictorial language. In 1503–1504 he
returned to his native city. He had
become a famous artist in Europe and
executed small works for the
Confraternity of Our Lady as well as
major commissions for high-ranking
collectors. Later in his career he began
to paint compositions with half-length
figures like the *Ecce Homo*, the
Crowning with Thorns, and the *Way to
Calvary*. Bosch's funeral took place in
the chapel of the Confraternity of Our
Lady on August 9, 1516.

Hieronymus Bosch
Cure for Madness
1475-1480
oil on wood, 19 × 13¾ in.
(48 × 35 cm)
Prado, Madrid

"Extract the stone: my
name is Lubbert Das
(crazy man)." This
inscription in gold letters
explains the unusual
subject of the painting.
The episode refers to the
Flemish expression "to
have a stone in the head,"
which means to be mad.
This scene contains
bizarre details like the
funnel-shaped doctor's
hat, the woman with
a book on her head, the
contradiction between the
jug with a lid offered by
the monk and the open
jug hanging from the
surgeon's belt. A liking for
proverbs, even among
intellectuals, is one of the
most interesting aspects
of Flemish and Dutch
culture: in 1500 the
Humanist Erasmus
of Rotterdam published
Adagia (Adages),
a collection of ancient
proverbs,

Hieronymus Bosch
The Triptych of the Hay Wain
central panel: *The Hay Wain*, side panels: *Original Sin; Infernal Constructions*, 1500-1502 oil on wood, central panel, 53 × 39½ in. (135 × 100 cm); side panels, 53 × 17¾ in. (135 × 45 cm)
Prado, Madrid

"The world is a mountain of hay: everyone snatches as much as he can." Once again, the key to interpreting this work, one of Bosch's masterpieces, lies in a proverb. This triptych begins with the left panel that depicts four separate episodes connected with the theme of man's damnation: the fall of the rebel angels, the creation of Eve, the original sin, and the expulsion of Adam and Eve from Eden. The vast central scene is dominated by a hay cart, the symbol of human greed, slowly drawn by horrible creatures. Corrupt mankind, already on the path to eternal damnation, throngs tumultuously around the cart, even cutting each other's throats or being mown down by the wheels in order to snatch a handful of hay. The countless figures also include the rulers of the earth (the pope, the emperor, the king), following the terrible procession on horseback. There are other scenes taking place as the cart passes, which give the painter another opportunity to vent his sarcasm: in the foreground, an obese friar looks on as busy nuns fill his large sacks with hay. A group of lustful lovers are on top of the cart.

In the right panel the devils drag the terrified sinners into a flaming Hell against the backcloth of an inextinguishable fire. There is one detail that makes this scene even more terrible: Hell is too small for all the damned and groups of demon-workers are building new and larger towers.

35

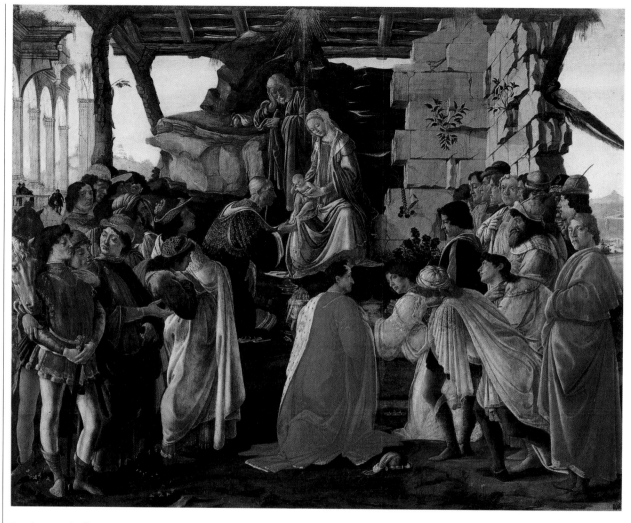

Sandro Botticelli

Alessandro di Mariano Filipepi
Florence, 1445-1510

A leading exponent of Florentine art in the last quarter of the fifteenth century, Botticelli is famous, above all, for his works commissioned by the Medici family and particularly for his large profane allegories. These reflect the tastes, the cultural climate, and refined return to classicism of Lorenzo the Magnificent and Neoplatonic Florentine culture. This was a sophisticated, refined, erudite, and serene period of the Italian Renaissance. During his life Botticelli came into close contact with other Florentine artists, and his training began in the workshop of Filippo Lippi, in the 1460s. When the latter moved to Spoleto in 1466, Botticelli became an assistant to Verrocchio, and thus came to know the master's other young pupils, including Perugino and Leonardo. The recurrent subject of Botticelli's early works was the Madonna and Child, which he repeated in numerous versions. In 1470 he painted the allegorical work *Fortitude* as part of a cycle of Virtues executed by Piero Pollaiolo (Uffizi, Florence). In 1472 he and his pupil Filippino Lippi were enrolled in the Florentine Painters' Guild. A series of portraits of the Medici were made by Botticelli, the ruling family's favorite artist, as is demonstrated by the commission he received in 1475 for the great *Adoration of the Magi*, now in the Uffizi. In 1477 the so-called *Spring* marked the beginning of the cycle of great mythological allegories, probably painted for Lorenzo di Pierfrancesco de' Medici (a cousin of Lorenzo the Magnificent), the first great paintings on profane subjects drawn from classical antiquity. Regarded as one of the leading masters, Botticelli was summoned to Rome in 1482 and involved in the task of decorating the walls of the Sistine chapel. He returned to Florence as the favorite painter of Lorenzo the Magnificent. For a decade Botticelli produced frescoes and altarpieces, as well as religious and secular paintings, that marked the end of the experimental stage of Humanism and the development of an extremely elegant linear approach. In 1492 the death of Lorenzo the Magnificent and the moral revolution brought about by Savonarola had a striking effect on Botticelli's style. He used pale colors, his compositions became taut and dramatic, and an intense mysticism reappeared in the choice of subjects. This period of spiritual turmoil saw the artist's last masterpieces, produced on the eve of the new century, which almost anticipate Mannerism.

Sandro Botticelli
Spring
1477-1482
tempera on wood
80 × 123¾ in.
(203 × 314 cm)
Uffizi, Florence

Produced under the supervision of the Humanist Marsilio Ficino for the Medici villa at Castello, Botticelli's great secular paintings stand at the heart of his output and represent the culmination of Florentine Neoplatonism. Painted for the young Lorenzo di Pierfrancesco de' Medici, a cousin of Lorenzo the Magnificent, the paintings had the didactic purpose of inculcating virtue and a taste for beauty.

Opposite
Sandro Botticelli
Adoration of the Magi
1475
tempera on wood
43¾ × 52¾ in.
(111 × 134 cm)
Uffizi, Florence

Commissioned by Giovanni del Lama (the figure turning toward the spectator in the group on the right), this painting is in actual fact a celebration of the Medici family, who had particular ties with the Magi, and of the powerful political and cultural circles in Florence at the time. All the most illustrious members of the ruling family are portrayed, beginning with the elderly Cosimo, next to the Holy Family, and his son Piero the Gouty, in the center of the scene wearing a red cloak. The young Lorenzo is also present, flanked by the Humanists Angelo Poliziano and Pico della Mirandola. Botticelli includes a portrait of himself, enveloped in a large golden yellow cloak, on the extreme right.

François Boucher
Paris, 1703-1770

Boucher, a brilliant decorator and colorist and a protégé of the Marquise de Pompadour, represented the elegant, refined taste of the court of Louis XV. He painted all his subjects with great perfection and taste, happy to try his hand at a wide range of genres and themes, from mythological subjects to pastoral scenes, from landscapes to portraits. After training in the workshop of François Lemoyne, he traveled to Italy in 1727, staying in Rome at the French Academy and for

brief periods in Naples and Venice. He painted mythological themes such as the *Birth of Adonis* and the *Death of Adonis* (both in the Matthieu Goudchaux Collection, Paris), and the pastoral scene *Women at the Fountain* (J. B. Speed Art Museum, Louisville). He returned to Paris in 1731, and was admitted to the Academy as a history painter in 1734, presenting *Rinaldo and Armida* (Louvre, Paris) as his *morceau de réception*. In 1735 he received his first official commission: the decoration of the Queen's room in the palace of Versailles with four *grisailles* depicting the virtues, in

which the Italian-influenced aspects of his style are given a more individual treatment. The following year he began to work with the Royal Manufactory of Beauvais, for which he produced the cartoons of fourteen tapestries in the series *Fêtes de village à l'italienne*, rustic scenes with brightly-colored figures in relaxed poses against a highly evocative background of woods and ruins. Despite the evident influence of Watteau, Boucher evolved an unmistakably individual pictorial language aimed at exalting beauty and eroticism. In 1742 he began to work with the Paris Opéra, producing

magnificent stage sets; this comes as no surprise, since his theatrical vocation is evident in both his painting and his drawing. In 1755 he was appointed painter to the king, after which he continued to alternate religious and pastoral subjects, landscapes and countryside or mythological scenes, confirming his fame as a charming painter of grace and joy.

Opposite
François Boucher
Nude Lying on a Sofa
1752
oil on canvas
23¼ × 28¾ in.
(59 × 73 cm)
Alte Pinakothek,
Munich

Gently reclining on the sofa, with a rather mischievous air, the girl's nudity is provocative yet graceful. The daring pose, the reflection of the light on the silk of the cushions, the curtain and the clothing, and the pink flesh create a perfect representation of the frivolity and sensuality of the age.

François Boucher
Portrait of the Marquise de Pompadour
1759
oil on canvas
35¾ × 27¼ in.
(91 × 69 cm)
Wallace Collection,
London

Commissioned for the Castle of Bellevue in 1758, the painting represents the Marquise in a small wood next to Pigalle's statue of *Love and Friendship*. The figure of the woman, with her noble pose and sumptuous dress, dominates the composition, which is almost entirely in shades of ocher.

Dieric Bouts

Haarlem, c. 1415-Louvain, 1475

The artist was born in the town of Haarlem in the northern Netherlands, where quite a lively school of painting developed in the second half of the century. His youth is shrouded in mystery, but the influence of van der Weyden can be detected in the early works produced around 1450. The presence of Bouts in Louvain, then a rapidly expanding city, is documented from 1457, and in 1468 he was appointed the city's official painter.

His most significant works include the *Last Supper Altarpiece* and the *Last Judgment Altarpiece*, which the Louvain City Council commissioned to rival Rogier van der Weyden's imposing work in Beaune. In addition to his large official works, however, Bouts' oeuvre includes many versions of the Madonna and Child. His lucid and controlled handling of space also allowed him to depict landscapes of great precision and beauty in which the figures are perfectly integrated, thus anticipating devices that were to be adopted by Gérard David.

Dieric Bouts
Virgin and Child
c. 1450
oil on wood
8½ × 6½ in.
(21.6 × 16.5 cm)
Metropolitan Museum
of Art, New York

Dieric Bouts
*Supper in the House
of Simon the Pharisee*
c. 1445-1450
panel, 16 × 24 in.
(40.5 × 61 cm)
Gemäldegalerie, Berlin

This early work shows the artist's interest in the rational arrangement of figures in space, which is evident in most of his paintings.

Bramante

Donato D'Angelo, Fermignano
(Pesaro), 1444-Rome, 1514

The greatest architect from the Milan
of the Sforzas to the Rome of Pope
Julius II, Bramante proved a splendid
and original interpreter of classical
antiquity in increasingly monumental
and daring forms. However, his debut
was made as a painter when he arrived
in Milan in about 1480, and although
he did produce a number of
architectural works at this time (Santa
Maria presso San Satiro, Santa Maria
delle Grazie, cloisters of
Sant'Ambrogio), it was his painting,
especially the rigorous monumentality
of the figures in solemn spatial
contexts, that influenced the Lombard
school. The Pinacoteca di Brera houses
the repositioned frescoes of *Men-at-
Arms* and *Christ at the Column*, the only
panel that can definitely be attributed to
him. The Sforza Castle contains his
symbolic fresco *Argus* which he painted
together with Bramantino. Bramante left
Milan after the fall of Ludovico il Moro
and settled in Rome (1499) and he
started his extraordinary
reinterpretation of antiquity (the small
temple next to San Pietro in Montorio
left a deep impression on the artists of
his time, including Raphael). He became
the most important architect at the
papal court. For Julius II he undertook
the redesign of the Vatican Palaces
around the Belvedere. From 1506
onwards he did fundamental work
on rebuilding St. Peter's which was later
to be carried on by Michelangelo.

Bramante

Christ at the Column
c. 1490
wood panel, 37 × 20¾ in.
(93.7 × 62.5 cm)
Pinacoteca di Brera, Milan

This was painted for the
Chiaravalle abbey. Christ's
torso, carved like a
column, is a fine example
of the geometrical
monumentality that was
Bramante's inspiration not
only as an architect but
also as a painter. Through
the window we can see a
landscape with many
watercourses. Light glints
realistically on Christ's
curly hair. Both of these
features can be related to
works made by Leonardo
during his stay in Milan.

Georges Braque
Argenteuil, 1882-Paris, 1963

A leading figure in avant-garde research between the early part of the century and the Second World War, Georges Braque moved to Paris at the age of eighteen to study Dufy and the late works of the Impressionists. Concentrating on landscape, he soon showed a tendency to handle colors with great freedom, even in an unnatural way, using large expanses of color defined by marked outlines. This was the road taken by the Fauves, with whom Braque came briefly into contact only to establish a close partnership with Picasso, around 1907. Alternating summers in the countryside with work at the legendary Bateau-Lavoir in Montmartre, Braque and Picasso created Cubism through a continual exchange of ideas. The themes of Cubist painting were rapidly fixed: analysis of the human figure (practiced mainly by Picasso) and still life. For these compositions, Braque gave up the vivid colors of his early period in favor of a rigorous investigation of forms, volumes, and lines. The first phase of "Analytical Cubism" (1908-1911), during which the collaboration between Braque and Picasso was so close that their work was almost indistinguishable, was followed by the period of "Synthetic Cubism" (1912-1914), in which Braque expressed himself with greater originality, especially through the insertion of numbers, letters, and various materials applied onto canvas in the new technique of collage. After the First World War, and the end of his friendship with Picasso, Braque continued his research into the decomposition and recomposition of objects set on a table with a small round top (*guéridon*), attaining effects of total abstraction. Like Picasso, Braque paid homage to the classical tradition in the twenties, painting imposing female figures and trying his hand at sculpture in bronze.

Georges Braque
Houses at L'Estaque
1908
oil on canvas, 23½ × 28¾ in.
(60 × 73 cm)
Kunstmuseum, Bern

The influence of Cézanne marks a turning point in Braque's painting. He spent his summers with Picasso, engaged in a quest for a sober simplification of color and geometrization of form.

Georges Braque
Violin and Palette
1910
oil on canvas, 36¼ × 16¾ in.
(92 × 42.5 cm)
Guggenheim Museum, New York

In his compositions Braque often included musical instruments and scores: "timeless" objects whose form has remained unchanged for centuries.

Bronzino

Agnolo di Cosimo di Mariano Tori
Florence, 1503-1572

Bronzino was the best portrayer of the frozen, rigid etiquette of the Grand Duke's court in Florence. His career is interwoven with the history of Mannerism on which he left his own mark. He happily established himself as the official painter of the Grand Duchy and as the enigmatic stylist of a small circle of cultured aristocrats.

Bronzino was first Pontormo's pupil and then for many years his close assistant. With his master he took part in many important jobs in Florence in the 1520s (frescoes in the Galluzzo Charter House and decorating the Capponi chapel in Santa Felicita). In 1530 he was summoned to the della Rovere court in the Marches and it was there that he began to paint portraits. It was not long before his outstanding talent in this direction became clear and he started to develop his own style, quite distinct from that of Pontormo. In fact, in addition to his master's almost maniacal insistence on accurate drawing, Bronzino added his own very personal use of color which he applied in a clear and compact fashion that almost gave the effect of varnish. By about 1540 he had undoubtedly become the darling of the Medici court and Florentine aristocracy, not least thanks to his literary talents, for he was also a poet. He alternated his production of smooth, almost crystalline portraits, with noteworthy decorative schemes, such as the frescoes in the Medici villas, the redecoration of the private apartments in the Palazzo Vecchio, or designing tapestries for the Grand Duke. From 1560 onward, he produced more religious paintings for altars in the major Florentine churches. These reveal his limits as a painter.

Bronzino
Portrait of Eleonora da Toledo
1545-1546
tempera on wood
45 × 37¾ in.
(115 × 96 cm)
Uffizi, Florence

The firm and glacial way that Bronzino draws outline and detail makes his portraits quite unmistakable. At the same time they possess an almost arrogant grandeur. This leads to a sense of immobile and timeless refinement which is particularly noticeable in his portraits of the Grand Duke's family. Archeological work in the tomb of Eleonora, the wife of Francesco I de' Medici, has revealed fragments of the dress worn in this portrait.

Ford Madox Brown
Calais, 1821–London, 1893

Though he trained and worked in England, Brown made long journeys on the Continent, studying the art of the past and entering into contact with the liveliest circles and movements in art. One of his most interesting encounters was with Overbeck's group of Nazarenes in Rome, who urged him to go back to the models of the fifteenth century. In this sense, Brown supplied the formal ideas that led to the formation of the Pre-Raphaelites though he was never actually a member of Dante Gabriel Rossetti's Brotherhood. Brown's painting is composed of figures and settings that are clearly delineated by refined draftsmanship and illuminated by a precise and diffuse light. The spacious and well-laid-out compositions hark back to the paintings of the Renaissance, including the much-admired Botticelli, from whom Brown also took the form of the tondo. His most important works were painted around 1850, when the artist was equally happy to tackle scenes drawn from ancient history and episodes of acute social relevance, playing an extremely prominent role in British intellectual debate.

Ford Madox Brown
The Last of England
1855
oil on panel
32¼ × 29½ in.
(82 × 75 cm)
City Art Gallery,
Birmingham

The melancholy and tender image of two emigrants illustrates an unfamiliar aspect of industrial and working-class society in Imperial and Victorian Britain.

Jan Bruegel the Elder
The Original Sin
c. 1620
oil on wood
20 × 32¾ in.
(52 × 83.5 cm)
Museum of Fine Arts,
Budapest

Repeatedly depicted by
Bruegel and his school,
this surprisingly fresh
painting belongs to the
"encyclopedic" genre of
the Baroque. The aim
was to contain within a
single work a whole
universe of scientific
and natural
observations. Domestic
animals and exotic
beasts, the
representatives of all the
continents and of all the
species, are depicted
with precision, the
pretext being the
reference to the garden
of Eden.

Jan Bruegel the Elder
Brussels, 1568-Antwerp, 1625

The son, though not the pupil, of the
great Pieter Bruegel the Elder (who died
before Jan was one year old), the future
leading exponent of the first period
of still life in Europe was raised by his
grandmother, Maria Bessemers—a
painter of considerable talent—together
with his brother, Pieter the Younger,
who also trained as a painter. Jan
Bruegel showed great talent and
considerable independence at an early
age. After a stay in Cologne in 1589, Jan
Bruegel went to Naples in 1590, where
he began an intense five-year period of
work and study in Italy. He spent most
of the time in Rome, where he became
one of the leading members of the
increasingly large colony of northern
artists. He and his painter friend Paul
Brill drew numerous views of the
ancient monuments (the study of Jan
Bruegel's exceptional drawings is
relatively recent and they are proving
to be a valuable source of information
on the former appearance of ruins that
have since been altered or destroyed),
and he successfully tried his hand at the
independent genre of landscape.
Stormy seas, Alpine views with rustic
hermits, or red-tinged mountains were
his first subjects. These were nearly
always small works, painted on copper,

and executed with typically Flemish
meticulous precision. The small works
in which Bruegel paints countless
objects or all kinds of animals verge
on pure virtuosity. This aptitude for
painstaking execution, which is almost
miniaturistic, can also be seen in the
religious and allegorical works painted
in tandem with Hans Rottenhammer.
After being noted by Cardinal Federico
Borromeo, a great connoisseur of the
arts and one of the first to appreciate
the emerging genre of still life, Jan
Bruegel began to paint bunches of cut
flowers and in a very short space of
time became a true specialist in this
field. In 1595, Cardinal Borromeo
invited him to Milan and became his
patron, a relationship that continued
even after the painter's return
to Antwerp, when it developed into
a regular correspondence.
Jan Bruegel painted a considerable
number of works for the cardinal,
which are still housed in the Pinacoteca
Ambrosiana in Milan, founded by
Federico Borromeo in 1618.
During the years he spent in Antwerp,
the demand for Bruegel's work from
collectors throughout Europe increased.
He therefore set up a large studio in
which his son Jan the Younger was also
an apprentice. Around 1615, Rubens
invited Bruegel to join his workshop
as his specialized assistant.

Jan Bruegel the Elder
Mouse with Roses
1605
oil on copper
3 × 4 in. (7.2 × 10.2 cm)
Pinacoteca Ambrosiana,
Milan

This very unusual
work of extremely fine
draftsmanship was
particularly admired
by Cardinal Borromeo,
and the painter gave
it to him as a gift.

Pieter Bruegel the Elder

Breda (?), 1525/30-Brussels, 1569

The life and artistic career of Pieter Bruegel the Elder unfolded in major centers of culture and during an eventful period of history, yet so little confirmed information about him has survived that it is difficult to reconstruct his personal and artistic life in any detail. The custom of signing and dating works does at least give a reliable chronology of paintings, drawings, and engravings. The first written evidence, dated 1551, is his enrollment in the Antwerp Painters' Guild, where he was admitted as a "master," a level that was awarded only after coming of age, usually between twenty-one and twenty-five years. He must therefore have been born between 1525 and 1530. The documentation reveals nothing about his place of birth and the earliest biographers give conflicting information on this point. According to the most credible hypothesis, he was born in Breda, but other towns in Brabant and Limburg have also been suggested. Very little is also known about his artistic training. The only consistent reference is to the Antwerp studio of Pieter Coecke, an artist and intellectual of great standing. He arrived on the art scene with landscape drawings dating from 1552. A significant aspect of the artistic *milieu* in Antwerp was the Italian connection; in fact, Bruegel's document of enrollment in the guild is countersigned by the Mantovan engraver Giorgio Ghisi. Perhaps this encounter gave him the idea of going to Italy, a journey he made between 1552 and 1556. From 1556 he worked for the printing works of Hieronymus Cock. His first dated painting, the *Parable of the Sower* (now in Washington, D.C.), and the fascinating Brussels *Fall of Icarus* were executed in 1557. His career developed in three parallel directions: drawing, engraving, and painting, but from 1562, painting was his main interest. In 1564 his firstborn, Pieter, also known as Bruegel the Younger, was born. His second son, Jan, born in 1568, was to become an excellent still-life painter, known by the nickname "Velvet" Bruegel. The cycle of paintings called the *Seasons* dates from 1565. By this stage Bruegel the Elder had become an established figure, his works taking on a new monumental dimension and leaving behind the multifarious details typical of the earlier period. He died in Brussels on September 5, 1569.

Pieter Bruegel the Elder
The Tower of Babel
1563
oil on wood, 44¾ × 61 in.
(114 × 155 cm)
Kunsthistorisches Museum, Vienna

46

Pieter Bruegel the Elder
Hunters in the Snow
1565
oil on wood, 46 × 63¾ in. (117 × 162 cm)
Kunsthistorisches Museum, Vienna

The inspiration for this very famous scene stems from human, social, climatic, and natural conditions, which acquire a timelessness going beyond the constraints of the cycle to become the very image of the freezing cold and silence of winter. It is part of the cycle of the *Seasons* in Rudolph II's collection, discussed on the previous page. Bruegel's composition is set higher in respect to the foreground and focuses on the fundamental contrast between the white of the snow and the black outlines of the people, trees, and buildings. The striking simplicity (such that Bruegel has erroneously been compared with naïf painters) highlights the exceptional luministic effects he achieved, especially in the background landscape. Bruegel, who came from rural low-lying Flanders, had been very struck by the experience of crossing the Alps on his journey to Italy. His memories of the snow-covered peaks and rocky outcrops take shape in an image in which reality and fantasy combine in an extremely evocative way. Few other works of art manage to communicate such a sense of icy air and imminent snow surrounding the highest jagged peaks. The leafless branches of the bare trees form a black screen against the solid background of the sky. Down on the floor of the valley the tiny village nestles at the foot of the enormous mountains. The children playing on the frozen pond add a delightful note and enliven the whole scene.

Gustave Caillebotte
Paris, 1848-Gennevilliers, 1894

A figure perhaps unjustly undervalued by the general public, Caillebotte is a painter of great interest, occupying a unique position within the Impressionist movement. He was invited to join the group by Monet in 1874, on the occasion of the historic exhibition in Nadar's studio. Caillebotte, while adopting the clear light, brilliant colors, and (at least in part) themes from bourgeois life so dear to the Impressionists, never turned his back on his original influences, which came not so much from landscape painting *en plein air* as from the Realism of Courbet. The

Floor-Scrapers (1875) is Caillebotte's most emblematic work, achieving a fine balance between the effect of the light entering through the window and the dark outlines of the workers. Monumental figures were to remain a constant feature of his painting, setting it apart from the other work shown at the Impressionists' joint exhibitions, in which he participated regularly up until 1882. It is interesting to note, however, that after the group had more or less broken up, Caillebotte too began to paint the sort of landscapes around the Seine and Argenteuil that had been characteristic of the initial phase of the movement.

Gustave Caillebotte
Paris, A Rainy Day
1877
oil on canvas
83½ × 108¾ in.
(212.2 × 276.2 cm)
Art Institute, Chicago

The streets of Paris were no less lively in bad weather, but Caillebotte (unlike Renoir and Pissarro when painting under similar conditions) takes advantage of the gloom to concentrate on the robust characterization of his figures.

Robert Campin

Master of Flémalle
Valenciennes (?), c. 1375-Tournai, 1444

There is little reliable information on
this artist, also known as the Master of
Flémalle, who is of crucial importance
for an understanding of how Flemish
painting gradually freed itself from the
earlier tradition. It is known, however,
that he spent much of his life at
Tournai in present-day Wallonia,
where a revolt led by representatives
of the craft guilds in 1423 weakened
the aristocratic ruling class and led to
broader participation in city
government. Campin played a leading
role in this middle-class society, where
he held such posts as dean of the
goldsmiths' corporation and head of
the painters' guild. He ran a thriving
and well-organized workshop, where
Rogier van der Weyden and Jacques
Daret completed their apprenticeship.
His fortunes seem to have waned
when changes occurred in the city at
the end of the 1430s. From then on his
life was complicated by legal
proceedings and trials that certainly
contributed to his fall from favor.
His realism, however, was to have an
extraordinary influence on the artists
of the following generation. Robert
Campin adopted an approach that was
different from that of his more famous
contemporary van Eyck and less
detached. Influenced by the painting
and sculpture of the Dijon School, he
developed a simple, unadorned style
to sympathetically depict surprisingly
inventive everyday scenes that
revitalize age-old iconographic
devices. Campin moved away from
the linear approach of his predecessors
and accentuated the exquisitely
human, physical presence of his
figures.

Robert Campin
Trinity
c. 1410
panel, 56¾ × 21 in.
(144 × 53 cm)
Städelsches
Kunstinstitut,
Frankfurt

This
monochromatic
painting possesses
all the power of a
sculpture. The
monumental figures
of God and the suffering
Christ emerge with
extraordinary power
from the niche, modeled
by a bright light that
emphasizes their
volumes. The restricted
space is dominated by
the limp body of Christ,
rendered with great
sensitivity, which God
the Father seems to
proffer to the spectator,
almost invading his
space.

Opposite, right
Robert Campin
St. Veronica
c. 1410
panel
59¾ × 24 in.
(151.5 × 61 cm)
Städelsches
Kunstinstitut, Frankfurt

Against the background
of rich brocade that
foreshortens the space,
St. Veronica is depicted
in absorbed
contemplation of the
mystical vision of
Christ's face.

Robert Campin
Nativity
c. 1425
panel
34¼ × 28¾ in.
(87 × 73 cm)
Musée des Beaux-Arts,
Dijon

In this panel the painter
once again concentrates
on the volumes of the
bodies and the folds of
the brightly colored
garments. The most
striking element in the
work is the sweeping
landscape stretching
from the foreground
toward the horizon. The
tiny figures, farms, and
trees along the road lead
to a distant bridge that
is the entrance to a
fortified village bathed
in light.

Canaletto

Giovanni Antonio Canal
Venice, 1697-1768

Canaletto is the leading figure in the history of the *veduta*, that particular, independent style of landscape art that was first introduced at the end of the seventeenth century by the Dutch painter Gaspar van Wittel, and spread all over Italy from Rome to Venice and Naples. He is also one of the world's best-loved painters. His tireless production of works for export to aristocratic collections is a constant hymn to beauty: the splendor of architecture, the wonders of the heavens, and the enchantment of nature. The most famous works are of course those depicting his native city. Canaletto's Venice is a fabulous city, both alive with the bustle of countless activities and transfixed eternally as a legend that history cannot mar, but only enrich with new episodes. It is certainly no coincidence that even now, over two centuries after his death, Canaletto's work remains constantly in great demand on the art market, regardless of changes in fashion and taste. The son of

a theatrical scene painter (this reference to his father's work is essential to understand the developments in technique and the type of image adopted by the artist), Canaletto followed his father's craft in the theaters of Venice and Rome. In Rome he had the opportunity to see and study the work of van Wittel, and came into contact with important painters of classical ruins. His first paintings were depictions of the ancient buildings and ruins of Rome that displayed a bold and theatrical handling of perspective. The first person to appreciate the young artist's work was a theatrical impresario, the Londoner Owen Mac Swinney, who drew the attention of his fellow countrymen to Canaletto. At the age of thirty, he began to paint views of Venice aimed primarily at European gentlemen on the Grand Tour. His choice of spectacular settings and clear blue skies soon brought him fame, and the British consul in Venice, the highly cultured collector Joseph Smith, commissioned him to paint dozens of paintings. These were subsequently bought en bloc by George III and now constitute an exceptional collection of Canaletto's

works, the largest and most important in the world, held by the British royal family at Buckingham Palace and Windsor Castle. Using his training as a painter of stage sets and his skill in perspective distortion to obtain spectacular effects, Canaletto established a model for views of Venice not only in paintings but also in drawings and engravings, which increased his fame still further. Links with Canaletto became synonymous with success throughout Europe, and it is no coincidence that his nephew Bernardo Bellotto was to adopt the pseudonym "Canaletto" outside Italy, almost as though seeking to pass himself off as his celebrated uncle. In 1746 he moved to London and spent a successful period of ten years in England, during which he painted a constant stream of views of Venice (based on detailed drawings he had taken with him). He also produced memorable views of the capital and the English countryside that were to provide inspiration for the local painters. On his return to Venice, he took up the chair in perspective at the Accademia di Belle Arti founded by Piazzetta and directed by Giambattista Tiepolo.

Canaletto
The Basin of St. Mark–Looking Eastward
c. 1738
oil on canvas, 49¼ × 80½ in. (125 × 204.5 cm)
Museum of Fine Arts, Boston

This canvas underscores the importance of Canaletto's use of optical instruments and his study of perspective. He assumes a raised viewpoint in the area of the Punta della Dogana at the mouth of the Grand Canal, where his horizon opens up with the effect of a wide-angle lens. Canaletto maintains a clarity of vision even in the furthest distances. The monuments lining the Riva degli Schiavoni do not constitute the final visual objectives, but are absorbed within a single, choral image.

Canaletto
*The Doge's Procession to
the Church of San Rocco*
c. 1735
oil on canvas
57¾ × 78¼ in.
(147 × 199 cm)
National Gallery,
London

Every year in the month
of August the painters
of Venice would exhibit
their works in front of
the Scuola di San Rocco
in a bustling fair that
displayed the progress
and development of the
local school.
This occasion also
enjoyed some official
recognition, and
Canaletto's painting
depicts the visit paid to
the exhibition by the
Doge (in the center,
beneath the parasol,
wearing heavy robes
of gold thread trimmed
with ermine at the
height of the summer!)
and the Venetian
senators. The paintings
were hung on the
façades of the buildings
and an awning was
extended over the route
to protect the visitors
from the sun.
The holes for the
poles used to support
the awning can still be
seen today in the square
adjacent to the Scuola
and the church of
San Rocco.

Alonso Cano
Granada, 1601-1667

A painter, sculptor, and architect of remarkable talent, Cano was trained by his father Miguel in his youth, and assisted him in producing painted carved altarpieces. He is one of the most interesting figures in seventeenth-century Spain, not only by virtue of his activities as a multifaceted artist, but also because of his complex life. His training was completed in Seville, in the workshop of Francisco Pacheco, together with Velázquez, his near contemporary. Cano shared his friend's admiration for the Italian art of the Renaissance, though he was not so concerned with the application of color and brushwork, but took a greater interest in the classical nude and anatomical drawings of great accuracy, which were also to prove useful for his highly esteemed work as a sculptor. On Velázquez's invitation, he moved to Madrid in 1637. At the court of Philip IV he distinguished himself as Velázquez's assistant, as a restorer of old paintings (including some masterpieces by Titian, damaged in the fire at the Buen Retiro palace in 1640), and as a painter of luminous religious compositions. The theme of the male nude continued to predominate and Cano preferred such scenes as the Scourging of Christ, the Deposition, the Pietà, and the Crucifixion. His career as court painter was dramatically interrupted when he was forced to flee from Madrid after being accused—perhaps unjustly—of the murder of his second wife. After a period spent in Valencia, Cano returned to Madrid, but he had by now lost favor. In 1652, he returned to his hometown and began the great task of decorating the façade of the cathedral. He also continued producing wooden sculptures—sometimes working together with Pedro de Meña—many of which were painted. He asked for permission to become a priest with the Chapter of Granada, but his acceptance was delayed until 1660. During this period he painted an impressive series of canvases with *Stories of the Virgin* for the niches in the choir of Granada cathedral, a task that continued until 1664.

Alonso Cano
The Dead Christ Supported by an Angel
c. 1645
oil on canvas, 54 × 39¼ in.
(137 × 100 cm)
Prado, Madrid

Caravaggio

Michelangelo Merisi
Milan, 1571-Porto Ercole, 1610

A short and adventurous life forms the dramatic setting for the work of Caravaggio, the artist who did more than any other to influence the development of seventeenth-century painting by introducing a realism and use of light and shade that were to be followed for centuries to come. Most probably born in Milan (his nickname being derived from the Marchese di Caravaggio, for whom the painter's father worked as an administrator), he received his training from Simone Peterzano, but above all he studied with keen intelligence the work of Leonardo da Vinci, Titian, and the sixteenth-

century masters from Brescia. This gave him a very strong leaning toward realism that was expressed through his handling of light and emotion. Around 1590 Caravaggio moved to Rome. The early years were grim, fraught with poverty and illness. An assistant in the workshops of established painters, Caravaggio found it difficult to make a name for himself. This period saw the production of some memorable paintings. Caravaggio brought the little world of the Roman alleys into painting: gypsies, cardsharps, prostitutes, ambiguous young "hustlers," street lads, and strolling musicians. His early works, characterized by a light neutral background, are milestones in the birth of genre painting. The descriptive details—flowers, fruit, and various

objects—are executed with the greatest care, and Caravaggio does not hesitate to endow them with an independent dignity as artistic subjects. The *Basket of Fruit* in the Pinacoteca Ambrosiana in Milan is a celebrated model for still-life painting. The early religious paintings (such as the *Rest on the Flight into Egypt* in the Galleria Doria Pamphili in Rome) were still influenced by the naturalism of the Lombard school, but there was to be a further breakthrough. In the monumental paintings for the church of San Luigi dei Francesi in Rome (1600), Caravaggio offered a radically new and highly dramatic interpretation of altar painting. The figures emerge from the dark background to create an unprecedented expressive impact. The great religious works painted in Rome

(1600-1606) triggered widespread heated debate; some of them were refused by clients shocked by their excessively brutal realism. Found guilty of murder and sentenced to death, Caravaggio was forced to flee from Rome (1606), thus beginning a human odyssey during which he produced masterpieces that were to become points of reference for European painting as a whole. After a stay in Naples, he went to Malta, where he was admitted into the Order of the Knights of St. John. This glory was, however, short-lived. He was imprisoned on Malta but succeeded in escaping, first to Sicily and then to Naples. Trusting that a papal pardon would be forthcoming, he prepared to sail for Rome, but, after a series of adventures, he died of malaria at Porto Ercole.

Previous page
Caravaggio
Basket of Fruit
1597-1598
oil on canvas
18 × 25½ in.
(46 × 64.5 cm)
Pinacoteca Ambrosiana,
Milan

Cardinal Del Monte
gave this extraordinary
canvas to Cardinal
Federico Borromeo,
Archbishop of Milan
and renowned art
collector. It marks the
beginning of the still-life
genre, and is poised
between a meticulous
imitation of reality and
sweeping poetry.
Federico Borromeo
wished to accompany
this work with another
basket of fruit, but as
he himself wrote, "since
none could match the
beauty of this one
and its incomparable
excellence, it has
remained alone."

Caravaggio
*The Calling
of St. Matthew*
1599-1600
oil on canvas
126¾ × 133¾ in.
(322 × 340 cm)
Contarelli chapel,
church of San Luigi
dei Francesi, Rome

The long and complex
contractual negotiations
for the decoration of the
Contarelli chapel in the
church of the French
community in Rome
came to an end with the
decision to engage
Caravaggio to execute
three paintings: the
altarpiece depicting St.
Matthew writing the

Gospel, flanked by two
works showing the key
moments in the life of
the evangelist.
Caravaggio produced
his first version of *St.
Matthew and the Angel*,
but the clerics found the
saint's expression too
crude and refused to
accept it. Before
beginning a new version
of the altarpiece (1602),
Caravaggio executed the
two side paintings,
which constitute an
epoch-making turning
point in the history of
art. With tremendous
force, he draws the
spectator into the
episode as it is actually
happening, when it has

reached its dramatic
climax. The *Martyrdom*
is a brutal execution,
with the killer bursting
into the church to strike
down the saint during
the celebration of mass.
Caravaggio interprets
the scene as an episode
of violent crime, with
the saint attempting to
defend himself while the
space is rent by the
figures of the killer and
of the choirboy fleeing
in terror. Much calmer
but by no means less
evocative is the scene
of the *Calling*. Christ
enters a guardhouse in
which soldiers and tax
collectors are seated on
benches. Followed by a

shaft of light, He raises
His arm and points to
the dumbfounded
Matthew, who responds
by placing his hand on
his breast.

Caravaggio
Christ Taken Prisoner
1602
oil on canvas
52½ × 66¾ in.
(133.5 × 169.5 cm)
National Gallery of
Ireland, Dublin

This is one of the most
recent and interesting
additions to the catalog
of Caravaggio's works.
Discovered in the
possession of the Jesuit
order in Dublin, the
work had previously
been regarded as lost
and was known only
through old copies. The
dramatic night scene
broken by the metallic
glint of armor highlights
the painter's ability to
convey gesture,
physiognomy, flashes of
anguish, terror,
excitement, and
brutality.

Below
Caravaggio
*Martyrdom of St. Peter;
Conversion of St. Paul*
1600-1601
oil on canvas, 90½ × 69
in. (230 × 175 cm) each
Cerasi chapel, church of
Santa Maria del Popolo,
Rome

The scenes unfold in
silence and solitude.
Three soiled and straining
laborers lift St. Peter
nailed upside-down
on the cross. Caravaggio
does not condemn the
executioners, but rather
underscores the painful
aspect of their task with
the rope that marks two
of them on the back and
arm, while the apostle
looks around, abandoned.
An equally new
interpretation is given of
the conversion of St. Paul,
whose fall takes place in
the darkness of a stable.

57

Vittore Carpaccio
Venice, c. 1455/60-1525/26

The most famous and fascinating works by Carpaccio come from his stupendous cycle of huge canvases on the subjects of St. George and St. Ursula. These reveal the painter's unusual ability to compose vast narrative scenes with crowds of main characters and onlookers against detailed urban backdrops. Even when the town portrayed is not Venice, the canvases still evoke the magical fascination of the city. Carpaccio's activities in his early years are not easy to piece together. In 1490, however, he began the cycle of *The Legend of St. Ursula* (Accademia, Venice). This took him several years to complete and contains remarkable evidence of his stylistic development. By the end he had achieved a perfect balance between anecdotal action, architectural perspectives, soft light, bright colors, and a wealth of descriptive detail. The canvases painted between 1502 and 1507 for the Scuola di San Giorgio degli Schiavoni (still in situ) reach the same level. The later cycles painted for the merchants from Venetian ports in Albania and S. Stefano, scattered between various Italian and foreign museums, seem less powerful. However, he achieved great emotional drama in the resplendent altar paintings produced in the first decade of the Cinquecento. They seem to ignore or reject the soft-toned paintings of Giovanni Bellini and Giorgione (*The Presentation at the Temple*, Accademia, Venice; *Meditation on the Passion*, Staatliche Museen/Preussischer Kulturbesitz, Berlin). Carpaccio also received a number of official commissions (*The Lion of St. Mark* in the Doge's Palace), but after his altarpiece for the church of San Vitale, his Venetian career foundered, partly because by then Titian dominated the scene. Carpaccio ended his career back in the provinces (Bergamo, Cadore, Istria) where his now out-dated style still attracted admirers. He was rediscovered in the nineteenth century and now ranks second only to Giovanni Bellini among Venetian fifteenth-century artists.

Vittore Carpaccio
Young Knight
1510
canvas, 85¾ × 59¾ in.
(218 × 152 cm)
Thyssen-Bornemisza Collection, Madrid

Vittore Carpaccio
The Legend of St. Ursula:
The Arrival of the English
Ambassadors
1495
canvas, 108 × 232 in.
(275 × 589 cm)
Gallerie dell'Accademia,
Venice

By combining the
geometrical rigor of
Renaissance perspective
with his own supremely
imaginative conceptions,
Carpaccio has
constructed a scene rich
in architectural
splendors and colors.
The English ambassadors
are delivering a letter
which requests the hand
of Princess Ursula in
marriage to the crown
prince of England. On
the right of the painting,
Ursula informs her
father of her conditions
for accepting the
marriage. This painting,
too, contains much
valuable documentary
evidence of the times.

Vittore Carpaccio
The Legend of St. Ursula:
The Dream of St. Ursula
1495
canvas
108 × 105 in.
(274 × 267 cm)
Gallerie dell'Accademia,
Venice

This is a most
fascinating
demonstration of
Carpaccio's versatility.
The scenes range from
measured courtly
dignity to this touching
and intimate episode. At
dawn, an angel bearing
the palm of martyrdom
enters the room in
which Ursula is sleeping.
He brings her a dream
about her approaching
death. The objects and
furnishings which
surround the sweetly
sleeping saint are all
reproduced with loving
and touching care. They
provide a reliable
inventory of the interior
of rich Venetian houses
at the end of the
fifteenth century.

Annibale Carracci
Pietà
c. 1599-1600
oil on canvas
61½ × 58¾ in.
(156 × 149 cm)
Galleria Nazionale di
Capodimonte, Naples

The dramatic nature of the subject is softened by the supple, modulated elegance of the execution. Painted during the period of his artistic maturity, at the same time as the frescoed ceiling in the Galleria Farnese in Rome, this splendid work demonstrates Annibale Carracci's ability to select elements from various artists of the past and blend them together in an original and highly successful fashion. While the soft, delicate treatment of drapery and flesh are reminiscent of Correggio, the poses of Christ and Mary are clearly modeled on Michelangelo's *Pietà* in the Vatican.

Annibale Carracci

Bologna, 1560-Rome, 1609

An illustrious member of a family of painters, Annibale Carracci played a crucial role in the transition from the Mannerism of the late Renaissance to the early Baroque. Together with his brother Agostino and cousin Ludovico, he founded the Accademia dei Desiderosi, the first well-structured form of cultural training for young artists, providing a model for the programs of academies of fine arts that was to last almost to the present day. Annibale himself probably trained with his older cousin Ludovico, with whom he also collaborated on a number of early works. Above all, Annibale and Ludovico shared the desire for a return to "natural" painting, a pure and simple style far removed from prestigious but complex and intellectual Mannerism. Annibale's first major public work, the *Crucifixion* for the church of Santa Maria della Carità in Bologna (1583), exemplifies this approach. In the following years, Annibale embarked on an impassioned study of Correggio and Titian, curbed the impetuous energy of his early years, enriched his palette, and softened his outlines. The result was a supple, delicate style, both classical and up-to-date, which soon proved to be the right choice. Around 1590 Annibale Carracci moved to Rome, where his academic approach was enriched through contact with the enormous repertoire of classical art. In an exhilarating environment, surrounded by stimuli and points of reference at the highest levels of the art of the day, he broadened his range of subjects considerably, and also laid the foundations for the specific development of the "ideal" landscape. His presence in Rome was of crucial importance also for the establishment of an actual colony of painters from Emilia, including Guido Reni. The culmination and quintessence of Annibale Carracci's work in Rome is the frescoed ceiling of the gallery in Palazzo Farnese, one of the greatest masterpieces of painting between the sixteenth and seventeenth centuries. Exhausted by the physical and intellectual energy expended on this work, Annibale Carracci never fully recovered and died in 1609, one year before Caravaggio.

Mary Cassatt
The Boating Party
1893-1894
oil on canvas
35½ × 46¼ in.
(90.2 × 117.5 cm)
National Gallery of Art,
Washington, D.C.

This painting was begun in the summer of 1893 at Antibes and reflects the many Impressionist works depicting Sunday outings or regattas on the Seine (as, for example, *Boating* by Manet, today in the National Gallery of Washington; Cassatt herself recommended its acquisition). The broad, sharply defined fields of color and the acute sense of line reveal the influence of Japanese prints. In 1890 Cassatt paid an enthusiastic visit to a large Paris exhibition of more than seven hundred colored prints from Japan; to her friend the painter Berthe Morisot, Cassatt wrote, "You couldn't dream of anything more beautiful ... I don't think of anything else."

Mary Cassatt

Allegheny City (today part of Pittsburgh), Pennsylvania,1844-Château de Beaufresne, Le Mesnil, 1926

One of the greatest and most influential female painters in the entire history of art, Mary Cassatt is an exemplary figure in the American school of the late nineteenth century. One of the original members of the Parisian Impressionists, she spent almost her entire life in France, but she made trips between the two sides of the ocean, partly to carry out her avowed goal of introducing Americans to "modern" painting. Daughter of a well-to-do family living in Philadelphia, Cassatt lived in Europe as a child. At the age of seven, together with her four brothers, she attended school in France and Germany. Following the death of one of her brothers, in 1855, the Cassatt family returned to Philadelphia. Despite her father's veto, Cassatt hoped to become

an artist; at sixteen she enrolled at the Pennsylvania Academy of Fine Arts. After several years of study, she traveled to France and Italy, ultimately settling in Paris. Prevented from following the regular course of artistic studies by the French academy's prohibition of female students, she studied under other artists. Her first success, and an authentic turning point in her career, came with a painting of a Spanish subject, *On the Balcony during the Carnival*, exhibited at the Salon of 1872, a work very close to the style of Manet and also reminiscent of Goya. In 1875 she moved definitively to Paris; a decisive factor behind this decision was her encounter with the painting of Degas. She first saw one of his works displayed in a gallery window, and the experience was like being struck by lightning. As she wrote years later: "How well I remember ... seeing for the first time Degas's pastels in the window of a picture dealer on the

Boulevard Haussmann. I used to go and flatten my nose against that window and absorb all I could of his art. It changed my life." Cassatt soon became an alert and original interpreter of the innovations of Degas, such as the unusual framing of the compositions, the apparently casual design, and the admiration for Japanese prints. Association with Degas and the other painters of the Indépendents group was not without its drawbacks: *Little Girl in a Blue Armchair*, one of her most famous works, completed thanks to the direct intervention of Degas in the painting of the background, was rejected by the jury of the Salon in 1878. The preceding year, she had been joined in Paris by her parents and her sister Lydia; thanks in part to their involvement, leading families of the financial and cultural elite in America were brought into contact with Impressionism, leading to the formation of a flourishing connection

between the American art market and French painters. One of the first and most astute collectors was Louisine Waldron Havemeyer, a personal friend of Cassatt's and the first American to purchase works by Degas. Cassatt spent summers in a villa at Marly (during vacations the Cassatts had Manet as a neighbor), and the experience shows up in her work, her palette growing paler and more luminous. These changes are further enlivened in her canvases set on the beaches of the coastal resorts she visited with her mother. Around 1890 her success was complete, and the Cassatt family moved into a splendid seventeenth-century castle near Le Mesnil, not far from Beauvais. Cassatt's activity was brought to an almost complete end at the close of the last decade of the nineteenth century, when vision problems prevented her from working.

Mary Cassatt
*Children Playing
on the Beach*
1884
oil on canvas,
38½ × 29 in.
(98 × 74.5 cm)
National Gallery of Art,
Washington, D.C.

The identity of the
two girls so absorbed
in playing in the sand
is not known, nor has
anyone recognized
the beach on which the
scene is set. In fact,
Cassatt visited several
seaside locales in 1884,
in both France and
Spain, while traveling
with her mother and a
nephew. With her usual
sensitivity she locates
the point of view in
a position dramatically
close to the children,
more or less the spot
where a mother would
sit while keeping an eye
on them. In so doing,
Cassatt concentrates
the viewer's attention
entirely on the two
delightful girls, to the
point of eliminating
even the shadows on
the sand, and all the rest
of the setting is lost in
a distant haze.

George Catlin

Wilkes-Barre, Pennsylvania, 1796-Jersey City, New Jersey, 1872

Catlin was a painter of Native Americans, and his works, accompanied by in-depth written reports, constitute invaluable documentation of many tribes—in some cases, the only surviving memory. He started out as a successful lawyer, but in 1821, driven by his passion for Native American cultures, he left that work to dedicate himself to painting and documenting American Indians. Beginning in 1830, following military expeditions exploring the West, he visited a vast territory, full of Indian settlements, painting and drawing as he went. Catlin was a self-taught painter, and his technique and his colors reveal the awkward conditions under which he worked. He traveled with about ten colors, transporting his canvases rolled up in cylindrical tubes; the speed at which he worked led to a certain terseness in his brushstrokes, with the colors reduced to the essential. During his many trips west Catlin brought back not only images but artifacts and notes on the lives of the indigenous peoples, all in all a vast quantity of material that, at the end of the 1830s, he put on display in his Indian Gallery. After visiting many cities along the Atlantic Coast, in 1840 he took the Indian Gallery to Europe, where it enjoyed great success. Between 1840 and 1846 it was in London, then in France, then again in London. In London the artist fell victim to speculators, went from debt to bankruptcy, and in 1852 was forced to sell his entire collection to his creditors. Retrieved by an American, the collection was brought back to Philadelphia, where it passed many years locked away in a warehouse. Donated by Catlin's heirs to the state, it is today in the Smithsonian American Art Museum in Washington, D.C. As for Catlin, unable to fit into urban American life, between 1852 and 1860 he went back to roaming among the native tribes; then he decided to explore the unspoiled world of the equatorial jungle in South America. He returned bitterly disappointed and died a financial failure in Jersey City.

George Catlin
*Buffalo Chase
on the Upper Missouri*
oil on canvas, 25¾ × 32 in. (65.4 × 81.3 cm)
Gerald Peters Gallery,
Santa Fe, New Mexico

The Missouri Territory, farthest border of the world inhabited by whites, offered views of an unknown reality. Catlin proved himself exceptionally capable at capturing and describing the characteristics of each tribe and at describing the details of customs.

**Giacomo Ceruti
"Il Pitocchetto"**
Milan, 1698-1767

An artist of great moral nobility, Ceruti was the leading exponent of the "pauperistic" trend in eighteenth-century European painting, firmly rooted in the wholly Lombard tradition of realism that also included Caravaggio. He worked mainly in Brescia for patrons from the solid provincial aristocracy who were capable of appreciating the innovations of his art.

A versatile artist, he also tried his hand at religious painting (admittedly with no great success). His portraits, still lifes, and above all the scenes illustrating the grim and bitter life of the poor were far more successful. Ceruti produced canvases of great intensity, with a capacity to move the viewer, equaled by few other paintings in the eighteenth century. Anticipating the moral and social philosophy of the Enlightenment, Ceruti drew attention to human problems seldom touched upon by previous painters.

He addressed these subjects with a solid technique of great energy and solemn monumentality. The protagonists of this everyday human adventure are not "minor" figures but are powerfully represented in a style of painting that does not hesitate to adopt an epic tone.

Giacomo Ceruti
Washerwoman
c. 1736
oil on canvas, 57 × 51 in.
(145 × 130 cm)
Pinacoteca Tosio-Martinengo, Brescia

In the poor courtyard setting, the youth and the washerwoman are deeply human figures. The painter expresses resignation and dignity.

64

Paul Cézanne
Aix-en-Provence, 1839-1906

As with many of the leading figures in the history of art, the importance of Cézanne only came to be understood rather late, but his influence, which can immediately be recognized as the basis of the Cubist movement, has been fundamental on the whole of that century's painting. Born into a wealthy bourgeois family in Provence, he went to school with Emile Zola and then commenced a career in banking. Eventually, however, his own desire to become an artist managed to prevail over his father's doubts, and, in 1861, he moved to Paris, at the

crucial moment of the transition from the Realism of Courbet to the Impressionism of Monet. Cézanne, who from the outset showed an independent preference for great rigor of composition and little inclination to abandon himself to the Impressionists' taste for pure light and color, made a thorough study of the works of Manet, with whom he shared a great respect for the art of the past. The initial vigor of his brushwork, with its broad strokes of dark color, gradually became more controlled. Persuaded by Pissarro to lighten his palette and devote himself to landscape painting *en plein air*, Cézanne spent time at Auvers-sur-Oise near Pontoise and, with the intention of "doing Poussin again, from

nature," inserted human figures, such as the first *Bathers*, into his landscapes. It was during this period that he started to conceive the landscape not as an "impression" of color, but as a mental construction of regular geometric solids (cubes, spheres, and cylinders). He took part in the historic exhibition of 1874, but after a series of disappointments at the shows of the seventies, gradually distanced himself from the movement (partly for reasons of character) and left Paris for the provinces. On the estate at L'Estaque he began to restrict the number of his subjects: portraits of himself and members of his family, still lifes with apples and other banal objects, card players. He painted repeated views

of certain places, such as the Mont Sainte-Victoire. In his creative solitude, Cézanne abandoned Impressionism completely in favor of a totally new conception of painting. His concrete and solid synthesis of form and color represents a link between the classical painters of the Renaissance and developments in contemporary art. Much admired by painters but little known to the public, Cézanne began to attract attention after an exhibition organized by the art dealer Ambroise Vollard in 1895. In 1907, one year after his death, the artist was celebrated with a retrospective that confirmed his role as the precursor of twentieth-century art.

Previous page
Paul Cézanne
The Card Players
1890-1892
oil on canvas
17¾ × 22½ in.
(45 × 57 cm)
Musée d'Orsay, Paris

Patient, thoughtful,
solitary, and silent,
card players exercised
a strong fascination on
Cézanne. It is likely that
the painter identified
with these figures and
their unhurried
reflection on ordinary
numbers and shapes,
seeking winning
combinations and new
solutions to the same
old problems.

Paul Cézanne
Mont Sainte-Victoire
1885-1887
oil on canvas, 25½ × 32
in. (65 × 81 cm)
Stedelijk Museum,
Amsterdam

The massive profile of
the mountain was visible
from the windows of his
studio. It is a looming
presence in all his
mature work. The series
of Mont Sainte-Victoire
shows a progressive
abandonment of the
attempt to reproduce
reality in favor of a
calculated disintegration,
until the landscape turns
into a mere pretext for
exercises in composition.

Paul Cézanne
Peaches and Pears
1890-1894
oil on canvas, 24 × 35½
in. (61 × 90 cm)
Pushkin Museum,
Moscow

Still lifes clearly reveal
the innovative character
of his art. The objects
and the compositional
layout go back to the
historical roots of the
genre in France. Their
representation, on the
other hand, is different
from that of the past: he
reconstructs the fruit and
other objects along the
lines of geometric solids,
pointing the way to
Cubism.

Paul Cézanne
Large Bathers
c. 1900-1906
oil on canvas, 50 × 77¼
in. (127 × 196 cm)
National Gallery, London

The imposing nude
female figures,
illuminated by the light
filtering through the
trees and reflected from
the waters of a pool, are
inspired by a long series
of precedents that
commenced with the
mythological scenes
from the Renaissance of
Diana bathing. Cézanne,
confirming his key role
in the history of modern
painting, anticipates the
simplification of
volumes of Cubism
and the graphic
insistence on outlines
of Expressionism.

Paul Cézanne
Large Bathers
1898-1905
oil on canvas
75 × 80¾ in.
(190.5 × 205 cm)
Philadelphia Museum
of Art, Philadelphia

The numerous
variations on the theme,
often on a large scale,
constitute an extremely
closely knit series,
painted over a fairly
short span of time. It is
an excellent
demonstration of
Cézanne's capacity to
concentrate on one
theme, tackled
analytically in a quest
for an ever more
effective solution, with
the patience and
meticulousness of a
chess player.

Marc Chagall
The Stroll
1917-1918
oil on canvas,
67 × 64¼ in.
(170 × 163.5 cm)
Hermitage,
St. Petersburg

The geometric forms and flat areas of brilliant color are concrete signs of the influence of various European avant-garde movements, from Fauvism to Orphism and Cubism, fused in a highly distinctive synthesis. Against the backdrop of an urban landscape, a male figure with one arm raised above his head holds on to the figure of a woman, floating in the air as if she were a kite. The figures can be identified as the artist himself and Bella, the woman he had always loved and whom he had at last married.

Marc Chagall

Vitebsk, 1887-Saint-Paul-de-Vence, 1985

Chagall's artistic career extends over a very long span of time, traversing the most advanced currents on the European scene and developing, with total originality and coherence, a body of work that centers around a few central themes: his family, the place of his birth, the life of peasants in the Russian countryside, and Jewish rites. During his first stay in Paris (1910-1914) he frequented Apollinaire's circle, where he was drawn to Orphism. Returning to Russia, he gave his enthusiastic support to the revolution of 1917 and, appointed commissar of fine arts in his native city, founded an academy to which he invited Constructivists and Suprematists. In 1923 he went back to Paris, where he made a series of engravings for Gogol's *Dead Souls*, La Fontaine's *Fables*, and the Bible. In the second half of the forties he settled in Provence, where he devoted himself to ceramics and sculpture and produced a number of large and monumental works, integrated with their architectural surroundings, such as the stained-glass windows for Metz Cathedral (1965-1968) and the decoration of the opera houses in Paris (1962-1964) and New York (1965).

Philippe de Champaigne
Brussels, 1602-Paris, 1674

After serving his apprenticeship in his hometown, in 1621 Philippe de Champaigne moved to Paris, where he met Poussin and was commissioned to work with him on the decoration of the Palais de Luxembourg. In 1628 Marie de' Medici appointed him court painter, a position he was to retain also during the reign of Louis XIII. His portraits, especially those of Louis XIII and Richelieu, were renowned both for their grandiose conception and for their acute insight, demonstrating a capacity to combine French elegance with a psychological penetration of Flemish origin. Richelieu commissioned him to decorate his Parisian residence (1636) and the church of the Sorbonne (1644) as well as his properties in the country. In 1648 he was one of the founders of the Academy together with Lebrun, but began to turn gradually away from official painting as he became more involved with the Jansenist movement. The intense spirituality and strict rules of moral conduct observed at Port-Royal by the followers of Abbé Antoine Arnauld, including the great mathematician and philosopher Blaise Pascal, gave renewed vigor to Champaigne's paintings. This is demonstrated by his portrait of Pascal (Moussalli Collection, Paris) and the *Ex-Voto* (Louvre, Paris) painted for the miraculous cure of his daughter, a nun in the convent of Port-Royal. Eliminating all Baroque gratification, his painting achieved a formal purity in its portrayal of ascetic, immobile figures, while retaining the grandeur of his early portraits.

Philippe de Champaigne
Triple Portrait of Richelieu
oil on canvas, 22¾ × 28¼ in. (58 × 72 cm)
National Gallery, London

Cardinal in 1623, master of the destinies of the French monarchy, he inspired and directed the events of Louis XIII's reign. The triple portrait is adopted in this case not as an artistic device but as an opportunity for greater analytic insight.

Jean-Baptiste-Siméon Chardin
Paris, 1699-1779

A controversial artist, at times almost a precursor of Cubism in his use of space, but at times capable of tender, contained emotion, Chardin was perhaps the only great painter of the eighteenth century who had no Academy training and who never traveled to Italy. The Academy did, however, manage to win him back: his painting *The Ray* (Louvre, Paris), shown in 1728 in Place Dauphine in an open-air exhibition, won him admission to the Academy as a "painter of animals and fruit." Success, however, only came after 1737, when he exhibited seven genre scenes at the Salon, including the *Girl with Racket and Shuttlecock* (Uffizi, Florence). In 1743 Chardin was elected counselor of the Academy, in 1755 he became treasurer, and from 1761 he was the "hanger" of the Salon. Taken up by these increasingly time-consuming duties, he reduced his output and began to paint copies and variations of previous works. From 1771 he turned to pastel, a medium that he used only for portraits, analyzing the features of his models with the same careful attention he had brought to fruit and game in his still lifes. Before him only Vermeer had matched the particular pictorial treatment evident in the *Bunch of Flowers in a White China Vase Decorated with a Blue Pattern* (National Gallery of Scotland, Edinburgh), with the subtle interplay of white and blue, in a milky light, that demonstrates an almost magical ability to combine power and simplicity.

Opposite
**Jean-Baptiste
Siméon Chardin**
The Young Schoolmistress
c. 1736
oil on canvas
24¼ × 26¼ in.
(61.5 × 66.5 cm)
National Gallery,
London

A central element in
the bare composition of
this painting is the long
hatpin with which the
sweet figure of the
young woman, seen in
profile, points out the
letter of the alphabet
to her young pupil. It is
not so much the careful
rendering of the features
as the subtle use of color
that allows Chardin
to bring out the
psychological depth
of the character.

**Jean-Baptiste
Siméon Chardin**
Self-Portrait
1775
pastel
18 × 15 in. (46 × 38 cm)
Musée du Louvre, Paris

Exhibited at the Salon
of 1775 together with
the portrait of his
second wife, Marguerite
Pouget, whom he
married in 1744, this
was much admired by
critics and public alike.
Writing about the
painting at the end of
the nineteenth century,
Proust praised Chardin's
eccentric originality in
portraying himself as an
old English tourist.

**Jean-Baptiste
Siméon Chardin**
*Pipes and Drinking
Pitcher*
c. 1737
oil on canvas
12¾ × 15¾ in.
(32.5 × 40 cm)
Musée du Louvre, Paris

Owned by the artist,
the painting was
described in detail in
the inventory drawn up
on the death of his first
wife in 1737: a
rosewood case with steel
handles, lined in blue
satin. Here, too, there
is a delicate harmony
of blues and whites.

71

William Merritt Chase

Franklin Township, Williamsburg, Indiana, 1849-New York, 1916

The life and career of William Merritt Chase distantly paralleled those of his more famous and more talented colleagues, beginning with the highly admired and envied Whistler. In terms of American Impressionists, Chase represents a truly unique case: His work is permeated by the aesthetic culture of France, but he himself never once made a trip to Europe. He received his training in a Bostonian setting and spent much of his life between Long Island and New York, making a name for himself as a highly valued teacher. His was an "easy" painting of immediate pleasures, in general little valued by critics but at the same time much loved by the public. In effect, Chase never achieved a truly original style, but his works always offer a sense of grace, amiability, and light. We are clearly a good distance away from the blunt, socially committed realism of such painters as Homer and Eakins, active during the same years.

William Merritt Chase
The Greenhouse
1890
oil on canvas
14½ × 16 in.
(36.5 ×40.5 cm)
Manoogian Collection, Detroit, Michigan

This small oil summarizes the most highly valued aspects of Chase's painting: pale colors, settings bathed in serenity, carefully balanced colors, and subtle sentimental allusions.

Petrus Christus

Baerle, c. 1410-Bruges, 1475/76

The artist belongs to what is commonly referred to as the second generation of fifteenth-century Flemish artists, which followed the generation of the "founding fathers" van Eyck, Campin, and van der Weyden. Little is known about his early training, but he probably made a careful study of the most acclaimed artists, especially van Eyck. In 1444 Christus moved to Bruges, where he was to spend the rest of his life, and immediately gained entry to the city's most important circles. He joined two confraternities dedicated to the Virgin Mary, whose members included aristocrats, rulers, powerful, high-ranking figures from the rising middle class. His numerous commissions were not restricted to paintings but also included sumptuous decorations and ceremonial items that the city displayed on important occasions, such as the wedding of Charles the Bold and Margaret of York (1468). The artist's highly personal approach to painting drew initially upon van Eyck's minutely detailed realism, but then concentrated above all on the handling of space. He is the first northern painter to adopt a rational form of spatial organization based on a single vanishing point. The innovative aspect of his work is not, however, confined to an attempted geometric arrangement of images, but also includes a palpable rendering of reality. These are not remotely symbolic images. His figures seem to bridge the distance separating the painted space from the space of the spectator, thus creating scenes with intimate, contemplative devotional overtones.

Petrus Christus
Portrait of a Carthusian
1446
oil on wood, 11½ × 8½ in.
(29.2 × 21.6 cm)
Metropolitan Museum
of Art, New York

The magnetism of this intense portrait stems from the extraordinary rendering of the sitter's physical traits, and, above all, from the innovative pose of the subject, who stands at a marble parapet looking straight at the spectator, almost as though inviting him or her to share the intimacy of this domestic scene.

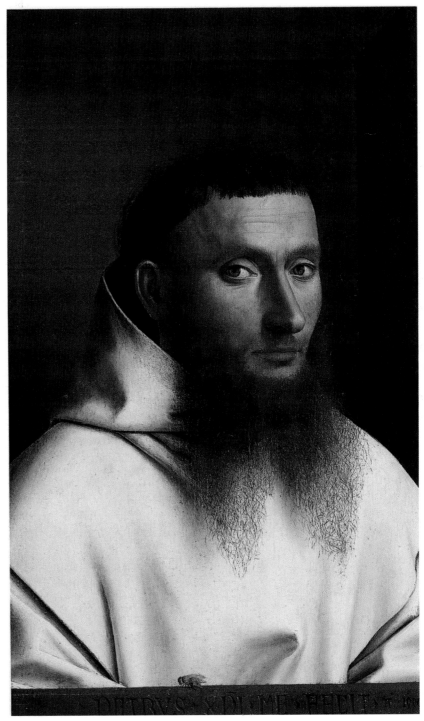

*St. Eligius as a
Goldsmith*
1449
oil on wood
38¾ × 33½ in.
(98 × 85 cm)
Metropolitan Museum
of Art, New York

This celebrated work
was commissioned by
the Bruges Guild of

Goldsmiths and
Silversmiths, whose patron
saint was St. Eligius. The
saint is portrayed behind
the counter of his
workshop intent on
weighing the wedding ring
that the couple wishes to
buy. The tools and
precious materials used in
the goldsmith's craft are
displayed on the shelves,
and a convex mirror

reflects the street in
front of the workshop
and two passers-by. The
artist succeeds in giving
an image with a wealth
of hidden, mysterious
meanings the
appearance of a genre
scene portraying an
episode of everyday life
in the rich middle-class
world of fifteenth-
century Bruges.

Above
Petrus Christus
Madonna of the Dry Tree
1465
oil on wood, 5¾ × 5 in.
(14.7 × 12.4 cm)
Thyssen-Bornemisza
Collection, Madrid

This unusual small
panel offers a devotional
image that was very dear
to the members of the
Confraternity of the
Madonna of the Dry
Tree, to which the artist
himself belonged.
The Virgin is depicted
in the center of the Tree

of Good and Evil,
which withered after
the original sin.
Thanks to her, the tree
would flower once
again, and mankind
would be saved through
the birth of Christ.
The work displays
a highly sophisticated
technique derived
from illumination.
Fine, transparent
brushstrokes alternate
with touches of pure
color that suggest
volumes in this
precious and delicate
image.

Frederic Edwin Church

Hartford, Connecticut, 1826-
New York, 1900

Undisputed leader of the second generation of landscapists in the Hudson River School, Church went against the tastes of the public and the critics to create an authentically American style of painting. Born into a prestigious Connecticut family, Church received a solid humanistic and scientific education, but his true apprenticeship took place under Thomas Cole: In 1844 he went to Catskill, where he painted with the master, developing the same enthusiasm for nature, grounded in the conviction that only attention to the smallest detail makes an understanding of the mysteries of creation possible. Church also shared Cole's ethical sense of the labor of an artist: A work of art must not merely imitate reality but make manifest what is sacred in it, selecting moral and religious subjects in nature. Church settled in New York, opening a studio there in 1849 and entering the National Academy of Design as an associate painter. Having achieved moderate success, Church progressively abandoned the well-known landscapes of New England and headed off in search of new subjects; first he traveled to the western states, then he went to South America, following in the footsteps of Alexander von Humboldt, the German naturalist and geographer who at that time was a popular figure in the United States. Humboldt had elaborated a method of research based on a synthesis between scientific observation and poetic contemplation, and Church found solid scientific and philosophic support for his own beliefs in Humboldt's writing. In 1853, and again in 1857, he visited Colombia and Ecuador, coming away with strong visual and existential experiences from which he drew inspiration for his mature production. The pilgrimages he made over the next decade brought him to the Middle East, where he visited thousand-year-old cities. In these far distant lands, so different from the pristine, unspoiled American landscape, he found signs of the divine power of nature. Following a custom begun by West early in the century, Church charged the public to view his large canvases, making the experience more exciting by designing suitable settings for the paintings with special lighting, sometimes enclosing a canvas in a windowlike frame flanked by tropical plants to increase the illusion of reality. Early in the 1880s, having arrived at the height of success, he found that his fame was beginning to wane. He left the artistic scene of New York to seek refuge in a castle on the banks of the Hudson.

Frederic Edwin Church
New England Scenery
1851
oil on canvas
36 × 53 in.
(91.4 × 134.6 cm)
George Walter Vincent Smith Art Museum, Springfield, Massachusetts

Cimabue

Cenni di Pepo
active between 1272 and 1302

Cimabue's work had a decisive effect on the early development of Italian art. Tradition, inspired by Dante's reference to him, regards his monumental compositions as marking the real foundation of the Florentine school, his work challenging the style and rules of Byzantine painting. His relationship with Giotto is the subject of one of the oldest and most famous legends in the history of art. After probably spending some time in Rome (1272), Cimabue started the huge task of painting a series of frescoes in the basilica at Assisi. Despite the erosion of the centuries (and recent earthquake damage), works like the *Crucifixion* in the Upper Church reveal a style which already had a well-defined, dramatic quality. The power of Cimabue's painting can be seen from his panel paintings of the Madonna in Majesty (in the Louvre, the Uffizi, and in Bologna in which the supple power of the painting grows progressively greater). This can also be seen in the panel paintings depicting the terror of the crucifixion (the best known of these was that from Santa Croce in Florence, destroyed in the 1966 flood) and in his cartoons made for the mosaics in the Baptistery in Florence and for Pisa's cathedral.

Cimabue
*Madonna
and Child Enthroned
with two Angels*
c. 1300
wood panel
Santa Maria dei Servi,
Bologna

This large modeled panel contributed to the development of the Madonna in Majesty, a theme also painted in the same years by Duccio and Giotto. In the sturdy structure of the throne, Cimabue confirms the Romanesque solidity so characteristic of his work.

François Clouet
Tours, c. 1515-Paris, 1572

A portraitist and painter of mythological scenes—executed in the Mannerist style of the Fontainebleau School—and spirited genre scenes, François Clouet took over from his father Jean as "*peintre et valet de chambre*" to Francis I in 1541. He broke away from the traditional half-length portrait and cold chromatic shades of the northern style in favor of a new approach and a warmer range of colors, as exemplified by *Francis I on Horseback*. In harmony with the fashion for antiquity that reached its peak in the reigns of Henry II (1547-1559) and Charles IX (1560-1574), François Clouet's portraits place the subject in the imaginary dimension of a narrative context, as documented by *Diana Bathing*, where the figures of Diana and the rider are identified as King Henry II and his mistress Diane de Poitiers.

Above
François Clouet
Diana Bathing
1550-c. 1560
oil on wood
52½ × 75½ in.
(133 × 192 cm)
Musée des Beaux Arts, Rouen

The wooded background of this mythological painting is dominated on the left by a figure on horseback, an imaginary portrait of Henry II. It depicts Diana surrounded by satyrs and nymphs. The precious ornaments and affected elegance of the poses reflect the sophisticated taste of the court at Fontainebleau.

Following page
François Clouet
Lady in Her Bath
c. 1570
oil on wood
36¼ × 32 in.
(92 × 81 cm)
National Gallery of Art, Washington, D.C.

This painting is characterized by a complex spatial composition embracing three different moments of a theatrical scene. The opening of the heavy drapes reveals a female nude in the foreground gently reclining in a bathtub. The coarse figure of a wet nurse feeding a baby on her right provides a striking contrast, while the center is occupied by a child reaching toward a basket of fruit. A second curtain opens to reveal a maid, who has an illustrious precedent in Titian's *Venus of Urbino*, and a window looking onto a garden. The figures are arranged in such a way as to highlight the female figure in the foreground, whose idealization is underscored by the vigorous Flemish-style realism of the remaining iconographic elements of the scene.

Jean Clouet
Brussels, c. 1485-Paris, 1540

This artist of Flemish origin established himself as a portrait painter at the court of Francis I. While only a small number of works can be attributed to him with certainty, including the two portraits of Francis I and Guillaume Budé, there are a great many drawings (one hundred and twenty-five in the Musée Condé at Chantilly). These are small-sized portraits in charcoal with touches of color depicting figures at the court of Francis I. Alongside the northern influence, it is possible to detect in his portraits an echo of the art of Leonardo, who lived in France from 1516 to 1519 as a guest of Francis I. In particular, in his drawings the soft outlines, sfumato surfaces, and rounded faces show the influence of a chiaroscuro technique peculiar to the late fifteenth century and to Leonardo. In 1533 Clouet was appointed "*peintre et valet de chambre*" to the king.

Above
Jean Clouet
Guillaume Budé
c. 1536
oil on wood
15¾ × 13½ in.
(19.7 × 34.3 cm)
Metropolitan Museum of Art, New York

This is a portrait of the celebrated humanist Guillaume Budé, who noted the name of Jean Clouet as the painter of this work on a page of his manuscript *Adversaria*, thus providing a decisive document for the identification of the artist's oeuvre.

Left
Jean Clouet
Francis I
c. 1525
tempera and oil on wood
37¾ × 29 in.
(96 × 74 cm)
Musée du Louvre, Paris

This portrait offers a typical display of pomp, and recalls Fouquet's *Portrait of Charles VII* in the imperfectly frontal presentation of the chest and the slight turn of the head. While the precious material of the embroidered garment and the precise draftsmanship show the influence of the artist's Flemish origins and the French tradition of illumination, the fleeting expression of the face is evidently derived from Leonardo.

Thomas Cole

Bolton-le Moors, Lancashire, England,
1801-Catskill, New York, 1848

Thomas Cole was the leading theorist
of the Hudson River School, the group
of American landscape painters that he
founded together with Asher B. Durand.
Born in England, Cole moved to the
United States in 1818; he was fascinated
by the immense, unexplored territory,
dense with unspoiled natural scenery.
Setting himself up in Philadelphia, he
attended the Pennsylvania Academy
of Fine Arts, but only briefly, such that
he remained a self-taught artist.
In New York in 1825, he began making
excursions into the Hudson River Valley.
Enthralled by the magical, mysterious
panoramas of the valley, he relocated his
atelier to be close to the river. Animated

by a deep spirituality, Cole saw the
majesty of the American landscape
as a manifestation of the divine
presence. In 1825 he wrote a short
poem, "The Vision of Life," in which he
expressed anxiety over the loss of this
earthly paradise, its natural state being
ruined by the rapid progress of the
industrialization that began in America
in the early decades of the century.
Among the founders of the National
Academy of Design, he held his first
exhibition there in 1826. His works met
with great success; in particular, his
paintings were bought by an important
collector who provided the funds for a
trip to Europe. Unlike most American
artists, Cole made several trips to
Europe; in 1829 he went to London,
where he visited the Royal Academy,
coming in contact with the works of

Claude Lorrain, Nicolas Poussin, and
William Turner; between 1829 and 1832
he was in Italy, a trip that made clearer
to him the differences in nature as
presented on the two continents.
Florence became his favorite city, and he
remained there twelve months, painting
the landscape of the Arno River, with its
many villas flanked by rows of cypress
trees. Back in the United States he
continued to paint views of the Arno,
commissioned by American collectors
who showed much appreciation for
paintings of Italian scenes. Between 1833
and 1836 Cole worked on the famous
cycle of five paintings depicting *The
Course of Empire* (New-York Historical
Society), commissioned by the wealthy
New York merchant Luman Reed, in
which he presents the history of a great
nation, from the state of nature to its

rise to power and its ultimate conquest
and destruction, demonstrating the
devastating effect of the hand of man on
nature. In 1836 he moved to the town of
Catskill in New York State, and there he
continued to paint with success until his
death. Although strongly affected by Old
World images and ideas—linguistic and
compositional debts to Friedrich and
Turner are often recognizable—Cole's
painting was anchored in the present and
strove to join the pragmatic to the moral.

Thomas Cole
*Distant View
of Niagara Falls*
1830
oil on panel, 19 × 24 in.
(47.9 × 60.6 cm)
Art Institute, Chicago

John Constable

East Bergholt, 1776-London, 1837

With Constable the English school of painting took a decisive leap forward, placing itself on the cutting edge of European art in the early nineteenth century. From his childhood Constable, the son of a mill owner, showed a deep love for the countryside and the restful rural landscape (while his contemporary Turner preferred the sea and mountains). In 1799 he moved to London to attend the Royal Academy of Arts. Thus he acquired a thorough grounding in the history of landscape painting, paying particular attention to the seventeenth-century masters of the idealized "classical landscape," whose methods of composition he adopted: making drawings, taking notes, and then making sketches from life before painting the final picture in the studio. Constable's work is characterized by his insistence on returning to the same subjects, painting the same views of the countryside several times or repeated versions of monuments like Salisbury Cathedral, anticipating what Monet and Cézanne were to do several decades later. On the one hand Constable sought out real views, corners of Suffolk to depict in an "objective" way (though within the obvious limits of this definition), without resorting to particular effects or "picturesque" and evocative viewpoints. Yet, as in early Romantic English poetry, Constable looked for and found harmony in nature, which he investigated with patient care and an intense sense of involvement. His landscapes attracted attention abroad especially after a show held in Paris in 1824, becoming an important model for the nineteenth-century interest in views of nature. But the painter did not achieve the success he deserved at home, partly because of his shy and reserved character preferring the countryside to society life. Constable was not given a post at the Royal Academy until 1829, when his painting began to lose the clarity of earlier years.

John Constable
The Mill at Flatford
1817
oil on canvas
39¾ × 50 in.
(101 × 127 cm)
Tate Gallery, London

Constable's landscapes are inspired by Suffolk, the county where he was born. Although he wanted to present a limpid and accurate image of nature, he was unable to conceal his feelings of affection for rural, often sunlit scenes, with the presence of a few human figures.

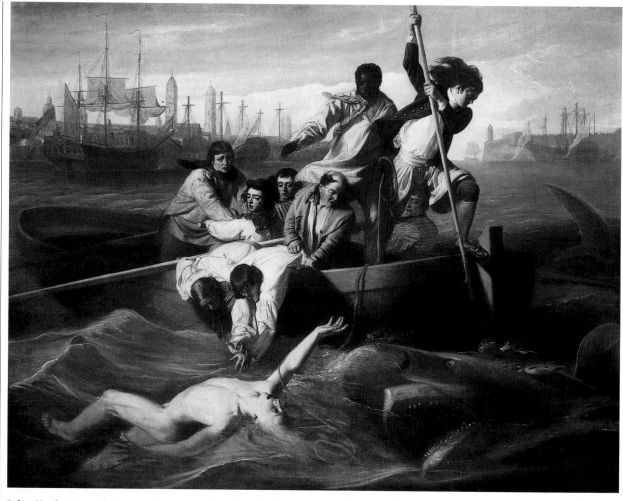

John Singleton Copley
Boston, 1738-London, 1815

In middle-class, commercial Boston, Copley did his apprenticeship in the workshop of the engraver Peter Pelham, his mother's second husband. Influenced at first by contemporary American portrait painters, he soon evolved a distinct style of portraiture all his own. His practice of mezzotint engraving was evident in his manner of painting, especially in the gradations of light and shadow and the refined, delicate use of colors. His portrait painting shows his evident desire to combine a formal, classical vision of society with an attempt to convey the freshness and spontaneity of everyday life. In 1774, encouraged by his fellow American Benjamin West, he began the Grand Tour that was to take him to London, Paris, Genoa, and finally Rome, which proved to be the decisive stage of his journey. It was in Rome that he heard the news of the American War of Independence, which broke out in 1775. He decided not to return to the United States, but to move with his family to London. Here his work was admired by George III, who made him a member of the Royal Academy in 1783. During his time in London he continued to practice portrait painting, although his work lacked the concrete yet refined simplicity and the psychological perception that had marked his American portraits. Following in the footsteps of West, he also devoted himself to modern history painting, confirming his bent for contemporary themes, and his desire to find in modern life the same examples of virtue, pride, and dignity found in ancient models.

John Singleton Copley
Brook Watson and the Shark
1778
oil on canvas
71½ × 90½ in.
(182 × 230 cm)
National Gallery of Art, Washington, D.C.

The first painting of contemporary history based on a personal story, this was commissioned by the English merchant Brook Watson, and depicts an episode that happened during his childhood: threatened by a shark in the port of Havana, he was saved by a group of sailors. Exhibited at the Royal Academy in 1778, the painting is striking for the grandeur of the composition, which is reminiscent of a biblical scene.

Jean-Baptiste-Camille Corot
Paris, 1796-1875

A refined master of landscape, Corot was one of the nineteenth century's most cultivated and gracious painters. His point of reference was the art of the great seventeenth-century painters: like Poussin and Lorrain, Corot spent a long time in Rome and other Italian cities. Corot's career got off to a relatively late start and his first truly interesting works date from his first stay in Rome (1825-1828). Financial security allowed Corot to produce two kinds of pictures: landscapes intended for public show and the market, of a fairly conventional character, and works of smaller size but great freshness. His landscapes and figures of peasant girls are a mark of Corot's

desire to capture the reality of nature, clearing the way for painting *en plein air*. Returning to France, Corot found a new source of inspiration in the forest of Fontainebleau. Following in his footsteps, many French painters went to live at Barbizon. Two further long stays in Italy rendered Corot's style even more assured and personal: the faultless handling of light and full recognizability of the locations never descend to the level of the picture postcard, but always remain interpretations of great lyrical force. Celebrated in his homeland and incredibly prolific (some five thousand pictures are now believed to be his own work), Corot continued with his free and delightful investigation of the values of light and color.

Below
Camille Corot
The Forest of Fontainebleau
c. 1830
oil on canvas,
69 × 95¼ in.
(175 × 242 cm)
National Gallery,
Washington, D.C.

Landscapes done directly from nature made Corot one of the pioneers in the representation of light and natural surroundings which, passing through the painters of the Barbizon School, came into its own with the Impressionists.

Following page
Camille Corot
Chartres Cathedral
1830
oil on canvas
25½ × 19¾ in.
(65 × 50 cm)
Musée du Louvre, Paris

Once again, Corot is at his most reflective and balanced in his handling of a theme that fascinated nineteenth-century artists: the Gothic cathedral. With its apparent simplicity, the church painted by Corot is equidistant from the Romantic and idealized celebration of

a national style on the part of the German Schinkel, the Englishman Constable's patient search for a solution to the nagging problem of representing light and shade, architecture and nature, van Gogh's desperate agitation, and Monet's investigation of the way light breaks down forms.

Correggio

Antonio Allegri
Correggio (Parma), 1489-1534

Known by the name of his native town,
Correggio first trained in Emilia (under
the Modenese terra-cotta sculptor
Antonio Begarelli, among others), then
in Mantua under the elderly Mantegna,
and finally, during the 1510s he sought
to give a free interpretation of the
works of Leonardo. By adding his study
of Raphael and the art of central Italy,
Correggio developed an independent
style that featured a narrative fluidity
mediated by Leonardesque sfumato, a
virtuoso control of perspective, and a
soft sense of color. During his career he
executed several fresco cycles in Parma:
the Camera della Badessa for
the Convent of San Paolo, (1518),
the decoration of the church of San
Giovanni Evangelista (1520-1523),
and the *Assumption of the Virgin* on the
dome of the cathedral (1526-1530). In
addition to the large frescoes, during
the 1520s Correggio also painted major
altarpieces, expressing a refined
sensibility through the softness of his
style and his attention to the elements
of composition. The relations between
the various figures are captured in
gestures and glances. In this respect,
the two altarpieces in the Galleria
Nazionale at Parma, the *Madonna
of St. Jerome*, and the *Madonna of the
Bowl*, are exemplary. The nocturnal
setting of the *Adoration of the Shepherds*
in Dresden (also known as *The Night*
and formerly in the church of San
Prospero in Reggio Emilia) led to
further developments in the use of light
in Italian art, influencing the Carraccis
in the late sixteenth century and also
Baroque painters. During the last few
years of his life Correggio painted
Jupiter and Antiope (c. 1528), and,
immediately afterwards, the cycle of
four canvases for Federico Gonzaga
depicting the loves of Jupiter: *Danaë*
(Galleria Borghese, Rome), *Leda*
(Staatliche Museen, Berlin), *Io* and
Ganymede (Kunsthistorisches Museum,
Vienna). These are fundamental works
in the history of mythological and
profane painting, perfectly poised
between a sensual, naturalistic
rendering and poetic idealization.

Correggio
Madonna of St. Jerome
1523
oil on panel
80¾ × 55½ in.
(205 × 141 cm)
Galleria Nazionale,
Parma

Francesco del Cossa
Ferrara, c. 1436-1477/78

Cosmè Tura's assistant and partner in Ferrara, Cossa diluted his master's harshness in his own more genial style of painting. His masterpieces are the allegories of the *Months* that he painted for the salon in the Schifanoia Palace in Ferrara (c. 1470). Here he combined mythological scenes and astrological references with episodes from the contemporary life of the Duke, the city, and the countryside. Dissatisfied with the remuneration he was receiving, Cossa left Ferrara and just after 1470 settled in Bologna. There he painted major altarpieces (*Merchants' Altarpiece*, Galleria Nazionale, Bologna; *Annunciation*, Gemäldegalerie, Dresden) and for the church of San Petronio he produced the ambitious *Grifoni Polyptych*. The plastic energy of his characters extends to Cossa's detailed landscapes and architectural backdrops as well.

Francesco del Cossa
St Peter; St John the Baptist
c. 1473
wood panels
44 × 21½ in. each
(112 × 55 cm)
Pinacoteca di Brera, Milan

Gustave Courbet

Ornans, 1819-Vevey, 1877

A central figure in the history of nineteenth-century painting, Courbet marks the end of lyrical and literary Romanticism and the start of a direct, forceful, and in some ways scandalous interpretation of reality. An irregular and unmethodical training led Courbet, who moved to Paris in 1840, to spend more time in the Louvre than at the studio of some more or less talented artist. Courbet keenly studied the great painters of the past, concentrating chiefly on Rembrandt and even making a trip to the Netherlands to see more of his work first hand. After showing a few already very interesting pictures at the Salons of 1844 and 1846, Courbet played a leading role in the uprisings of 1848: it was at this time that he began to paint scenes of huge size with groups of life-sized figures, like the *Burial at Ornans*. Courbet realized that he had opened up a new direction: that of Realism. And so, in polemical opposition to official culture, he organized one-man shows in which his gigantic and dark pictures, free from any indulgence in mysticism or sentimentality, depicted everyday life in energetic fashion. In 1855 Courbet summed up the themes

and figures of his art in a vast composition, *The Artist's Studio*. Shortly afterward he painted *Young Women on the Banks of the Seine*, a picture that scandalized the bourgeois public. Courbet's life went through another upheaval in 1871, when the fifty-year-old painter took part in the insurrection that established the Paris Commune. Arrested after its fall, he was sentenced to six months in prison. He was tried again in 1874 and a heavy fine imposed on him for his presumed role in the destruction of the Vendôme Column: he was forced to flee to Switzerland and his works were sold at auction. And so the life of an "accursed," non-rhetorical and powerful painter came to an end, on a personal note that likened his fate to that of his beloved Rembrandt.

Above
Gustave Courbet
*Courbet with
a Black Dog*
1844
oil on canvas
18 × 22 in. (46 × 56 cm)
Musée du Petit Palais,
Paris

The cocky attitude is reminiscent of the early self-portraits of Rembrandt, the artist of the past to whom Courbet felt closest. The presence of a dog is characteristic.

Gustave Courbet
The Artist's Studio
1854-1855
oil on canvas
141¼ × 235½ in.
(359 × 598 cm)
Musée d'Orsay, Paris

Here the self-portrait is transformed into the manifesto of a new perception of the role of art and the artist in society. Courbet is seated at the easel and painting a landscape. He is surrounded by a nude model, a white cat, and a child, all clearly recognizable symbols of purity and naiveté. Just as in a grand Renaissance composition, two symmetrical groups of figures are arranged around the center of the canvas (which is also the most luminous and brightly colored point): on the right we see the artist's relatives, friends, and collaborators; on the left, people taken from everyday life, an expression of the eternal conflict between winners and losers, rich and poor. The artist places himself in the middle, as the interpreter and mediator of this reality: the painting is charged with ideological significance.

Gustave Courbet
Burial at Ornans
1849
oil on canvas
124 × 263 in.
(315 × 668 cm)
Musée d'Orsay, Paris

Another canvas of
enormous size and another
decided statement. With
an indomitable spirit of
concreteness, expressed
through the life-size
figures and dark and
earthy colors, Courbet
orchestrates a parade of
peasants dressed in black,
minor notables, stunned
relatives, priests, and altar
boys, while the mystery
of death hovers over
the narrow horizons
of a provincial graveyard.

Above
Gustave Courbet
The Meeting (Bonjour, Monsieur Courbet)
1854
oil on canvas
50¾ × 58¾ in.
(129 × 149 cm)
Musée Fabre,
Montpellier

Through this painting,
depicting an early
morning meeting with
the collector Alfred

Bruyas, Courbet puts
across a free-and-easy
image of the artist.
Refusing to shut himself
up in his studio,
Courbet goes in search
of inspiration in the
open air, with his
painting equipment
on his back.

Gustave Courbet
The Bathers
1853
oil on canvas
89¼ × 76 in.
(227 × 193 cm)
Musée Fabre,
Montpellier

Somewhere between
Ingres and Cézanne,
here Gustave Courbet
depicts a majestic and
hefty nude.

Lucas Cranach the Elder

Kronach, 1472-Weimar, 1553

Son of a painter, Cranach trained in Bavaria. In 1498, being inclined to novelty and fantasy, he embarked on a journey that followed the course of the Danube. This was an important period for art in southern Germany and Austria that saw the emergence of a new style of painting, which was characterized by an impassioned interest in nature. At the same time, Maximilian I of Hapsburg established new cultural centers at Vienna, seat of the university, and in Tyrol, where the court resided. Cranach became one of the leading artists in the Danube School through the magical exuberance of his fairy-tale rendering of nature and the incisive force of his figures. In 1505 he was invited to Wittenberg by the elector of Saxony, Frederick the Wise, who also commissioned works from Dürer and upheld a refined Humanism that promoted the depiction of classical myths set within the German context of his day. Cranach was the major exponent of this style. Influenced by his contact with Dürer, his figures became more substantial and they are sometimes set against dense, black grounds, while in time, his rapid draftsmanship acquired a more elaborate elegance that became almost abstract, the German response to Italian Mannerism. Until his death, almost fifty years later, Cranach was employed by the court of Saxony, becoming one of the most long-lived and active artists of the German Renaissance. His style ranged from the legendary expressionism of his early period to the intellectual, decorative predominance of graphic elements in his last works. He worked in many different genres, including engraving, and executed altarpieces, classical nudes, portraits, allegories, hunting scenes, and Lutheran propaganda subjects. Cranach was one of the first artists to support the Reformation and painted many portraits of Martin Luther, his wife Catharina von Bora, and Melanchthon, as well as large religious paintings on the themes of Reformation doctrine. He also produced illustrations for the Bible translated into German by Luther during the period he spent in Saxony under the elector's protection. Although, as time passed, his flourishing workshop, in which the leading figure was his son Lucas Cranach the Younger, turned out works on a scale that could virtually be called "mass production," Cranach, however, remains one of the most versatile masters of the sixteenth century in central Europe.

Lucas Cranach the Elder
Judith with the Head of Holofernes
c. 1530
oil on wood
34¼ × 22 in.
(87 × 56 cm)
Kunsthistorisches Museum, Vienna

An unforgettable figure, displaying Cranach's exceptional skill in depicting textures and in the sumptuous use of the color red, Judith can also be interpreted as a symbolic heroine, an allegory of sexual restraint. Holofernes meets his tragic end because he attempts to seduce Judith and his severed head is a warning not to give in to lustful temptations.

Following page
Lucas Cranach the Elder
Double Portrait of Duke Henry the Pious of Saxony and His Wife Katherine of Meclemburg
1514
oil on wood transferred to canvas and divided in two, 72½ × 32½ in. each (184 × 87.5 cm)
Gemäldegalerie, Dresden

An extremely unusual celebratory painting, this is both a portrait of the aristocratic Saxon couple and a coat of arms. Cranach does not set a dividing line between the depiction of the figures (the striking, aggressive, almost picaresque man and the apparently docile, but at heart, spirited woman) and the spectacular, enameled heraldic decoration in gold, blue, and red.

Carlo Crivelli
Madonna of the Taper
c. 1490
wood panel
85¾ × 29½ in.
(218 × 75 cm)
Pinacoteca di Brera,
Milan

This was the central
piece of a dismantled
polyptych. It takes its
name from the slender
candle in the bottom
left of the picture.

Carlo Crivelli
Venice, c. 1430/35-the Marches, 1494/95

Crivelli was born in Venice and received
his early training in the Vivarini studio
before moving to Padua. The young
Crivelli experienced misfortunes which
led him first to Istria (1459) and then to
the Marches where he lived from 1468
until he died. In the provinces Crivelli's
creativity flourished best and he
became one of the most individual
Italian artists in the second half
of the Quattrocento. He was obviously
familiar with the most advanced
perspective and classical monumental
art. However, in his hands this was
dressed in splendid and exuberant
ornamental trapping. He even
reintroduced the old gold background.

Carlo Crivelli
Annunciation
1486
wood panel
81½ × 57½ in.
(207 × 146 cm)
National Gallery,
London

Salvador Dalí
Figueras, 1904-1989

An egocentric artist—he liked to describe himself as "El Unico"—Dalí passed through the most significant avant-garde movements of the early part of the century, from Futurism to Metaphysical Art, Cubism and Surrealism, which he took up in 1929. In a vulgar and indecorous fashion Dalí applied his own peculiar interpretation of Surrealism to daily

life as well, cultivating what he himself described as a "paranoiac-critical" state. According to psychiatric tests, the paranoiac critical is an individual who, blinded by a feeling of omnipotence, interprets the world in terms of a delirious vision but is able to rationalize the delirium. In 1934, repudiated by Breton, he left the Surrealist group in Paris and in 1939 moved to the United States, where he spent the war years, publishing his autobiography

The Secret Life of Salvador Dalí in 1942. After the war he kept up his prolific output, trying his hand at illustration and graphic art as well. His hallucinatory and deserted landscapes, filled with symbolic elements, and the series of limp and melting watches, intended to symbolize the transience of time, gave way to a more academic style, which he used to revise and correct the same themes as he had tackled in his early work.

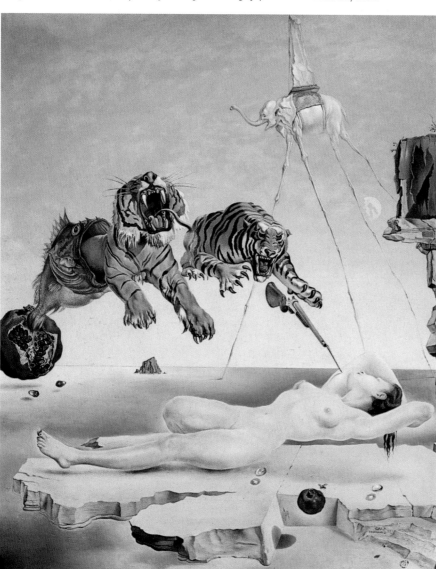

Salvador Dalí
Dream Caused by the Flight of a Bee around a Pomegranate One Second before Waking
1944
oil on canvas
20 × 16¼ in.
(51 × 41 cm)
Thyssen-Bornemisza Collection, Madrid

The "paranoiac-critical" method was a sort of self-induced hallucination that allowed the artist to create behind every image another one ready to take its place. Thus reality can suggest other realities, just as legitimate. Everything depends on the faculty of interpretation of the subject.

Honoré Daumier

Marseilles, 1808-Valmondais, 1879

A versatile and ingenious artist,
Daumier alternated his work
as a painter with that of a satirical
cartoonist and even a sculptor.
In the early part of his career he faced
serious economic difficulties and legal
problems over his lampoons of King
Louis-Philippe published in *La
Caricature*, a weekly that was closed
down by the censors in 1834. Up until
1860 Daumier devoted himself almost
exclusively to charcoal drawing and
lithography: he developed a sensitive
mastery of light and shade and
eventually decided to try its effect in
oil painting. The result was excellent
and totally original: renouncing his
customary sarcasm, which found
brilliant expression in his lithographs
for the magazine *Charivari*, Daumier
painted the trials and tribulations of
the poor, exploring the world of third-
class railroad cars, washerwomen, and
apprentices. Once again faced with
financial problems, he was forced
to give up painting and go back to
producing lithographs for illustrated
magazines. In 1866 his friend Corot
gave him a small house in the country
and Daumier went to live there.
His last works include a series
of interpretations of the story
of *Don Quixote*.

Honoré Daumier
The Laundress
1863
oil on panel
19¼ × 13 in.
(49 × 33 cm)
Musée d'Orsay, Paris

Daumier did not paint
many pictures. Little
inclined to let himself
be seduced by vivid
color and bright light,
Daumier transferred the
expressive characteristics
and techniques of
engraving into painting.
A sharp contrast
between the illuminated
and shaded parts of the
picture renders the
figures monumental,
isolating them in the toil
of their daily life.

Gérard David

Oudewater, c. 1455-Bruges, 1523

The last great artist active in fifteenth-century Bruges was born in the province of Holland in the northern Netherlands. He was probably trained in his father's workshop before setting off on travels that took him first to Haarlem and then south. In 1484 he settled in Bruges and his style began to change considerably. Either to satisfy the demands of patrons or under the influence of Memling's sober, detached approach, David began to produce works of greater serenity and restraint that immediately found favor with the public, to such an extent that he was obliged to expand his workshop. Toward the end of the century, when contacts between Flanders and Italy became more intense, David was one of the first to introduce Renaissance elements into his work. The most innovative aspect of his oeuvre, however, is unquestionably the importance attributed to landscape, depicted in all its vibrant, tangible aspects in a way that anticipates Joachim Patinir's extraordinary paintings.

Gérard David
Landscapes, exterior side panels from the *Nativity Triptych*
c. 1510-1515
panels, 35½ × 12 in. each (90 × 30.5 cm)
Mauritshuis, The Hague

The exterior panels of the triptych are of exceptional importance, since the artist depicts a densely wooded scene with no figures apart from the minute shapes of the grazing oxen and the donkey lying down near the stone building. This was the first time that a landscape had ever played such a dominant role and excluded any human presence. The naturalistic depiction of the forest is sustained by a masterly rendering of atmosphere. The landscape thus assumes deep religious significance as the element that introduces the spectator to the scene of the Nativity. It is as if the artist were inviting us to undertake a pilgrimage leading us through the woods into the presence of Christ.

Gérard David
Nativity Triptych
c. 1510-1515
oil on wood transferred to canvas
central panel, 35¼ × 28 in. (89.6 × 71.1 cm)
side panels, 35¼ × 12¼ in. (89.6 × 31.4 cm)

Jules S. Bache Collection, Metropolitan Museum of Art, New York

This scene of homage being paid to the newborn Child is bathed in a tranquil atmosphere. The figures include the two donors.

Jacques-Louis David
The Oath of the Horatii
1784-1785
oil on canvas
130 × 167¼ in.
(330 × 425 cm)
Louvre, Paris

This painting is regarded as a symbol of European Neoclassicism. The perfect combination of an uncompromising intellectual conception, a formally impeccable execution, and a content of intense moral significance makes it the manifesto of an era. The restrained strength and statuesque gestures (not just of the men but of the women too) are derived directly from models of Hellenistic sculpture. Through a spectacular display of artistic virtuosity, David sets out to make us admire the civil virtues of the protagonists. The large canvas summarizes the lessons absorbed by the artist during his long stay in Rome.

Jacques-Louis David
Paris, 1748-Brussels, 1825

David epitomizes the origin, development, and decline of Neoclassicism. Ever since his earliest works David showed a clear preference for historical and mythological subjects, and it was through these that he embarked on a brilliant academic career. In 1775 he won the greatly coveted Prix de Rome, which allowed him to spend five years in Italy. There he made a thorough study of the great

exponents of seventeenth-century classicism, from the Carracci to Poussin, though his calculated academicism was toned down by the influence of Raphael. With links to the cultural circles of Winckelmann and Mengs, David also took a passionate interest in the study of classical statuary, admiring its purity and perfect composure. To David, classical art was not just a stylistic model but also the reflection of a higher morality. Consequently, on his return to Paris, David painted a series of large classical

scenes as monumental examples of private and public virtue. The most celebrated of these is *The Oath of the Horatii* (1784-1785): a closed form, perfectly defined by rigorous drawing, dignified and almost sacred poses, carefully studied colors, and a sense of drama expressed in a restrained way and yet conveying the impression of an explosion. With the outbreak of the French Revolution, David became the great illustrator of the events and figures of the political upheaval: the most unforgettable canvas from that

period is *The Death of Marat*. With the fall of Robespierre he was imprisoned and reacted symbolically by painting the great picture of *Sabine*, a plea for moderation and reconciliation. When Napoleon appeared on the scene, he became his official glorifier, cloaking his conquests in the aura of a timeless epic. He became the stylistic model for an entire generation of artists, including Ingres. With the defeat of Napoleon, he fell into disgrace and was exiled to Brussels, where he went back to painting mythological scenes.

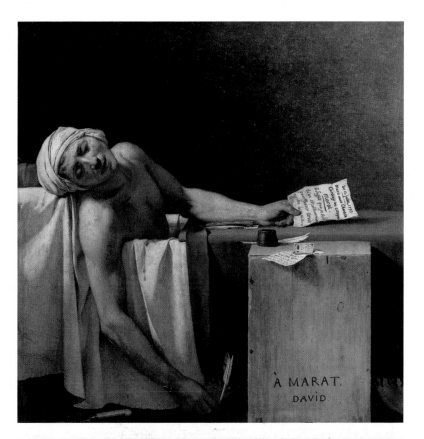

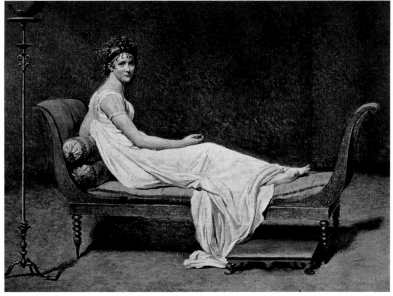

Above, right
Jacques-Louis David
The Death of Marat
1793
oil on canvas, 63¾ × 49¼
in. (162 × 125 cm)
Musées Royaux des
Beaux-Arts, Brussels

The image of Marat
stabbed to death in his
bath has become almost
an artistic summary of
the French Revolution.

Jacques-Louis David
*Portrait of Madame
Récamier*
1825
oil on canvas, 67 × 94½ in.
(170 × 240 cm)
Musée du Louvre, Paris

David never abandoned
his formal composure,
even when he shows
penetrating insight into
the psychology
of his sitters.

Stuart Davis
Philadelphia, 1894-New York, 1964

Son of the art director of the *Philadelphia Press*, Stuart Davis, like most of the artists of his generation, began his artistic career as a graphic illustrator. A decisive aspect of his artistic training was his familiarity with Robert Henri, who contributed to the *Press*. Born in Philadelphia, Davis moved with his family to New Jersey, and in 1910 he left school to take painting classes with Henri in New York. He began by painting the life of the streets of the city, using its colors, forms, and music while adopting the range of dark tints so dear to Henri. The 1913 Armory Show had a deep impact on the development of his painting. Impressed by the simplification of forms and, most of all, by the decorative colors used by the Fauvists, he decided to become a "modern" artist, elaborating upon his own personal style characterized by a palette of bright colors. In 1917, after meeting Demuth and Sheeler, he oriented his work more in the direction of abstractionism, no longer painting directly from nature and moving his attention from color to structure, from Fauvism to Cubism. Drawn to abstract art, he spent the year 1928 studying it in Paris. He then returned to New York, the preeminent city for an artist wishing to express his or her art. Davis declared he did not want to copy Matisse or Picasso; rather, he wanted to paint the American scene, thus making clear his allegiance to the new, modernist culture. He began teaching at the Art Students League in 1931 and continued to uphold the modernist point of view even during the general realignment of American art with the forms of a renewed realism. In 1933, as part of the Federal Art Project, he made three abstract murals and, politically active, was elected president of the Artist's Union and director of its official organ, *Art Front*.

Stuart Davis
Swing Landscape
1938
oil on canvas
85¼ × 173½ in.
(217 × 441 cm)
Indiana University Art Museum, Bloomington

In search of an art capable of expressing the vitality of American culture, Davis took jazz, the characteristic American music, and strove to translate its rhythms onto canvas.

Giorgio de Chirico

Volos (Greece), 1888-Rome, 1978

The son of an Italian engineer employed on the construction of railroads in Greece, de Chirico always regarded the fact that he was born in the land of myths and gods as a sign of destiny. Throughout his life, like his brother Alberto Savinio, he felt that he had a profoundly "classical" identity, and this proved to be the constant essence of his work, despite his various shifts in style and readiness to compare his work with developments elsewhere in the art world. Operating completely outside the sometimes rather provincial schemes of Italian art, de Chirico was in fact far more interested in the tendencies in culture that were emerging elsewhere in Europe. Trained in Munich, he came under the sway of Nietzsche's philosophy and the late Romantic painting of Böcklin, both strongly imbued with a feeling of nostalgia for the classical world. In 1910 de Chirico went to Paris, where he formed a close friendship with Guillaume Apollinaire and watched developments in Cubism with interest. It was in these years that de Chirico's most characteristic vein of inspiration took shape, the one linked to images of great power, set in disturbing, dreamlike contexts, filled with allusions. A fundamental impetus in this direction came from his celebrated meeting with Carrà and De Pisis at the military hospital of Ferrara in 1916: this marked the "official" birth of Metaphysical painting, one of the most important and original Italian avant-garde movements of the twentieth century. Its typical themes were mannequins, statues, silent and deserted "squares of Italy," knife-edged shadows, backdrops of empty buildings, and objects of everyday use presented completely outside their usual context. In 1918 de Chirico along with Carrà helped to found the magazine *Valori Plastici*, which gave the Metaphysical movement a literary underpinning. Dissatisfied with the evolution of Italian painting in the twenties, de Chirico returned to Paris, where he established links with the Surrealists and stepped up his investigation of archeological themes and motifs. This reexamination of the past led, in the thirties, to a "Neo-Baroque" style in which he painted horses, still lifes, and portraits. Over the rest of his long career de Chirico went back several times to themes he had already tackled, and in particular those of the Metaphysical period.

Giorgio de Chirico
The Red Tower
1913
oil on canvas
29 × 39½ in.
(73.5 × 100.5 cm)
Peggy Guggenheim
Collection, Venice

Exhibited at the Salon d'Automne in 1913, the composition has a polycentric structure, marked by the divergent lines of perspective of the porticoes that enclose the square. In the background an equestrian monument and a circular tower are set.

Edgar Degas

Paris, 1834-1917

The son of a banker of noble origins (his surname was written de Gas until the painter decided to adopt a less pretentious form), he received a strict classical training. Degas is often described as "the most Parisian of the Impressionists." In reality, he remained on the edges of the group: Degas chose to go in a direction of his own, showing little interest in nature and instead paying great attention to the expressions, gestures, and emotions of human figures, especially women. This choice was strongly influenced by his love for the Italian painting of the Renaissance, which he studied through visits to the Louvre and a long stay in Tuscany. During the sixties, when he found himself at the heart of Parisian artistic life, he made friends with Manet, with whom he shared a classical education and elevated culture. Degas was also attracted by forms of expression that had only recently been introduced into Paris, such as Japanese prints and photography. At the beginning of the seventies, when the Impressionist group was already firmly established, Degas concentrated on two of his favorite subjects: the worlds of the theater (musicians, singers, and above all dancers) and horse racing. He preferred the lights of the Opéra and the sporting and fashionable atmosphere of the Longchamp racecourse to popular dances at the Moulin de la Galette. After a visit to New Orleans (1873), Degas started to draw inspiration from the simple daily life of washerwomen, housemaids, and seamstresses in their modest apartments. In his inquiry into the human body, he investigated the attitudes of laundresses and women combing their hair or washing themselves in a tub. Partly as a consequence of failing eyesight, which was eventually to lead to blindness, Degas made his brushwork rapid, almost cursory, and in the end took to modeling in clay and wax.

Edgar Degas
Ballerina in the Photographer's Studio
1875
oil on canvas
25½ × 19¾ in.
(65 × 50 cm)
Pushkin Museum, Moscow

This splendid painting, with its masterly harmony of grays and blues, combines two of Degas's main interests: the limber movements of the ballerina and his love of photography. Degas, an extremely refined draftsman, did not share the Impressionist's fascination with light and color: what interested him rather was the subtle point of contact between movement and balance displayed by a ballerina on point, while the recent development of photography suggested new and unpredictable angles for the image. The view of the roofs of Paris seen through the windows is memorable.

Edgar Degas
*Singer with a Black
Glove*
c. 1878
oil on canvas
20¾ × 16¼ in.
(53 × 41 cm)
Fogg Art Museum,
Cambridge (Mass.)

Edgar Degas
*The Orchestra of the
Opéra*
1869-1870
oil on canvas
22¼ × 18¼ in.
(56.5 × 46.2 crn.)
Musée d'Orsay, Paris

Edgar Degas
*The Rehearsal
of the Ballet Onstage*
1874
oil and watercolor on
paper mounted on
canvas, 21½ × 28¾ in.
(54.3 × 73 cm)
Metropolitan Museum
of Art, New York

An assiduous frequenter
of the Opéra, Degas did
not participate in
popular dances or
Sunday outings on the
Seine. His favorite milieu
was the world of the
theater, surrounded by
the stars of the ballet, the
players of the orchestra,
and famous singers.
Perhaps the most effective
of his paintings are the
ones that do not
represent a moment in
the performance of an
opera, concert, or ballet,
but dance schools or the
choreographer giving
advice. He makes us
breathe the always frantic
atmosphere that precedes
the opening night, taking
us behind the wings to
show us the myriad
personages of the theater.

Pieter de Hooch

Rotterdam, 1629-Amsterdam or
Rotterdam, c. 1684

A poetic painter of peace and quiet,
of the calm cleanliness of Dutch
domestic interiors, de Hooch is an
artist who has always been well-
known, but has recently been receiving
greater attention. In fact, though
not possessing Vermeer's gift of
psychological penetration, de Hooch
reveals in all his works great lyrical
finesse, and a poised elegance of
composition, color, and expression,
which make him one of the greatest
genre painters of all time. De Hooch
was a pupil of Nicolaes Berchem, and
ever since his youth he was attracted
to simple, serene themes. He
completed his artistic training by
spending some time in Leyden where
the legacy of Rembrandt and the
example of Dou led him to refine his
painting further, making it even more
subtle and precise. The turning point
in his career was his lengthy stay in
Delft (nearly a decade from 1654 on),
during which he measured himself
directly with Vermeer. Some of his
themes are similar, in particular the
secret world of domestic intimacy, but
the feeling is different. Vermeer always
captures the human element of the
situation; de Hooch affectionately and
meticulously depicts the context, the
episodes, and the figures, creating, in
his most successful works, symbolic
images of Dutch culture in the mid-
seventeenth century. Around 1663
he moved to Amsterdam, where his
works met with the approval of
bourgeois collectors, partly because
of his remarkable handling of
perspective. In his later works he tends
to comply with the tastes of the new
Dutch clientele, who are attracted by
affected gestures and somewhat cold,
aristocratic ostentation.

Pieter de Hooch
The Mother
c. 1660
oil on canvas
20¾ × 24 in.
(52.5 × 61 cm)
Rijksmuseum,
Amsterdam

The magic of the light
shining through the
window and spreading
through the house is
depicted with a perfect
mastery of perspective,
stressed by the converging
lines on the floor. The
mother is looking for
possible lice in the hair
of her little daughter, who
is kneeling at her feet.
A necessary and private
task, which in figurative
Dutch culture of the
seventeenth century was
considered the symbol
of the mother's role, the
metaphor of lice indicates
that the mother was
responsible for removing
all manner of physical
and moral "dirt" from the
home and the children.

Pieter de Hooch
The Linen Cupboard
1663
oil on canvas
28¼ × 30½ in.
(72 × 77.5 cm)
Rijksmuseum,
Amsterdam

One of de Hooch's most
famous works, this
painting dates from
between the end of the
period spent in Delft and
his move to Amsterdam.
Since he was working
for a public with more
demanding tastes, one can
understand why there is
greater monumentality
than in his earlier works.
However, the painting is
extremely appealing. The
lady is tidying the linen,
helped by her
housekeeper, while the
little girl, who is supposed
to be learning how to do
household tasks, seems to
be irresistibly attracted by
the sunlight outside, on
this bright spring day.

Willem de Kooning

Rotterdam, Netherlands, 1904-
East Hampton, New York, 1997

A restless and rebellious figure, de Kooning made his way through the principal languages of modern European painting without ever accepting a stylistic dogma. Born in Holland, he performed his apprenticeship at the Rotterdam Academy of Fine Arts and Techniques, a decisive experience for the elaboration of a pictorial technique in which design is the preliminary phase. Arriving in the United States in 1927, he opened a studio in New York and initially made works of a commercial character, most of which have since been destroyed. Only toward the mid-1930s did he dedicate himself completely to painting. His first paintings are in an eclectic style influenced by European avant-garde movements. De Kooning inserts biomorphic forms into a Cubist space and then treats those forms in a curiously experimental way, steadily distancing himself from his initial figuration. In this way he expresses his own response to the contemporary political situation, and his painting rises to become a means of social protest. While the roots of his imaginative expression may well lead back to surrealist art, the works of his mature phase show a preference for simpler fantasies incorporating fragments of color form. Beginning in 1945, with the work *Pink Angels*, de Kooning conceived a new genre with a psychodynamic composition in which the unity of the painting takes form as the organization of energies transmitted directly to the canvas through the action of the painter's hand. His fame, already affirmed within art circles, became public in 1948 with his first one-man show, at the Charles Egan Gallery in New York, in which he exhibited the black-and-white paintings he had been making over the past two years. De Kooning's originality became completely apparent in his abstract works of the 1940s: His individuality and his restlessness find full expression in increasingly broken-up images for which he adopted rapid brushstrokes, broad and incisive, and used new materials, including black enamels.

At the end of a long, gradual stylistic experimentation period, de Kooning asserted himself in the 1950s as one of the masters of the new Action Painting, representing, alongside Pollock, its dominant force while developing an array of vital pictorial concepts and a point of departure for further explorations.

Willem de Kooning
Pink Angels
c. 1945
oil and charcoal
on canvas
51 × 39½ in.
(130 × 100 cm)
Mr. and Mrs. Frederick Weisman Collection, Beverly Hills, California

With this work de Kooning brings the process of figural fragmentation derived from Cubism to a kind of conclusion; totally dismembered bodies become sinusoidal pink forms against a yellow background.

103

Eugène Delacroix

Charenton-Saint-Maurice, 1798-
Paris, 1863

The artist who is more representative than any other of French Romanticism was born to a family of high state officials. Trained in the studio of a Neoclassical artist, he formed a close friendship with Géricault around 1819, even posing for one of the figures in the *Raft of the "Medusa"* and Antoine-Jean Gros, famous for his huge history paintings. Another factor to bear in mind if we want to understand Delacroix is the great attention he paid to the masters of the past: Michelangelo's nudes, Titian's lush color, and Rubens's exuberance of composition would remain constant points of reference throughout his career. He made his official debut in 1822: *The Barque of Dante*, exhibited at the Paris Salon, immediately stirred interest in the young painter, who chose unusual themes and at once tried his hand at pictures of large size. With *Liberty Leading the People* (1830), Delacroix painted a genuine, though somewhat bombastic, "manifesto" of patriotic and revolutionary sentiments. All these works, painted during the early part of his career, show a complete command of an extraordinary range of compositions. In 1832 Delacroix's style underwent a profound change, following a visit to Spain and Morocco. His contact with Goya's painting and the experience of Africa gave his work an even greater dramatic intensity and dynamism, often conveying a vibrant sense of the erotic. Numerous paintings, drawings, and watercolors from the 1830s record his journey. Back in Paris and playing a leading role in cultural and literary circles alongside writers like Dumas, Baudelaire, and Victor Hugo, Delacroix devoted himself to ambitious cycles of frescoes and decorations, including those of the Apollo Gallery in the Musée du Louvre and the church of Saint-Sulpice in Paris, his last work on a grand scale.

Eugène Delacroix
Women of Algeria
1834
oil on canvas,
70¾ × 90¼ in.
(180 × 229 cm)
Musée du Louvre, Paris

The exotic costumes, the eroticism of the languid girls, and the cool shadows and lighting of the harem make this painting one of the earliest examples of Orientalism. Delacroix tackles an unusual theme, veined with a hint of forbidden sensuality.

Eugène Delacroix
The Barque of Dante
1822
oil on canvas
70¾ × 94½ in.
(180 × 240 cm)
Musée du Louvre, Paris

This was Delacroix's
first work to make a
great impact. The
unusual and fascinating
subject, the
monumentality of the
composition, the violent
and contrasting
handling of the paint,
very different from the
noble and statuesque
calm of Ingres, caught
the attention of the
critics and public alike.

Eugène Delacroix
Liberty Leading the People
1830
oil on canvas,
102¼ × 128 in.
(260 × 325 cm)
Musée du Louvre, Paris

In explanation of this
painting, Delacroix wrote:
"If I have not won battles
for my country, at least I
shall paint for it." He had
played a fairly lukewarm
part in the popular
uprisings in Paris in 1830
and, perhaps exaggerating
his own role, portrayed
himself as the man with
a top hat. The fruit of a
mix of Romantic and
literary culture, the canvas
is a singular blend of
realism and propaganda,
rhetoric and observation
of contemporary events.
Amidst the chaos of the
barricades the heroine,
embodying free France,
appears semi-naked,
wearing a Phrygian cap,
holding a flag in one hand
and a gun in the other.
He transformed a battle
scene into a collective
manifestation of
the nation's destiny
and history.

Georges de La Tour
The Fortune Teller
c. 1632-1635
oil on canvas
40¼ × 48½ in.
(102 × 123.5 cm)
Metropolitan Museum
of Art, New York

Three young women
and an old gypsy are
symmetrically arranged
around a young
gentleman with whom
they are exchanging
intense glances.
Here La Tour combines
the Caravaggesque
theme of the fortune
teller, which was
relatively common
during the first half of
the seventeenth century,
with the originally
French theme of the
prodigal son robbed
by women.

Georges de La Tour
Vic, 1593-Lunéville, 1652

A painter who was long overlooked,
La Tour's oeuvre has only recently
been reconstructed and assessed
by modern criticism. This revival,
which began in the twenties, has
reattributed to La Tour works that
were previously considered to be by
other Caravaggesque painters,
especially Valentin and Honthorst.
The 1972 exhibition in Paris, the first
devoted to La Tour, was pivotal
in this respect since it displayed over
thirty original paintings by the artist.
His biography is also uncertain.
Little or nothing is known of his
training, which is likely to have taken
place in Nancy. It is possible that
he journeyed to Italy between 1610
and 1616, which would explain his
knowledge of Caravaggio's works
and his circle, whose influence
can be seen in his painting. However,
recent studies have revealed that

he was an unusual artist who
developed an individual, consistent,
extremely modern language. Though
in his early years La Tour faithfully
followed Caravaggio's model, in his
maturity he moved toward a
simplification of composition and a
stylization of the figures, attributing
a moral value to realism, in line with
the severe style of French classicism.
From 1620 on, his presence is
documented at Lunéville, his wife's
hometown, where he spent a happy
period and established himself both
socially and artistically. In the
following decade Lorraine was
devastated first by the plague and
then by war. Lunéville, a garrison
center, was put to fire and sword and
plundered; thus all traces of the artist
and most of his early works were lost.
In 1643 La Tour was back in Lunéville,
where he remained until he died from
an epidemic fever, contracted in 1652,
which had already caused the death
of his wife. Though the chronological

order of his paintings is uncertain,
it is possible to trace a line
of development from the "daytime"
paintings to the large "nocturnal"
compositions, in which candlelight
is a kind of leitmotif.

Opposite
Georges de La Tour
Magdalene with a Lamp
c. 1638-1643
oil on canvas,
50½ × 37 in.
(128 × 94 cm)
Musée du Louvre, Paris

This is the only signed
canvas devoted to the
saint. It presents a more
severe image than the
others; having chosen
solitude and austerity,
Mary Magdalene is
depicted in tranquil
poverty.

Maurice Quentin de La Tour
Saint-Quentin, 1704-1788

An artist who recorded the pomp and the official side of contemporary life in France with considerable professional skill and an eye for psychological analysis, he painted portraits, all of them in pastel, that are evidence of a society that was only concerned with appearances, and toward which he adopted a detached, ironic, and at times scornful attitude. After his training in Paris in the workshop of J. Spoëde, a painter of still lifes, in 1725 he went to England, where he stayed for two years. On his return to Paris he received numerous commissions for portraits, and in 1737 he was admitted to the Academy, taking part regularly in the Salons. He painted portraits of Louis XV and the Marquise de Pompadour (both in the Louvre), of members of the aristocracy, and of great intellectuals, including the encyclopedists Voltaire, Rousseau, and D'Alembert. The medium he used for these portraits was pastel, which had become popular in France after the stay in Paris (1720-1721) of the well-known Venetian pastelist Rosalba Carriera. Pastel proved to be the medium best suited to his nervous temperament; his rapidity of execution was matched by a rapidity of vision that allowed him to capture his sitters in vibrant tones. His search for luxurious, refined effects, achieved through extreme technical virtuosity, does not undermine the spontaneity of pastel painting.

Maurice Quentin de La Tour
Portrait of M.lle Ferrand
1753
oil on canvas
28 × 23 in. (73 × 60 cm)
Alte Pinakothek, Munich

A cultured young lady portrayed as she takes a pause from her reading of a work on Newton. In the mid-eighteenth century, the ideas of the English scientist, who had died in 1727, had reached a vast public, including women, with the publication of works like the 1737 *Il Newtonianismo per le dame* (Newtonianism for Ladies), by Francesco Algarotti.

Robert Delaunay
Paris, 1885-Montpellier, 1941

Robert Delaunay and his wife Sonia are considered the founders of Orphism: references to the Cubist breakdown of the object in space were mixed with an investigation of rhythm in color, of an almost musical harmony that favored soft and circular forms. Initially influenced by the Symbolist currents and an admirer of Cézanne, Delaunay showed a very early interest in the theater. The various views of Paris he painted around 1910 reveal his taste for color, combined with a division of the image into geometric planes. It is interesting to note his contacts with the Blaue Reiter group in this period: thus he provided a unique link between the Parisian avant-garde and the research under way in Munich. The example of Seurat's experiments and a scientific interest in optics and the refraction of light led him to develop the characteristic circular patterns, almost whirlpools of color, that mark the historic phase of Orphism. For some years he alternated periods of return to the figurative with an ever clearer trend toward abstraction, which finally won out from 1930 onward.

Robert Delaunay
The Eiffel Tower
1910
oil on canvas
78¾ × 53¾ in
(200 × 136.5 cm)
Peggy Guggenheim
Collection, Venice

The great iron tower is the totem of Delaunay's figurative painting. The unmistakable shape of the tower is made to rotate, bend, and collide with other elements. Far from being a faithful representation, a souvenir of Paris, his *Eiffel Tower* is an endless modular structure, used for experiments in composition.

Robert Delaunay
The Cardiff Team
1912-1913
oil on canvas, 125¾ × 80 in. (326 × 208 cm)
Stedelijk van Abbe Museum, Eindhoven

Robert Delaunay
First Simultaneous Disk
1912
oil on canvas
diam. 52¾ in.
(134 cm)
Burton Tremaine
Collection, Meriden
(Conn.)

Orphism, the movement founded by Delaunay and his wife Sonia, entailed careful analysis of color transitions, drawing on scientific techniques for the investigation of the refraction and composition of light.

109

Sonia Delaunay-Terk
Gradizhsk (Ukraine),
1885-Paris, 1979

Trained in Russia, Sonia Terk moved to Paris, where she met and married Robert Delaunay, collaborating with him on the research into color and poetics known as Orphism. In particular, Sonia developed the theme of "simultaneous painting," a free expression of color, often arranged in concentric circles of gradated tones. Sonia carried out her first experiments in the field of book illustration and collage. A separate mention should be made of her costume designs for Diaghilev's Ballets Russes, as well as her clothing designs, which were to have a considerable influence on the Parisian fashion of the twenties and thirties. Around 1914 Sonia played an active part in the artistic and scientific experiments conducted by her husband into the retraction of light. Later on, Sonia showed a distinct preference for abstract painting, with compositions entitled "rhythm-color," and for the production of cartoons for tapestries.

Right
Sonia Delaunay-Terk
Illustration for Blaise
Cendrars's *La Prose
du Transsibérien et de la
petite Jehanne de France*
1913
oil and tempera on
paper, 76¼ × 7¼ in.
(193.5 × 18.5 cm)
Centre Pompidou, Paris

A fine example of a "simultaneous book," an original blend of words and color devised by the painter.

Sonia Delaunay-Terk
Electric Prisms
1914
oil on canvas
98½ × 98½ in.
(250 × 250 cm)
Centre Pompidou, Paris

Paul Delvaux

Antheit, 1897-1994

A Belgian painter, he did not discover Surrealism until 1934, when he saw Magritte's work at the exhibition "Minotaure," held at the Palais des Beaux-Arts in Brussels. So he decided to destroy the works of his Expressionist period, just as he had destroyed his Post-Impressionist ones after coming into contact with the painting of Ensor. Though he adopted Surrealism wholeheartedly, he was still able to develop a personal style. In his pictures he expressed the dreamlike dimension of reality, creating visionary disturbing compositions. They combine the Metaphysical space of de Chirico with Magritte's process of enigmatic estrangement. Classical architecture and bourgeois interiors are peopled with disquieting female figures, often naked, possessing an arcane sensuality. He showed his work at the movement's main exhibitions and staged his first retrospective in Brussels in 1944.

Paul Delvaux
Woman in the Mirror
1936
oil on canvas
28 × 35½ in.
(71 × 92.5 cm)
Thyssen-Bornemisza
Collection, Madrid

A picture pervaded by a dreamlike and mysterious sensuality, whose cold and tenuous colors render the female figure recondite and inscrutable.

Paul Delvaux
*The Staircase
(Nude on the Stairs)*
1946
oil on panel
48 × 59¾ in.
(122 × 152 cm)
Museum voor Schone
Kunsten, Ghent

A complex setting, serving as a reminder of the fact that Delvaux studied architecture while training in Brussels, is dominated by two enigmatic female nudes, figures from a dreamworld clearly derived from de Chirico.

111

Charles Demuth
Lancaster, Pennsylvania, 1883-1935

Along with his contemporary Charles Sheeler, Demuth was a primary exponent of precisionism, the American modernist style also known as Cubist realism. The two men shared a passion for photography, architecture, and industrial design. After apprenticeship at the Pennsylvania Academy of Fine Arts, Demuth studied at the Académie Julian in Paris from 1912 to 1914. Elegant and ironic, both unconventional and conservative, he attracted the friendship of writers and artists. His exposure to Cubism provided him with the means to become one of the first modernist experimenters in America. He blended the original matrix of Cubism, however, with several typically American inclinations, chief among these a preference for urban and industrial subjects and a sense of proportion and expressive immediacy. He had his first personal show in 1915, at the Daniels Gallery in New York; he then took part in the avant-garde shows of Stieglitz, with whom he exhibited at the 291 Gallery before the war and, between 1926 and 1929, at the Intimate Gallery. A skilled illustrator, Demuth directed his attention to architecture and, more in general, to the urban and industrial settings of New York and Lancaster, the industrial city where he spent most of his life, prevented from traveling by a serious form of diabetes. He followed the themes established by Sheeler, but developed them further in accordance with his own expressive modalities. After simplifying the geometry of a scene he flattens the surfaces and crosses them with lines of force that do not penetrate or disarrange the forms and instead rhythmically divide them, modulating light and color. In the 1920s, inspired by Picabia, he produced a series of portrait-posters honoring his contemporaries. These compositions are populated by objects, letters, and numbers following modalities that recall Cubist collages while at the same time anticipating the more advanced forms of pop art.

Charles Demuth
My Egypt
1927
oil on panel
35¾ × 30 in.
(90.8 × 76.2 cm)
Whitney Museum of American Art, New York

With his spare, rarefied style, Demuth gives an image of grain elevators near Lancaster the timelessness usually associated with the architecture of ancient Egypt.

Maurice Denis

Granville, 1870-Saint-Germain-en-Laye, 1943

The founder and leading light of the Nabis group, he combined his activity as a painter with that of theorist and art critic: in 1890 he published the movement's manifesto in the magazine *Art et Critique*. Thus he exercised an influence on the numerous men of letters with whom he came into contact, as well as on artists. The decisive influence on his development came not from his studies at the Académie Julian in Paris, but from his meeting with Gauguin and the critic Emile Bernard, at Pont-Aven in 1888. Here, together with Sérusier and Bonnard, he worked in close contact with nature, seeking not to record its appearance but to re-create its inner essence. Consequently Denis renounced the Impressionist premises of his style and chose to place the emphasis on decoration, laying on the paint in flat areas of color with clear outlines. In his manifesto of Symbolism, Denis reminded painters that "a picture—before being a war horse, a nude, or an anecdote of some sort—is essentially a flat surface covered with colors assembled in a certain order." The simplicity of the themes chosen by the Nabis (very different from the sophisticated work of Parisian artists), the use of pure colors, and Gauguin's emphasis on morality induced Denis to give the group a mystical connotation. The peremptory character of their pictorial representations, their fondness for allusive scenes and mysterious landscapes, and the idealization of their figures place Denis and his group at the origins of European Symbolism. Thus his most mature manner, in which the forms of objects, landscapes, and figures are reduced to colored silhouettes, can be regarded as the precursor of abstractionism. Toward the end of the century, after a visit to Italy where he was able to study the work of the Renaissance masters, Denis adopted a more monumental approach. A new chapter in the evolution of his style opened, with an inclination toward sumptuous decoration and the depiction of classical, mythological, and religious themes. In 1913, returning to the tradition of large-scale mural painting, he decorated the dome of the Théâtre des Champs-Elysées in a manner inspired by a complacent and intellectual type of Catholic mysticism. This work and his subsequent decoration of the Petit Palais made the artist popular with the public as an illustrator of sacred themes. Denis, who was deeply religious, had always shown great interest in the genre of sacred art, going so far as to found the "ateliers de l'art sacré" with Rouault.

Maurice Denis
September Evening
1910
oil on canvas
25¼ × 36½ in.
(64 × 93 cm)
Musée de Brest, Brest

Figures seen in languid positions fill the foreground of this painting in which we can discern the tendency toward transposition of the ideal into figures, settings, and situations drawn from everyday life.

Fortunato Depero
My "Plastic Ballets"
1921
oil on canvas
74½ × 70¾ in.
(189 × 180 cm)
Private collection

Here Depero evokes the staging of mechanical ballets and puppet shows. After the early phase of Futurism, he kept alive the cheerful vision of a "Futurist Reconstruction of the Universe."

Fortunato Depero

Fondo in Val di Non, 1892-
Rovereto, 1960

The phase of critical reassessment of the prolific activity of this versatile and brilliant artist, the only one to really attempt the Utopian enterprise of the "Futurist Reconstruction of the Universe," has now been brought to a happy conclusion. Joining the Futurist group at a very young age, Depero was still in the middle of his formative stage when the war broke out. He formed a partnership with Balla that yielded some imaginative projects. Depero regarded painting as just one of his many activities, in which commercial art played a significant role. Nevertheless, his paintings sum up the key features of his style, such as the presence of mechanical mannequins, cut-outs painted in glowing colors, and complicated machinery operated by automatons. A set designer and director of plays, Depero called his home-cum-studio in Rovereto "the Magician's house." From it emerged a continual flow of creative marvels, such as the large decorative panels described by their author as "mosaics of cloth." He received official recognition for his work, not least an invitation to spend two years in New York (1928-1930), where Depero, fascinated by the "Futurist" impetus of skyscrapers, contributed to a number of prestigious magazines. After 1930, however, Depero's activity was restricted to the narrow confines of Fascist autarky.

André Derain
Waterloo Bridge
1906
oil on canvas
31¾ × 39¾ in.
(80.5 × 101 cm)
Thyssen-Bornemisza
Collection, Madrid

In Derain's work
Fauvist expressionism
developed into
an intensification
of Impressionism. This
picture makes use of
just a few fundamental
tones: reds and yellows,
greens and blues.

André Derain
Chatou, 1880-Garches, 1954

A friend and fellow student of Matisse and Vlaminck, with whom he founded the Fauvist movement, Derain showed a deep interest in reality right from the beginning of his career. In contrast to Matisse's lyricism and Vlaminck's aggressiveness, he was able to establish a masterly balance between a free and highly imaginative use of color and control over form, in a deliberate challenge to the Impressionist tradition. A very interesting example of this is provided by the group of canvases he made of views of the Thames in 1905, an updated version of Monet's celebrated series. From 1908, after the conclusion of the decisive Fauvist period, he came under the influence of Cézanne's work, brought to prominence by the Cubists. But, rather than being stimulated to break down volumes geometrically, Derain found in Cézanne the inspiration for reinterpretation of the traditional plastic values in landscape painting and scenes of real life, seen in comparison with the products of non-European artistic cultures. As more and more avant-garde movements sprang up with provocative proposals, Derain felt the need to return to the roots of Realism in the work of Caravaggio and Courbet, though mediated by the ancient Roman art which he rediscovered on a visit to Italy. In this sense his work was in line with the "return to order" that characterized the Italian culture of the twenties.

André Derain
Woman in Chemise
1906
oil on canvas
39¼ × 32 in.
(100 × 81 cm)
Statens Museum for
Kunst, Copenhagen

Derain juxtaposes warm
colors (orange and
pink) with cold ones
(blue and green) to
achieve a perfect balance
of tones.

Barthélemy d'Eyck
Active in France from 1447 to 1470

Active at the court of René of Anjou at Angers, in Naples, and then for a long period in Provence, according to documents from the years 1447 to 1470, Barthélemy d'Eyck is described by contemporary biographers as one of the greatest artists of his day. Although there are no references to any of his works, critics are unanimous in identifying him as the Master of the Annunciation of Aix and the Maître du Coeur,

author of the *Livre du Coeur d'Amour Epris*, one of the marvels of fifteenth-century European illumination. Trained in Flemish artistic circles and probably related to the van Eyck brothers, Barthélemy d'Eyck is distinguished from those he followed both by the strength of his painting, which shows the influence of the Burgundian master Claus Sluter, and by the function assigned to light, which unifies space and figures in ways that were to be taken over by the Avignon School.

Barthélemy d'Eyck
Annunciation
1443-1445
oil on wood, 61 × 69¼ in. (155 × 176 cm)
Sainte-Marie-Madeleine, Aix-en-Provence

Painted for the Corpici chapel in the church of the Savior, this triptych was subsequently taken apart. The central panel is in the church of St. Mary Magdalene at Aix,

while the side panels are in the Musées Royaux in Brussels and in the Rijksmuseum in Amsterdam. The central scene is endowed with extraordinary force and originality by the balanced handling of mass, the symbolic use of light, and the deft mastery of space. The figure of the Archangel Gabriel occupies the left side of the painting,

framed by two pillars and surmounted by the figure of God the Father. A ray of light passes from his hand raised in blessing through the rose window to illuminate the face of the Virgin, The church opens up on the right into two aisles that open the space obliquely to emphasize the Virgin and underscore her symbolic role as mother of the Church.

Jim Dine
Cincinnati, 1935

Follower of Neodadaism but also influenced by Russian constructivism, in particular Ivan Puni, Dine worked out a pictorial language characterized by a highly personal relationship to the object, whether it is painted or, more often, applied directly to the canvas. Dine arrived in New York in 1958 and held his first "happening" at the Judson Gallery the very next year. In 1962 he organized his first one-man show, causing quite a sensation: He exhibited *Green Suit* and *Flesh Tie*, a suit and tie painted following gestural art. Dine declared that his painting is made of objects that he intends to transfer to the canvas without changing or distorting them romantically, since what interests him is only their presence. The articles of clothing of his first works were soon joined by tools—saws, hammers, pliers, screwdrivers—all of them hung on the canvas, sometimes upside down, always in a way that forces them to show themselves off in an isolated, frontal presentation so as to create a face-to-face relationship between the viewer and the painting. The factor of perception takes on a central role. The act of seeing is neutral, but observation, while passive, hides an interrogating, scrutinizing tension that in some ways recalls the attitude of the detective faced with the photo of a suspect. More recently, Dine has preferred palettes and chromatic scales in which he shows himself treating color on the same level as an object.

Jim Dine
Shoe
1961
oil on canvas
Property of the artist

Exhibited at the Venice Biennale in 1964, this work is an eloquent simplification of Dine's pictorial procedure. At other times and places, artists use the object as a model, isolating it on the canvas and presenting it using the tools of painting; in this case, the object is absent, and what remains is its trompe-l'oeil imitation.

Otto Dix

Untermhaus, 1891-Singen, 1969

Dix studied at the art schools of
Dresden and Düsseldorf (1910-1914).
His early works appear to lie completely
outside the avant-garde currents
of German Expressionism and to be
influenced, if anything, by
Impressionism. The call to arms in the
First World War brought about an
abrupt change in his style. When he
emerged from the horrors of the war,
Dix seems to have been shocked by the
physical and moral wounds that had
been opened in the body of German
society. Thus he developed a means
of expression in which he took a drastic
and biting realism to the point of
absurdity. A typical example is the
Match Seller, in which a disabled soldier,
his legs reduced to stumps, squats on
the sidewalk as people pass by with
indifference. The paintings of social
protest were combined with a prolific
output of portraits, characterized by
their incisive and penetrating line.
Dix went on to explore the roots of
Expressionism in the tradition of
German painting and, together with
George Grosz, founded the movement
called Neue Sachlichkeit ("New
Objectivity") in 1924. Dix's preferred
themes were social satire and the
denunciation of violence, offering an
interesting parallel with the films of
Fritz Lang and the hard-hitting cabaret
of Berlin. The polemical violence of his
paintings did not prevent Dix from
pursuing an academic career. The
advent of Nazism (1933) coincided with
his grotesque picture, the *Seven Deadly
Sins*, which included a vicious caricature
of Hitler. His work was declared
"degenerate art" and about 250 of his
canvases were burned in public. In 1939
Dix, accused of involvement in a plot to
kill the Führer, was arrested and
imprisoned. After the war he went back
to live on Lake Constance, where he
continued to work for many years,
choosing themes from the Bible and
adopting a much gentler style than that
of the Berlin period.

Otto Dix
Triptych of the War
central panel and predella
1929-1932
mixed media on canvas
80¼ × 80¼ in.
(204 × 204 cm)
Gemäldegalerie Neue
Meister, Dresden

Domenichino
Diana the Huntress
1614
canvas
88½ × 126 in.
(225 × 320 cm)
Galleria Borghese, Rome

The story of how this festive picture came to be painted is very unusual.

Cardinal Aldobrandini commissioned it as a sequel to Titian's *Bacchanals* which he had recently added to his collection. The comparison with such an illustrious model brought out the best in Domenichino, especially his ability to handle light, and spurred him to take a fresh approach. Unlike Titian, he was willing to avoid explosive use of color and movement. Instead he seemed content to concentrate on a serene contemplation of the beauty of girls, animals, and the countryside.

Domenichino

Domenico Zampieri
Bologna, 1581-Naples, 1641

Domenichino was perhaps the most sophisticated painter of the seventeenth century, so much so, in fact, that at times his work can seem rarefied. He studied under the Carracci cousins, first in Bologna and then in Rome (where at the beginning of the century he assisted Annibale who was then working in the Farnese Gallery and on the large lunettes in Palazzo Doria-Pamphili). He was completely bowled over by the simple, classical, and elegant beauty of Raphael's art, having a deep admiration for all the great masters of the early sixteenth century. His career was mainly spent trying to revive that wonderful era of the High Renaissance, but he did this with a completely up-to-date critical and intellectual approach. His output typically included altarpieces (*The Communion of St. Jerome* painted in response to Agostino Carracci, Rome, Vatican Gallery), and secular and religious fresco cycles, such as those painted for Villa Aldobrandini at Frascati, for the St. Nilo chapel in the abbey at Grottaferrata (1610), or the murals in the St. Cecilia chapel of San Luigi dei Francesi in Rome (1611-1614), located opposite Caravaggio's St. Matthew canvases painted in such a different style a dozen years earlier. His career stalled slightly after the failure of his frescoes in Sant'Andrea della Valle (1624-28). Embittered by their poor reception, he moved to Naples, where he painted the chapel of the Tesoro in the cathedral.

Domenico Veneziano
Domenico di Bartolomeo
Venice, c. 1410-Florence, 1461

Domenico Veneziano's complex and rich artistic background, learning his craft between Rome and Florence, gave him a composite style that was very personal. His surviving work dates mainly from the middle decades of his life when he was working in Florence. Of his outstanding works, we should mention the *Adoration of the Magi* (Staatliche Museen/Preussischer Kulturbesitz, Berlin). This was painted just before he started the frescoes (now almost completely vanished) in the church of Sant'Egido in Florence on which he worked together with Andrea del Castagno and Piero della Francesca. In 1447 Domenico Veneziano completed his masterpiece, the *Altarpiece of St. Lucy of the Magnolias* (Uffizi, Florence). It was this work that definitively marked an end to the use of polyptychs as altar paintings.

Domenico Veneziano
Altarpiece of St. Lucy of the Magnolias
1445-1447
wood panel
82 × 85 in
(209 × 216 cm)
Uffizi, Florence

Dosso Dossi

Giovanni di Niccolò Luteri
between Mantua and Ferrara,
c. 1490-Ferrara, 1542

We do not know exactly either where or when Dosso was born. He was to become the outstanding painter in the Ferrara school of the whole sixteenth century. In its timing and thought his work was in perfect harmony with that of Ludovico Ariosto, who was then the court poet to the Este family. Dosso's early training brought him into close contact with Giorgione's circles. In about 1510 he was in Mantua and from 1514 he became court painter in Ferrara. He was called almost immediately to work alongside Bellini and Titian on the decorative mythological scheme for Alfonso d'Este. Thanks to frequent travels

(mainly to Venice but also to Florence and Rome), Dosso stayed in constant contact with what was going on in the world of painting and his style evolved at the same pace as most of sixteenth century art. In the long years he worked for the Este family he produced both altarpieces (sometimes in collaboration with Garofalo, such as the grandiose *Polyptych* now in the Ferrara National Gallery) and noteworthy decorative cycles on pagan literary or mythological themes. Dosso's main stylistic reference is Venetian art, and he long continued Giorgione's romantic landscape style. But he quotes from Ferrara's own tradition, as well as possessing his own narrative vein close to Ariosto's poetry. The frescoes in the Villa Imperiale in Pesaro and Buonconsiglio Castle in Trent were painted in collaboration with his brother Battista in about 1530.

Dosso Dossi
*Jupiter Painting
Butterflies, Mercury,
and Virtue*
c. 1522-1524
canvas
44 × 59 in.
(112 × 150 cm)
Kunsthistorisches
Museum, Vienna

A highly imaginative creator of fanciful tales, Dosso Dossi from Ferrara often drew inspiration from mythology to create episodes not to be found in classical texts and art. His work is wholly infused with the spirit of the Renaissance, the last great cultural flowering of the Italian courts, before developments in international politics and the emergence of large states rendered the fragmentation of power into small local dukedoms anachronistic.

121

Gerard Dou
Leyden, 1613-1675

Dou has gone down in history for being Rembrandt's first pupil, between 1628 and 1630. He is one of the most typical exponents of the Fijnschilderei or "fine painting" characteristic of Leyden. Rembrandt's early, precise,

meticulous style remained Dou's point of reference throughout his career, to the extent that it became an actual mania. According to sources, Rembrandt and Dou worked together on several paintings, but it has been very difficult to identify these to date. Dou was obsessed by formal clarity, and his extremely accurate small or

very small works are painstaking. Naturally such paintings took a very long time to complete, and their market price during the seventeenth and eighteenth centuries was extremely high, which encouraged imitators who were not always so successful. The son of a glass painter, from 1632 on Dou was the most

famous painter in Leyden after Rembrandt moved to Amsterdam and Jan Lievens left for England. He established the local painters' guild in 1648. Dou frequently set his pictures in an arched window frame or an illusionistic picture frame.

Left
Gerard Dou
The Young Mother
1658
oil on wood
29 × 21¾ in.
(73.5 × 55.5 cm)
Mauritshuis, The Hague

The descriptive details are painted with an accuracy reminiscent of Jan Bruegel's crowded allegories and the earlier paintings and miniatures of the Flemish "primitives."

Gerard Dou
The Seller of Game
c. 1670
oil on wood
22¾ × 18 in.
(58 × 46 cm)
National Gallery, London

Dou's gifts of patience and minute handling in the representation of details and surfaces clearly emerge in the exuberant still lifes that he often paints in the

foreground, creating almost illusionistic effects despite their small size. There are no particular variations in style throughout the painter's career and he always remains faithful to his early manner acquired in Rembrandt's studio in Leyden.

Duccio di Buoninsegna
Siena, c. 1260-1318

The great age of the Sienese School started with Duccio. At the beginning of the fourteenth century Siena was vying with its neighbor, Florence, for political and artistic supremacy in central Italy. A faithful follower of Byzantine painting, Duccio managed to give to his traditionally painted figures fresh humanity and life with his newfound sensitivity to color and line. While his paintings may seem rooted in the Byzantine tradition, we can discern the first signs of the International Gothic art that was to influence Simone Martini and the Lorenzetti brothers. The most important features of Duccio's work were his supple draughtsmanship and use of clear colors. This was apparent in the *Madonna Rucellai* in the Uffizi (1285) and in the round choir window for Siena cathedral (1288). Although as a young man Duccio probably worked in Assisi, he spent virtually his entire life in Siena. Nonetheless it appears that he was aware of the new ideas in Florentine art. The delicate Madonnas now in Perugia, London, and also Siena provide wonderful examples of Duccio's poetic rendering of feeling. They preceded his masterpiece which encapsulated both his own work and the very spirit of an age in transition. This is the splendid *Maestà* he painted for Siena cathedral, now in the Museo dell'Opera.

123

Previous page
Duccio di Buoninsegna
*Window Showing
the Life of Mary*
c. 1287-1288
stained-glass
Cathedral, Siena

This is the oldest and the
most important surviving
example of Italian stained
glass. The technique
was widespread across
northern Europe,
especially in France,
but is rare in Italy.

Left
Duccio di Buoninsegna
Madonna Rucellai
c. 1285
wood panel
177 × 114 in.
(450 × 290 cm)
Uffizi, Florence

This altarpiece was once
attributed to Cimabue but

is typical of the young
Duccio's output. Working
within the Byzantine
tradition, he created images
fascinating for their
insubstantial quality that
seem held together by
magic. The Virgin's robes
fall almost sinuously,
foreshadowing the elegance
of Gothic painting .

Duccio di Buoninsegna
Maestà (front)
1308-1311
wood panel
83 × 167¾ in.
(211 × 426 cm)
Cathedral Museum,
Siena

The celebrated
masterpiece that the
inhabitants of Siena
carried in procession
from Duccio's studio to
the High Altar in the
Cathedral, the *Maestà* is
a very large and
complex picture.
Over the years, the
original frame and some
other parts have been
lost, but the main body
of the picture is
substantially preserved.

The front shows a large
image of the enthroned
Virgin which is still
based on Byzantine
models. The patron
saint of Siena is
surrounded by
wondering, dreamy
angels looking toward
her. Set square in the
center is the massive
marble block with
decorations that
remind us of the
Cosmati work found
in many Roman
mosaics. The inscription
around the base of
the throne contains
two prayers. The Virgin
is being asked to grant
peace to Siena and glory
to Duccio who has
painted the scene.

125

Marcel Duchamp

Blainville, 1887-Neuilly, 1968

An irreverent and provocative artist, he broke with the traditional conception of art and the concept of the work of art itself, in an attempt to demonstrate the artist's absolute freedom within society. After an early Fauvist phase, he moved on to Cubist decomposition, taking its principles to an extreme. In 1912 he took part in the exhibition of the Section d'Or, which comprised works by the dissident Cubists who belonged to Apollinaire's circle. The following year saw him break away from the Cubists and head in a direction unconstrained by the techniques of painting itself: the "work of art" was transformed into an object of everyday use, detached from reality and elevated to the status of an art form. Out of this came the first "ready-mades": a bicycle wheel fixed to a stool, a bottle rack and, more embarrassingly, a ceramic urinal turned upside down and signed with the apparent pseudonym R. Mutt, which concealed the key to the interpretation. In 1915 Duchamp moved to New York where, together with Francis Picabia and Man Ray, he created the American Dada movement publishing the sole issue of the magazine *New York Dada* (1921). In addition to his ready-mades, the artist produced a large work on glass, *The Big Glass,* which he left incomplete in 1923 when he gave up art for the game of chess. After a long pause he resumed an intense activity, producing ironic and paradoxical objects such as the *Boîte-en-valise,* a suitcase containing miniature copies of his most significant works. He completed his *Etant donnés* (1966): a female nude against the backdrop of a landscape and viewed through a keyhole. The installation was set up in a room at the Philadelphia Museum of Art, and inaugurated after his death. The themes of virginity and maternity return, no longer set in a space dominated by forms alluding to modern technology, but in a sort of theater of nature, offering an optimistic vision of the world.

Marcel Duchamp
*Nude Descending
a Staircase*
1912
oil on canvas
58¼ × 35 in.
(148 × 89 cm)
Philadelphia Museum
of Art, Philadelphia

Raoul Dufy

Le Havre, 1877-Forcalquier, 1953

A member of the Fauves, Dufy represented that side of the group most attracted to the beauty of the world and nature. While Vlaminck took the emotional use of violent color to its extreme consequences, Dufy preferred a refined style, working with brief and light brushstrokes in compositions that take on the appearance of precious and original arabesques. Trained at the municipal school of art in Le Havre, he received a grant in 1900 that allowed him to move to Paris and enroll in the studio of Maurice Bonnard. Here he studied Impressionist and Post-Impressionist painting until he joined forces with Matisse in 1905, struck by the painting *Luxe, Calme et Volupté,* shown at the Salon d'Automne the previous year. The Fauve experience at an end, a reexamination of Cézanne brought him to Cubism, as the 1910 painting *Boats in Marseilles Harbor* testifies. But Dufy did not find the strict rationality of the Cubists congenial and decided to head off in a direction of his own, quite distinct from the currents that dominated the European scene. He developed a flowing, concise, and extremely rhythmic style, covering the canvas with broad expanses of color (with a particular emphasis on shades of blue) overlaid with a dense and elegant mesh of tiny motifs, analyzed in every detail. He also produced fine drawings and textile designs that led him to experiment with new techniques of decoration.

Raoul Dufy
*The Big Tree
at Saint-Maxime*
1942
oil on canvas,
25½ × 31½ in.
(65 × 80 cm)
Musée des Beaux-Arts,
Nice

Against a background
of vibrant tones, obtained
by the skillful treatment
of oil colors so that
they assume the fluidity
of tempera, the
representation takes
on an elegant lightness.

Albrecht Dürer
Nuremberg, 1471-1528

Dürer was the greatest German painter and one of the leading intellectuals of the Renaissance. His art and ideas dominated the central European cultural scene in the early decades of the sixteenth century. Always at the center of debate, in direct contact with princes and emperors, ready to travel frequently, in touch with artists and intellectuals, a committed participant in the great historic events of his time, Dürer is a figure that exerts an eternal fascination. After his apprenticeship first to his father, and then to Michael Wolgemut's workshop, at the age of nineteen he set off on a long journey during which his artistic culture acquired a European dimension. He stayed away from Nuremberg for four years, from April 1490 to May 1494. He spent some time in Basel where he became acquainted with the works of Konrad Witz. Continuing down the Rhine valley he then moved to Colmar in Alsace and stayed with three sons of Martin Schongauer, whose paintings and engravings he studied assiduously. His next stop was Strasbourg. His journey to Venice completed his training, which, after his return to Nuremberg, launched him on an exceptional career as a painter and engraver, also in the service of Maximilian of Hapsburg. From 1505 to 1507 Dürer returned to Italy. This journey was an encounter at the highest level between the greatest German artist and the culture of the Italian Renaissance in all its splendor. He spent a long time in Venice, when the local school was experiencing the transition between the style of the Bellinis and Carpaccio and the new generation of Giorgione, Lorenzo Lotto, and Titian. Midway through the first decade of the sixteenth century, this culminated in one of the most brilliant periods in the whole history of European painting. His later compositions are wide-ranging in monumentality and perspective. Another journey in 1521 took him to Antwerp and the Netherlands where he came into contact with Metsys and Lucas van Leyden. In his last years, he sought to attain a difficult balance in art and moderation between the tensions that were rife in Germany. Dürer is a universal artist, open to extremely varied themes, formats, and techniques. He also constantly furthered the development of painting, by producing treatises and technical writings.

Albrecht Dürer
Self-Portrait
1498
oil on wood
20½ × 16 in.
(52 × 41 cm)
Prado, Madrid

Dürer's life is a compelling mix of a highly successful career and public image and, by contrast, a tormented spirit. At many stages during his existence Dürer hovered between a satisfied awareness of his growing success and the dark, lonely abyss of depression. This conflict makes the artist's personality particularly fascinating and enriches his works with a deep introspective, psychological component. In this self-portrait painted in his youth, when he was already successful and aware of having acquired a high social status, Dürer looks self-satisfied with his appearance and the renown he has gained. He is no longer a craftsman like his father, who was a goldsmith, but a sophisticated intellectual. His slanting eyes that indicate his distant Mongolian origins confer an aristocratic touch on the portrait.

Albrecht Dürer
The Four Apostles
1526
panels, 84¾ × 30 in. each
(215 × 76 cm)
Alte Pinakothek, Munich

The pairs of apostles
(John and Peter, Mark
and Paul) personify man's
four basic temperaments
that reflect the humors
and are, respectively,
sanguine, phlegmatic,
choleric, and melancholic.
The long inscription
at the bottom invites
the spectator to seek
moderation and
reconciliation and to
listen to others. During
the last years of his
life, he strove to understand
the changing times in
which he lived, the great
historical events and
radical psychological,
social, and religious
changes he had witnessed.
An awareness that had
remained hidden for so
long, a dark presentiment
that was coming true,
matured in him:
an awareness of the
limitations of art, and the
contrast between
Humanist utopias and
reality. Dürer continued
to seek a mathematical
formula to describe and
define beauty, but it
always eluded him.
Meanwhile the myth of
man as the measure of all
things was being
shattered by the blows of
the Protestant schism and
the bitter bloodbath of
religious wars. In his last
years Dürer executed
some of his finest
masterpieces, which
display his anxiety to
leave a lasting legacy for
posterity, but also his
awareness that some
of the ideals on which
he had based his entire
existence were doomed
to failure.

129

Thomas Eakins
Philadelphia, 1844-1916

Openly opposed to the stylish habit among many of his colleagues of moving to Europe, Thomas Eakins represents, together with Homer, the most direct and intense version of American realism at the end of the nineteenth century. Born into a well-to-do middle-class family, and thus relieved of any financial preoccupations, Eakins created for a select few people, primarily intellectuals, to whom his paintings offered a radical alternative to the aesthetic elegance of John Singer Sargent and the painters tied to Impressionism. After studies at the Philadelphia Academy of Fine Arts, and also after following a course in medicine, Eakins did, however, spend a period in Paris, where he encountered and highly esteemed Manet. From 1873 on, he remained in Philadelphia, where the controversial *Surgical Clinic of Professor Gross* (1875) earned him much fame. As a realist painter, Eakins affirmed the necessity of understanding and studying reality, including by way of science and the advances in the field of photography, but without any sprinkling of European culture dust. "Nature," he wrote, "is just as varied and just as beautiful in our day as she was in the time of Phidias." He began a collaboration with the photographer Eadweard Muybridge in 1884, and under the auspices of the University of Pennsylvania, he assembled a large collection of images of human and animal locomotion, published in 1887 as *Animal Locomotion*, a spectacular volume illustrated by more than seven hundred images arranged in sequence. This scientific attitude directed his career as a painter, free of the usual conventions, including any need to please the public. Public exhibitions of Eakins's works were rare and invariably controversial; he preferred smaller shows, at which he sought the approval of a limited circle of intellectuals, the same people who posed for his portraits, from university professors to the poet Walt Whitman. Only at the posthumous show held in New York in 1917 did American artists, and in particular the members of the Eight, discover the importance, commitment, and solid concision of his noncelebratory realism.

Thomas Eakins
Portrait of Frank Jay Saint John
1900
oil on canvas
23½ × 19½ in. (60 × 50 cm)
Fine Arts Museums of San Francisco

In portraits, too, Eakins revealed his desire to be free of European schematics, seeking to be faithful to the truth instead.

Opposite
Thomas Eakins
The Surgical Clinic of Professor Gross
1875
oil on canvas
96 × 78 in. (244 × 198 cm)
Thomas Jefferson University Art Museum, Philadelphia

This is Eakins's best-known work, commissioned to celebrate the famous surgeon Samuel Gross; in it Eakins does not limit himself to making a portrait of the professor but instead locates him in the dramatic and disturbing setting of an operation being carried out in public in the anatomy theater of Jefferson Medical Hospital, where Eakins himself had studied.

Rejected by the judges of the artistic commission for the large show for the 1876 Centennial Exposition in Philadelphia, the work was presented to the public in the section reserved for medicine, where its immediate and brutal realism awakened lively reactions, among them nausea and fainting.

Adam Elsheimer
Frankfurt, 1578-Rome, 1610

A great artist of the same generation as Caravaggio, Rubens, and Guido Reni, Elsheimer unfortunately died very young, thus interrupting the development of a poetical style of painting that had begun with great delicacy in works of rarity and charm. Attracted from an early age by Italian Renaissance art, he moved to Venice in 1598, where he came into contact with Hans Rottenhammer (who had worked with Jan Bruegel in previous years) and studied Tintoretto's work. This Venetian experience gave rise to Elsheimer's most ambitious religious works, whirling celestial visions directly inspired by Tintoretto's paintings in the Doges' Palace in Venice. In the fateful year of 1600, a watershed that was not merely symbolic but also real for many early Baroque masters, Elsheimer moved to Rome, where he spent the last ten years of his short life. In the lively circles of "Romanized" Nordic painters, Elsheimer altered his style to focus primarily on landscape painting, as did his friend Paul Brill. In this field, Elsheimer struck a note of intense expressive originality that was both classical and romantic, idealized and scientific. Keenly interested in the artistic movements of his day, Elsheimer was familiar both with the Caravaggesque handling of light and the tranquil sweeping views of the Roman countryside by Annibale Carracci. His own technique was, however, to remain firmly linked to his northern roots, and was characterized by exquisite, painstaking execution impeccably suffused with light.

Adam Elsheimer
Flight into Egypt
1609
oil on copper
12¼ × 16¼ in.
(31 × 41 cm)
Alte Pinakothek,
Munich

This enchanting nocturnal elegy is unquestionably Elsheimer's best-known work. Despite its small size, it can be regarded as one of the most fascinating paintings produced in the early seventeenth century, as well as a real cornerstone in the early history of landscape painting. The perfect depiction of the heavenly vault, where the Milky Way and the constellations sparkle in a sky illuminated by a full moon, demonstrates Elsheimer's great interest in the world of science, and the work of Galileo in particular.

James Ensor
Ostend, 1860-1949

A voluntarily isolated and unconventional artist, Ensor was a figure of great significance in the European painting that came after Impressionism. Making his debut in the crucial 1880s, he came into direct contact with the leading currents of the time, from Symbolism to Decadentism, but quickly went in a direction all of his own, explicitly detached from groups and movements and openly challenging the views of the art critics. In a surprising anticipation of what would later be known as Expressionism, Ensor peopled his pictures with grotesque and troubled figures, often wearing bizarre or macabre masks. His skeletons and harridans, clowns and demons can be interpreted as so many satires of bourgeois hypocrisy. The climax of this ironic and yet disquieting painting, at times even obsessive in the suffocating presence of the sneering and unrecognizable faces that throng his pictures, was reached in Ensor's masterpiece, the *Entry of Christ into Brussels* (1888), an extravagant and singular painting of overwhelming chromatic force. Every now and then, even Ensor permitted himself a break by painting or drawing solitary landscapes. After the turn of the century the creativity and potency of the Belgian artist's images tended to fade.

James Ensor
Little Church of Mariekerke
1901
oil on canvas
21¼ × 26½ in.
(54 × 67 cm)
Museum voor Schone Kunsten, Ostend

Ensor's pale and tenuous landscapes represent an interval of silence and poetry in the noisy, brightly colored and lively comedy of the world staged by the artist. The delicate composure of the scene is still reminiscent of Corot.

James Ensor
*Entry of Christ
into Brussels*
1888
oil on canvas, 100 × 169¾
in. (254 × 431 cm)
Musées Royaux des
Beaux-Arts, Antwerp

The painter's greatest
masterpiece, the work
harks back to the
sixteenth-century models
of Bosch and Bruegel in
its *horror vacui*, with the
main subject (Christ is in
the background,
underneath the banner
with the inscription "Vive
la Sociale") almost
suffocated by an
overflowing mass of
humanity, made up of
caricatured faces, macabre
apparitions parading like
mannequins.

James Ensor
Theater of Masks
1908
oil on canvas
28¼ × 33¾ in.
(72 × 86 cm)
Thyssen-Bornemisza
Collection, Madrid

A characteristic example
of the Belgian artist's
taste for illusion and
bitter irony, in which
it is not easy to tell
whether the "masks" are
worn by the actors on
the stage or the people
in the audience. James
Ensor turns the
relationship on its head,
challenging the public
to look at itself without
hypocrisy.

Max Ernst
Untitled-Dada
c. 1922
oil on canvas
17 × 12½ in.
(43.2 × 31.5 cm)
Thyssen-Bornemisza
Collection, Madrid

The painting
deliberately sets out
to create a sense of
bewilderment. The
random combination
of objects in everyday
use and totally invented
forms produces an
ironic and arbitrary
composition.

Max Ernst
Bruhl, 1891-Paris, 1976

The anti-systematic philosophy of
Nietzsche and Freudian psychoanalysis
played a decisive role in the
development of this German painter
and sculptor, who followed his own
line of research without ever
becoming fully involved in any
of the avant-garde movements with
which he came into contact.
Only to Giorgio de Chirico did Ernst
profess the devotion due to a master,
whose teachings were beyond
question. He shared de Chirico's
conviction that the marriage between
artistic creativity and industrial
production, the objective
of the Weimar school, was totally
impracticable: art was the only
medium that ensured freedom
and made it possible to strip away
the grotesque mask of power.
In 1921 Ernst took part in the
exhibition organized by Breton in
Paris, moving to the city the following
year and establishing links with the
Dada group and then Surrealism,
but following a course that could not
be assimilated with their approach.
He invented new techniques, such
as *frottage*, based on the child's game
of taking an impression of the texture
of a material by rubbing, and
produced works of a visionary
character, but always extremely lucid.
After a period in the United States
(1939-1953), he returned to France,
where he continued to work intensely,
producing graphic art
and totem-like sculptures as well.

135

Giovanni Fattori
Livorno, 1825-Florence, 1908

A painter of great force but also deep feelings, and an excellent engraver, Fattori was one of the most important Italian artists of the nineteenth century. He spent the whole of his life in Tuscany but, through his contacts with the art dealer and critic Diego Martelli, was able to keep constantly abreast of developments elsewhere. As a result the research of the Macchiaioli (the group of which he was the most ardent and enduring spirit) was consciously carried out in parallel with that of the Impressionists and European Realism in general. After training first in Livorno, he moved to Florence to study at the academy there. His early paintings include huge pictures of historical subjects and his first portraits, a genre that he practiced throughout his life to great effect. His meeting with Signorini, Lega, and many other artists at the Caffè Michelangelo led Fattori to put aside the traditional chiaroscuro of Romanticism and go in for a more immediate style, based on a dynamic and realistic relationship between light and color: the *macchia* ("stain" or "blob"). Around 1860 Fattori applied this new technique to paintings of contemporary battles, represented with a profound and non-rhetorical sense of participation. These were followed by numerous scenes devoted to work in the fields, in which his love for the Maremma region and the bare coast around Livorno were combined with a human and social empathy for the toil of the peasants. Fattori's realism also found expression through his choice of colors imbued with light and a draftsmanship that inherits the tradition of Tuscan art. His inclination for painting in the open air and the great luminosity of his pictures may in part recall the parallel work of the Impressionists in Paris, but the robust brushwork, with synthetic "blobs" of color, is wholly original. After the seventies, when the Macchiaioli group began to break up, Fattori devoted himself chiefly to portraits and engravings.

Giovanni Fattori
On the Lookout
1872
oil on panel
14½ × 22 in.
(37 × 56 cm)
Private collection, Rome

Lyonel Feininger
New York, 1871-1956

Feininger was an artist of great originality and independence of mind. Influenced by the main currents of German Expressionism and yet inclined to develop a poetics all of his own, he managed to create a unique blend of German and American culture, the two sources of his inspiration. Born to a family of musicians of German origin, he went back to Germany to study music. But he decided to become a painter instead, studying first in Hamburg and then in Berlin. Between 1890 and 1910 he earned his living drawing caricatures and cartoons for German and French magazines. Several stays in Paris brought him into contact with the avant-garde. In particular, he formed a close friendship with Robert Delaunay. The process of development of his style was slow, but deep. In 1913 Feininger was invited to take part in the historic exhibition staged by Kandinsky and Marc's Blaue Reiter group. This gave him an opportunity to demonstrate the independence of his style, confirmed by his first one-man show (Berlin, 1917) and by a flourishing activity as a graphic artist. Stimulated by his contacts with Cubism and Futurism, Feininger started to break down the image into three-dimensional planes, geometric shapes, and regular parallelepipeds. The most interesting characteristic of this approach (applied not only to human figures but also and above all to architectural scenes) was the artist's great sensitivity to light, which permeated all his pictures and produced effects close to abstraction. At the end of the First World War, Feininger was called by Walter Gropius to work at the Bauhaus, where he chiefly taught engraving. In 1926 Feininger formed the group known as Die Blaue Vier, "The Blue Four," with Kandinsky, Klee, and Jawlensky. But the political situation was growing hostile: in 1933 Feininger's works were placed on the list of "degenerate art." A few years later, in 1937, Feininger was forced to leave Germany and return to the United States, where he spent the final part of his career observing and representing the skyscrapers of Manhattan.

Lyonel Feininger
The White Man
1907
oil on canvas
26¾ × 21 in.
(68 × 53.3 cm)
Thyssen-Bornemisza
Collection, Madrid

The lean figure loping through the city late in the evening is an apt allegory of Feininger's subtle and refined role in the art of the early twentieth century. Apart from the period spent at the Bauhaus, Feininger cannot be pinned down or associated with a particular avant-garde, following a course of his own that led him to build a bridge between Germany and the United States. The density of the paint in his prewar pictures was later to give way to sophisticated light effects and transparent tones.

Domenico Fetti
Rome, 1589-Venice, 1623

This singular artist, who worked
in Mantua as painter to the Gonzaga
court for practically the whole of his
career, is still undergoing a process
of critical reappraisal. With his late
Renaissance training, Domenico Fetti
found himself in a somewhat unusual
position. While Mantua could boast
a long and illustrious artistic and
cultural tradition, on the eve of the
seventeenth century, the ancient state
of the Gonzaga family appeared to be
drastically impoverished, and occupied
a marginal position in both historical
and economic terms. And yet, there
was no lack of opportunity for
encounters at the highest level. In fact,
at the beginning of the seventeenth
century, Rubens drew a salary from the
Gonzaga family for a number of years,
despite the fact that he worked mainly
in Rome. Fetti independently
developed an unusual and brilliant
style of his own, which is a blend of
influences and ideas from different
sources. His direct relations with
Rubens, and his taste for Dutch and
Flemish painting in general, led him
to adopt thick, rich brushstrokes,
which can be clearly seen in the highly
inventive series of small and medium-
sized paintings of Apostles, or the
delightful little images of his New
Testament parables, interpreted almost
as genre scenes. In his larger works—
including altarpieces, the frescoes in
Mantua cathedral, and the enormous
lunette with the *Miracle of the Loaves
and Fishes*, now in the Palazzo Ducale
in Mantua—the compositions are
more complex, dynamic, and dramatic.
Fetti remains best known, however, for
his contemplative, solitary figures lost
in ecstasy, in concentrated thought, or
in a dream world. Such images won
immediate success, to such a degree
that the painter took to repeating them
in a number of versions. Fetti spent
the last years of his life in Venice,
where he was instrumental in leading
local painting to break away from the
worn-out late-Renaissance tradition
and move in the direction of the new
Baroque models.

Domenico Fetti
Meditation or Melancholy
c. 1622
oil on canvas
70½ × 55 in.
(179 × 140 cm)
Gallerie dell'Accademia,
Venice

Georg Flegel

Olomouc, 1566-Frankfurt, 1638

Little is known about the training and career of this artist, who was a fundamental point of reference for the early development of "archaic" still-life painting north of the Alps. The evident links with the Flemish painting of the fifteenth century and the Renaissance period make it very likely that he initially worked in the Netherlands. This tradition also accounts for Flegel's delight in the precise reproduction of objects, accurately observed and painted with respect to shape, volume, material, and differences in the refraction of light. Flegel's works also mark a significant step forward compared to late sixteenth-century Flemish and Dutch painting, since they are among the first examples of pure still life without figures. Stress should also be laid on his complete independence with respect to Italian art, which exercised great influence on many German masters in the early seventeenth century.

Georg Flegel
Cabinet with Shelf
c. 1610
oil on canvas
36½ × 24½ in.
(92 × 62 cm)
Národní Galerie, Prague

One interesting compositional invention by Flegel consists of paintings depicting cupboards, cabinets, or display cases with various objects arranged like small collections of rare items. This was a very popular genre in the seventeenth century, particularly with art collectors in central and northern Europe, and some masters developed these compositions so that they practically verged on *trompe-l'oeil*. Flegel conveys a sense of order, satisfaction, harmony, and delight in the painstaking representation of elegant objects, feelings that were to be subtly undermined by the disquieting impact of Stosskopf's metaphysical canvases.

Jean Fouquet
Tours, c. 1420-1481

Jean Fouquet, the greatest figure in fifteenth-century French painting, was trained by painters of illuminations, probably under the influence of the Bedford Master. His stay in Italy from 1445 to 1447 was of crucial importance, since he became acquainted not only with the most recent perspective techniques, but also with the whole battery of classical architectural devices including columns, capitals, arches, and friezes, which were to feature in his subsequent output. During his stay in Rome—which is documented by the lost portrait of Pope Eugenius IV that once hung in the sacristy of Santa Maria sopra Minerva—he met Beato Angelico, then working in the Vatican. The latter's influence can be detected in the illuminations of the *Hours of Etienne Chevalier*, especially the scene of the *Annunciation*. On his return to France, Fouquet found work in the court of Charles VII and then of Louis XI, whose official painter he became in 1475. His artistic career is sparsely documented. Two works are identified as preceding his stay in Italy, namely a *Portrait of Charles VII* and the *Pietà of Nouans*, which are devoid of Italianate devices and display the influence of Jan van Eyck and the severe sculpture of the Burgundian master Claus Sluter. Fouquet's patrons include state officials such as Guillaume Jouvenel des Ursins, the chancellor of France, and Etienne Chevalier, the treasurer. It was for the latter that Fouquet painted the work known as the *Melun Diptych*, around 1450, as well as the extraordinary illuminations of the *Hours of Etienne Chevalier*. Between 1470 and 1475 he illustrated the *Antiquités Judaïques* by Josephus Flavius, the only work that can be attributed to him with certainty, and the one that has made it possible to identify his entire oeuvre. Heir to the great Gothic tradition, as revealed by his use of glowing color, Fouquet nevertheless distanced himself from the fantastic unreality of the later Middle Ages by forging a new style that combines the perspective techniques acquired during his stay in Italy and the naturalistic discoveries of Flemish art.

Jean Fouquet
Etienne Chevalier with St. Stephen, panel from the *Melun Diptych*
c. 1450
panel
36¾ × 33½ in.
(93 × 85 cm)
Gemäldegalerie, Berlin

Etienne Chevalier is depicted kneeling in prayer with St. Stephen, his name saint, in a sumptuous gallery faced in marble. The plastic density of the forms and the austere simplicity of the faces suggest a setting whose realism contrasts sharply with the other panel of the diptych to create a sort of juxtaposition between the earthly and divine worlds.

Below, left
Jean Fouquet
*Descent of the Holy
Ghost,* from the *Hours
of Etienne Chevalier*
c. 1452-1460
tempera on parchment
7¾ × 5¾ in.
(19.7 × 14.6 cm)
Metropolitan Museum
of Art, New York

The scene represents the
descent of the Holy
Ghost upon the faithful,
a subject suggested by
the epigraphic text. The
rendering of medieval
Paris—the façade
of Notre Dame can
be recognized together
with the once-covered
Pont Saint Michel—
arouses particular
interest because of
the realism that denotes
the influence of the
northern style.

Jean Fouquet
Madonna and Child,
panel from the *Melun
Diptych*
c. 1450 panel
36 × 32 in.
(91 × 81 cm)
Musée des Beaux-Arts,
Antwerp

In her great solemnity,
the *Madonna and Child*
is the divine
transfiguration of Agnès
Sorel, the favorite of
Charles VII. Chevalier
was her executor. The
absorbed downward
gaze of the Virgin,
depicted frontally
with the traditional
accoutrements of gems
and veils in a sort of
pyramid-shaped icon,
and the substantial
volumes of the red and
blue angels crowded
into the background,
in no way detract from
the essential unreality
of the composition,
in which the deft handling
of light creates a
strongly idealized
atmosphere.

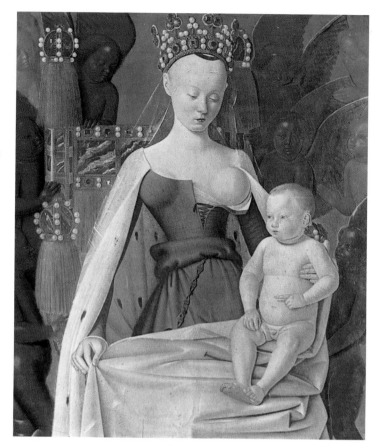

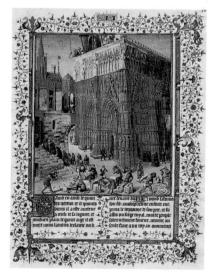

Jean Fouquet
*Building the Temple in
Jerusalem,* from the
Antiquités Judaïques
c. 1465
tempera on parchment
8½ × 7 in.
(21.3 × 18 cm)
Bibliothèque Nationale,
Paris

Around 1465 Fouquet
was commissioned
by Jean d'Armagnac to
complete the decoration
of the illuminated
codex of Josephus
Flavius, left unfinished
after the death of Jean
de Berry. The dramatic
history of the Jewish
people is freely
interpreted by the
artist, who fills the
scene with deftly
marshaled multitudes
against a background of
imposing architectural
structures that echo the
greatness of the events.

Jean-Honoré Fragonard
Grasse, 1732-Paris, 1806

The last great master of Rococo, he trained in Paris. After spending a few months in the workshop of Chardin, in 1750 he was accepted as a pupil of Boucher, and helped to produce the cartoons for the tapestries for the Gobelins and Beauvais manufactories. In 1752 he won the Prix de Rome with *Jeroboam Sacrificing the Golden Calf* (Louvre, Paris), and the following year

he entered the Ecole Royale des Elèves Protégés, directed by Jean-Baptiste van Loo. He remained there until the autumn of 1756, when he left for Rome, staying at the French Academy for four years. Here he devoted himself to landscape painting, influenced by great Italian masters such as Tiepolo, who taught him to draw and to paint with light, and Barocci for the brilliant composition. In 1761 he returned to Paris. In 1765 he was elected a member of the

Academy, but he remained independent, choosing his patrons from the bourgeoisie and the new nobility. For them he painted mainly sweeping landscapes in the Dutch style, and "small paintings" of gallant subjects or of everyday life. Around 1780 his painting took a neoclassical turn, although he maintained his own personal touch. Some of his distinctive characteristics, such as the swathes of color applied without any preparatory drawing, the brushstrokes, and the

striking colors, remained constant throughout his career, whatever genres he tackled. His versatility led him to make use of those he considered to be his masters, from Rembrandt to Rubens, Tiepolo, Watteau, and Boucher, with confident ease, as if to test out his ability. A painter of gallantry and nature, though also of domestic scenes and childhood, he left an extremely varied oeuvre that seems to evoke all that had been dear to eighteenth-century society.

143

Previous page
Jean-Honoré Fragonard
La Gimblette
(The Ring-Biscuit)
c. 1765-1772
oil on canvas
27½ × 34¼ in.
(70 × 87 cm)
Fondation Cailleux,
Paris

A frankly libertine scene
depicting a reclining
young woman as she
plays with a lapdog. The
light enhances the pink
flesh tones of her body
in a composition
characterized by a sort
of parallel between
the girl's face, lit up
by a slight smile,
and the raised legs
and right arm, which
attenuate the sensuality
of the scene.

Jean-Honoré Fragonard
Music
1769
oil on canvas
31½ × 25½ in.
(80 × 65 cm)
Musée du Louvre, Paris

The figure of the
musician, seen from
behind, with his face
turned to the viewer, is
bathed in an uneven
light that creates strong
contrasts. The
composition, based
mainly on shades of
ocher, is one of the
group of portraits
symbolizing poetry,
singing, theater,
and music.

Jean-Honoré Fragonard
The Reader
c. 1776
oil on canvas
32¼ × 25½ in.
(82 × 65 cm)
National Gallery of Art,
Washington, D.C.

Considered one of
Fragonard's
masterpieces, this is a
scene of bourgeois life
from his series of young
women intent on their
private occupations.
Portrayed against a
vague background, the
girl's expression is rapt,
while the pose of the
hand holding the book
is deliberately affected.

Jean-Honoré Fragonard
Venus Refusing a Kiss from Cupid
c. 1760, oil on canvas
14½ × 13½ in.
(37 × 34 cm)
Private collection

Caspar David Friedrich

Greifswald, 1774-Dresden, 1840

The most important exponent of German Romantic painting, capable of making artistic and existential choices of great courage, he was trained in the classical atmosphere of the Copenhagen Academy. In 1798 he moved to Dresden, where he became involved in a vibrant cultural, philosophical, and literary environment centering on Goethe's poetry and the latest developments in idealism. The exceptional liveliness of the time and the desire to fix the characteristics of an authentically "German" art led Friedrich to refuse to make the customary journey to Italy, placing him in open opposition to the Nazarenes, German painters active in Rome. In 1808 the artist underlined this choice in polemic fashion: asked to paint an altarpiece, he painted *The Crucifix in the Mountains*, a mountainous and deserted landscape containing nothing but a slender cross. Thus the traditional themes of sacred art gave way to the new Romantic awe of nature, in which admiration for the spectacles of the sea, mountains, mist, and sun was mixed with a sense of human impotence. Nature and its contemplation are the heart of Friedrich's pictures, sustained by a faultless handling of light. Human figures often appear, but always with their backs turned, in a thoughtful or even ecstatic attitude. With the passing of time, Friedrich's landscapes were enriched with more and more symbolic contents, to the point of using variations in light and situation to allude to the age of man. The rather rare architectural elements are confined to Gothic ruins and confirm the artist's radical choice: to spurn the Neoclassical backdrops of academicism for national settings, landscapes, and sentiments.

Caspar David Friedrich
The Crucifix in the Mountains
c. 1807
oil on canvas
45¼ × 43¼ in.
(115 × 110.5 cm)
Gemäldegalerie Neue Meister, Dresden

With this painting Friedrich earned himself a place in the debate over developments in art in the early nineteenth century, by urging a new relationship with tradition and nature. Setting the picture inside a carved and gilded frame, Friedrich overturns the concept of the altarpiece by depicting a "mystical" chain of wooded mountains on which stands a cross. The painter, taking his cue from contemporary German poetry, is suggesting an attitude of admiration and respect for nature, capable of conveying profound emotions.

145

Right
Caspar David Friedrich
The Sunset (Brothers)
1830-1835
oil on canvas, 9¾ × 12¼
in. (25 × 31 cm)
Hermitage,
St. Petersburg

Even in paintings
of small size like this,
the German artist is able
to conjure up highly
evocative atmospheres.
Especially in the works
from the latter part of
his career, the muted
tones of the dying light
and the dark outlines
of the figures are
obvious symbols of
death.

Caspar David Friedrich
Monk by the Sea
1808-1810
oil on canvas
38½ × 50½ in.
(98 × 128 cm)
Nationalgalerie, Berlin

This is Friedrich's most
"abstract" work,
surprising in its almost
total lack of form and
color. A brooding sky,
covered with gray
clouds, looms over
a thin strip of sand,
lapped by dark waves.
In this threatening
setting, the tiny figure
of a monk once again
alludes to the
relationship between
the mystery of the
divine and nature.

Nicolas Froment

Uzès, c.1435-Avignon, 1483

Froment did his apprenticeship in northern France and after 1468 was summoned to the court of René of Anjou, where the sovereign had established a cultural center of great vitality. Froment was a leading figure among the artists of the Avignon School, who contributed toward the creation of a new approach in fifteenth-century French painting. The presence of Froment's *Raising of Lazarus*—his first known work, signed and dated 1461—in the Uffizi Gallery has led some writers to suggest a stay in Florence. Evidence to the contrary is, however, provided by the form of the triptych with hinged panels, the harsh, contracted style, and the crowd of figures with contorted faces, all features denoting a strong Flemish influence. His *Triptych of Mary in the Burning Bush*, the only work that can be attributed to this artist with absolute certainty, was commissioned by René of Anjou (possibly together with *the Diptych of René of Anjou and Jeanne de Laval*, now in the Louvre). It displays some differences in approach but is still in the Flemish tradition.

Nicolas Froment
The Madonna and Child Appear to Moses, from the *Triptych of Mary in the Burning Bush*
1475-1476
panel
120 × 87½ in.
(305 × 225 cm)
Saint-Sauveur,
Aix-en-Provence

This work is a personal reworking of the northern style that is more faithfully adopted in the *Annunciation*. The monumental nature of the composition, the vast landscape in the background, and the skillful use of light to envelop the figures in the foreground all denote the influence of Italian art, which played a crucial role in the formation of the Avignon School. The position of Provence at the center of cultural exchanges between Italy and northern Europe made it an extraordinary vantage point for the artistic movements in a crucial period of the European Renaissance.

Johann Heinrich Füssli
Zurich, 1741-London, 1825

After profound literary studies and training to be a priest in Switzerland, Füssli decided to devote himself to art and poetry, which he thought would allow him to express his feelings with full freedom. In 1736, spurred on by his desire for independence, he moved to London. Sir Joshua Reynolds encouraged him to concentrate on painting, but for the time being he preferred to carry on in his role as a critic and man of letters of international repute: among other things, he translated the writings of Winckelmann into English, making a fundamental contribution to the development of Neoclassicism in

Great Britain. In 770 Füssli went to Rome: he was to stay in Italy for three years, almost overwhelmed by his admiration for classical antiquities and the works of Michelangelo. During his time in Italy, Füssli perfectly embodied the new aesthetics of the "sublime," the feeling of awe and profound unease inspired by the spectacles of art and nature that seem to tower over us. Returning to London, Füssli chose to settle in England permanently and anglicized his name to the more easily pronounceable Henry Fuseli. From this time on he alternated a prolific output of paintings with his activity as an acute art critic and scholar. Along with Blake, Füssli anticipated many of the themes of English Romanticism, such as the exploration

of the world of nightmares and visions, the intertwining of the heroes of Greek myths with the settings of medieval sagas, and a subtle but penetrating eroticism. One distinctive aspect of his work was the pictorial interpretation of the great poems of Dante, Homer, Milton, and Shakespeare. In his illustrations of the culminating moments of tragedies and of classical and medieval epics, Füssli achieved results characterized by their energetic composition and graphic force.

Johann Heinrich Füssli
Paolo Malatesta and Francesca da Polenta Surprised by Gianciotto Malatesta
1786
oil on canvas
47¾ × 52 in.
(121 × 132 cm)
Cantonal Museum of Art, Aarau

Füssli's pictorial work rendered unmistakable by the efficacy and force of its execution, covers a remarkably eclectic range of subjects, situations, and sentiments. In this early canvas, still inspired by the grace and lightness of Rococo painting, the artist anticipates the vogue for themes drawn from Dante or the medieval world that was to characterize at least two generations of painters and writers on the threshold of the nineteenth century. In fact it should be remembered that Delacroix also took an episode from Dante's *Inferno* as the subject of one of his first pictures.

Thomas Gainsborough

Sudbury, Suffolk, 1727-London, 1788

Gainsborough differed from his great rival Reynolds in both temperament and artistic style. Whereas Reynolds's art was solemn and objective, Gainsborough's was characterized by a delicate, lyrical approach, learned from French art, which was much in fashion in eighteenth-century England. Reynolds himself, in the famous *Discourse* delivered at the Royal Academy several months after Gainsborough's death, acknowledged his rival's greatness, his "powerful intuitive perception," and his impeccable art hidden behind an apparently facile, coarse language. The son of a cloth merchant from Suffolk, he trained in London, where he worked as an assistant to Hubert Gravelot, a French draftsman and engraver. On his return to Sudbury in 1749, he began to work as a portrait painter for local customers (magistrates, tradesmen, minor nobles) who demanded portraits that presented a good likeness, but were simple and, above all, inexpensive. Throughout his life, from his first stay in London on, Gainsborough also devoted himself to landscape painting, the genre in which he regarded himself to be most gifted, despite the lack of commissions. In actual fact, his talents were equally distributed between landscapes and portraits, for he was able in both genres to achieve a perfect marriage of nature and culture, spontaneity and artifice. In 1759 he moved to Bath, the fashionable spa town, where he began to be appreciated and sought after, even though his natural, vigorous painting still lacked elegance and depth. In 1774 he returned to London, where he worked for important patrons and achieved a new height of refined elegance. The favorite painter of George III and Queen Charlotte, he painted numerous portraits of members of the royal family. In 1784 he painted the *Portrait of the Three Eldest Princesses*, a splendid work that was cut in vandalistic manner to one third of its original size in order to hang it above a door in one of the rooms of Windsor Castle, where it is still held. Toward the end of his career his technique became more fluid, his brushwork free and sensual, and his compositions highly individual. Gainsborough combined what was his true artistic vocation, landscape painting and figures, and it is precisely from this marriage between subject and background, between fiction and nature, that his portraits take shape, escape from the confines of traditional portraiture and gain the favor of the most demanding public.

Thomas Gainsborough
Conversation in a Park
c. 1740
oil on canvas
28¾ × 26¾ in.
(73 × 68 cm)
Musée du Louvre, Paris

The current identification of the painting dates back to 1806, when it was sold at a Christie's auction, and is still highly debated. The strongest doubts relate to the male figure; the bright red clothes, the book resting on the legs, and above all the sword, not a fitting emblem for an artist, all point to a young nobleman. However, the work does undoubtedly portray a married or engaged couple, and the detail of the sword, like the temple in the background, heightens the romantic atmosphere.

Thomas Gainsborough
Mr. and Mrs. Andrews
1750
oil on canvas
27½ × 47 in.
(69.8 × 119.4 cm)
National Gallery, London

The figures portrayed may be Robert Andrews and his wife Frances Carter, or it may be a simple marriage portrait. Frances Carter brought a dowry of a property, which came into the possession of Robert Andrews in 1750. The painting that bears this date can therefore be read as a triple portrait: of Robert Andrews, his wife, and his property.

Paul Gauguin

Paris, 1848-Marquesas Islands, 1903

Gauguin started to paint in his free time while working as a stockbroker. Continually beset by financial problems he saw Paris as a suffocating prison from which he tried to escape. His first flight was to Pont-Aven in Brittany, in 1885: an obscure village in a poor farming region, which he made into one of the principal centers of late nineteenth-century art. Spurning the Impressionist fascination with light and nature, Gauguin set out to simplify forms into large, flat areas of color separated by distinct outlines, used unnatural colors, and abandoned perspective. His objective was to go beyond the sensory limits of Impressionism, with the avowed intention of seeking "suggestion rather than description," shifting attention from the physical world to that of the mind. Faraway places, uncontaminated by civilization, exercised a powerful fascination on the artist. After a brief stay in Panama in 1887, and then on Martinique, he returned to Pont-Aven and assembled an eclectic group of young artists and intellectuals. Out of the quest for a fusion between natural and supernatural came a new style, Synthetism, the vehicle for an anti-naturalistic and symbolic vision. In 1888 he went to stay with van Gogh in Arles, but their friendship ended in a quarrel. He returned to Pont-Aven, only to set off once again in search of uncorrupted places. Taking refuge on Tahiti, surrounded by the colors of the tropics and the beautiful dark-skinned girls, he gave vent to all his passion for the exotic and primitive, which he observed with a sense of ecstatic contemplation as the image of a lost paradise. His primitivism should not be seen as a form of exoticism, however cultivated and eclectic, but as an ethical need to get away from modern society, where there was no longer room or time for the imagination. The arrival of electricity on Tahiti and his financial problems drove him further and further from civilization, as far as the Marquesas Islands, where he died in 1903.

Paul Gauguin
Te Tamari No Atua
(Nativity)
1895-1896
oil on canvas,
37¾ × 50¾ in.
(96 × 128 cm.)
Neue Galerie, Munich

151

Geertgen tot Sint Jans
Haarlem (?), c 1460–c. 1490

The artist is a major exponent of painting in the northern Netherlands. His apprenticeship took place in Haarlem, where Albert van Ouwater had a flourishing workshop. Later he probably followed the custom of the time and completed his training with a journey to Flanders, thus coming into contact with the artistic circles of Ghent and perhaps also Bruges. The byname "tot Sint Jans" (of St. John) derives from the fact that he lived in Haarlem with the Knights of the Order of St. John, where he worked as a painter and assistant. It was for the Order that he produced his most important work, an altarpiece of which only two panels have survived, the *Lamentation over the Dead Christ* and the *Julian the Apostate Burning the Bones of St. John the Baptist*. While his early works display a somewhat static, schematic style the influence of Hugo van der Goes, whose work the artist studied with great attention, soon becomes apparent. The images are thus enriched with a greater sense of space and movement accentuating both their narrative and dramatic effect.

Geertgen tot Sint Jans
Julian the Apostate Burning the Bones of St. John the Baptist
c. 1480-1490
oil on wood
69 × 54¾ in.
(175 × 139 cm)
Kunsthistorisches Museum, Vienna

The subject of this work is connected with the founding of the Order of St. John, and involves various episodes regarding the saint's life and the fate of his relics. In addition to its religious significance, however, stress is laid on the present-day relevance of the scene. The men depicted in dark garments behind the sepulcher are in fact representatives of the Order, and this section can be described as the first group portrait in the painting of the Netherlands.

Geertgen tot Sint Jans
Holy Kinship
c. 1475
oil on wood
54 × 4½ in.
(137.5 × 105 cm)
Rijksmuseum, Amsterdam

In this early work the artist portrays Christ's closest kin gathered in a large church. The figures in the foreground are stylized and abstract, and appear far beyond human reach.

Geertgen tot Sint Jans
The Nativity at Night
c. 1480-1485
oil on wood
13¾ × 10 in.
(34 × 25 cm)
National Gallery,
London

This splendid depiction of the Nativity at night is one of the most intense and lyrical religious works in fifteenth-century Flemish painting. The figure of St. Joseph can barely be discerned in the darkness of the cattle shed, the divine light emanating from the Christ Child illuminates the faces of the Virgin and the angels bending tenderly over the crib. Light plays the major role in this painting, revealing the forms of the human figures and animals, but also glimpses of the landscape in the background. In this intimate and exquisitely human composition the artist succeeds in making the revelation of the divine an experience that is also accessible to human beings, who are thus encouraged to join the Virgin in prayer.

Gentile da Fabriano
Valle Romita Altarpiece
c. 1410
tempera on wood, central
panel, 62 × 31½ in.
(157.2 × 79.6 cm), lower
side panels, 46¼ ×15¼ in.
(117.5 × 40 cm) upper
side panels, 19¼ × 15 in.
(48.9 × 37.8 cm)
Pinacoteca di Brera, Milan

Set in a late nineteenth-
century neo-Gothic
frame, the panels display
motifs of the International
Gothic style. The great
central scene of the
Coronation of the Virgin
seems to float in the richly
glittering gold of the
heavenly background,
with the figures enveloped
in the folds of their
superb, exquisitely
depicted robes. The small
angel musicians below are
set on the celestial vault
and the painter's signature
can be read on the starry
sky beneath them. The
four saints portrayed in
the side panels advance
through the grass and
flowers of a wonderful
garden, slender figures
with sweet expressions in
the timeless atmosphere
of a fairy tale dream. The
same atmosphere reigns
in the small narrative
scenes, where four
episodes in the lives of the
saints are depicted against
urban settings and rocky
landscapes.

Gentile da Fabriano
Fabriano, 1370/80-Rome, 1427

During the first twenty-five years
of the fifteenth century, Gentile da
Fabriano from the Marches region
was Italy's most celebrated painter. He
traveled widely and left memorable
works in the great cities of art as well
as in so-called "minor" centers, thus
making a crucial contribution to the
training of an entire generation of
painters and to the spread of the late
Gothic style. Gentile's painting is the
most fascinating expression of the
transition between the height
of Gothic decorative art and the
beginning of Humanism. The *Valle
Romita Altarpiece* is an example of this
master's early stylistic development,
which was influenced by the schools of
Rimini and Lombardy. The result was
an art of extraordinary finesse,
characterized by the use of precious
materials, which focused on the
precise depiction of naturalistic detail.
In 1408 Gentile da Fabriano frescoed
some rooms in the Doges' Palace
in Venice. Although these works have
been lost, they influenced all of early
fifteenth-century Venetian art. He
then spent some time in Lombardy before
returning to the Marches. As his fame
spread he decided to move his
workshop to Florence in 1419. Gentile
came into contact with Humanism,
though he did not abandon his
individual style and in fact,
accentuated the fairy tale aspect of his
figures. His most celebrated work, the
Adoration of the Magi for the Strozzi
chapel in the Church of S. Trinità, now
in the Uffizi, dates from 1423. This
was followed by the *Quaratesi
Altarpiece* (divided between museums
in Florence, London, and New York,
and the Vatican Gallery), which
is influenced by the frescoes painted
by Masolino and Masaccio in the
Brancacci chapel. After spending some
time in Siena and Orvieto, Gentile
moved to Rome early in 1427 to start
decorating the Church of St. John
Lateran, a great project suddenly
interrupted by the artist's death in
August of the same year.

Théodore Gericault

Rouen, 1791-Paris, 1824

An untimely death cut short the career of one of the most interesting and courageous of early nineteenth-century artists, perhaps the first to seek a compromise between the flawless technique and figurative culture of Neoclassicism and the early Romantic sensibility that was beginning to take its place. In spite of his short life, Géricault displayed an extraordinary capacity for the composition and execution of images, not just as a painter but also as an engraver and sculptor. Moving to Paris as a child, he received his training from artists working in the late eighteenth-century tradition like Vernet and Guérin. While studying the masterpieces of the past in the Louvre he attended meetings of the Jacobins and of soldiers returning from Napoleon's campaigns that were held in Guérin's studio. This stirred a desire for liberty in the young Géricault: not just personal and political freedom, but also an artistic one that prompted him to look for new forms of expression. It is no accident that one of his favorite subjects was the horse, often frisky, rearing, or at any rate brimming with energy. A journey to Italy in 1816 brought him into contact with the works of Michelangelo and Caravaggio, from which he acquired his fascination with the human body, dramatic handling of light, and capacity to take on monumental enterprises. Returning to Paris in 1817 and stimulated by his friendship with the young Delacroix, Géricault painted his greatest masterpiece, *The Raft of the "Medusa,"* exhibited at the Salon of 1819. The huge picture caused a sensation, becoming almost a symbol of a rudderless moment in history, when the end of the Napoleonic era opened up new horizons. Subsequent works revealed Géricault's strong interest in the world of medicine, both physiology (some of his studies of anatomical specimens or the severed heads of condemned criminals are truly macabre) and psychiatry (his portraits of mental patients are unprecedented in the history of art).

Théodore Géricault
The Raft of the "Medusa"
1818-1819
oil on canvas
193¼ × 282 in.
(491 × 716 cm)
Musée du Louvre, Paris

In 1816, the ship *Medusa* sank off the coast of West Africa. About 150 people were left drifting on an improvised raft and had to face many days at sea in conditions of terrible hardship. In the end only fifteen survived. Struck by this dramatic episode, which seemed like a metaphor for the ruinous fall of Napoleon, Géricault carried out meticulous research in order to depict the castaways in a painting of exceptional size and power.

Giorgione

Castelfranco Veneto (Treviso),
c. 1418-Venice, 1510

The "mysterious" aspects of Giorgione's life (his "obscure" origins, his untimely death, and the very small number of works generally attributed to him) have created a legend around the painter, which in the past has made critical analysis difficult. In all probability, he was a pupil of Giovanni Bellini, and was quick to assimilate the influences of the "foreigners" who passed through Venice, like Leonardo and Dürer. A constant feature of his work is the search for a warm, enveloping natural atmosphere. The outlines of the figures and elements of

the landscape appear to be slightly blurred, while the gradations of light and color predominate. His whole oeuvre was executed by the end of the first decade of the sixteenth century. His untimely death in 1510 put an abrupt end to a career. It is, however, possible to trace a stylistic development from his early works, which were deeply influenced by Bellini, to the turning point constituted by the altarpiece in the Cathedral of Castelfranco Veneto (1504), where the traditional composition of the *Sacre Conversazioni* is set in a sweeping landscape bathed in natural light. Giorgione ran a flourishing workshop that also produced works executed by more than one painter. In 1508,

together with his pupil Titian, he executed the frescoes on the façade of the Fondaco dei Tedeschi, on the Grand Canal, but only a few faded fragments of these now remain. His small and medium-sized works painted for private collectors fared better. The most popular genres were portraiture and religious subjects (*Nativity, Virgin and Child*) depicted in vast natural settings, but he also introduced profane subjects, moralizing scenes, allegories of the "three ages of man," concert scenes, female half-figures, and refined mythological or literary themes. All of these were new iconographic forms. On his death, some of his unfinished works were completed by Titian and Sebastiano del Piombo.

Giorgione

Adoration of the Shepherds (Allendale Nativity)
c. 1504
oil on wood, 35¾ × 43½ in. (90.8 × 110.5 cm)
National Galley of Art, Washington, D.C.

He follows the example set by Giovanni Bellini and develops the placement of figures in landscape. The small crib is not set at the center and the left-hand section of the panel opens onto a natural setting.

Giotto

Vespignano c. 1267-Florence 1337

Giotto rivaled his fellow Florentine and contemporary Dante in his richness of emotional expression and radical innovations. His stays in Padua, Rimini, Milan, and Naples produced local schools of artists, the "Giotteschi." Traditionally, Giotto was Cimabue's pupil. His training was completed, however, when he got to know the Roman school while working in Assisi with other artists. Critical argument still rages over whether Giotto's early days as an artist were spent working on the fresco scaffolds in Assisi's Upper Church painting the famous cycle of the *Life of St. Francis*. In 1304 Giotto went to Padua where he undoubtedly painted the frescoes in the Scrovegni chapel. His human figures possess a real physical presence. They are set against natural backgrounds or fully three-dimensional architectural settings. Among his paintings in Florence, we still have the two frescoed chapels (Bardi and Peruzzi) in the church of Santa Croce after 1320. In his later years Giotto also worked in Naples, Rome, and Milan.

157

Previous page
Giotto
Homage of a Simple Man
1295-1300
fresco
Upper Church, Assisi

Giotto
St. Stephen
1320-1325
wood panel, 33 × 21 in.
(84 × 54 cm)
Horne Museum,
Florence

This wood panel is in
good condition. It was
originally part of a
polyptych which is now

scattered among the
collections of several
museums. The central
panel was the *Madonna*
currently in the
National Gallery of Art
in Washington. *St.
Stephen* is one of the
works in which Giotto
paid close attention to
the transparency of the
colors.

Giotto
*Madonna Enthroned
All Saints' Altarpiece*
1306-1311
wood panel, 128 × 80¼
in. (325 × 204 cm)
Uffizi, Florence

This composition, which
has recently been
restored, adheres to the
Tuscan tradition of
Virgins painted against a
gold background on a
pentagonal panel.

The solid presence of
the Madonna and Child,
deliberately framed by
regular solids, stands
out against the Gothic
throne which appears by
contrast flimsily elegant.
The sense of perspective
of the pierced seat
breaks completely with
the massive thrones seen
in the Madonnas in
Majesty painted by
Duccio and Cimabue.

Opposite
Giotto
*View of the Interior
Toward the Apse*
1304-1306
fresco
Scrovegni chapel, Padua

Enrico Scrovegni built
the chapel in expiation
of his father's sins of
usury. The chapel is
quite small and very
simple in structure,
perhaps at Giotto's own

suggestion. At the
bottom, false marble
skirting has grisaille
(painted in grayish
tones) images of *Vices*
and *Virtues*. Along the
walls and around the
chancel arch three
successive tiers showing
*Scenes from the Lives of
Joachim and Anne, the
Virgin and Christ*. There
are also roundels
showing the *Evangelists*
and the *Doctors of the*

Church. The work is
completed by a scene
showing *The Last
Judgment*. The fine state
of preservation of these
frescoes enables us to
appreciate Giotto's
innovations in regard to
his depth of vision and
his portrayal of real
human emotions.

Giulio Romano

Giulio Pippi

Rome, 1492/1499-Mantua, 1546

Giulio Romano was a noted architect as well as one of the first painters of the emerging Mannerist school. As Raphael's chief pupil, all of his training and early work was done in Raphael's studio before he became his master's right-hand man. In this capacity he oversaw some of the most important decorative cycles, such as the Vatican rooms and loggias, the Farnesina and Villa Madama. A supple plastic quality and a preference for metallic colors mark his *Martyrdom of St. Stephen* (S. Stefano, Genoa) or *The Madonna of the Cat* (Capodimonte, Naples). In these works we can also discern the tendency toward distorted, rhetorical gestures and expressions that is the hallmark of early Mannerists. When Raphael died (1520), Giulio Romano took over the studio and successfully completed the work in hand, the Constantine Room in the Vatican, which required considerable expertise. In 1524 he moved to Mantua. From then until his death Giulio dominated the art of the Gonzagas' highly civilized Renaissance court. For the Gonzagas he designed extraordinary fresco cycles and ambitious building projects such as the Palazzo Tè, Mantua Cathedral, and the Abbey of S. Benedetto Po. He also undertook the renovation of ancient buildings, with new apartments in the Ducal Palace, and designed cartoons for tapestries and elaborate jewelry. Many Gonzaga residences have since been damaged or demolished so much has been lost. Of what survives, his most complex enterprise is the design and decoration of the Palazzo Tè. Begun in 1526, this is one of the first true Mannerist buildings which flouted the rules of classical architecture. Each room contained new and original, even bizarre, decorative ideas. In the Sala de' Giganti, his illusionistic masterpiece, the whole room is painted from floor to ceiling to give the impression of giants hurling down rocks.

Giulio Romano
General View of the Cupid and Psyche Room
c. 1526-1528
fresco
Palazzo Tè, Mantua

When he decorated the Gonzagas' residence, he let loose his riotous fantasy, creating surprises in every room. Classical scenes flow freely into one another around the walls while the ceiling is divided into separate sections. He delighted in playing with illusions of false perspective: the figures seem to jump out of all the scenes, which illustrate ancient myths.

Natalia Goncharova
Ladzymo, 1881-Paris, 1962

Goncharova was a highly innovative painter and the founder of Rayonism, a current of painting that represented a brilliant fusion of elements from Orphism, Cubism, and Futurism. At the beginning of the century, together with Mikhail Larionov (whom she later married), she proposed a return to traditional forms of expression in Russia, such as icons and popular prints, abandoning the tendencies of nineteenth-century Realism. After a primitivist phase, Goncharova placed herself at the head of a group of young Muscovite artists that set out to combine the roots of the local visual arts with the most advanced expressions of the international avant-garde. After coming into contact with the work of the Blaue Reiter group, she drew up the manifesto of Rayonism in 1913. This was based on an intense dynamism that adapted the forms of reality to produce a highly expressive image in bright and simplified colors. In 1914 Goncharova and Larionov left Russia for Paris, where they continued their research in collaboration with the French avant-garde and achieved renown as costume and scene designers for Diaghilev's Ballets Russes.

Natalia Goncharova
Springtime in the City
1911
oil on canvas,
27½ × 35¾ in. (70 × 91 cm)
Abram Filippovich
Cudnovsky Collection,
Moscow

The tradition of nineteenth-century Russian Realism represented by Repin and the Wanderers was shattered to permit the emergence of a style fully comparable with the products of the contemporary Expressionism, but with a greater subtlety of interpretation. She was one of the century's most interesting woman painters, although the evolution of her style ran its course within a fairly short period of time. Here we can note her ability to conjure up atmospheric sensations and subtle hints of exchange between the figures notwithstanding the abbreviated lines and forms.

Francisco Goya
The Parasol
1777
oil on canvas
41 × 59¾ in.
(104 × 152 cm)
Prado, Madrid

This is one of the finest and most celebrated of the cartoons prepared by Goya for the royal tapestry factory: an extremely demanding cycle, which saw him assume the role of the heir to Giambattista Tiepolo as decorator of the residences of the Spanish court. Immersed in the elegant climate of Rococo, he interpreted popular themes with a sense of gay participation. The compositions, in view of their transformation into tapestries, are relatively simple, while the combinations of colors achieve a marvelous harmony, certainly in line with the tradition of luminous Venetian painting.

Francisco Goya y Lucientes
Fuendetodos, 1746-Bordeaux, 1828

The Spanish painter was the first to grasp the radical turning point in history and art that was marked by the end of the eighteenth century, and he interpreted it in a more intense manner than any other artist. The course of Goya's human and stylistic development is remarkable: from the freshest and most indulgent of Rococo to the brink of nineteenth-century realism, passing through an extraordinary series of experiments, almost all of them anticipating cultural tendencies that were later to spread throughout Europe. His laborious artistic training, begun in the provinces and culminating in a journey to Italy in 1771, led the young Goya to acquire a vast figurative culture. This was clearly evident in his first large-scale works of decoration, such as the frescoes in the church of Pilar at Saragossa. In 1774 Goya was given an important post at the court in Madrid, making cartoons for the tapestry factory. Adopting the style of Tiepolo, Goya depicted the elegant world of eighteenth-century Madrid with the lightest of touches. The success of these cartoons (now in the Prado) made Goya the most celebrated artist in Spain and from 1789, official painter to the king. For the court and nobility of Madrid, Goya painted numerous portraits that reveal a careful study of Velázquez. Gradually, however, Goya's figures lost the richness of color and confident look of the early years and were presented in empty spaces, with a fixed hallucinatory gaze. His sense of solitude increased after 1792, when the painter was struck by an illness that left him almost deaf. On the other hand, while his individual figures withdrew into a troubled incommunicability, Goya observed the movements of the crowd and the habits of the people with great sensitivity, interpreting proverbs with ironic and fanciful subtlety. His frescoes in S. Antonio de la Florida in Madrid (1798) are spectacular, and were immediately followed by the engravings of *Los Caprichos* and the extraordinary *Family of Charles IV*, a group portrait that has the flavor of the end of an era, filled with twilight characters and moods. In the early years of the nineteenth century, Goya frequently painted female figures, culminating in the two *Maja*, using brushstrokes laden with paint that would have been worthy of Titian.
In 1808 Spain was invaded by Napoleon's troops: it was a moment of terrible tragedy, to which Goya gave grim expression in the *Disasters of War* and, later on, in the two paintings dedicated to the insurrection in Madrid and the executions which brought it to a close. After 1810 Goya's brushwork grew loose and blurred, his colors dark and gloomy, in a crescendo of bitterness that ended in the dramatic *Black Paintings* executed by the artist on the walls of his house in the country.
In 1824 Goya left Spain for Bordeaux, where he spent the last years of his life in relative tranquillity. This stay made Goya's influence on subsequent nineteenth-century French painting even more direct.

Francisco Goya
La maja vestida,
La maja desnuda,
c. 1803
oil on canvas,
37½ × 74¾ in.

(95 × 190 cm)
Prado, Madrid

These two extremely
famous paintings were
in all likelihood

conceived as a pair: the
canvas showing the girl
with her clothes on
would have covered the
picture of her naked,
forming a lid that could

be raised by the owner.
The identity of the
model is still open
to debate, as is that
of the person who
commissioned the

canvases, perhaps
the minister Godoy.
There remains the keen
fascination of two
paintings that echo
Titian's historic figure of

the reclining Venus, but
with an unforgettable
quiver of coquetry.

Right
Francisco Goya
The Second of May 1808

Below
The Third of May, 1808
1814
oil on canvas
104¾ × 135¾ in.
(266 × 345 cm) each
Prado, Madrid

In May 1808 the population of Madrid rebelled against the troops of the French invaders, but the revolt was ruthlessly put down. In 1814, with the return of the Bourbons, Goya was asked to illustrate "the heroic actions of our glorious insurrection against the tyrant of Europe." The painter's response carefully avoided rhetoric. In the scene of the execution two groups face one another: on the right the soldiers of the firing squad carry out their orders in mechanical fashion; opposite them the rebels are seized by terror. These are no heroes ready to die for their country, but ordinary people crushed by history. Ragged and terrified, the condemned men seem to be crying out for mercy and make us understand that the history of peoples is written in men's blood: a workman's shirt is turned into the standard of a universal denunciation of war.

Benozzo Gozzoli
Benozzo di Lese
Florence, c. 1421-Pistoia, 1497

Benozzo Gozzoli is famous for only one work but that is one of the most delightful in the whole Renaissance. Originally trained as a goldsmith, he was Fra Angelico's assistant in Rome.

In 1450 he was in Montefalco in Umbria where he left frescoes in the churches of S. Fortunato and S. Francesco. After revisiting Rome in 1458 he received the most important commission of his career: to decorate the private chapel in the Palazzo Medici in Florence. The subject chosen was the *Journey of the Magi* which he

used to portray various members of the Medici family, with its young princes handsomely, even flamboyantly dressed and all set against a wonderful landscape, creating a fairy tale of the Renaissance. Between 1464 and 1466 he was located in San Gimignano where he painted the frescoes in the collegiate church and in S. Agostino.

Benozzo Gozzoli
General view of the
Journey of the Magi
1458-1460
fresco
Palazzo Medici
Riccardi, chapel
of the Magi, Florence

El Greco

Domenikos Theotokopoulos
Crete, 1541-Toledo, 1614

Born in Crete, he moved to Venice and came into contact with Titian, Tintoretto, and Jacopo Bassano. He acquired a feeling for rich and glowing color, and his early works indicate careful study of Tintoretto's elaborate perspectives. Around 1572, while still a young man, he arrived in Rome, where he studied the works of Michelangelo and enrolled at the Accademia di S. Luca. In 1577 he moved to Toledo, the city that was to become his adopted home. From this time on, his real name was definitively replaced by the nickname by which he became famous and that recalled his distant but never forgotten homeland. In alternating altarpieces, medium-sized devotional works, and highly intense portraits, El Greco marked a radical turning point in Spanish art, and acted as a bridge between Renaissance and Baroque. His painting gradually took on visionary, fantastic overtones, with figures elongated beyond the limits of verisimilitude, phosphorescent colors, and dizzying compositional layouts. In the closing years of the sixteenth century and especially in the works painted in the seventeenth century, El Greco moved still further toward a visionary, magical, and tautly evocative style. Among his later works, attention should be drawn to the extraordinary *Laocoön* in the National Gallery of Art in Washington, the only work in the artist's vast output with a literary or mythological subject. El Greco played a crucial role in Spanish painting by breaking with the tired repetition of worn-out models and opening up an era of courageous innovation. Despite the well-equipped workshop set up in Toledo with numerous assistants and copyists, El Greco's style had practically no followers, and thus was truly unique in the panorama of European art on the threshold of the Baroque era.

El Greco
Healing the Blind
1572-1576
oil on canvas
19½ × 24 in. (50 × 61 cm)
Pinacoteca Nazionale, Parma

This is one of the most interesting youthful compositions. Influenced by the Venetian style, it dates from the Italian period, the years when El Greco was described as a "worthy follower" of Titian.

Opposite
El Greco
*Burial of the Count
of Orgaz*
1586-1588
oil on canvas
181 × 141¾ in.
(460 × 360 cm)
St. Tomé, Toledo

This is the painter's
greatest masterpiece and
one of the most striking
works of the late
sixteenth century.
In the lower portion
of the painting, the
count, clad in shining
armor, is laid to rest at
a solemn funeral in
which a number of
saints participate. In the
mystical upper portion,
the nude count presents
himself in heaven before
the luminous figure of
Christ his judge.

El Greco
Baptism of Christ
1608-1614
oil on canvas
130 × 83 in.
(330 × 211 cm)
Ospedale Tavera, Toledo

El Greco's favorite
format for large-scale
compositions is a highly
elongated rectangle with
the height measuring
over twice the width.
These unusual
proportions accentuate
the tapering vertical
impetus of the figures
and make it possible to
depict scenes on two
levels, one above the
other. In the lower
portion, which is often
painted in darker
shades, the figures have
greater earthly
corporeality. In the
upper portion, reserved
for heavenly
apparitions, the light
explodes to the point
where it dissolves the
image.

George Grosz
Berlin, 1893-1959

A painter and draftsman of pungent and dramatic power, Grosz was the most typical exponent of German art after the country's defeat in the First World War. Right from his debut (an album of drawings representing obscene, scandalous, erotic, and immoral subjects), Grosz showed himself to be totally uninhibited by bourgeois tastes and the demands of the art market. Even his stylistic technique, based on an abbreviated and almost childish line in both his graphic work and his painting, avoided any concession to either academicism or the avant-garde. From 1918 onward Grosz's favorite subjects were scenes denouncing physical and moral degradation: disabled soldiers, profiteers, the shady characters who peopled the turbid political and social world of the Weimar Republic. He was truly prophetic in his caustic depiction of figures that seem to anticipate Nazism with their outbursts of militarism, thirst for profit, desire for revenge, and myths of heroism that were unable to conceal the squalid backdrop of abjection and greed for power. During the twenties Grosz and Otto Dix founded the Neue Sachlichkeit group and played an enthusiastic part in the seething theatrical world of Berlin. In 1933 the Nazis banned Grosz's paintings and drawings and he at once decided to emigrate to the United States. There, while toning down the most openly political aspects of his art, Grosz continued to use his biting line and bittersweet brushwork to point out the discrepancy between morality and vice, looking on with growing anguish as the world stumbled toward a new war.

George Grosz
Gray Day
1921
oil on canvas, 45¼ × 31½ in. (115 × 80 cm)
Nationalgalerie, Berlin

A desolate image of postwar, the painting represents a morning on the outskirts of Berlin. In the foreground we see the protagonist, a state official in charge of pensions for disabled soldiers. Dressed with scrupulous care (a decoration is pinned to the lapel of his jacket) and with a *pince-nez* over his eyes, the bureaucrat is the very image of an evasive and pedantic type of assistance, which the man keeps locked up in the briefcase he is carrying under his arm. Symbolically, a wall of bricks and indifference separates the functionary from the veteran who is supposed to be receiving his help. A black marketeer is the hidden but real puppet master of this squalid scene.

Mathis Grünewald

Mathis Niethart Gothart
Würzburg, c. 1480-Halle, 1528

The name "Grünewald" was coined by
a seventeenth-century biographer and
was the result of a misunderstanding.
In actual fact, this artist's first name
was Mathis and his surname was
Niethart which means "full of evil." To
counterbalance this he added a second
surname Gothart ("full of God").
In documents, however, he is usually
referred to by his Christian name.
Until 1505, when "Meister Mathis" was
commissioned to paint an epitaph at
Aschaffenburg, we do not have any
records of his life. His first dated work
is the *Mocking of Christ*, Munich
(1503). From 1510 on, Grünewald
worked between Mainz and Frankfurt,
alternating painting and hydraulic
engineering. From 1511 on, this

versatility gained him the position
of court painter to the archbishop of
Mainz, Uriel von Memmingen. The
following year he embarked on the
work that was to be the masterpiece
of his career, the *Isenheim Altar* (now
in Colmar) that was completed in
1516, when Grünewald entered the
service of Cardinal Albert of
Brandeburg, archbishop of Mainz,
who also commissioned works from
Dürer, Cranach, and Holbein. As a
result he came into closer contact with
the other great masters of the German
Renaissance. In 1520 Grünewald and
Dürer attended the coronation of
Charles V at Aachen. Though still
in the service of the archbishop
of Mainz, Grünewald became
increasingly interested in the
Reformation, with dire consequences.
The repressions after the defeat of
Thomas Müntzer's peasant followers

forced Grünewald to leave Mainz and
move to Frankfurt, where he virtually
stopped painting and devoted himself
to selling paints and to producing a
soap with pharmaceutical properties.
In 1527 he was in Halle where he
worked as a hydraulic engineer.
He died the following year.
The possessions he left behind
included sumptuous clothes in
precious materials and also several
Lutheran books in a sealed box.
Grünewald's works are a very fine
testimony of a dramatic moment in
history interpreted by a spirit sincerely
involved in the crisis of religious
and social renewal. "Mathis der Maler"
came to symbolize a genius in
the face of tragedy and Paul
Hindemith has based one of the
most intense and important operas
of the twentieth century
on this symbolic figure.

Mathis Grünewald
High Altar from the
Church of the Abbey of
St. Anthony at Isenheim,
first wall
1515
oil on wood
central panel
Crucifixion
106 × 121 in.
(269 × 307 cm)
fixed panels
St. Sebastian;
St. Anthony the Hermit
91¼ × 29½ in. each
(232 × 75 cm)
predella
Deposition of Christ
26½ × 134¼ in.
(67 × 341 cm)
Musée d'Unterlinden,
Colmar

Mathis Grünewald
High Altar from the
Church of the Abbey of
St. Anthony at Isenheim,
second wall, side wings
of the *Nativity;
Annunciation;
Resurrection of Christ*
1515
oil on wood
106 × 56 in. each
(269 × 142 cm)

172

Musée d'Unterlinden,
Colmar

Grünewald's panels were
hinged to a structure
with wings. The sides
were opened or closed
depending on the
liturgical calendar, at
Advent, Lent, and
Easter. The general
scheme must have been

designed by Guido
Guersi, who had a great
mystical culture and
gave original
interpretations of the
Bible. It is not difficult
to imagine what the
atmosphere must have
been like on Good
Friday, in the silent
church, dimly lit by
the candles of the

Sepulchre, in front
of the empty altar
dominated by the
tortured image of the
great, suffering,
crucified Christ, gory
and horrifying against
the dark sky. Then on
Easter Sunday, as the
sound of the creaking
hinges of the altarpiece
mingled with the

ringing church bells,
there would appear the
joyful, hopeful rainbow
of the *Resurrection*,
reminiscent of the bond
between God and Noah,
in an explosion of
divine joy that joins
the angel concert
of the *Nativity*. In an
impressively inventive
use of color, Grünewald

paints a vortex
resembling a column
of ice rising from
the empty tomb,
and as it rises it seems
to be heated by an inner
fire, until it explodes
in an iridescent circle
around the face
of Christ, who is
transfigured by the
light.

Mathis Grünewald
High Altar from the Church of the Abbey of St. Anthony at Isenheim, third wall, side wings of the sculpted box
Conversation between St. Anthony the Hermit and Paul of Thebes; Temptation of St. Anthony
1515
oil on wood

104¼ × 55½ in. each (265 × 141 cm)
Musée d'Unterlinden, Colmar

The Isenheim monastery in Alsace was the mother house of the congregation of St. Anthony, an order subject to the rule of St. Augustine, but closely associated with the aristocracy and medicine. Devoted to St. Anthony the Abbot (patron saint of animals and particularly pigs), these monks were considered the best physicians of the time, especially as regards the treatment of herpes or "St. Anthony's fire," syphilis, epilepsy, and the plague. Thanks to his contact with this order, Grünewald was able to develop his passion for medicine, which is evident in various works, and can also be seen in his subsequent study of chemistry and his production of medicaments. One of the devils attacking St. Anthony in the scene of the *Temptation* appears to be a patient from the Isenheim hospital. He is in a semireclining position, bloated, and covered in boils. He is not beating the hermit, but seems to be overcome by the fever and pain caused by his suppurating sores.

Francesco Guardi
Venice, 1712-1793

Guardi remained in Venice all his life.
He never ventured abroad, and his
rapid, impulsive, often dramatic
technique gained him far less success
with travelers and collectors. His images
of a weary, impoverished Venice in
decline are, however, moments of lofty
and heart-rending poetry in the
European art of the late eighteenth
century. Brother-in-law of Giambattista
Tiepolo, Francesco Guardi started
painting views at an advanced age after
abandoning his earlier career as a
painter of religious scenes and copyist.
His views are often those depicted
in celebrated and dazzling works by
Canaletto, but given a completely
different interpretation so that the
triumphant image of Venice
shimmering in the wondrous beauty of
its palaces reflected in the canals gives
way to a subdued, faded city inhabited
by poor people forced to work hard for
their living.

Francesco Guardi
*The Fire at the Oil
Warehouse at San
Marcuola*
1789-1790
oil on canvas,
16¾ × 24 in.
(42.5 × 62.2 cm)
Alte Pinakothek, Munich

Francesco Guardi
Gondola on the Lagoon
c. 1780
oil on canvas, 9¾ × 15 in.
(25 × 38 cm)
Museo Poldi Pezzoli,
Milan

These two works
symbolize the decline
of Venice and date to
Guardi's last years. The
gondola seems to float
on a timeless horizon,
suspended between sea
and sky in a general
blurring of outline.

Guercino

Giovan Francesco Barbieri
Cento, Ferrara, 1591-Bologna, 1666

The works produced in Guercino's long career may appear contradictory. At one end, we have a style of painting full of dramatic impetus and chiaroscuro; at the other, smooth, precise images of perfect classicism. actual fact, over decades of prolific activity, Guercino effectively summarizes the general developments in taste and the predominant trends in seventeenth-century Italian art. According to tradition, Guercino was practically self-taught, trained through his admiration for Ludovico Carracci. The early works, painted for his hometown or places in the surrounding area, are characterized by strong chiaroscuro, sharp contrasts, and broad vigorous brushwork, only superficially similar to Caravaggio and actually developed directly from the Ferrara school and Titian. Noted by Cardinal Serra (the papal legate in Ferrara), Guercino painted a series of works characterized by intense personality and crude drama, very different from the work executed in Emilia at the time. In 1621 he was called to Rome by Pope Gregory XV. This began a period of reflection in which Guercino progressively attenuated his use of chiaroscuro, but without abandoning daring compositions, unusual perspectives, and dynamic gestures. This is the central period of the artist's career, a crucial phase if we are to understand not only the progressive development of his own style toward classicism but also the more general shift affecting all art in Rome, from Caravaggio to the "ideal" painting of the Bolognese school. On his return to Cento in 1623, Guercino was already an established master. His very active workshop produced altarpieces and religious paintings for towns large and small in such quantities as to establish consolidated iconographic traditions. On the death of Guido Reni in 1642, Guercino left his hometown and moved to Bologna, where he became the new leader of the local school. This marked another step toward the controlled, noble classicism and intelligently academic approach that were to characterize all the works produced in the master's last years.

Guercino

Erminia and Tancred
1618-1619
oil on canvas, 57× 73½ in. (145 × 187 cm)
Galleria Doria Pamphili, Rome

Among the early works characterized by strong chromatic contrasts, this illustration of Tasso's *Jerusalem Delivered* stands out for its intense beauty, an interlude of amorous passion in the middle of the tragic tale. The wounded hero still wears part of his armor, and the metal contrasts effectively with Erminia's soft garments.

Frans Hals

Antwerp, c. 1580-Haarlem, 1666

Frans Hals is one of the most appealing portraitists in the whole history of art. He was a painter who specialized in one genre of painting, and yet he was so imaginative and brilliant that he always invented new compositions, ranging from the bust of a single person to vast scenes representing large animated groups of people. Little is known of his training and early work. In 1616, when he was no longer young, Frans Hals painted his first large group portrait, *Banquet of the Officers of the St. George Militia*, now in the Frans Hals Museum in Haarlem. After this work, the painter displayed great freedom from the earlier rigid schemes, portraying groups in movement, rendered vibrant and lively by his rapid brushwork and rich use of color. The dazzling chromatic effects and rapid execution, which does not linger over details but captures the fleeting expressions of the characters, are characteristic of Frans Hals's portraits until 1640. Having become acquainted with the Carvaggesque style through the painters of the Utrecht school, Frans Hals often uses diagonal light and neutral grounds, while his dense, thick color is reminiscent of Rubens and the Antwerp school. A painter of great renown (he had an efficient workshop with many pupils and followers), Frans Hals painted large official portraits as well as pictures of aristocratic patrons or, in some cases, models taken from everyday life, such as common people, drinkers, fishermen, and young women, all depicted with an emotional and communicative immediacy. Without making preparatory drawings or sketches, Frans Hals painted his canvases using a technique that we might call "impressionistic," and that was, in fact, studied by some nineteenth-century French masters. After 1640, as in Rembrandt's late painting, Frans Hals developed a cool palette and tended to concentrate on black and white, which at times created an emotional dramatic tension.

Frans Hals
Portrait of Willem van Heythuysen
c. 1635
oil on canvas
80½ × 53 in.
(204.5 × 134.5 cm)
Alte Pinakothek, Munich

Above, left
Frans Hals
Malle Babbe
c. 1635
oil on canvas,
29½ × 25¼ in.
(75 × 64 cm)
Gemäldegalerie, Staatliche
Museeen, Berlin

This old woman
nicknamed "Malle Babbe"
was a familiar figure in
Haarlem's taverns. He
portrays her with an
enomous tankard of beer
and a paradoxical owl on
her shoulder. Stylistically
speaking the painting is
extraordinarily powerful
despite its small range
of colors. As usual Frans
Hals has painted it
without making a
preparatory drawing
or sketch.

Above, right
Frans Hals
Portrait of an Officer
c. 1645
oil on canvas,
33¾ × 27¼ in.
(86 × 69 cm)
National Gallery of Art,
Washington, D.C.

This painting dates from
the middle period of
Frans Hals's output,
between the chromatic
richness of his early
period and the almost
monochrome works of his
last years. The pleasant
character (an officer who
does not look very
military and is evidently a
bon vivant) is depicted in
three-quarter profile, one
of Hals's favorite poses,
with his hand on his hip
and wearing a broad-
brimmed hat. The colors
that are predominantly
shades of brown, yellow,
and rust are reminiscent
of Rembrandt's.

Frans Hals
Gypsy Girl
c. 1630
oil on wood
22¾ × 20½ in.
(58 × 52 cm)
Musée du Louvre, Paris

This canvas, with its
remarkable naturalness
and unbridled
exuberance, is one of
Hals's freest paintings,
executed for pleasure
and not on commission.
Works like this were
to make a great impact
on nineteenth-century
French painting,
particularly that
of Manet.

Keith Haring

Reading, Pennsylvania, 1958-New York, 1990

Haring belongs to that generation of young artists who see the city, with its endless walls and surfaces ready to bear the bright images of advertising, as their natural habitat. Theirs is an art movement that, without seeking to undo the world of machines and technology, takes aim at the ills created by it in terms of social injustice, isolation, and discrimination. These are the so-called graffiti artists, and although Haring remained anchored to traditional concepts of art, their world was his world. Having learned drawing from his father, he enrolled in the Ivy School of Professional Art in Pittsburgh in 1976, while studying the art of Pollock and Tobey on his own. He exhibited his drawings at his first one-man show, held in the Pittsburgh Center for the Arts. He moved to New York in 1978 and attended the School of Visual Arts; in 1980 he took part in the Times Square Show, a counterculture exhibit. In 1981 Haring abandoned paper in favor of found materials, such as used plastic garbage bags and the black coverings put over expired advertising posters in subway stations. On these he created symbolic figures that were simple but at the same time disconcerting. The artist declared that he wanted to create universally legible images, immediately understandable by anyone; but his works, most of them untitled, leave much to the individual interpretation of the viewer, who must struggle to respond to the existential questions posed by the artist on such topics as religion, racism, sex, and work. His career brought him meteoric fame, and by the late 1980s he had stopped doing subway drawings and was busy creating murals in cities around the world, including Sydney, Rio de Janeiro, and Amsterdam. His life was cut short by AIDS at the beginning of the next decade.

Keith Haring
Tree of Life
1984
acrylic and oil on canvas
118 × 145¾
(300 × 370 cm)
Silvana Coveri
Collection, Monte Carlo

Francesco Hayez
Venice, 1791-Milan, 1882

Hayez trained in Venice at a time when eighteenth-century graciousness was still predominant. After some time in Rome as a young man, where he fell under Canova's and Ingres' classical influences, most of his long artistic career was spent in Milan. He first moved there in 1820 and later became director of the Brera Academy. By following phases in his painting over seven decades, we can trace the most important turning points in the development of Italian art in the nineteenth century. Hayez learned a perfect drawing technique, as can clearly be seen from his penetrating portraits, which stand comparison to those painted by Ingres. He used his technique mainly to create huge historical canvases. His tone was unashamedly Romantic, something that particularly appealed to the Viennese court, although his style remained mainly classical. He painted the Emperor's portrait and frescoed the ceiling in the Caryatid Room of the Palazzo Reale in Milan (destroyed during bombing in 1943). Hayez became one of an intellectual set in Milan that included Rosmini, Manzoni, and Rossini. Through his work he at times conveyed moral and civil feelings that must be read in the light of the Risorgimento. His school influenced generations of Lombard painters from the Neo-Classical period right through to late nineteenth-century Verism.

Francesco Hayez
The Kiss
1859
oil on canvas
44 × 34½ in.
(112 × 88 cm)
Pinacoteca di Brera, Milan

The canvas has quite rightly become one of the symbols of Italian Romanticism. It sprang from the sentimental and melodramatic strand of medieval costume drama that Verdi so beautifully captured in his operas.

179

Ferdinand Hodler
Bern, 1853-Geneva, 1918

Hodler's work occupies a unique position in the European art of the late nineteenth century, standing somewhere between Symbolism, the last current of historical and nationalist painting, and the beginnings of Expressionism. Hodler is considered one of the painters who was best able to interpret the landscape of Switzerland and the country's pride in its strength and freedom, through a line of bounding energy and sharp and limpid colors. Hodler received his training in Geneva, in an environment permeated by Symbolist ideas, while his style appears to hark back directly to the Northern European graphic art of the Renaissance, in particular Holbein. Hodler painted his most significant works during the last decade of the century: portraits of women, mountainous landscapes with a rarefied and transparent atmosphere, and above all elongated canvases representing allegorical subjects, with figures repeating supple gestures, forming a choreography of absorbed rhythms.

Ferdinand Hodler
The Sacred Hour I
1910
oil on canvas
69 × 30¼ in.
(175 × 77 cm)
Argauer Kunsthaus,
Aarau

The painting is a large-scale preparatory sketch for a huge mural. His elongated, sinewy figures, imbued with a piercing sense of disquiet, bring Hodler close to the grand themes of Central European Expressionism. However, the Swiss painter's work stands out clearly for its dazzling gleams of light, inspired by the high mountains. While his figures are defined in a realistic manner, with sharply incised expressions, features, and outlines, the Alpine landscapes tend to summarize the image in terms of the drastic contrasts between the blue-white of the ice and snow and the dark outcrops of rock.

William Hogarth
London, 1697-1764

An engraver and art theorist, Hogarth's first approach to painting came in the workshop of Sir James Thornhill, the most successful painter in England in the early eighteenth century, whose daughter he married in 1729. The heir to Thornhill's school, the Great Queen Street Academy, active from 1711 to 1720, he was mainly attracted by subjects of contemporary life, despite returning on various occasions to historical or mythological themes. His fame initially rested almost exclusively on book illustrations and satirical prints in which the influence of the minor Dutch artists can be seen. He began to devote himself to painting around 1728; his first works are conversation pieces and portraits, whose distinctive feature is a lively feeling for the representation of scenes, a completely new development in English painting. In 1732, driven by a desire to increase his earnings and to reach a wider audience, Hogarth created a new form of art: the modern moral subject. He translated stories of contemporary life into paintings and engravings, conceived as theater scenes, in which it is possible to discern the influence of Lord Shaftesbury's ideas on the moral duties of art, ideas that were widespread among the English public. Fielding himself used Hogarth's cycles to draw inspiration for some of the characters in *Tom Jones*. Opposed to the official academy that leads to excessive rigidity in ideas about art and to the codification of artistic practice and development, Hogarth upheld the freedom of the market and the deregulation of the academy. Hogarth always lived in England, apart from a brief trip to Paris in 1743 with the painter F. Hayman. In 1757 he became court painter, an appointment made by George II and renewed by George III. In 1753 he published *The Analysis of Beauty*, a theoretical treatise in which he argued against classicism and outlined the characteristics of the English school of painting, of which he is considered the true founder.

William Hogarth
Marriage à la Mode, After the Wedding.
1734-1735
oil on canvas
27 × 36 in. (70 × 91 cm)
National Gallery, London

For the six scenes *Marriage à la Mode*, he drew inspiration from the growing fashion for matrimonial alliances between the old aristocratic families and wealthy middle-class merchants, who were willing to do anything to obtain social prestige, even if they had to purchase it.

Hans Holbein the Younger
Augsburg, 1497/98-London, 1543

Son and pupil of Hans Holbein the Elder, Holbein trained in the town where he was born, one of the main centers of Renaissance art in southern Germany. He embarked on his career with his brother Ambrosius in 1516, first working in Basel and then in Lucerne (1517-1519). His most interesting early works include the frescoes that decorated the façade of the Town Hall in Lucerne, destroyed in 1825, but known from preliminary studies. The results of a journey he made to Lombardy can be seen in his early half-length female figures and portraits that are unmistakably influenced by Leonardo, though they already display penetrating psychological insight and a precise rendering of the physical traits of the sitters. One of the most striking is the profile of *Erasmus of Rotterdam*. During the 1520s Holbein painted mostly religious works, including the impressive *Dead Christ*, now in the Kunsthalle, Basel, and he also executed cartoons for glass paintings and engravings. Holbein's religious works show that he had acquired a serene, classical monumentality, updated by the latest developments in Italian art, and they also display an intense realism and an almost obsessive, meticulous research into detail. There are, however, some echoes of Grünewald's harsh style. From 1526 to 1528 Holbein lived in England, where he was under the patronage of the intellectual Sir Thomas More. He then executed new outdoor frescoes in Basel, followed by a journey to Italy, during which he became directly acquainted with Lotto's portraits. The spread of the Reformation and the consequent lack of commissions for religious art in the German-speaking countries drove Holbein to settle in London in 1531. From 1536 on (the year in which Henry Vlll married Jane Seymour), he became portraitist to the royal court and the English aristocracy. He died of the plague in 1543. Holbein's portraits precisely depict his subjects' symbols of rank, but they do not stop at appearances. In his awareness of volumes, his psychological insight, and realistic accuracy, Holbein is one of the most balanced and outstanding portraitists of the European Renaissance.

Opposite
William Hogarth
Lobster-Seller
c. 1740
oil on canvas
25 × 20½ in. (63.5 × 52.5 cm)
National Gallery, London

**Hans Holbein
the Younger**
Venus and Cupid
c. 1525
tempera on wood,
13½ × 10¼ in. (34.5 × 26 cm)
Kunstmuseum, Basel

This is one of the paintings in which the influence of the Milanese style and of Leonardo is most evident. The woman in the portrait seems to have been the wife of a nobleman from Basel notorious for his libertine ways.

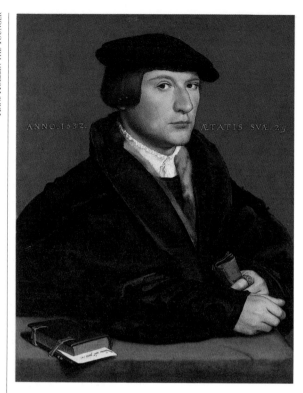

**Hans Holbein
the Younger**
Portrait of Herman Wedigh
1532
tempera and oil on wood
16¾ × 12¾ in.
(42.2 × 32.4 cm)
Metropolitan Museum
of Art, New York

Based on the strong
contrast between
the dense, smooth, blue
ground and the somber
black jacket, this is the
portrait of a German
merchant, working in
the German
confraternity in London
("Stalhof") at the time.
After his return to
Germany he played
an active role in the
political life of Cologne.

**Hans Holbein
the Younger**
Edward VI as a Child
1538
oil on wood, 22½ × 17¼
in. (57 × 44 cm)
National Gallery of Art,
Washington, D.C.

Born in October 1537,
the Prince of Wales,
heir to the throne of
England, is just over one
year old. The moralizing
inscription in pompous
Latin couplets, signed by
the court poet Richard
Morrison, and the
child's elaborate official
dress create a striking
contrast with his tender
expression and very
delicate somewhat sad
features, which seem
to indicate that he is
mourning his mother,
Jane Seymour, who died
in childbirth. Holbein
also depicts the prince's
favorite toy, a little
golden bell with a
handle.

Opposite
**Hans Holbein
the Younger**
The French Ambassadors
1533
oil and tempera on wood
81½ × 82½ in.
(207 × 209.5 cm)
National Gallery,
London

Holbein's greatest
masterpiece and one
of the most sublime
examples of Renaissance
portraiture, this can be
considered a painting
in the genre of works
depicting a special
event. In fact, it records
the visit paid by Georges
de Selve (the figure in
somber though refined
ecclesiastical attire, on
the right) to his friend
Jean de Dinteville,
French ambassador to
London, at Easter 1533.
The two young men,
respectively twenty-five
and twenty-nine years
old, had a meteoric
diplomatic career. De
Selve became a bishop
when a mere boy, was
accredited to the Holy
See, then ambassador to
Venice, and was very
involved in attempting
to bring about a
reconciliation between
Protestants and
Catholics. De Dinteville,
Lord of Polisy, was one
of the most trusted
advisers on
international affairs
to the king of France.
In this striking painting,
however, Holbein goes
beyond a mere portrait
of his subjects. There
are valuable musical and
scientific instruments
that are subtly symbolic
arranged on the piece of
furniture, covered with
a typically Holbein-style
carpet, that the two
diplomats are elegantly
leaning against. The
severe theme is the
transitoriness of beauty,
art, and harmony. The
almost unrecognizable
object in the foreground
is also linked to this
allegory; it is a human
skull painted in
a virtuoso, distorted
manner known as
anamorphosis, which
Leonardo also adopted.

**Hans Holbein
the Younger**
*Portrait of Henry VIII
Aged Forty-Nine*
1539-1540
tempera on wood
34¾ × 29½ in
(88 × 75 cm)
Galleria Nazionale
d'Arte Antica, Rome

The king is wearing
the sumptuous attire
for his fourth marriage,
to Anne of Cleves on
January 6, 1540, after his
failure to win the hand
of Princess Christine of
Denmark. This painting,
almost unanimously
considered by experts
to be by Holbein's hand
and brilliantly executed,
is probably the last
portrait of Henry VIII
to be painted by the
artist. There have been
many copies made of it
with the king in full
frontal position, obese
enough to take up all
the available surface;
in fact, his right elbow
seems raised in an
attempt to make more
room for himself.

ANNO · ETATIS ·   · SVÆ · XLIX ·

Winslow Homer

Boston, 1836-Prouts Neck, Maine, 1910

Gifted with natural talent, which he used as the witness and interpreter of an epoch of enormous change, Winslow Homer was the most powerful of the late nineteenth-century American realists. At nineteen, while working as a lithographer in Boston, he sent several of his etchings to the illustrated periodical *Harper's Weekly*. His sense of realism, his ability to quickly grasp and convey the spirit of situations, scenes, and figures, soon made him a popular magazine illustrator, among the first "artist-correspondents" sent to make illustrations of the Civil War. In New York (where he had been living since 1859) the canvases he made based on his war experiences enjoyed great success. With the end of the war, his preferred themes became scenes of family life and the New England

landscapes so dear to the American public. In 1866–1867 he made his first trip to Europe, experiencing the colors of Paris under the sway of the Impressionists; he also saw and studied Japanese prints. One result of this visit was that he changed the technique he used for life sketches, going from pencil to watercolor. Upon his return to America he dedicated himself primarily to the world of children and, with growing interest, to the sea. In 1881–1882 Homer returned to Europe but, surprisingly, set himself up on the English coast of the North Sea, in a fishing village near the mouth of the Tyne River. He now set about creating the best-known works of his career, images of the struggle of man against the natural elements. Back home, he settled in the Maine town of Prouts Neck, where he found the atmosphere suited to his paintings, which now recorded the epic in scenes of daily life, with stylistic richness and sober, solemn colors.

Winslow Homer
Gloucester Farm
1874
oil on canvas
20¾ × 30 in.
(52.7 × 76.6 cm)
Philadelphia Museum of Art, Philadelphia

This work dates to the middle period of Homer's career, when he was influenced by the pale, bright colors of the French Impressionists. During this period Homer tended to construct his works using solid volumes, simplified and essential, almost in a preview of the painting of Edward Hopper and other artists of the years between 1920 and 1940. Unlike the masters of the

Hudson River School, Homer did not see the American landscape as a natural setting to be contemplated and instead took it for a place where people live; he looked at it with unblinking realism, stripped bare of any celebratory or rhetorical intentions. The gestures are simple, neither grandiose nor declaiming, with no trace of the "literate" sensibility so dear to the elite intellectuals of North America. Because of his unenchanted, straightforward view, Homer became an awkward character in the American painting of the late nineteenth century. There is a

certain eloquence in this ambiguous, almost embarrassed judgment of Homer from Henry James: "He not only has no imagination, but he contrives to elevate this rather blighting negative into a blooming and honorable positive. He is almost barbarously simple, and to our eye, he is horribly ugly; but there is nevertheless something one likes about him."

Winslow Homer
Breezing Up
1876
oil on canvas
24 × 38 in.
(61.5 × 97 cm)
National Gallery of Art,
Washington, D.C.

The more sophisticated critics of Homer's day found themselves in difficulty when faced with his dark but at the same time oddly compelling works. As Henry James wrote, "Mr. Homer goes in, as the phrase is, for perfect realism, and cares not a jot for such fantastic hairsplitting as the distinction between beauty and ugliness. He is a genuine painter; that is, to see, and to reproduce what he sees, is his only care; to think, to imagine, to select, to refine, to compose, to drop into any of the intellectual tricks with which other people sometimes try to eke out the dull pictorial vision—all this Mr. Homer triumphantly avoids." But in truth Homer was not at all the natural painter James took him for; he made abundant sketches from life and then carefully recomposed and translated them into paintings in his atelier.

Edward Hopper
Automat
1927
oil on canvas, 28 × 36 in.
(71.5 × 91.5 cm)
Des Moines Art Center,
Des Moines, Iowa

No painter can match Hopper in the eloquent expression of the loneliness and isolation that are constant aspects of modern life. The extreme realism of his vision leads to other levels of reading, deeper and more introspective possibilities of meaning; in fact, every Hopper image can be taken as the transcription of an archetypical state of mind. A woman seated alone at a table in a self-service restaurant is absorbed by her thoughts; the seat across from her is empty, the window behind her, in a cunning play of mirrors, reflects the artificial lights of the interior of the Automat, hiding the darkness of the city outside. The only touch of life, also from a chromatic point of view, is the bowl of fruit. Even the title has a double meaning: the kind of diner is an Automat but the woman, alone with her expression of emptiness, could be mistaken for an automaton.

Edward Hopper
New York, 1882-1967

The melancholy, silent realism of Hopper and the chaotic, disruptive abstract expressionism of Jackson Pollock represent the twin poles of American painting, the two souls that form the essence itself of twentieth-century American art. Hopper lived through a period of the twentieth century marked by profound historical, cultural, and artistic change; but through it all he stayed faithful to himself, making no changes to his way of painting and not even leaving New York except for brief trips. He remained isolated in his laconic world, motionless and suspended. Hopper dedicated himself to painting from an early age, studying at the New York School of Art from 1900 to 1906, beginning with classes in advertising illustration and then studying art under Robert Henri. After these studies he made his first trip to Europe. He visited France, Britain, Holland,

Germany, and Belgium, although he spent most of his time in Paris, where he had the chance to encounter Picasso and the Fauvist painters, admiring in particular the works of Matisse and Albert Marquet. Back in New York he worked as an illustrator and exhibited his paintings for the first time, in 1908, in a group show set up with other Henri students in the former Harmonie Club building in New York. The next year he returned to Paris; in 1913 he exhibited one painting at the Armory Show. Between 1915 and 1923 he made about fifty etchings in which he examined the themes he would return to again and again throughout his career: figures gazing out windows, figures alone within the urban setting, isolated buildings set down in landscapes. During the summer of 1923 he went to Maine, a habit he would continue for the rest of his life; sometime around that period he began painting with watercolors. In 1933, when he was fifty-one, the Museum of Modern Art in New York held

a large retrospective exhibit of his works. During the 1940s and 1950s he made several trips to the West Coast and Mexico. Beginning in the 1930s Hopper was looked upon as the leading member of the regionalist movement in American art known as the American scene—although he himself denied any such association. The movement was dedicated to the most realistic and accurate representations of American life and American experience in its many different aspects. As Hopper himself stated, truly great art is art that reflects the genuine character of a nation. With powerful eloquence, his evocative and deeply moving paintings present images of solitude, alienation, loneliness, the lack of communication between individuals. In 1964 the Whitney Museum of American Art dedicated an important retrospective show to Hopper's works, and among its many enthusiastic fans were numerous avant-garde artists.

Edward Hopper
Gas
1940
oil on canvas
26¼ × 40 in.
(66.7 × 102.2 cm)
Museum of Modern Art,
New York

Here we find ourselves
on the border between
civilization and nature,
in this case on the edge
of a dense, impenetrable
forest, along a deserted
road that leads into
darkness and cuts the
image in half. To one side
of the road is nature, to
the other is civilization,
symbolized by a gas
station. The visible word
Mobilgas emphasizes the
allusion to contemporary
reality. The man is alone,
no one is nearby, all
action is suspended,
the artificial illumination
suggests that evening
is coming. The chasm
between civilization and
nature cannot be closed.

Edward Hopper
Pennsylvania Coal Town
1947
oil on canvas
28 × 39¾ in.
(71 × 101.5 cm)
Butler Institute
of American Art,
Youngstown, Ohio

In 1933 Hopper said,
"My aim in painting
is always, using nature
as the medium, to try
to project upon canvas
my most intimate
reaction to the subject
as it appears when I like
it most." The sense of
solitude and sadness
that pervades his works,
giving them a universal,
timeless value, is based
on the unbridgeable
distance that separates
people from one
another and from the
environment in which
they live.

Jaume Huguet
Valls (Tarragona), 1414-
Barcelona, 1492

An acute observer of reality, his work is a blend of Italianate and Flemish elements. Little is known of his training, which must have taken place in Barcelona, where the Catalan tradition was very strong and the influence of French painting filtered through the border region of Roussillon. Huguet rejects the Flemish style and insists on adopting the earlier tempera technique with gold grounds to create the emotion infused into the figures by his renowned sensitivity. He first worked in the province of Aragon, mainly at Saragossa; in 1448 he settled in Barcelona, where he married in 1454 and was active until 1487. A large number of works have been attributed to him and documented, though it is evident that they have been executed by many different hands. He had so many commissions that he set up a workshop that was responsible for most of the production. The *Altarpiece of St. Abdon and Senen* (church of Santa Maria Terrassa), executed between 1458 and 1461, is the best of those that have come down to us. The slim figures of the titular saints have an exquisite melancholy and expressiveness. During the artist's long career his panels became increasingly sumptuous in decoration and contain more imposing groups of figures; they include glimpses of blurred landscapes in the distance and poignant scenes of everyday life. His later works owe much to his assistants, especially the members of the Vergós family: the glittering brocades and jewelry, the heavy gold grounds, and the gleaming, bejeweled scrolls and borders are typical of the tendency to take the decorative aspect to the extreme, which is a typical feature of Aragonese art. The style developed by Huguet spread throughout the whole of Aragon, to Catalonia, and even to Corsica and Sardinia. However, after these excesses, the Barcelona School entered a long period of obscurity and inactivity.

Jaume Huguet
The Archangel St. Michael
1456
tempera on wood
84 × 53½ in.
(213 × 136 cm)
Museo de Arte de
Cataluña, Barcelona

Jean-Auguste-Dominique Ingres
Montauban, 1780-Paris, 1867

The figure of Ingres dominates the scene of early nineteenth-century European art from the height of an absolute perfection of style and technique, but for a long time this has permitted only a partial appreciation of the artist. He has been criticized for a certain "coldness," a lack of emotional involvement in the work, as if the painter's work were confined to a quest for academic perfection. This is, of course, a grave misunderstanding. Ingres belonged to a generation full of doubts, of leaps forward and steps back: his art, though undoubtedly self-absorbed, is the expression of a search for higher, lasting values, within the bounds of a classical tradition of which Ingres felt himself the proud heir. In 1797, after studying at the Toulouse Academy, he became David's pupil and soon distinguished himself by his great skill and ability to compose imposing scenes on historical themes. It was with one of these that he won the prestigious Prix de Rome in 1801, earning himself the right to a period of study in that city. The campaigns waged by Napoleon (of whom Ingres painted a large formal portrait) prevented him from making the journey for several years, and he did not reach the city until 1806. Ingres stayed in Italy for eighteen years, first in Rome and then in Florence, entering into the heart of classical and Renaissance artistic culture and taking up its suggestions and influences in eclectic fashion. Working chiefly as a portraitist, he attracted attention with his first large female nudes, painted with a limpid rigor that was still capable of conveying a passionate sensuality. Returning to Paris in 1824, he showed a large picture at the Salon that was immediately acclaimed and held up in contrast to the early work of Delacroix, initiating a dialectical rivalry: Ingres was considered the champion of the academic tradition and was given official posts of growing prestige, while Delacroix embodied the new Romanticism. In reality, Ingres took the great myths of the past and gave them pictorial form, effectively blending a wide variety of references to tradition in which Raphaelesque elements frequently played a large part. Nor was his work always in line with "official" currents, as is demonstrated by his controversial return to Italy between 1835 and 1841. Alongside numerous portraits, paintings of historical or literary subjects, and large commemorative compositions, he produced a great deal of graphic work.

Previous page
Jean-Auguste-Dominique
Ingres
Madame Moitessier
1851
oil on canvas
57½ × 39 ½ in.
(146 × 100 cm)
National Gallery,
Washington, D.C.

Jean-Auguste-Dominique Ingres
The Turkish Bath
1863
oil on canvas
diam. 43¼ in. (110 cm)
Musée du Louvre, Paris

Trying his hand at the treacherous format of the tondo, Ingres arranges a group of naked women with undeniable attention to form, but also with an equally powerful sensuality. The figures of Ingres's bathers look motionless and monumental in the perfection of style attained by the painter: a purified form, an ideal of beauty pursued and achieved. There is nothing to suggest that paintings like these, through the reinterpretation of the Impressionists and Cézanne, would form the basis for such a "revolutionary" picture as Picasso's *Les Demoiselles d'Avignon.*

Jasper Johns
Augusta, Georgia, 1930

Immune to any classification or stylistic label, Jasper Johns represents a link between abstract expressionism and pop art. Following university studies in South Carolina, he moved to New York in 1949 and made friends with the painter Robert Rauschenberg, the dancer Merce Cunningham, and the composer John Cage, relationships he later claimed had been fundamental to his artistic formation. His first *Flag* appeared in 1954, soon followed by bull's-eyes and other motifs, each translated to the canvas with respect to its shape, size, and color while paradoxically preserving an abstract expressionist language. Johns turned his attention not to the objects themselves but to how they are

perceived, which involves several levels of reading, running from the most immediate, superficial meaning to deeper interpretations. The artist's own perception loses all meaning in the moment the work is offered to the public, for the public will use it as it pleases, often obliterating the artist's original intention. Johns's first one-man show, at the Leo Castelli Gallery in New York in 1958, put him at the forefront of the New York art scene. The next year he met Marcel Duchamp, another decisive moment in his career, for that friendship led him to introduce real— decontextualized—objects to his works, beginning the movement that, since it follows the path of the Dadaists, came to be called New Dada. By applying Dadaist ready-mades to the language of abstract

expressionism, Johns negated both the individualism of the abstract expressionists and the metaphysical and psychological essence of the Dadaists. Johns's constant concern is the relationship between painting and reality, in which he maintains the supremacy of painting. Common objects like crutches, rulers, spoons, or balls are inserted into the pictorial surface of the canvas, enclosed in a doughy paint following the technique of encaustic. Although it follows a strict iconography, his work is not without expressive freedom. The flags, targets, numbers, and maps of the United States lose their usual meaning to reveal visual qualities that are exalted by the freshness and creativity of the brushstrokes.

Jasper Johns
Map
1961
oil on canvas
78 × 124 in.
(198.2 × 314.7 cm)
Museum of Modern Art,
New York

Jacob Jordaens
Antwerp, 1593-1678

Jacob Jordaens is the third of the great masters of the Antwerp school, after Rubens and van Dyck, who led the city on the Scheldt to the height of European painting in the first half of the seventeenth century. Unlike his two famous colleagues, Jordaens did not spend long periods studying in Italy. His art remains attached to the firmly established, flourishing Flemish tradition, while the many ideas drawn from Italian art are always filtered through his completely independent style. Jordaens was drawn into the orbit of Rubens's vast workshop and soon became established as a versatile painter, not as a specialist in a particular genre like his fellow artists Jan Bruegel (still life) and van Dyck (portraiture). He therefore closely collaborated with Rubens, but was also, above all, an independent master, highly skillful at developing the stimulating innovations of Caravaggio and Michelangelo, in a style based on broad brushwork, thick with paint. Caravaggio's influence, which is most evident in the light effects of his early works, becomes more attenuated as the years pass, and is replaced by a style of painting that is more popular and immediately enjoyable, simple and full-bodied. Among his religious works, the scenographic altarpiece with the *Martyrdom of St. Apollonia* deserves a special mention, but his paintings of rustic subjects or natural produce are also very noteworthy. Late in life Jordaens often returned to subjects that were dear to him, such as crowded festive scenes and Aesop's fable about the peasant and the satyr. After the death of Rubens in 1640 and of van Dyck in 1641, Jordaens became the leading Flemish painter of his day.

Juan de Flandes

Ghent (?), c. 1450-Palencia, 1519

Originally Flemish, he arrived in Spain by way of Italy, where he probably traveled with Giusto of Ghent, whose school he belonged to. He was active in Spain from 1496 on, in the service of Isabella the Catholic, who promoted the spread of Flemish art and for whom he executed an altarpiece with scenes from the life of Christ. This polyptych—now dismembered—consisted of forty-six panels, twenty-seven of which have been preserved (fifteen are in the Royal Palace in Madrid). Their format is unusual and their small size—8 × 6 inches (20 × 15 cm)—must have forced the artist to adopt an almost miniaturistic technique. When the queen died in 1504, after a brief stay in Salamanca, where he executed the *Altar of St. Michael* in the cloister of the old cathedral and the high altar in the university chapel, Juan de Flandes moved to Palencia where he was active until 1519. His painting is characterized by the minute detailing typical of the Flemish tradition and by a delicate, sensitiveness to light and color.

Opposite
Jacob Jordaens
Self-Portrait of the Painter with His Family
1621-1622
oil on canvas
71¼ × 73½ in.
(181 × 187 cm)
Prado, Madrid

Juan de Flandes
Joanna the Mad;
Philip the Handsome
1496-1500
oil on wood
14¼ × 10 in. each
(36.4 × 25.5 cm)
Kunsthistorisches
Museum, Vienna

This pair of portraits, executed on the occasion of the betrothal of the two subjects, reveals the artist's extraordinary talent not only in religious works but also in portraiture, the only secular genre permitted in Catholic Spain.

197

Wassily Kandinsky
Moscow, 1866-Neuilly-sur-Seine, 1944

Even the life of this great painter of Russian origin, the founder of one of the most significant and enduring currents in contemporary art, Abstract Expressionism, displays some surprising aspects. Kandinsky came to painting very late. Trained in law, he was heading for a university career as a professor of jurisprudence, while studying Russian folk culture almost as a hobby and admiring the paintings of Monet, brought to Moscow by collectors like Shchukin and Morozov. At the age of thirty, he suddenly decided to go to Munich and study painting. At the academy he met his fellow student Paul Klee, with whom he was later to work at

the Bauhaus. Kandinsky's early paintings, though very interesting, can be placed within the late nineteenth-century tradition: landscapes and scenes of life among the Russian people are depicted in a technique reminiscent of Divisionism, while using the attractive colors of Art Nouveau. In 1908 he went to live iin Murnau, where he painted a series of landscapes in which the naturalistic image progressively dissolved into areas of strongly contrasting color. It is possible to discern parallels with the contemporary work of the Fauves, but his evolution was extremely rapid: as early as 1909 he was already venturing into abstraction, covering the canvas in spots and bands of color laid on with great freedom. He accompanied his painting by essays and other writings,

which formed the theoretical basis for the birth of the group called Der Blaue Reiter, founded in Munich in 1911 with Marc and Macke. Returning to Moscow in 1914, his took part in the Russian revolution and was given a post as a teacher at the Muscovite art workshops, where he began to carry out Constructivist research. This tendency toward modular forms, very different from the Munich years, was confirmed after his return to Germany (1922) and collaboration with Klee and the Bauhaus at Weimar. Henceforth his pictures were more geometrical in appearance, though he never abandoned his intensely lyrical use of color. After publication of the important *Point and Line to Plane* (1926), he continued to work at the Bauhaus until its closure in 1933.

Wassily Kandinsky
Landscape with Church
1913
oil on canvas,
30¾ × 39¼ in.
(78 × 100 cm)
Museum Folkwang,
Essen

The great shift to Abstract Expressionism came between 1910 and 1914, the years of the Blaue Reiter group's most intense activity and of Kandinsky's links to the composer Arnold Schönberg. This canvas still maintains traces of the figurative.

Wassily Kandinsky
The Railroad near Murnau
1909
paperboard, 14¼ × 19¼ in. (36 × 49 cm)
Lenbachhaus, Munich

The theme of the moving train has been a stimulating one for modern painting: the image of the railroad, with its dynamism, steam, and technology, repeatedly drew the attention of European artists. For Kandinsky, the dark silhouette of the passing train offered the opportunity to depict a field of energies.

Wassily Kandinsky
Composition VII
1913
oil on canvas
118 × 78¾ in. (300 × 200 cm)
Tretyakov Gallery, Moscow

This is the largest and most important painting of Kandinsky's early abstract phase. He carried out a lengthy preparation for the work through drawings and watercolors which testify to his intense commitment and progress toward a definitive structure.

Ernst Ludwig Kirchner
Street, Berlin
1913
oil on canvas
47¾ × 37½ in.
(121 × 95 cm)
Brücke-Museum, Berlin

In his lively urban scenes, which look as if they might have been sketched on the spot in the streets of Berlin, it is possible to discern the painter's delight in creating successions of rhythmic lines, almost in the manner of Art Nouveau. One of the leaders of the group Die Brücke, Kirchner used accentuated contours and forceful lines. There is a striking difference between these elegant streets—through which the smartly dressed and highly strung representatives of a "gilded youth" pass with a rather bored air, their faces bearing the simpering expressions of mannequins—and the sidewalks crowded with human relics and ambiguous figures painted by Grosz and Dix after the war.

Opposite
Ernst Ludwig Kirchner
Self-Portrait as Soldier
1915
oil on canvas
27¼ × 24 in. (69 × 61 cm)
Allen Memorial Art
Museum, Oberlin (Ohio)

This is a symbolic image of the artist during the war. Kirchner, in a soldier's uniform, feels as if he has been maimed, with his right hand cut off, owing to the impossibility of painting. His face screwed up in a tense grimace, with a cigarette dangling from his lips, is an expression of the brutalization of people and the loss of human relationships in an existence that has been rendered almost bestial.

Ernst Ludwig Kirchner
Aschaffenburg, 1880-Davos, 1938

Founder of the Die Brücke group, Kirchner is perhaps the most typical and consistent exponent of the German group of Expressionists. Kirchner started painting almost by chance. As a student of architecture in Dresden, he was able to study the artists of the German Renaissance (Cranach, Dürer) in the city's museums, along with a few pictures by Munch and van Gogh. The common denominator of all these works was their distortion of reality and intensity of line simplified and dramatic in its effect. In 1905, Kirchner and some of his fellow students set up Die Brücke, an artistic movement which published writings and engravings in a magazine of the same name. Kirchner was the driving force: he painted landscapes and portraits in brilliant colors, characterized by their energetic distortions of expression.
In 1911 he went to live in Berlin, where his attention was caught by street scenes, urban landscapes, and the people who made up the city's variegated social panorama, emaciated figures represented with blunt and spiky outlines. During the war Kirchner moved to Switzerland, where he concentrated on Alpine and forest scenes, further accentuating the dissonance of color and line.

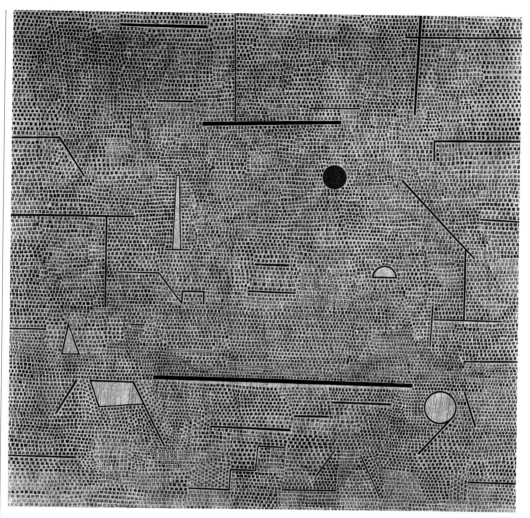

Paul Klee
Light and Other
1931
watercolor and varnish
on canvas
37½ × 38¼ in.
(95 × 97 cm)
Private collection

A perfect example
of Klee's painstaking
analysis of every
element of the
composition. The Swiss-
German painter follows
a hidden plan,
determining the
position of lines, points,
and areas of light and
color. At first glance,
it looks like an exercise
in mathematics, but on
close examination we
discover all the charm,
poetry, and intimate
beauty of the world laid
bare by Klee.

Paul Klee

Münchenbuchsee, 1879-Muralto, 1940

An extremely precocious talent, he was
encouraged to paint by his musician
parents. He trained first in Bern and
then in Munich, during the Jugendstil
period. Throughout the first decade
of the century the young Klee traveled,
wrote, drew, and studied artists of
the past and present, gaining a truly
thorough understanding of
developments in painting. He was most
impressed by Cézanne, but displayed
an extraordinary eclecticism, in graphic
art as well as painting. In contact with
Kandinsky, he exhibited in Berlin with
the artists of the Blaue Reiter in 1912. In
particular, he formed a close friendship

with August Macke, with whom he
made a memorable journey to Tunisia
in 1914. At the end of this immersion
in the light of the Mediterranean, Klee
declared "color and I are one and the
same thing: I am a painter." This
marked the beginning of an important
phase in which the artist commenced
his patient, solitary, and poetic
investigation of gradations of light
and color. Appointed a teacher at the
Bauhaus in Weimar in 1920, Klee
managed to pull off the far from easy
trick of remaining true to a strictly
constructivist and scientific approach
while preserving a strong element of
lyricism in images that never completely
lost touch with the real world. In 1924
he founded the group of the "Blue

Four" with Kandinsky, Feininger, and
Jawlensky. Klee saw his paintings of the
twenties, almost all on a small scale,
as miniature idylls, in which the color
was laid on in a regular, geometric, and
abstract way, while the graphic signs,
barely hinted at, evoke objects, animals,
and elements of reality. Over the years he
produced not only paintings, drawings,
and engravings but also theoretical
writings and gave fundamental lectures
on color at the new seat of the Bauhaus
in Dessau. Condemned as a degenerate
artist by the Nazis, Klee gave up his
teaching post and returned to Bern. In
the last years of his life, plagued by grave
illness, Klee painted bitter pictures, laden
with gloomy omens and characterized
by dark and heavy lines.

Gustav Klimt
Vienna, 1862-1918

To comprehend the gilded and glittering refinement of Klimt's art it is perhaps necessary to go back to the work of his father, a goldsmith and engraver. The young Gustav quickly made a name for himself as a talented decorator of theaters and baths, with allegorical scenes of pleasing ornamental effect. This sort of activity was to characterize Klimt's production for a long time, up until such fundamental and highly innovative works as his decoration of the great hall of Vienna University (1893), the allegory of Beethoven for the exhibition of the "Sezession" (1902), and the extraordinary frieze for the Palais Stoclet in Brussels (1909-1911). By the beginning of the twentieth century Klimt, despite some controversy, was the most influential painter in Vienna. At the center of an extremely lively circle of philosophers, writers, and musicians, Klimt founded the movement known as the *Sezession* in 1897, one of the most interesting of the tendencies that preceded the emergence of the avant-garde. The "Secession" proposed a shift away from the pompous academic style of late nineteenth-century art and toward a luminous and refined painting, of supple and modular elegance, with a considerable emphasis on decoration. A series of journeys through Europe made for the purposes of study placed Klimt at the center of the debate over Art Nouveau. One of the places he visited was Ravenna, where the Viennese painter studied the technique and chromatic effects of mosaic in order to be able to reproduce them in painting. The faces and attitudes of his figures are almost completely surrounded by precious tesserae. Another frequent characteristic of Klimt's pictures is the contrast between the decorative, abstract parts and the great realism of the figures, often highly symbolic in content. After 1910, in parallel with the evolution in Kokoschka and Schiele's style, Klimt turned more decisively in the direction of Expressionism.

Gustav Klimt
Salome
1909
oil on canvas
70 × 18 in.
(178 × 46 cm)
Ca' Pesaro, Venice

This macabre painting epitomizes the fundamental characteristics of the Austrian painter: a precious opulence cloaks the gilded figures with iridescent ornaments, while their forceful personality emerges from the colored patterns. The hands and face are depicted with penetrating psychological realism.

Gustav Klimt
Danaë
1907-1908
oil on canvas
30¼ × 32¾ in.
(77 × 83 cm)
Private collection, Vienna

The huddled pose of the mythical maiden as she receives the shower of gold in her womb is an extraordinary demonstration of the painter's skill with form.

Oskar Kokoschka
Pöchlarn, 1886-Villeneuve, 1980

A leading figure in the most intense period of Viennese Expressionism, Kokoschka started out as a pupil and follower of Klimt in the movement of the Sezession. However, following the advice of his friend Adolf Loos and the example of international currents, Kokoschka abandoned the ornamental style and glowing colors of the Sezession in the first decade of the twentieth century for a deeper involvement in the artistic and literary movement of Expressionism. Major works of drama, penetrating portraits, and paintings of great chromatic force emerged out of Kokoschka's intense activity during the years around the First World War, at the end of which he moved to Dresden. Although part of a continuous network of links with other contemporary painters, maintained in part through his frequent travels for the purposes of study and to keep in touch with the latest developments, Kokoschka represents an isolated case. Some features of his style, such as the use of the sinuous brushstrokes of Austrian Baroque painting, set him decisively apart from the various groups and avant-garde movements of international Expressionism. Over the course of the twenties Kokoschka abandoned his more intense themes, such as psychologically revealing portraits, for works on a large scale, chiefly views of cities. In spite of this new tranquillity, his work was banned by the Nazi regime. Kokoschka moved first to Prague and then to London, where he painted large allegorical cycles.

Left
Oskar Kokoschka
Portrait of Gino Schmidt
1914
oil on canvas
35½ × 22¾ in.
(90 × 57.5 cm)
Thyssen-Bornemisza
Collection, Madrid

The picture was painted during the years of Kokoschka's greatest success as a portraitist of the Viennese upper middle class. It has an unusual history: the three Schmidt brothers, proprietors of a thriving interior decoration firm with branches in Vienna and Budapest, originally commissioned the artist to paint them all together on a single canvas. Subsequently, Kokoschka split the large picture into three separate portraits.

Oskar Kokoschka
Portrait of Adolf Loos
1909
oil on canvas
29¼× 35¾ in.
(74 × 91 cm)
Nationalgalerie, Berlin

The young Kokoschka and Loos, one of the boldest and most severe architects of the twentieth century, formed a firm friendship, based on mutual admiration. Kokoschka openly defended Loos during the dispute that arose in 1910, on the occasion of the inauguration of his unadorned building on Michaelerplatz, right opposite the emperor's study. Franz Joseph considered the "house without eyebrows" offensive, dragging Loos into a fierce controversy. The architect played an important role in Kokoschka's entry into the *Sturm* ("storm") group based in Berlin.

Mikhail Larionov

Tiraspol, 1881-Fontenay-aux-Roses, 1964

Fellow student and then husband of Natalia Goncharova, Larionov was strongly committed to a shift away from the repetitive painting of the late nineteenth century and a return to the sources of Russian art, brought into line with developments in the international avant-garde. During the first decade of the century Larionov painted in an almost naïve manner, with deliberately simplified forms of a popular and primitive flavor. Through an extensive series of writings, exhibitions, and encounters, he contributed to the foundation of Rayonism, a movement that Larionov saw as a springboard for abstract art, unlike his wife, Goncharova, who always maintained a figurative

approach. An important stimulus for Larionov was the dynamic breakdown of forms carried out by the Futurists, applied to figures in movement. In 1914, Larionov accompanied the ballet company led by the celebrated choreographer Diaghilev to Paris, where he concentrated chiefly on stage design.

Mikhail Larionov
The Brawl
1911
oil on canvas
28 × 37 in.
(71.3 × 94 cm)
Thyssen-Bornemisza
Collection, Madrid

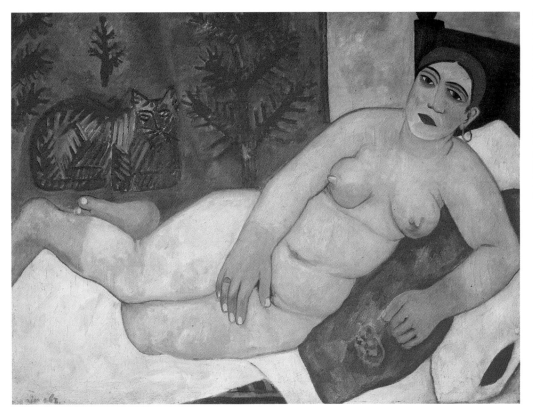

Mikhail Larionov
Venus of Kazapsk
1912
oil on canvas
39¼ × 51 in.
(99.5 ×129.5 cm)
Thyssen-Bornemisza
Collection, Madrid

This painting belongs to the most characteristic phase of Larionov's career, when he was attempting to fuse the great models of the European avant-garde with the Russian tradition.

Charles Lebrun
Paris, 1619-1690

The dominant personality in the French school of Baroque classicism, Lebrun was the supreme arbiter of taste at the court of Louis XIV. In 1634 he entered the workshop of Simon Vouet, where he produced paintings revealing an already acquired mastery of technique. In 1642, despite his appointment as court painter, Lebrun decided to complete his artistic apprenticeship in Rome on a grant provided by Chancellor Séguier. Between 1642 and 1646 he studied sixteenth-century Roman works with Poussin and also came under the influence of the painters working in the capital at that time. Poussin's teaching had a decisive impact on his style that can be seen in his mature works, where dramatic feelings are depicted with calculated poise and proportion. On his return to France, he received important commissions for religious paintings and decorative works. He decorated the castle of Hesselin in 1649, the palace of President Lambert in 1650, the castle of Vaux between 1658 and 1661, and the Apollo Gallery in the Louvre in 1663. As a protégé of Jean-Baptiste Colbert, Louis XIV's superintendant of finances, he was appointed first painter to the king in 1662 and began the most fertile period of his career. He was made a chancellor in 1664 and prince of the French Academy two years later. He decorated the Galerie des Glaces in the palace of Versailles (1771-1784): canvases glorifying the sovereign for the ceiling and colored marbles, gilded bronzes, and mirrors for the walls. On Colbert's death in 1683, Lebrun fell into disgrace.

Charles Lebrun
The Holy Family with the Sleeping Child
1655
oil on canvas
34¼ × 46½ in.
(87× 118 cm)
Musée du Louvre, Paris

Charles Lebrun
Chancellor Séguier
c. 1656
oil on canvas
116¼ × 137¾ in.
(295 × 350 cm)
Musée du Louvre, Paris

Silvestro Lega

Modigliana (Forlì), 1826-Florence, 1895

Lega spent his youth in Florence which left an indelible mark on him. This was not merely from an artistic standpoint either. He was still studying at the Academy of Fine Arts, learning the rigorous formal rules of Romantic and purist art, when he became involved in republican political circles and the Risorgimento. He was just 22 in 1848 when he took part in the ill-fated conspiracy of the Tuscan students at Curatone. Upon his return to Florence, he used his training as a traditional painter to produce canvases about contemporary history. Although he was among those who met in the Caffè Michelangelo, the birthplace of the Macchiaioli movement, for a long time Lega remained committed to a Romantic style of painting. He did, however, change to new subjects, such as minor episodes from the wars of independence that were increasingly popular. In 1861 he set up his own studio in the hills at Pergentina which became the laboratory of the central and most important phase in the development of the Macchiaioli movement, to which Lega by now was unreservedly committed. Landscapes painted *en plein air* and poetic images of everyday scenes were his preferred way of painting. His style retained overtones of the tradition of classical painting: the light colors of his palette, his clear draughtsmanship, monumental figures, and tranquil gestures all bring fifteenth-century painting to mind. In the 1860s he produced his freshest works, centered around his search to capture intimate feelings, country settings, and interiors always with a simple and serene feel to them. Later on, his color became much brighter and he seemed to be looking for stronger effects.

Silvestro Lega
The Folk Song
1867
canvas, 55 × 33¾ in.
(140 × 86 cm)
Florence, Palazzo Pitti,
Galleria d'Arte Moderna.

This is a good example of his lyrical intimate quality. As tranquil day-to-day life rolled by, he seemed on the look-out for small moments of emotion.

Fernand Léger

Argentan, 1881-Gif-sur-Yvette, 1955

In order to understand the development of Léger's style it is important to know that he started his career as a technical draftsman in an architect's studio. A fondness for the exact definition of objects, for geometric solids, and for line was to remain a constant feature of his work. Entering the pulsating artistic world of Paris in the first decade of the century, Léger quickly identified the works of Cézanne and the early Cubists as the principal road he wished to follow, though he was also influenced by the simple and essential style of Rousseau *Douanier*. Around 1910 he carried out experiments in the decomposition of the image into geometric planes along with Picasso, Braque, and Delaunay, but he found Analytical Cubism too cerebral and detached from reality. Perhaps partly under the influence of the Futurists, Léger sought and found inspiration in modern industrial civilization, to which he devoted a number of interesting writings. Combining horizontal and vertical elements, sharply defined volumes, and dense colors laid on in tightly controlled areas, Léger created rigorous compositions that are sometimes reminiscent of cross-sections of machinery, in which cones, cylinders, and parallelepipeds fit together with ingenious precision. These themes (machines, workshops, factories) are characteristic of the largely abstract pictures Léger painted after the First World War. In the twenties, especially after receiving commissions for large-scale murals, Léger returned to the human figure, celebrating artisans, laborers, and builders in paintings based on the three primary colors (blue, yellow, and red) and defining the personages with broad and precise lines.

Fernand Léger
Composition
1918
oil on canvas
57½ × 45 in.
(146 × 114 cm)
Pushkin Museum,
Moscow

Léger's art represents a highly personal development of Cubism and early Constructivism. After the First World War, Léger began to place more emphasis on contemporary themes: the city, the workplace, the factory and mechanical progress provided the inspiration for compositions made up of lines, colors, and regular volumes that conveyed a feeling of modern life, riding a knife edge between the figurative and (as in this case) abstraction.

Louis Le Nain
Laon, 1593-Paris, 1648

Diametrically opposed to the classical school of French painting represented by Poussin, Louis Le Nain distinguished himself as the leader of the school specializing in paintings of an elegiac rural life, a seventeenth-century form of genre painting better known in Italy through the work of the so-called *bamboccianti*. We have little information regarding Louis Le Nain's life. Born in the country near Laon, a town in northern France, with one older and one younger brother who were also painters, Le Nain spent his childhood in close contact with the peasant world. Little is known about his artistic training. After a period in the workshop of a Flemish master in his hometown, he probably made a journey to Rome

between 1629 and 1630 before settling in Paris, where he soon acquired a certain reputation. Louis Le Nain worked throughout his life in the same workshop as his brothers, where all the works were signed with the surname alone, thus making attribution of the paintings often difficult, despite the difference in their artistic temperaments. Antoine is traditionally indicated as a painter of miniatures and portraits. Louis Le Nain produced mythological and religious works, but his fame rests on his canvases portraying the peasant world with measured realism. Mathieu devoted his energies to historical and religious subjects and continued the peasant genre after his brother's death.

Louis Le Nain
Peasant Family
1642
oil on canvas
44½ × 62½ in.
(113 × 159 cm)
Musée Louvre, Paris

This is a sober, rustic setting with austere figures frontally arranged, like actors on a stage, their intense, severe gaze directed toward the viewer. The soft, still light and the sober coloring of browns and grays combine to give an interpretation of the peasant world that is both authentic and solemn.

Leonardo da Vinci

Vinci, Florence, 1452-Cloux Amboise, 1519

Leonardo, the "universal" genius *par excellence*, occupies a key position between the serene certainties of fifteenth-century Humanism and the impassioned quest for a new understanding of the world, mankind, and the cosmos. Painting, described by Leonardo as "the most perfect of all the sciences," became both a medium of expression and a tool of research, opening up hitherto unknown horizons. He trained in Verrocchio's workshop in Florence, and this early experience played a crucial role in broadening his interests in various artistic and technical applications, which were always preceded by preliminary drawings. After starting out as Verrocchio's assistant, Leonardo embarked on an independent career and soon displayed a talent for portraiture and for the depiction of nature. In 1482, at the age of thirty, he left the Florence of Lorenzo the Magnificent for the court of Ludovico the Moor, and entered so deeply into the Lombard spirit that he made Milan his second home. He spent a total of about twenty-five years in Lombardy, divided into two long periods, 1482-1499 and 1506-1513. During this quarter of a century Milan and Lombardy became Leonardo's great "laboratory," offering him not only financial security and positions of the utmost prestige, but also a lively cultural environment with stimulating contacts. Painting and filling notebooks with innumerable notes and observations (the celebrated *codices*) are two different but complementary aspects of extremely versatile creativity. The works of the first Milanese period include the *Virgin of the Rocks* (begun in 1483; Louvre, Paris) and *The Last Supper* (1494-1498). Leonardo fled from Milan on the arrival of the French troops, and visited Mantua and Venice before returning to Florence, where he competed with Michelangelo to paint the lost frescoes of scenes from two battles in Palazzo Vecchio. During this Florentine sojourn he started work on the *Mona Lisa*. He returned to Milan in 1506, and completed the *Virgin and Child with St. Anne*, now in the Louvre. Finally, in 1513 Leonardo accepted the invitation of Francis I of France and moved to Amboise, taking with him a few paintings, thousands of papers and drawings, and a small court of pupils.

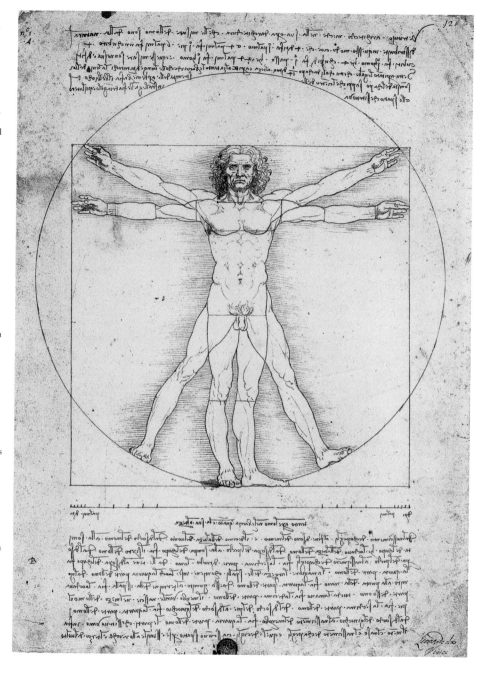

Leonardo da Vinci
Human Proportions According to Vitruvius
c. 1500

drawing and hand-written notes
Gabinetto dei Disegni, Accademia, Venice

Leonardo da Vinci
Mona Lisa
1503/06-1513
panel
30¼ × 21 in.
(77 × 53 cm)
Musée du Louvre, Paris

Idolized, derided, imitated, stolen, and then returned, in a bad state of preservation and always awaiting extremely difficult restoration, enigmatic in expression, ambiguous in pose, controversial as regards identification of the precise geographical location, put to the most bizarre uses in advertising, the *Mona Lisa* is one of the most worn-out "icons" in art, and yet capable of arousing new emotions every time you see it. As always, Leonardo took several years to develop this image, and reworked it a number of times, taking it with him from Florence to Milan and then to France. The result of this long process is a constantly changing and elusive work that overturns the very concept of a precise and permanent rendering of personality. The *Mona Lisa* remains inscrutable, and almost seems to reflect the misty atmosphere and jagged peaks of the landscape of water and mountains behind her. The relaxed pose with one hand upon the other and the slight turn of the bust were promptly taken up by Raphael for the female portraits he executed during his stay in Florence.

Leonardo da Vinci
The Last Supper
1495
tempera and oil
on two layers of plaster
181 × 346½ in.
(460 × 880 cm)
Refectory, Convento di
Santa Maria delle Grazie,
Milan

Work began on the *Last Supper* in 1494, when Ludovico the Moor decided to convert the Dominican church of Santa Maria delle Grazie into his personal mausoleum. Bramante was responsible for alterations to the building and Leonardo was commissioned to decorate the rear wall of the refectory with the traditional subject of *The Last Supper*, surmounted by the Sforza crests. Preferring to work slowly, he decided against the fresco technique, which guarantees lasting results but demands rapid execution. *The Last Supper* was not completed until 1498, but soon began to show signs of the dramatic deterioration that has required repeated restoration over the centuries. The most recent of these operations reveals a work that is very different indeed from the damaged version. It depicts a vast hall opening up behind the figures and illuminated on the left side by the real windows of the refectory, while the suffuse yet clear light of early evening enters through the three large apertures painted at the back of the scene. The disciples' shocked emotional reaction to the announcement of betrayal makes a strong impact in this evocative architectural setting enhanced by the play of light and the perspective. Every detail contributes to the physical and psychological dynamism of the scene.

Roy Lichtenstein
New York, 1923-1997

Determined to create painting for a vast public, Roy Lichtenstein achieved an art of extraordinary vitality by transcribing pictorial motifs drawn from the world of mass media. He studied under Reginald Marsh at the Art Students League in 1939-1940, concentrating on the painting techniques of the Renaissance. He then enrolled in Ohio State University, which he attended until called into the army in 1943, later returning to get his degree. In 1946 he began painting genre subjects and works of a Cubist or expressionist inspiration. At his first one-man exhibition, held in 1951 at the Carlebach Gallery in New York, he exhibited his first mixed-media paintings. Until 1957 he worked as a commercial artist, sometimes doing window displays. From 1957 to 1960 he taught at the State University of New York at Oswego. During this time his art stayed within the orbit of abstract expressionism, but the cosmopolitan setting and differing artistic opinions, most of all the new ideas in New York galleries and those he encountered through the Fluxus group, directed him more and more toward pop themes. His first pop works date to 1961 and show inspiration drawn from comics and other mass-media images, including reproductions of historical art masterpieces; these he exhibited in his first one-man show, in 1962 at the Leo Castelli Gallery. His goal was the creation of images at the highest level of objectivity, with no concern for the social or cultural background that generated the image, much less for the creative action of the artist. The design of a comic strip, with its elementary but complete dimension, constitutes a microcosm of imagination parallel to life and, functioning like a single frame, makes its way directly into the visual sphere of the viewer. Using the morphology of the comic strip, including the Benday dots used in the printing of real comics, Lichtenstein reformulated the images to arrive at a transfiguration of reality that includes a strong abstract component. Over the course of the 1960s he participated in numerous group shows, such as the "Six Painters and the Object" exhibit at the Guggenheim Museum in 1963 and the Venice Biennale in 1966. A retrospective of his work was held at the Guggenheim in 1969 and later visited other cities.

Roy Lichtenstein
Blam
1962
oil on canvas
68 × 80 in.
(172.7 × 203.2 cm)
Yale University Art Gallery, New Haven, Connecticut

Lichtenstein often uses battle scenes, clichés that comics borrow from movies. The flames of the explosion become red and yellow strips, while the jet itself, presented in extreme close-up perspective, takes on the appearance of a shiny metal toy.

Pol, Hermann, and Jean de Limbourg
Nijmegen, late XIV century-(?), 1416

Active in France in the early fifteenth century, the Limbourg brothers brought about an authentic revolution in the field of illumination. They were trained in the workshop of a goldsmith in Paris and under the supervision of their uncle, the successful painter Jean Malouel. Around 1402 they were working for Philip II the Bold of Burgundy. After his death they were employed at the court of Jean de Berry, for whom they produced their most celebrated work, the *Très Riches Heures du Duc de Berry*, an illuminated book of hours that was left unfinished on their death in 1416. Although it is difficult to distinguish the individual work of each brother, it is probable that the more talented was Pol, a favorite of the duke, who appointed him *valet de chambre* in 1413. Despite their links with the calligraphic aesthetic of French tradition, the brothers displayed a sure knowledge of the most modern Flemish and Italian developments even in their earliest work, an illuminated Bible for Philip the Bold and the *Belles Heures*. But it is the large full-page illuminations of the *Très Riches Heures*, begun in 1413, that give the strongest proof of their extraordinary talent. This is true in particular of the pages dedicated to the months, where the freely modeled figures of peasants and the nobles captured in stiff poses of courtly abstraction are set in the largest landscapes hitherto produced in illuminations. Northern realism and an Italian-style handling of space reach their height in these works. There can be no doubt that the duke's sophisticated culture and the example of the works of art contained in his collections certainly made a contribution to this achievement.

Pol and Jean de Limbourg
The Astrological Man
from the *Très Riches Heures du Duc de Berry*
1415-1416
tempera on parchment
11½ × 8¼ in.
(29 × 21 cm)
Musée Condé, Chantilly

This singular composition appears as an appendix to the *Très Riches Heures* and summarizes the astrological beliefs of the Duke of Berry. In the center two nude figures symbolize the male and female principles. The diamond-shaped frame and the female body are decorated with signs of the zodiac. The sinuous line and sophisticated modeling are evidence of an original reworking of Italian and Flemish models.

215

Jean-Étienne Liotard
Geneva, 1702-1789

After his apprenticeship in Geneva in the workshop of Daniel Gardelle, where he mainly learned the technique of miniature painting on china, in 1723 Liotard moved to Paris, where he began to work as a miniaturist and engraver. Individualism was both his limit and his strong point. Having failed in his attempt to enter the Academy in 1733, he devoted himself exclusively to portrait painting, establishing himself as a master of pastel, a medium introduced into France by Rosalba Carriera. Unlike other masters who exploited the semi-tones and the sfumato transitions of pastel, Liotard defined his figures with clear lines, avoiding any form of lyricism. A cosmopolitan artist, he painted the Austrian, French, English, and Dutch nobility, leaving out the whole array of curtains, drapes, crowns, and other frills that characterize court portraiture. He depicts his characters with remarkable simplicity, with clear, well-defined surfaces, as though they are engraved, without recourse to elegant, cloying formulas. From 1779 on he received no more commissions. Concerned by the development of political events, he retired to his country house in a village to the southeast of Geneva, where he painted still lifes of naive beauty and unexpected modernity. He died in 1789, one month before the beginning of the French Revolution.

Jean-Étienne Liotard
The Chocolate Girl
1744-1745
pastel on parchment
32½ × 20¾ in.
(82.5 × 52.5 cm)
Gemäldegalerie,
Dresden

Liotard's masterpiece, it was already praised by his contemporaries for the technical perfection achieved in the use of pastels. Count Francesco Algarotti, who purchased the painting in 1745 in Venice for the royal collections of Dresden, praised its astonishing likeness. The refined use of a limited range of colors is particularly effective: the white apron stands out against the background tones of gray, pink, and ocher, which are also used for the pattern on the cup.

Filippino Lippi
Prato, c. 1457-Florence, 1504

If his birth proved embarrassing for his parents, Fra Filippo Lippi and Sister Lucrezia Buti, who were both in holy orders, Filippino certainly compensated for this by being a true infant prodigy. He assisted his father from a tender age and had only just turned 12 when Filippo died. Nevertheless, Filippino was able to complete the frescoes in Spoleto cathedral. Straight afterwards he went on to assist Botticelli during what was destined to be a fruitful period in his early work. The two painters worked very closely but Filippino developed a more robust use of line and form than his master. Filippino's first certain works are characterized by an uneasy sweetness and a sinuous rhythm to his draughtsmanship over which he still retained total control. This can be seen in his first major work, completing the frescoes started by Masaccio and Masolino in the Brancacci chapel (c. 1484-1485). It is also apparent in the *Otto de Pratica Altarpiece* for the Palazzo Vecchio (now in the Uffizi), in the *Vision of St. Bernard* (1486, Badia, Florence), in the *Nerli Altarpiece* for Santo Spirito (c. 1488), and in the start he made on the frescoes in the Strozzi chapel in Santa Maria Novella which were only finished in 1502. Thanks to Lorenzo the Magnificent's intervention, Filippino was called to Rome in 1488 to paint the frescoes in the Carafa chapel in Santa Maria sopra Minerva. Struck by recent archeological discoveries, Filippino worked on antique ornamental motifs. Back in Florence, the painter was one of the first and most lucid to respond to the crisis in art caused by the death of Lorenzo the Magnificent and Savonarola's sermons. His paintings became bizarre, fantastical, and tend increasingly to seem hallucinatory in a highly inventive way. Among his last works is the *Deposition of Christ* (Accademia, Florence) which was completed by Perugino.

Filippino Lippi
Apparition of the Virgin to St. Bernard
c. 1486
wood panel
82¾ × 76¾ in.
(210 × 195 cm)
Badia, Florence

Painted at a time when Filippino was fully committed to finishing Masaccio and Masolino's frescoes in the Brancacci chapel, this dazzling altarpiece is one of the unquestioned masterpieces of Tuscan painting produced towards the end of the fifteenth century. Filippino rivaled the Flemish masters in his perfect depiction of detail and the vivacity of his colors. However, this work shows the first signs of the sense of unease and melancholy that appear to gnaw at the souls of Filippino's characters.

217

Fra Filippo Lippi
Florence, c. 1406-Spoleto, 1469

Filippo Lippi was an artist of vital importance to the development of Florentine painting, forming a link between Masaccio, whose pupil he probably was, and Botticelli. He first appeared on the artistic scene at the start of the 1430s. Among his early works are the frescoes in the Carmine Friary where some years earlier he had taken his vows as a monk. In 1434 he visited Padua, but his art was moving in another direction, becoming more linear and filled with decorative motifs –thin fluttering draperies, brocades. Filippo then began his monumental work, the *Coronation of the Virgin* (Uffizi). This was surrounded by numerous altarpieces which used Domenico Veneziano's rules of perspective. But they are all characterized by the delicacy and detail which touched even Leonardo. In 1452 Lippi moved to Prato where he painted what may be his masterpiece, the frescoes in the cathedral choir as well as other works. His long stay in Prato has to be viewed in the light of the scandal which broke over his relationship with the nun Lucrezia Buti, by whom he fathered Filippino. Back in Florence once more, Filippo received prestigious commissions, such as the *Nativity* for the Magi chapel in the Palazzo Medici, now in Berlin. It was after receiving another Medici commission that Filippo started his last work, the frescoes in the choir of Spoleto cathedral.

Filippo Lippi
Coronation of the Virgin
detail
1466-1469
fresco
Cathedral, Spoleto

The frescoes telling the *Life of the Virgin* in the conch of Spoleto cathedral apse were the last and most ambitious of Filippo Lippi's works. They remained incomplete at his death but were finished a couple of months later, in December 1469, by his son Filippino who was still very young at the time. The images have a priestly grandeur.

Johann Liss

Oldemburg, c. 1595-Venice, 1629

Like his friend and near contemporary
Domenico Fetti, Liss died very young.
The few short years of his career were,
however, generously filled with work
spanning a broad range of subjects
and stylistic points of reference,
journeys, and close relations with the
collectors of the time and other artists.
As a result of his delight in travel and
contact with different cultures, Liss
became an intelligent exponent of
various forms of figurative expression,
especially during the third decade
of the seventeenth century. While his
best-known works draw inspiration
above all from sixteenth-century
Venetian art, his career began with a
series of journeys to the Netherlands
and stays in Antwerp, Amsterdam, and
Haarlem. These provided important
opportunities for contact with
Rubens's studio and Flemish and
Dutch Caravaggesque painters like
Jordaens and Terbrugghen. His taste
for genre scenes and peasant festivities
of clearly Flemish derivation dates
from this period. He arrived in Italy
in 1621 and studied in Rome from the
following year to 1624, thus gaining
first-hand experience of the different
versions of the Caravaggesque style
produced by the northern masters.
The decisive turning point came with
his move to Venice. In a somewhat
mediocre period of Venetian painting
characterized by the tired repetition
of models drawn from Tintoretto, the
arrival of Liss was a breath of fresh air.
His richly sparkling, luminous
painting inspired by Veronese and
Titian gave the Venetian school a
timely jolt, thus paving the way for the
imminent arrival of Bernardo Strozzi
and, in the longer term, laying the
foundations for the renewal of
Venetian art in the eighteenth century.

Johann Liss
The Finding of Moses
c. 1626-1627
oil on canvas
61 × 41¾ in.
(155 × 106 cm)
Musée des Beaux-Arts, Lille

The scene is flooded with
an all-enveloping wave
of soft, radiant color,
from which the shapely forms
of scantily clad maidens
emerge with sensual force,
despite the remote biblical
source of the subject.

Fernando Llanos
active in Spain from 1506 to 1525

A painter originally from Valencia, active during the first quarter of the sixteenth century, Fernando Llanos, together with Fernando Yáñez, is the main exponent of the Valencia Renaissance school. He probably became acquainted with Leonardo's work during a stay in Italy before 1506, the year in which he worked with Yáñez in the cathedral at Valencia, which marked the beginning of a long artistic partnership that was to last until 1515. The two artists executed for the cathedral the *Altarpiece of SS.*

Cosmas and Damian (1506-1507) and the wings of the altarpiece for the high altar, that faithfully echo the manner and stylistic elements of Leonardo and the serene balance of Raphael, and in which the two hands are barely distinguishable. However, some subtle differences may be observed: Yáñez's compositions have a more grandiose architecture, his figures are elegant and serene; by contrast, Llanos's style is more nervous, his figures are more expressive and depicted in everyday situations. After 1515 he continued to work in the cathedral at Valencia. His activity is documented until 1525.

Fernando Llanos
Rest on the Flight into Egypt
1507
panel
76½ × 89½ in.
(194 × 227 cm)
Cathedral, Valencia

From 1507 on, the artist worked with Yáñez on the wings of the altarpiece for the high altar in the cathedral, executing twelve rectangular panels dedicated to the life of the Virgin. Despite the objective difficulty in distinguishing the contributions of the two artists, critics agree on attributing the *Rest on the Flight into Egypt* to Llanos, who prefers to render his figures less majestic and more expressive by accentuating movement.

Stefan Lochner

Meersburg, c. 1400-Cologne, 1451

Lochner is the most representative figure of the lively artistic climate found in Cologne in the middle of the century, when the cultural horizons of Germany began to open up to Flemish and Italian innovations. He was born in a small town on Lake Constance, where he probably stayed for a few years before making a journey to the Netherlands, where he became directly acquainted with the works of Jan van Eyck and Robert Campin. He settled definitively in Cologne around the year 1437, and was soon in great demand for both public and private commissions. Evidence of the great respect and fame that Lochner enjoyed is provided by the fact that in 1447 he was appointed to the city council, the most prestigious and representative body in Cologne.

The artist's work is in what is known as the Soft Style; his Madonnas have thin oval faces and elegant measured gestures. At the same time, however, he also injects new life into the exhausted courtly repertoire by introducing a more accentuated plastic quality and giving his compositions greater breadth. In some works, such as the central panel of the *Altarpiece of the Patron Saints of the City* in Cologne Cathedral, the use of a gold ground and the highly detailed depiction of fabrics and jewelry reflect the aristocratic taste of his patrons. Lochner combines these traditional elements, however, with an involved portrayal of the figures, who never appear to be abstract or distant, and a Flemish-style attention to naturalistic detail. He thus creates an individual and harmonious style that was to be admired also by Albrecht Dürer.

Stefan Lochner
Last Judgment
c. 1435
oil on wood
49 × 67¾ in.
(124 × 172 cm)
Wallraf-Richartz-Museum, Cologne

This work is the central panel of an altarpiece produced for the parish church of St. Lawrence in Cologne. The center of the work is dominated by the figure of Christ seated on two rainbows and granting the prayers of intercession for mankind from the Virgin and St. John, who kneel at his feet. These monumental figures are juxtaposed with the bustling scene on a smaller scale taking place beneath them, where angels and devils struggle to separate the souls of the damned from those admitted to heaven. The contrast between heavenly joy and terror is conveyed through numerous imaginative details. Desperation and ruin reign in hell. Lochner produces a stark and ruthless depiction of the monstrous creatures and human beings of all social classes torn apart by their irredeemable sins. This grim section contrasts with the luminous scene of the redeemed souls as they wait for admittance to the kingdom of heaven through an imposing gate.

221

Stefan Lochner
Adoration of the Magi,
central panel of the
*Altarpiece of the Patron
Saints of the City*
c. 1440-1445, panel,
102½ × 112¼ in.
(260 × 285 cm)
Cathedral, Cologne

This work was
commissioned for the
chapel of the City Council
of Cologne and moved
to its definitive location
in the cathedral only in
1810. The scene is imbued
with a strong symbolic
significance, as the Magi
are the patron saints
of the city. The finely
characterized individual
figures are arranged
harmoniously and
symmetrically around the
enthroned Virgin. The
solemnity is accentuated
by the rich jewelry,
gleaming armor, and
sumptuous garments.

Stefan Lochner
Madonna with Violets,
detail, c. 1435-1440
panel, 83½ × 40¼ in.
(212 × 102 cm)
Diözesanmuseum,
Cologne

Lochner here creates
an idyllic atmosphere.
The sophisticated
combination of colors is
enhanced by the natural
light and the clear blue
of the sky, which
emphasizes the delicate
profile of the Virgin.

Stefan Lochner
*SS. Mark, Barbara, and
Luke,* c. 1445-1450
panel, 3½ × 23 in.
(100.5 × 58 cm)
Wallraf-Richartz-
Museum, Cologne

This is a mature work,
probably produced
shortly before his death.
The figures occupy the
space with naturalness
and the sculptural quality
of their bodies is
accentuated by their soft
garments.

Pietro Longhi
Venice, 1701-1785

The son of a goldsmith (his real surname was Falca), Pietro Longhi tried without much success to become one of the group of eighteenth-century Venetian painters so much in demand for large-scale decorations. His youthful work included frescoes in the Palazzo Sagredo which reveal his lack of talent in this field. But at about the age of 40, Longhi managed to find his own creative voice which soon made him a specialist in a highly successful new genre. Drawing on his memories of youthful studies with Giuseppe Maria Crespi (an important precursor to Longhi's brand of genre painting), he began painting small canvases on everyday subjects, showing real places and people. Unlike most view painters at the time, normally forced to seek foreign patrons, Longhi mainly worked for local patrons and collectors, including the noble families of Grimani, Barbarigo, and Manin. Longhi prepared his work by making careful preparatory sketches. He concentrated almost exclusively on small-scale canvases depicting the modest day-to-day activities of aristocratic Venetian families. The wonderful amiability of these episodes of no earth-shaking importance is marked by an observant, often gently satirical touch. The playwright Goldoni called Longhi a "man seeking the truth," but his was not a very harassing quest. In later life Longhi also produced two interesting cycles of paintings. One was a series showing the *Seven Sacraments* while the other depicted *Hunters in the Valley.* Both are now in the Pinacoteca Querini-Stampalia in Venice.

Pietro Longhi
The Painter in His Studio
1740-1745
canvas
17¼ × 20¾ in.
(44 × 53 cm)
Ca' Rezzonico, Museo del Settecento Veneziano, Venice

We are given here a shadowy self-portrait of the artist's profile against the light. At the same time a mute dialogue between the lady who is sitting for him and the artist himself seems to be deliberately interrupted by the presence of the man who appears to be rather worried about the painter's work.

Pietro Longhi
The Tailor
1741
canvas
23½ × 19 in.
(60 × 49 cm)
Gallerie dell'Accademia, Venice

This picture belongs to the Contarini Collection. Once again, Longhi proved his perfect taste in the way he blends the color harmonies. The painting centers around the contrast between the professionally smooth gestures of the tailor who is showing off the costly fabric and the lady who almost seems bewildered.

Ambrogio Lorenzetti

Siena, active between 1319 and 1348

It is not uncommon to find two brothers whose careers run at times together but who are really quite different in style. The Lorenzetti brothers provide a classic example: Pietro's robust solemnity is countered by Ambrogio's cheerful amusement with all aspects of life which enabled him to turn reality into fable and, vice versa, to give concrete, tangible form to divine characters or abstruse political allegories. In both cases, the brothers' artistic progress started with Duccio. They pursued separate paths, Ambrogio being notably more of an innovator, only linking up again in the 1340s. They then shared the same terrible fate, both probably dying from the Black Death in 1348. Although he always remained one of the finest representatives of Sienese art, Ambrogio Lorenzetti established crucial contacts with Giotto and artistic circles in Florence where he probably lived between 1319-1327. His early work was fairly static in depicting gesture, even though his use of expression was already observant. During the 1320s Ambrogio's confidence grew until he was ready to produce monumental works (*Maestà*, Massa Marittima, Palazzo Comunale) for particularly complex environments (*Presentation in the Temple*, Uffizi, Florence), as well as scenes with a dynamic content (frescoes in the church of St. Francis in Siena and in the St. Galgano chapel at Montesiepi). Alongside these, there are also lesser but nonetheless charming works such as the *Madonna of the Milk* in the Palazzo Arcivescovile in Siena. The masterpieces that sum up his achievements are the allegories of *Good and Bad Government* in the Siena Palazzo Pubblico (1337-1340). They depict scenes from everyday life, crammed with incidents and yet newly naturalistic in his treatment of architecture.

Ambrogio Lorenzetti
Effects of Good Government in the City and in the Countryside
detail
1337-1340
fresco
Palazzo Pubblico,
Sala dei Nove, Siena

This is perhaps the most famous and impressive image of a medieval city ever painted. The towering cityscape forms the backdrop to the swarming activity of its citizens, from builders on the roofs to merchants, a school teacher, and the group of girls dancing happily in the foreground.

224

Claude Lorrain
Chamagne, Nancy, 1600-Rome, 1682

One of the greatest seventeenth-century landscape painters, Claude Lorrain moved to Rome in 1613 and remained there until his death except for one stay in Naples from 1619 to 1621 and another in his native Lorraine from 1625 to 1627.
His apprenticeship took place in the workshop of the Roman landscape painter Agostino Tassi; 1629 saw the beginning of his association with Joachim von Sandrart, with whom he learned to draw from life, freeing himself from Tassi's academic models. He gradually developed a tendency to give concrete shape to nature through the continuity of space and light. The remains of classical architecture, the great trees silhouetted against the sky, the distant peaks, and the still seaports combine to produce an ideal and yet recognizable landscape based on the Roman countryside or *campagna*, the hills of Latium that the artist never tired of exploring and recording in hundreds of precious drawings. The extraordinary series of *Morning, Afternoon, Dusk,* and *Night* at the Hermitage demonstrates Lorrain's highly personal use of light in relation to the specific hour dictated by the subject. Light from the left indicates morning and suggests cold tones for the landscape and the sky. Light from the right represents evening and allows the use of warm tones with skies ranging from fiery pink to orange. The cosmopolitan atmosphere of seventeenth-century Rome had a positive effect on Lorrain's long career, enabling him to combine very different experiences—Poussin's classical restraint, the landscapes of the Bolognese school from Carracci to Guercino, and the Caravaggesque handling of light—in a synthesis of remarkable originality that anticipates Turner and the Impressionists.

Claude Lorrain
Landscape with Dancing Figures
Marriage of Isaac and Rebecca
1648
oil on canvas
58¾ × 77½ in.
(149 × 197 cm)
National Gallery, London

Under the influence of Domenichino and Annibale Carracci, Lorrain's style became more elevated and serene. Having abandoned fantastic *vedute* ("views") and picturesque motifs, the artist began to base his landscapes on the nearby Roman countryside.

Lorenzo Lotto

Venice, c. 1480-Loreto, 1556

Born in Venice, Lotto trained under Giovanni Bellini and alternated trips to the great art cities (Venice and Rome) with longer stays in "minor" towns. He thus discovered his ideal dimension as a "provincial" artist, a term that should not be interpreted in a negative sense, but indicates a tendency to develop alternative forms on the margins of the intellectual debate that dominated the major cities. At the end of his apprenticeship, influenced by Bellini but also by the clear light and draftsmanship of northern European art, Lotto became involved in the initiatives of the Bishop of Treviso, Bernardo de' Rossi, and showed a leaning toward portraiture and the search for innovation in the execution of altarpieces. After two stays in the Marches, separated by a difficult period in Rome at Raphael's side (1508–1510), Lotto settled in Bergamo from 1513 to 1526. This was by no means a period of isolation, but the most productive in his career. He came into contact with the work of Gaudenzio Ferrari, and perhaps that of Correggio, resumed his relationship with northern European art, tried his hand at a variety of techniques, and furthered his development of portrait painting. Moreover, in Bergamo, the tastes of clients and painter coincided. They oriented toward an original blend of Venetian art and the Lombardy tradition, Leonardo and everyday realism. During the 1520s, when he painted a series of portraits and fine altarpieces, Lotto also executed works that seem to stem from a reflection on the religious events of the time and on the spread of Protestant ideas, but his religious feeling remained contradictory, bearing witness to an inner unrest that he never resolved. Lotto developed a broader, more undulating brushstroke that also characterizes his portraits, which aim at conveying an "intimate image" of the sitters and revealing their innermost emotions. In 1526 he returned to Venice after completing several fresco cycles in Bergamo and the surrounding area (the *Oratorio Suardi* at Trescore Balneario). Venetian artistic circles, dominated by Titian, seemed, however, reluctant to welcome a painter who had returned after working for twenty years in other parts of Italy. Lotto thus continued to maintain relations with the Marches. Shortly after his return to Venice, he

sent the *St. Lucy Altarpiece*, very similar to his output in Bergamo, to Jesi, and the *Annunciation*, a famous example of the psychological dynamism that animates his work, to Recanati. The few paintings that he executed for churches in Venice were not a great success. The most significant is *St. Antoninus Dole*, painted in 1542 for the Basilica of SS. Giovanni e Paolo. In 1549, almost destitute, he left Venice to return once again to the Marches, where he spent his last years in the monastery of the Santa Casa at Loreto.

Lorenzo Lotto
Portrait of a Young Man with a Book
c. 1526
oil on panel
18½ × 15 in.
(47 × 38 cm)
Castello Sforzesco, Milan

Lucas van Leyden
Lucas Hugenszoon
Leyden, c. 1489-1533

A child prodigy with great natural talent for drawing, Lucas trained in the Dutch city of Leyden, first with his painter father and later in the studio of Cornelis Engebrechtsz, the best local artist in the late fifteenth century. He was already working as an engraver, his technical skill, inventive power, and deft draftsmanship putting him on a level with Dürer. Alongside engravings of biblical subjects, some of which have a powerful visionary atmosphere, genre subjects appeared in Lucas' work: characters and situations from a rural context, such as the milk woman, and later, the dentist and surgeon of the village. The two main features of Lucas' work, which also appear in his painting, are his

capacity to innovate traditional iconographies and his desire to introduce new topics that anticipated seventeenth-century realism by nearly a hundred years. Fine examples of this are found in his various paintings of card players and chess players. His style shows traces of the nearby Italianate Antwerp School, but can be even more closely linked to the German Renaissance, to the rich pure Humanism of Dürer, with whom Lucas established a close friendship. After a wild adolescence, in 1517 he married Elyzabeth Boschhuyzen, a member of one of the richest and most powerful families in the city. His marriage introduced him to an elite circle, a position ratified by his significant economic success. The work before 1520 has a tendency to focus on portraiture In 1521-1522, a period spent in Antwerp persuaded

him to "modernize" his style, bringing it into line with the classical style of Mabuse and van Scorel. His interpretation was, however, highly individual. Forsaking the architectural compositions beloved of his colleagues, he arranged figures in an apparently random fashion, within large landscapes, to the point where it is sometimes difficult to identify the subject. His mature triptychs, such as the Amsterdam *Golden Calf* and the Leyden *Last Judgment*, are masterful. In 1527 he set sail with Mabuse on a trip round the regions of Flanders, Zeeland, and Brabant, during which Lucas enjoyed himself like a true prince of the arts. But there was a dramatic aftermath: he spent the last six years of his life in bed suffering from tuberculosis. He nevertheless continued to paint and produce etchings.

Lucas van Leyden
Madonna and Child, Mary Magdalene, and Donor
1522
oil on wood, 20 × 26¾ in. (50.5 × 67.8 cm)
Alte Pinakothek, Munich

This is one of the few paintings that have been dated. This carefully balanced composition, matched by the formally arranged relationship between the figures and the landscape, clearly displays Lucas van Leyden's draftsmanship, particularly well expressed in his strikingly accurate and clearly defined figures.

August Macke

Meschede, 1887-
Perthes-les-Hurlus, 1914

An intense and tragic figure from the
early period of German Expressionism,
Macke represents the lyrical side of the
movement. Trained in the tradition
of late nineteenth-century Germany,
he changed his style following a
repeated series of visits to Paris. He was
particularly attracted by the free and
expressive use of color made by Matisse
and the Fauves, but was also influenced
by the transparency of light in
Delaunay's work and the lively
composition of the Futurists. Out
of all these experiences came a painting
of great dynamism and imagination,
devoid of the harshness of line and
violent themes typical of other German
artists. In 1911 he joined Kandinsky's
Blaue Reiter movement, but the
journey he made to Tunisia in 1914
in the company of Klee and the Swiss
painter Louis Moilliet had an even
greater influence on the limpidity
of his color and the simplicity of his
landscapes. It was an exotic time, filled
with the fascination and light of the
Mediterranean, but destined to come to
a dramatic end just a few months later.
He enlisted on the outbreak of war and
was killed during one of the first
offensives on the Western front.

August Macke
Three on a Stroll
1914
oil on canvas,
22 × 13 in. (56 × 33 cm)
Thyssen-Bornemisza
Collection, Madrid

In this touching image
of contemplative calm,
we can perhaps detect
a distant echo of Caspar
David Friedrich in the
decision to represent
the figures from behind,
as well as a more recent
reference to the
Intimism of Vuillard.
Sent off to fight like his
friend Franz Marc,
Macke too sought
liberation from the
anguish of the trenches
in the themes most
congenial to him. Thus,
while Marc painted his
beloved animals, he
chose to depict figures
communing with one
another and with nature.

Alessandro Magnasco
Genoa, 1667-1749

Son of a minor Genoese painter, Alessandro Magnasco trained in his home town before moving to Milan when he was still young. There he worked for many years in Filippo Abbiati's studio. His meeting with Sebastiano Ricci marked a turning point in his art. Their acquaintance was renewed during a stay in Florence (1703-1709) at the court of Grand Duke Ferdinand of Tuscany. Soon afterwards Magnasco gave up painting large figures (he only produced a handful of these in his later years) and instead concentrated on his unmistakable canvases with fantastic landscapes or interiors peopled with weird characters. At the start he stuck to windswept countryside and ruins with beggars. But during his second and longer stay in Milan (1709-1735), he applied his typically vivid style to scenes set in monasteries, torture chambers, seascapes, masques, and bacchanals. His output was extremely well received in Milanese scholarly circles. The critical jury is still out as to any deeper meaning of these canvases, which mingle the macabre with the burlesque, simple description with powerful melodrama. Magnasco went back to Genoa in old age and it is there that we find his last, visionary and transfigured works.

His art later influenced Marco Ricci and Francesco Guardi.

Alessandro Magnasco
Sacrilegious Robbery
1731
canvas, 63 × 94½ in.
(160 × 240 cm)
Quadreria Arcivescovile, Milan

The painting illustrates a crime committed on January 6, 1731. Thieves were trying to force an entry into the church of Santa Maria in Campomorto at Siziano (Pavia) to steal the holy vessels used for mass. They were seen off by skeletons which issued from the graves in the surrounding cemetery. The macabre scene is a large votive piece. The events are watched by the Virgin who we see in the top right–hand corner organizing the skeletons' sortie and decreeing the punishment for the thieves, who were subsequently hanged. The canvas belongs to the church where the attempted sacrilegious robbery took place but for safety reasons it is kept in the Diocesan Museum in Milan.

René Magritte

Lessines, 1898–Brussels, 1967

After working in the Cubist and Futurist styles, Magritte's attention was caught, in 1922, by a reproduction of de Chirico's mysterious *Love Song* (1910). It seemed to him a new vision in which the observer "rediscovers his isolation and perceives the silence of the world." In the spring of 1927 Magritte moved to Paris, where he met Breton and joined the Surrealists, though continuing to go his own way. There is no space in his pictures for figures that transcend everyday reality: they are crowded with banal objects rendered bizarre by their gigantic proportions or distortions of their appearance. The result is an absurd and disquieting image of reality, as full of snares as a nightmare. In 1930 Magritte returned to Brussels, where he frequented a select circle of Surrealist friends and wrote the manifesto *L'action immédiate* in 1934, documenting his ties with Breton and his plan to bring Surrealism into the field of political struggle. After a short stay at Carcassonne, where he painted *Homesickness* (1940), he spent the rest of his life in Brussels, briefly adopting the style of Renoir before returning to his more usual manner.

Following page
René Magritte
Homesickness
1940
oil on canvas
39¼ × 31½ in.
(100 × 80 cm)
Private collection

Immobility and silence impart a sense of loss to the image as a whole which is cut in half by a balustrade, separating two irreconcilable realities. On the right-hand side, a man-angel leans against the balustrade, gazing at the city that is faintly visible in the distance. A street lamp stands in the background, on the left. In the foreground, in the middle of the picture, the figure of the lion harks back to the iconography of Venetian painting in the fifteenth century.

René Magritte
The Key of the Fields
1936
oil on canvas
31½ × 23½ in.
(80 × 60 cm)
Thyssen-Bornemisza Collection, Madrid

If the window opening onto nature is a clear metaphor for the human condition, the shards of broken glass, representing the elimination of the barrier between container and content, interior and exterior, humanity and reality, are a metaphor for painting, which was Magritte's instrument of choice for deepening his understanding of the world.

231

Juan Bautista Maino

Pastrana, Guadalajara, 1580-
Madrid, 1649

The son of a Lombard painter, from an early age Maino was involved in the work on the Escorial. Critical studies are now gradually rediscovering this artist, who was a celebrated painter in his day, but was later overshadowed by other great masters of the golden age of Spanish painting. An essential element in his formation was Caravaggesque realism, which he probably encountered in Italy, both in Lombardy and during a period of study in Rome. In 1611 Maino was living in Toledo, where he took the vows of the Dominican order. Very solid forms, clearly defined by the light and rich in color, predominate in his work. Noted by intellectuals and courtiers for his rich, sumptuous style, Maino was summoned to the court in Madrid, where he became the painter who most reflected the tastes of Philip IV. In his official capacity, and with the support of the all-powerful conde-duque de Olivares, he played a key role in bringing Velázquez to Madrid in 1623 and introducing him at court. As the mentor of this talented young painter from Seville, it was probably Maino who encouraged Velázquez to study Italian art, and Caravaggio in particular.

Juan Bautista Maino
*Reconquest of Bahia
in Brazil*
1625
oil on canvas
121¾ × 154 in.
(309 × 391 cm)
Prado, Madrid

This canvas celebrates the victory won on Brazilian soil by Don Fadrique de Toledo in 1625. Painted for the Buen Retiro palace, it provides a good example of a celebratory work before Velázquez's masterpieces, such as the *Surrender of Breda*, painted ten years later. The scene is divided into two parts: on the right, he depicts the historical episode, almost buried beneath layers of symbolic reference. Below a precious canopy, the victorious general shows a small group of kneeling officers a tapestry in which Philip IV is being crowned with a laurel wreath by an incongruous couple, the corpulent conde-duque de Olivares and the allegorical figure of Victory, standing on the bodies of Heresy, Wrath, and War. In the foreground to the left, we have what is definitely the most interesting and lively section of the painting: a wounded soldier being tended with great concern and a group of women, children, and peasants commenting on the scene. His greatest gifts come to the fore in this area of the canvas, and the influence of Caravaggio's early paintings is evident.

Kazimir Malevich
Kiev 1878-St Petersburg, 1935

Founder of the Suprematist movement, Malevich was one of the principal points of reference for the emerging international tendency of abstractionism. In his case, the quest for an "absolute," nonfigurative form of expression entailed the use of purely pictorial means, only later going on to develop the relationship with Constructivism that many Western artists were finding in the same years through their links with the Bauhaus. In fact, critics have persuasively suggested that the legacy of Byzantine and Orthodox art played a considerable role in the birth of abstractionism in Russia.

After training in Moscow along Neo-Impressionist lines, Malevich came into contact with Larionov around 1907, and this opened him up to influences from abroad, ranging from the Fauves to Léger and from the Cubists to Italian Futurism.
A surprising capacity for the assimilation and reworking of these ideas renders the pictures he painted between 1910 and 1914 particularly fascinating, presenting as they do a catalogue of his highly personal themes and solutions. In 1915, vigorously asserting the "supremacy" of abstractionism in the arts, Malevich painted the symbolic *Black Square on a White Ground* (Russian Museum, St. Petersburg). This was followed, after a period of return to color, by the still

more rarefied *White on White* (1918, Museum of Modern Art, New York). After the Russian Revolution, Malevich became aware of the political significance of his art, drawing a parallel between the social and economic innovations of Communism and the new painting, free of academic rules and attentive to the development of modern technologies. So, from 1920 on, Malevich devoted more and more of his energy to teaching, taking on increasingly responsible posts until he was appointed director of the Institute for the Study of Artistic Culture in St. Petersburg. Though he now painted few pictures, Malevich was already one of the most important names in contemporary art: his works proved

particularly popular in Germany and the Netherlands. However, on the rise to power of Stalin Malevich's lofty ideas about the order of things were dismissed as a mystical and idle utopia. The official art of the Soviet regime went back to a nondescript and popular realism and Malevich (after serving time in prison for subversive activity in 1930) was forced to repudiate abstraction and call for a return to figurative painting. For at least two decades after his death one of the greatest exponents of abstract art was forgotten, and his rediscovery was one of the most sensational critical developments of the sixties.

Kazimir Malevich
Suprematism-Abstract Composition
1915
oil on canvas
31½ × 31½ in.
(80 × 80 cm)
Museum of Figurative Arts, Ekaterinberg

The painting takes its name from the movement founded by Malevich, one of the most interesting currents in avant-garde Russian art. Believing m the "supremacy" of pure form and geometry, Malevich composed arcane abstract scenes, in which flat and smooth elements are arranged on the surface of the picture.

Edouard Manet

Paris, 1832-1883

Raised in the traditional environment of a well–to–do bourgeois family, given a classical education, and groomed for a career in the navy, Manet obtained permission to devote himself to painting only on the condition that he pursue a regular course of academic studies. Thus he received an excessively restrictive formal training, within which he began to develop an at once rigorous and independent style of his own. In the fifties he made a thorough study of the masterpieces in the Louvre as well as repeated journeys to Italy, Flanders, the Netherlands, and Germany to see the paintings of the great artists of the past firsthand. Manet's profound artistic culture was based on a few fundamental sources of inspiration: Titian, Rembrandt, and, after an important visit to Spain, Goya and Velázquez. His contacts with Baudelaire and, more generally, he circles of literary Realism (Zola, Mallarmé) led him, from 1858 onward, to tackle subjects drawn from everyday life. The success of his picture *The Spanish Singer* (Metropolitan Museum of Art, New York), exhibited at the Salon of 1861, was followed by the scandalized reaction of the right-minded public and critics to paintings that they considered provocative and outrageous. The biggest fuss erupted over two large and fundamental canvases painted in 1863 (*Le Déjeuner sur l'Herbe* and *Olympia*, both now in the Musée d'Orsay, Paris), dominated by imposing female nudes and rendered even more "modern" by the fact that they were openly based on themes and compositions by Titian and Giorgione. This was one of the first "scandals" caused by an artist who was later to be regarded as one of the Impressionists. The strong outline that detaches the figures from the ground, the use of black, and the expressive force of the figures would all be reinforced by Manet's journey to Spain: his full-length portraits are out-and-out tributes to Velázquez, while the Spanish tradition inspired pictures of unexpected violence, such as the series devoted to bullfighting or the *Execution of Emperor Maximilian of Mexico*. During the seventies Manet had frequent contacts with the group of Impressionists. His palette grew lighter and he started to tackle subjects similar to those of other painters (Sunday trips along the banks of the Seine, scenes of cafés–chantants, waitresses in bars), but his style remained highly personal,

drawing on a large range of cultural references. For Manet the confrontation with the tradition of painting and the human figure (he was also a penetrating portraitist) always took precedence and his attention remained centered on form and composition.

Edouard Manet
Boy with Sword
1861
oil on canvas
51½ × 36¾ in.
(131.1 × 93.3 cm)
Metropolitan Museum of Art, New York

The Salon of 1861 brought Manet his first public success: with a refined feeling for classical painting, the painter presented a series of portraits of standing figures, mostly in Spanish costumes, directly inspired by Velázquez. The artist's greatness lay in his ability never to turn his back on the lesson of the past, while bringing it to life by a sense of realism and burning immediacy.

235

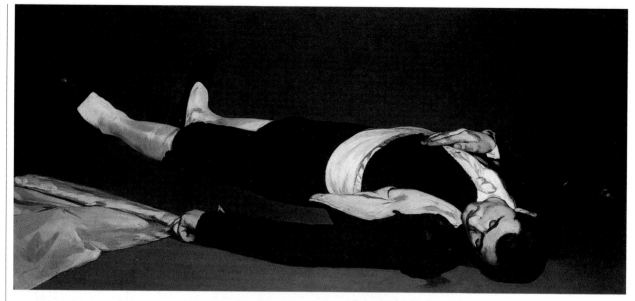

Above
Edouard Manet
The Dead Toreador
1865
oil on canvas, 30 × 60¼
in. (75.9 × 153.3 cm)
National Gallery,
Washington, D.C.

The painting is actually
only a fragment: the
upper part, representing
the bullfight, is now in
the Frick Collection in
New York. It was Manet
himself who, dissatisfied
with the composition,
split the picture in two.

Edouard Manet
Le Déjeuner sur l'Herbe
1863
oil on canvas, 82 × 104
in. (208 × 264 cm)
Musée d'Orsay, Paris

A celebrated and
controversial
masterpiece, it divided
the critics and public. It
marks a crucial point in
the history of art, a
deliberate turning away
from the schemes of
classical painting to
present a direct image of
nature and everyday life.

Andrea Mantegna

Isola di Carturo, Padua, 1431-
Mantua, 1506

The son of a humble carpenter
and initially trained as a craftsman,
Mantegna had the good fortune
to be accepted as an apprentice in the
eclectic workshop of Francesco
Squarcione in Padua, at the very time
when great Tuscan masters such as
Donatello and Paolo Uccello were
working in the city. From a very early
age Mantegna displayed a precocious
and "modern" talent oriented toward
the innovations in perspective and
classical monumentality. His career
developed rapidly. The frescoes in the
Ovetari chapel in Padua were followed
in 1451 by his marriage to Giovanni
Bellini's sister Nicolosia, a tie that was

also to become an artistic relationship
with the leading family of Venetian
painters. Mantegna's early period
ended with the spectacular altarpiece
for the church of San Zeno in Verona
(1456-1459), and in 1460 he moved to
Mantua to take up the position of
court painter. He was to live and work
in the city ruled by the Gonzaga
family from then until the end of his
life with one interval studying in
Rome (1489-1490). The master
performed the customary duties of a
court artist at Mantua, which included
the design of furniture and fittings,
and being responsible for the rulers'
"public image." Above all, he
succeeded in effecting a radical change
in taste from late Gothic decorative art
to Humanism and an emphasis on
archeology and perspective. *The*

Camera degli Sposi provides the most
complete and effective example of
Mantegna's style, which is marked by
superb draftsmanship. Conversely,
despite his relations with Giovanni
Bellini and subsequently with
Leonardo, Mantegna was never to
adopt—not even at an advanced age—
the techniques of tonal color and
sfumato, preferring his own clear,
infallible visual precision to the very
end. With very few exceptions,
Mantegna's works are no longer in
Mantua but have been dispersed like
the princely collections of the Italian
Renaissance. The great series of
tempera works depicting the *Triumph
of Caesar* (1488-1492) and
constituting the height of Mantegna's
classicism are now at Hampton Court
Palace. The Louvre owns the *Madonna*

della Vittoria (1496) and the two
extraordinary allegorical canvases
begun in 1497, which once hung
in Isabella Gonzaga's study. The
Pinacoteca di Brera has the grim *Dead
Christ*, one of the painter's last works.

Andrea Mantegna
The Gonzaga Court,
north wall
c. 1474
fresco and tempera
a secco
317 × 317¾ × 273 in.
(805 × 807 × 693 cm)
Camera degli Sposi,
Castello di San Giorgio,
Mantua

Franz Marc

Munich, 1880-Verdun, 1916

The art and life of Franz Marc are closely bound up with those of his friend August Macke, right up to the tragic fate of both men, killed in battle during the First World War. After studying philosophy and theology at the university in his native city, Marc moved to Paris where he came across the painting of Gauguin and the Nabis, whose love and sense of almost mystical reverence for nature he shared. In 1906 Marc embarked on the most characteristic phase of his painting: a painstaking study of animals. In 1910 he met August Macke, who had a similar taste for bright and transparent color. Along with Kandinsky, the two of them founded "Der Blaue Reiter", making a wholly original contribution to the movement. In fact Marc started out from a profound understanding of animal anatomy and then went on to paint them in a non–naturalistic, almost abstract way. The shapes of the animals, always recognizable, become part of a carefully modeled rhythm of lines, forms, and colors that freely expresses his feelings about the natural world. This tendency was further accentuated after 1912, through his contacts with Delaunay and Orphism. Enlisted as a soldier in 1914, he assembled an album of war drawings in the trenches, but this work was interrupted by his death in battle, at Verdun.

Franz Marc
Painting with Calves
1913-1914
oil on canvas
Neue Pinakothek,
Munich

Although able to convey the movements and attitudes of animals with great effectiveness, displaying a grasp of their anatomy and behavior worthy of a keen zoologist, Marc tended to place all the elements of the painting on the surface, fitting together areas of limpid color as in an old and radiant stained-glass window. The effect is comparable to the tonal gradations used in the Orphism of the Delaunays with whom Marc was in contact. The use of sweeping curves to link the various parts of the picture can also be associated with the Parisian movement of Orphism.

Simone Martini
Siena c. 1284-Avignon 1344

Simone Martini was a seductively refined artist of international importance. His genius lay in anticipating the developments that produced the courtly style of the International Gothic. If the parallel between Giotto and Dante can appear forced, the association of Simone Martini's name with Petrarch is historically and stylistically relevant. Both the painter and the poet spent long periods in Avignon, and there is an obvious connection between the erotic imagery of Petrarch's poetry and the lyrical sweetness of Simone Martini's painting. The 1317 *Maestà* in Siena's Palazzo Pubblico shows Simone's art as already mature. Immediately after finishing this first masterpiece, he went to Naples. In 1320 he painted the great polyptychs of Orvieto and Pisa, followed by the *Life of St. Martin* in the Lower Church in Assisi. This was his greatest achievement as a creator of narrative scenes. There has recently been controversy over the attribution of the famous *Guidoriccio da Fogliano at the Siege of Montemassi* (1328). Simone Martini balanced realistically solid individual detail against a fabulous background, as in the *Annunciation* (1333, Uffizi, Florence), one of the masterpieces of fourteenth-century Italian painting. Simone Martini spent his last years in Avignon, to which the popes had moved. Thanks chiefly to his work there, Avignon became a major center of International Gothic art.

Simone Martini
Annunciation
1333
wood panel,
104¼ × 120 in.
(265 × 305 cm)
Uffizi, Florence

This is his masterpiece and perhaps the greatest work of the International Gothic. Blazing gold surrounds the profiles of the two main characters, while a vase of lilies in the center adds an extra touch of elegance.

Masaccio

Tommaso di Giovanni Cassai
San Giovanni Valdarno (Florence),
1401-Rome, 1428

Despite his early death at the age of
twenty-seven, Masaccio was one of the
most innovative painters in the whole
history of art. All his works were
executed within the span of five short
years and must be seen in the dynamic
setting of the Florence of Brunelleschi
and Donatello. He followed the lead of
these artists of the previous generation
by abandoning the refined, dreamlike
late Gothic style in favor of an
innovative use of perspective and the
creation of solid, imposing figures.
His career started in the provinces
with a triptych for the church
of San Giovenale at Cascia di Reggello
(1422), and then developed in

Florence in close association with
Masolino da Panicale. They jointly
produced the *Madonna and Child with
St. Anne* in the Uffizi (c. 1424), and
commenced a cycle of frescoes
destined to alter the course of the
history of painting in the Brancacci
chapel in the church of Santa Maria
del Carmine. While Masolino adopted
a flowing, elegant style chracterized
by the use of glowing color, languid
poses, and appropriate classical
references, Masaccio concentrated on
the expressive power of strong figures
in urban or natural settings. This
marked a return, one century later,
to Giotto's approach, but with the
addition of the latest techniques
of representation in depth. These
elements are also evident in the works
he produced alone: the altarpiece with
a gold ground for the church of the

Carmelite Order in Pisa (1426), the
Madonna of Cardinal Casini in the
Uffizi, and the splendid *Trinity* fresco
in the church of Santa Maria Novella
in Florence (c. 1427). At the end of
1427 Masolino and Masaccio again
collaborated on a series of commissions
in Rome. Masaccio assisted Masolino
in executing the frescoes in the Branda
Castiglione chapel in the church
of San Clemente. He was preparing
to complete the wall decorations in
St. John Lateran, which had been left
unfinished on the death of Gentile
da Fabriano, but died in 1428 under
mysterious circumstances. The few
works left by this very young master
had a great impact on Florentine
painting and indicated a path that was
soon to be followed by artists such
as Paolo Uccello, Fra Angelico, and
Filippo Lippi.

Masaccio
Baptism of the Neophytes
rear wall, right of
window, second register
1424-1425
fresco
88½ × 63¾ in.
(225 × 162 cm)
Brancacci chapel, Santa
Maria del Carmine,
Florence

The celebrated
restoration of the
chapel, which brought
to light previously
unknown and well-
preserved areas of
painting such as the
decorative band visible
here, has clarified
Masaccio's role in the
work in the Brancacci
chapel. The apparent
contrast with Masolino,
more marked when the
painted surfaces were all
coated in grime, is now
seen to be less evident
because of the use of
very similar colors.
Compared to Masolino's
elegance, Masaccio
strikes a coarser, more
direct, and concrete
note. This sparing use of
descriptive elements in
order to focus on the
expressive power of the
human figures justifies
Vasari's description of
Masaccio as "*senza
ornato,*" without
ornamentation. He was
not interested in the
decorative aspect. At the
same time, however, he
truly emphasizes man's
physical and moral
dimension. The solemn
gravity of St. Peter's
gesture is juxtaposed to
the shivering neophyte
huddling in the cold,
and the kneeling youth
has the proportions of a
classical nude.
Masaccio's frescoes in
the Brancacci chapel
were to become
prototypes of Humanist
painting and influence
the works of Paolo
Uccello and Piero della
Francesca in the
following decades.

241

Masolino da Panicale

Tommaso di Cristofano Fini
Panicale in Valdelsa, 1383-
Florence, 1440

Masolino was a pupil of Ghilberti and, according to one tradition, Masaccio's teacher. His major works can be found from Florence to Lombardy, Umbria to Rome. Masolino managed to combine the decorative and fantastic tastes of late-Gothic art with the conquest of perspective. His scenes are imbued with warm light and delicate colors. Masolino made his appearance at the start of the 1420s with works in both Florence and Empoli. In 1424 the

Virgin and Child with St. Anne (Uffizi, Florence) marked the start of his partnership with Masaccio which culminated in the Brancacci chapel in Santa Maria del Carmine. In 1425 he broke off his work in Florence and left for Hungary in the train of Cardinal Branda Castiglione. In 1428 the Cardinal invited him to Rome to paint the frescoes in the private chapel of the church of San Clement's. The frescoes were dedicated to the *Scenes from the Life of St. Catherine of Alexandria*. Some of his panel paintings also date from his Roman years. In 1432, on the other hand, he produced a delightful fresco of the

Madonna and Child for the church of St. Fortunato in Todi in central Italy. Cardinal Castiglione summoned him again in 1435, this time to Castiglione Olona in Lombardy. Together with other major Tuscan artists he painted the frescoes in the Collegiate choir, some of the rooms in the Cardinal's palace and, most importantly, a spectacular section of the Baptistery.

Masolino da Panicale
Herod's Banquet
1435
fresco
Baptistery, Castiglione
Olona (Varese)

Long porticos of truly classical purity connect the three separate episodes. The descriptive details still seem rooted in the late-Gothic style, but the monumental scale of his work is already inspired by Renaissance classicism.

Henri Matisse
Le Cateau, 1869-Cimiez, 1954

An important role in Matisse's apprenticeship as a painter was played by his frequenting of the Parisian studio of Gustave Moreau, where he learned that color "had to be thought, dreamed, imagined." It was by following Moreau's example that Matisse abandoned the traditional principle of imitation in order to make creative use of color. Other significant impetuses in this direction, which would lead Matisse to banish from the canvas any element apart from pure color, came from the painters van Gogh and Gauguin, as well as from his encounter with Japanese woodcuts, Persian ceramics, Moorish textiles, and African art. He spent the summer of 1905 working at Collioure, together with André Derain. Returning to Paris, he exhibited his works at the Salon d'Automne in October, thereby launching what would come to be known as the Fauvist movement. This took the form of a Mediterranean response, based on light and color, to contemporary German Expressionism, founded essentially on the graphic line. The decisive moment in Matisse's career came in 1906 when he showed the *Le bonheur de vivre* at the Salon des Indépendants. The picture sparked a controversy in which Picasso intervened by painting *Les Demoiselles d'Avignon*, intended as a violent rebuttal of Matisse's work: an angular, harsh, almost monochromatic work, where the *Le bonheur de vivre* was curvilinear, exuberant, and brightly colored. At the end of the Fauvist experience, Matisse drew closer to Cubism, though he retained a brilliant, highly contrasting, and yet harmonious palette. His journeys to Morocco (1912-1913), the United States, and Tahiti (1930) were important. In his maturity his activity extended to embrace theatrical decoration, tapestries, ceramics, and even sculpture, to which Matisse had in fact devoted himself right from the beginning of his career, under the influence of Rodin. He produced important drawings and illustrations for literary works, such as the poems of Baudelaire and Mallarmé.

Henri Matisse
The Dessert, a Harmony in Red
1908-1909
oil on canvas
70¾ × 96¾ in.
(180 × 246 cm)
Hermitage, St. Petersburg

243

Henri Matisse
The Dance
1912
oil on canvas
75 × 45 in.
(190.5 × 114.5 cm)
Pushkin Museum,
Moscow

The panel of *The Dance* can be seen as a lyrical response to Picasso's *Les Demoiselles d'Avignon*. Like Picasso, Matisse reduces and simplifies the outlines of his figures, but unlike that of the Spanish artist, his color remains rich and brilliant. The motif of dancers in a ring, which first appeared in the *Bonheur de vivre*, was the artist's earliest attempt to depict figures in movement, introducing a dynamic element into the picture that seems to animate the surrounding space, whether it is that of an interior or a landscape.

Franz Anton Maulbertsch

Langerargen, 1724-Vienna, 1796

German by birth but Austro-Hungarian in terms of style and where he was active, Maulbertsch is one of the most interesting exponents of European Rococo. He trained in Vienna, where he assimilated Troger's teaching and admired Andrea Pozzo's bold style. Maulbertsch was an international artist, capable of appreciating the brilliant taste of the southern German courts and the rapid, fragmented, luminous brushstrokes of Venetian masters such as Sebastiano Ricci and Piazzetta. He made a particularly close study of Giambattista Tiepolo's works, and actually met the Venetian master during his stay at Würzburg. Tiepolo was a twofold source of inspiration for Maulbertsch, both for his impetuous style as an easel painter and for his decoration of vast spaces with light, airy frescoes. Aristocratic and imaginative, Maulbertsch had a brilliant career at court and with ecclesiastical patrons in Austria (attention should be drawn to the frescoes in the Piarist church in Vienna and the Hofberg in Innsbruck), Bohemia, Slovakia, and Hungary.

Franz Anton Maulbertsch
The Education of Mary
c. 1755
oil on canvas
23½ × 11¾ in.
(60 × 30 cm)
Kunsthalle, Karlsruhe

Maulbertsch's most characteristic work consists of easel paintings that display all the briskness and momentum of sketches, but are independent compositions in their own right. The subject, repeatedly painted in the history of art in the customary terms of delicate domestic intimacy, is treated by Maulbertsch as an opportunity for a highly imaginative work featuring a flight of angels, a handling of light that illuminates some parts but leaves others in shadow, and an all-enveloping sense of dynamism that is brilliantly controlled.

Melozzo da Forlì
Melozzo di Giuliano degli Ambrogi
Forlì, 1438-1494

Renowned in his own lifetime
for his great skill in perspective and
illusionism, as a painter Melozzo
da Forlì played a very significant role
in the development of Renaissance
painting in central and eastern Italy,
from the Marches to Rome. His early
work was in Forlì and was indebted to
Piero della Francesca. In 1469 he was
in Rome where he produced a
sacerdotal banner which is still in the
church of San Marco. In the 1470s
he was very busy at the cosmopolitan
court of Urbino, where he designed
a private study and the library for
Federico da Montefeltro. He returned
to Rome in 1475, this time to carry out
prestigious commissions. Honored
by Sixtus IV with the position of *pictor
papalis* (official Vatican painter),
between 1475-1477 he painted the
fresco decorations in the Apostolic
Library. All that remains is a noble
commemorative scene which is now
in the Vatican Gallery. He was then
employed by Giuliano della Rovere
(the future pope Julius II) to work on
refurbishing the church of SS. Apostoli.
He painted the frescoes in the apse
showing the *Redeemer and a Concert
of Angels*. Various fragments of this
ambitious composition can still be seen
in the Quirinal Palace and the Vatican
Gallery. In about 1484, and by now
backed up by his own efficient studio,
Melozzo was in Loreto to paint the
murals for the Treasury chapel at the
sanctuary. Nothing remains of his later
work which was carried out between
Forlì, Rome, and Ancona. In 1944 his
frescoes in the church of San Biagio in
Forlì were also destroyed by bombs.

Melozzo da Forlì
*Sixtus IV Appointing
Platina Prefect of the
Vatican Library*
1477
fresco (detached)
Pinacoteca Vaticana,
Vatican

This courtly scene of
great nobility provides
a quintessential image
of fifteenth-century
culture, not least because
it demonstrates the
relationship between
the literary and artistic
worlds, both nurtured
by great patrons.

Encapsulated in a space
with perfect perspective
which owes its rhythm
to the theories of Alberti,
the occasion depicted
is not without solemnity.
This is confirmed by the
long epigraph with its
perfect Latin characters.
Pope Sixtus IV
(who built the Sistine
chapel) is founding the
Vatican Library, putting
a famous Renaissance
scholar in charge of it.
The calm, noble
seriousness of the
characters recalls the style
of Piero della Francesca.

Hans Memling
Seligenstadt, c. 1440-Bruges, 1494

This Flemish artist, who played a leading role in Bruges in the second half of the century, was born in a small hamlet near Mainz and hence was of German origin. During his youth, Memling must have come into contact with the works of the Cologne School, whose elegant, refined interpretation of reality was to be the hallmark of all his own work. He moved to Flanders and served his apprenticeship in Rogier van der Weyden's workshop. When the latter died in 1464, Memling settled in the prosperous city of Bruges. The fact that he was not a member of the painters' guild suggests that he enjoyed a privileged position in the city's middle-class society, or that he had influential patrons. During his long career, the artist received no public commissions, but his clients came from the ecclesiastical sphere and the elite circles of court dignitaries, and powerful merchants and bankers. At a time when Petrus Christus's fame was beginning to decline, Memling filled an important gap with his extraordinary series of devotional paintings and portraits. His works can be regarded as the fruit of a refined and idealistic culture and won him immediate acclaim. He reworked the elements of the great Flemish tradition to create a measured, harmonious style where all tension and excess are replaced by calm, formal perfection. His magnificent realism does not seek to plumb the depths of the material world or to express deep emotion, but employs a masterly technique to create images revealing a universe more beautiful than the real one.

Hans Memling
Still Life with Jug of Flowers on a Rug
c. 1485-1490
oil on wood, 11½ × 9 in.
(29.2 × 22.5 cm)
Thyssen-Bornemisza
Collection, Madrid

This splendid still life is the reverse of a panel showing a young man in prayer before the Madonna. The small pottery vase stands on a valuable oriental rug in a niche.

Following page
Hans Memling
Wedding of St. Catherine
c. 1474-1479
panel
76¼ × 76¾ in.

(193.5 × 194.7 cm)
Memlingmuseum,
Bruges

The composition of this *sacra conversazione*

is symmetrical and monumental.
The clear perspective of the pictorial planes, the precise architectural elements, and the

arrangement of the saints around the Virgin's throne create a scene that focuses on the gestures of the Child and St. Catherine.

Anton Raphael Mengs

Aussig, 1728-Rome, 1779

A painter and theorist of great importance in the history of art, Mengs is rightly regarded as one of the founders of Neoclassicism or, to be more precise, as the leading figure in the phase of transition between the late Baroque and the changes brought about in art and culture by the Enlightenment. Trained by his father Ismael (a miniaturist at the Saxon court), Mengs spent his childhood and early youth between the Dresden of Augustus III of Saxony and Rome. During his travels in Italy, the young Mengs developed a passion for the study of archaeology and came under the spell of Raphael's painting. While such interests are hardly unheard of—similar tastes had been displayed a century earlier by Guido Reni and Poussin—in this case they constituted a theoretical stance intended as a radical alternative to the dynamic virtuosity and animated, but often excessive, style of Baroque art. Even a journey to Venice, where the great eighteenth-century school of Tiepolo was then developing, did nothing to change Mengs's mind. After settling in Rome, Mengs became the advocate of a return to a serene, intellectual form of art grounded in the classical rules of decorum, harmony, and composure, and imparted these precepts as director of the Accademia Capitolina. In 1755, the arrival in Rome of the philosopher and writer Winckelmann marked the beginning of a noble period devoted to the study and revival of ancient art. The fresco *Parnassus* on the ceiling of Villa Albani (1761) summarizes the return to Raphael and classicism. The spreading of Enlightenment ideas and aesthetics paved the way for a radical change in taste. In 1762, Mengs published the first edition of his treatise *Reflections on Beauty and Taste in Painting*, a fundamental theoretical study soon known throughout Europe, and he established himself as an outstanding cultural authority in the fields of art and ideas. His highly controlled and aristocratic frescoes for the royal palace in Madrid, where he worked for two long periods, gave the definitive *coup de grâce* to Tiepolo's creative exuberance and put forward a new model that ushered in the neoclassical era.

Anton Raphael Mengs
Glory of St. Eusebius
1757
fresco
Ceiling, church
of Sant'Eusebio, Rome

Adolf von Menzel
Wroclaw, 1815-Berlin, 1905

An artist of great significance in the German painting of the nineteenth century, Menzel is the perfect representative of Biedermeier culture and that bourgeois taste for a solid, concrete, and agreeable realism that was reflected in the literature and applied arts of the time. The son of a lithographer, Menzel was a self-taught genius. Working initially as an illustrator, he started to paint around the age of thirty, adopting the serene manner of the Berlin school of Realism. After the critical phase of the revolutionary upheavals of 1848, Menzel embarked on an official career that culminated in his appointment as professor of painting at the Berlin Academy. During the fifties his work acquired greater breadth and complexity, as he moved away from bourgeois interiors to paint vast compositions set in the open air. In 1867 he went to Paris, where he came into contact with the Impressionists, lightening his palette and painting the scenes of Parisian life that were beginning to meet with great success on the international market. Returning to Germany, Menzel spent the final part of his career as a painter investigating the world of work and industry, producing pictures of factories and steel mills with his customary sense of realism.

Adolf von Menzel
*Religious Service
at the Mission in the
Buchenhalle near Kösen*
1868
oil on canvas
28 × 22¾ in.
(71 × 58 cm)
Szépművészeti Múzeum,
Budapest

Menzel's dignified realism found precise echoes in the bourgeois tastes of Prussian culture in the second half of the nineteenth century, in close parallel with the novels of Theodor Fontane.

Quentin Metsys
Quinten Metsijs
Louvain, 1466-Antwerp, 1530

After training in his hometown, first learning the craft of his father Josse, a renowned blacksmith and clockmaker, and then in Dieric Bouts' workshop, Metsys embarked rather late on his career as a painter. He spent his youth, however, in the artistic climate of the last Flemish "primitives." Though his career was to lead him to be the leading exponent of new Antwerp painting, and to open the path toward the Italianate style of the early sixteenth century in the Netherlands, he was never to abandon completely the influences of the great tradition of van der Weyden and Memling. The small hammer that Metsys sometimes used as a symbol of his signature is linked to his early work as a blacksmith making artistic wrought-iron objects. Enrolled in the Antwerp Painters' Guild since 1491, Metsys soon became the leading exponent of the local school. He was frequently commissioned by the craft guilds of Antwerp and Louvain. During the first decade of the sixteenth century he made a journey to Italy, during which he must have visited Milan and Venice, and been especially interested in the art of Leonardo. His style became enriched by this experience and as a result of this introduction to Humanist culture, his intellectual interests broadened. In 1517, thanks to Pieter Gillis, he met Erasmus of Rotterdam and Sir Thomas More, while his friendship with Patinir and his contacts with Holbein, Lucas van Leyden, and Dürer became closer. The proof of his financial success can be seen from the fact that he bought and decorated a luxurious house in the center of Antwerp in 1521. His rather untimely death brought to a halt his flourishing career. Nonetheless, Metsys' works remained a longstanding and highly appreciated model in Antwerp; in fact, Rubens was to copy some of them a century later.

Quentin Metsys
*Portrait of Erasmus
of Rotterdam*
1517
panel, 22¾ × 71¾ in.
(58 × 45 cm)
Galleria Nazionale
d'Arte Antica, Rome

Following page
Quentin Metsys
*The Money Changer
and His Wife*
1514
panel
28 × 26¾ in.
(71 × 68 cm)
Musée du Louvre, Paris

This very famous signed and dated painting was imitated and copied several times during the sixteenth century. An overt tribute to the tradition of the Flemish "primitives," it echoes the precisely detailed composition of *St. Eligius* by Petrus Christus. Unlike the fifteenth-century model, however, Metsys does not depict a religious subject but creates a lively, realistic, and direct image.

Michelangelo
Holy Family
(Doni Tondo)
1504-1505
tempera on panel
diam. 47¼ in.
(120 cm)
Uffizi, Florence

This is the only completed panel that is entirely the work of Michelangelo. The circular panel was a characteristic of Florentine painting, and Michelangelo followed the tradition. Executed for the family whose name it takes, the painting depicts the Virgin and Child with St. Joseph, with St. John in the middle ground, and a disturbing series of nude figures in the background. The clarity and precision of the execution are in deliberate contrast to Leonardo's sfumato. The complicated, turning poses of the figures, and the relations between them constitute the premises for the developments in Tuscan art during the sixteenth century.

Michelangelo Buonarroti

Caprese Arezzo, 1475-Rome, 1564

The long life and titanic oeuvre of Michelangelo Buonarroti represent the most elevated and moving synthesis of the Renaissance. As a young man, Michelangelo shared its hopes and successes; in his maturity, he led its developments in various fields of art, from painting to architecture, poetry, and sculpture, which he was to consider throughout his life the most direct expression of his soul. Finally, as an old man, he witnessed the collapse of the Renaissance ideals, and depicted human destiny with terrifying, dramatic lucidity. After studying in the refined atmosphere of the court of Lorenzo the Magnificent, Michelangelo divided his time between Florence and Rome. Year after year, his style continued to develop and change as he sought new forms of expression, to the extent that he was well in advance of his time, and became a keystone and yardstick for the whole of modern culture. His architectural achievements (like the dome of St. Peter's and the Capitoline Square) were fundamental to the birth of Roman Baroque, while his marble sculptures still remain a model. The recently restored frescoes in the Sistine chapel continue to be one of the greatest masterpieces in the entire history of art. Michelangelo is a perfect example of the versatile artist, capable of achieving the highest results in different techniques and forms. His natural inclination was, however, to marble sculpture, which he tackled "by removing the superfluous." In the following celebrated lines of poetry, he describes his state of mind as he stands before a block of rough marble, freshly hewn from the quarries in the Apuan Alps: "The excellent artist has no concept / that a block of marble does not contain within itself / together with the superfluous, and only this is touched / by the hand that obeys the intellect." In other words, the hand and the chisel simply follow the directions of the intellect to eliminate the superfluous and free the idea contained within the marble. The evolution of Michelangelo's art can be clearly seen if we observe the way he treated the surface of his sculptures. His early works (like the *Pietà* in the Basilica of St. Peter's in Rome) are precise and polished, with soft drapery. Later, he gradually tended to make the "skin" of the figures less smooth, leaving rough, grainy areas. In his last works, he chose not to polish the surface at all, and even left some areas deliberately "unfinished," using a technique similar to that adopted in painting, around the same time, by Titian.

Michelangelo
Stories of the Creation
general view
of the ceiling
1508-1512
fresco
511¾ × 1417½ in.
(13 × 36 cm)
Sistine chapel, Vatican

Michelangelo designed
the composition of this
immense fresco as a
celebration of divine
creation and the beauty
of the human body.
The lunettes above
the windows contain
the series of frescoes
depicting the genealogy
of Christ, while the four
large corner lunettes
depict scenes from the
Old Testament. On the
ceiling itself are the
magnificent, intensely
expressive figures of the
Prophets and the *Sibyls*,
while the central
portion is divided
into nine rectangles
containing *Scenes from
Genesis*; the smaller
rectangles are flanked
by naked athletic
figures.

Michelangelo
Last Judgment, rear wall
1537-1541, fresco
539½ × 480¼ in.
(13.7 × 12.2 cm)
Sistine chapel, Vatican

The *Last Judgment* was
begun on October 31,
1541, under the eye
of Pope Paul III, and
became one of the most
astounding and
controversial works in the
history of art. Freeing
himself from traditional
canons, Michelangelo
created this intensely
compelling image. This
is the *Dies irae*, almost the
opposite of the *Creation*
scenes painted on the
Sistine chapel ceiling,
though the gesture made
by the figure of Christ the
Judge dividing the elect
from the damned is very
similar to that of God the
Father as he divides the
earth from the waters.
Against a limpid sky,
the dynamic Christ is the
focus of an exuberant
scene with over four
hundred figures. An
astonishing mass of
bodies, nearly all of them
naked, is suspended
between Heaven and Hell,
in a terrifying confusion
in which the presence
of a superior controlling
intellect can, however,
be perceived. There is no
longer anything heroic
about the nudes; they
are the shadows of men
terrified, battered,
deafened by the sound
of trumpets. In the Hell
scenes we can clearly see
the influence of the
Divine Comedy, but
Michelangelo's vision
is almost the opposite
of Dante's. The judgment
overwhelms both the
flesh and the spirit.
The Humanist man
of the early Renaissance,
the very man that
Michelangelo had
celebrated in the *Nudes*
on the ceiling, is now
crushed, finished.
He no longer has any
illusions.

John Everett Millais
Southampton, 1829-London, 1896

A member of the Pre-Raphaelite Brotherhood, he was one of the movement's most gifted exponents and his works quickly gained the favor of the critics and public. Between 1850 and 1860 Millais painted some of the most significant of all Pre-Raphaelite works, such as *Ophelia*, a picture of the Shakespearean heroine that was shown at the annual exhibition of the Royal Academy of Arts in London in 1852. Glaring contradictions soon emerged within the group, but Millais was able to fuse the romantic medievalism of Rossetti with the hyperrealism of Hunt, with the common intent of challenging academic art. The following year, however, he was elected an associate member of the aforementioned academy in London and entered the painting establishment. As the Pre-Raphaelite Brotherhood broke up, Millais, relying on the popularity he had already attained and attracted by the idea of making easy money, rapidly gave up the narrative genre and the group's rigid and severe technique to paint sentimental subjects and society portraits. From the sixties onward he produced pictures in decidedly Victorian taste, achieving economic success and greater popularity than his colleagues, who had remained faithful to the principles of the group even after its dissolution. In 1863 he was made a full member of the Royal Academy and in 1896, the year of his death, received its highest accolade when he was appointed its president.

John Everett Millais
Ophelia
1852
oil on canvas
30 × 43¾ in.
(76 × 111 cm)
Tate Britain, London

The protagonist of this moving picture, inspired by one of Shakespeare's plays, is Ophelia, depicted at the moment of her suicide, a desperate gesture to which she is driven by the apparent madness of her beloved Hamlet. Not just the subject but even the flowers and plants, reproduced with botanical accuracy, are drawn from the text of the play, where the willow is associated with abandoned love, the nettle with sorrow, and the daisy with innocence. It is said that, to make the picture as realistic as possible, the model Elizabeth Siddal had to pose in a tub filled with water heated by oil lamps from below. She became seriously ill as a result.

Jean-François Millet
Gruchy 1814-Barbizon, 1875

Raised in the country, Millet celebrated the simple and strong morality of rural life in epic, almost mystical tones, contrasting it with the confused and profane immorality of the city. Moving from Brittany to Paris in 1837, he studied the paintings in the Louvre at length, drawing inspiration from them for portraits and mythological pictures. His meeting with Daumier led him to devote himself to themes of social concern and his success was based on the presumed social and political messages of his scenes of peasant life.

In 1848 Millet settled permanently in Barbizon, on the edge of the forest of Fontainebleau, in close proximity to the landscape painters of the local school but not directly linked with them. Millet's most characteristic work dates from the fifties: this was the period in which he painted his large and famous pictures of peasants: workers in the fields are glorified by compositions in which they are presented as heroic figures charged with pathos. From 1863 onward, following the example set by Théodore Rousseau, Millet too turned his attention to landscape, while in his later works the themes are imbued with Symbolistic values.

Jean-François Millet
The Angelus
1858-1859
oil on canvas
33¾ × 43¾ in.
(86 × 111 cm)
Musée du Louvre, Paris

A break from work in the fields for prayer inspired Millet to paint a picture of contemplative suspense. The image, which was to become famous and was often copied or parodied, clearly marks the point of contact between the Realism of the mid nineteenth century and the subsequent mystical Symbolism of the Nabis.

Jean-François Millet
Spring, 1868-1873
oil on canvas, 34 × 43¾ in. (86 × 111 cm)
National Gallery, Washington, D.C.

Joan Miró

Barcelona, 1893-Palma, Majorca, 1983

Miró's love for Catalonia, the land of his birth, was a prime source of inspiration in his work. This tie is particularly evident in the early phase of his career, strongly influenced by recent developments in European art, from Cézanne to the Fauves, Expressionists, Cubists, and Futurists. Moving to Paris in 1919, he frequented Dadaist circles and events, meeting Picasso and Tzara. In 1921 he made friends with André Masson and came into contact with the Surrealist writers Artaud, Eluard, Aragon, and Péret. He ceased making any further attempt at representation in his painting and developed a lyrical abstraction based on carefully considered graphic signs, sometimes disturbing and at others joyful, which expressed the impulses of his memory

and unconscious. It was in this period that he painted works like *Harlequin's Carnival* (1924-1925), in which his highly personal interpretation of Surrealism, characterized by a fabulous vision of the world, is evident. In 1928 the masterpieces of Dutch seventeenth-century painting, seen on a visit to the Netherlands, inspired the series of *Dutch Interiors*, in which forms defined by contrasting colors or the same black line used to enclose images and geometric shapes and, at the same time, reconstruct them, stand out against a flat background. After the outbreak of the Spanish Civil War in 1936 and his enforced exile, his work grew darker and less monumental. This was the period of his *papiers collés*, with insertions of material, and the gouaches of the series *Constellations* (1940-1941). The latter, all of the same format, represent an extension of the process of deconstruction to which the

artist subjected the system of signs that he had himself created. This happened at a time when he was in close contact with Klee, though where Klee was sinking and exploring the depths, he was rising to the surface. In 1954 the Venice Biennale awarded him its international prize for graphic art, one of Miró's many fields of interest. Two years later he went to live in the house-cum-studio designed for him at Palma on Majorca by the architect José Luis Sert. He developed closer ties with the United States, where he received the Guggenheim Prize in 1959. In 1966 major retrospectives were dedicated to him in Japan (Tokyo and Kyoto) and the influence of Zen and the tradition of calligraphy induced him to eliminate any residue of narrative or aesthetic elements from his pictures, in a quest for essentiality. When he died in Palma tributes were paid to him all over the world.

Joan Miró
Harlequin's Carnival
1924-1925
oil on canvas
26 × 36¾ in.
(66 × 93 cm)
Albright-Knox Gallery,
Buffalo

He fills the transfigured space of his studio with natural and symbolic elements, in a fertile blend of the figurative and the abstract. Motifs with obvious echoes of Bosch, are reduced to graphic signs and float to the surface of the painting. Two serpentine forms, one white and the other black, intersect in the middle of the picture.

Amedeo Modigliani

Livorno, 1884-Paris, 1920

The son of a Tuscan man and a Frenchwoman, Modigliani was trained at academies in Italy (Florence and then Venice). However, he spent the whole of his short career as a painter in Paris, the city that he started to frequent in 1905 and where he moved permanently in 1909. Even in the similarity of sound between his French nickname Modi and the word *maudit*, Modigliani embodies the figure of the "accursed" artist, constantly in search of a satisfactory form of expression that is always out of reach. Living in one of the poorer quarters of Paris, among the crumbling buildings of Montparnasse, and steeped in the fumes of drugs and alcohol Modigliani turned out to be one of the greatest and most poetic artists of the early twentieth century. His conscious acceptance of a continuity with an age-old artistic tradition of the translation of feelings and emotions into lines and volumes places Modigliani firmly within the history of Italian art. His Italian—or rather Tuscan—training is manifest in the absolute rigor of his drawing and his emphasis on the human figure. Although thoroughly familiar with the Cubists, the artist from Livorno was never particularly attracted to the rationality of their vision. Influenced, if anything, by the synthetic simplicity of African sculpture, the forceful brushwork of Toulouse-Lautrec, and the works of Constantin Brancusi, Modigliani for several years limited his output of paintings to concentrate on sculpture. As some well-known stories about his life indicate, Modigliani had a difficult relationship with the medium of sculpture. At the urging of the poet and art dealer Leopold Zborowski, he returned to painting and from 1915 until his death in 1920 at the age of only thirty-six (followed a few days later by the suicide of his despairing wife) produced some three hundred oils, almost all of them portraits. The unmistakable elongation of his figures (Modigliani's necks have become proverbial) enhances the solitary and supple elegance of the images, while the expressions are rendered with a penetrating simplicity. Inclined by nature to hold aloof from avant-garde currents or movements, Modigliani remains a great and isolated figure. His work gave rise to no school, even though it was comparable in its power to what was being produced by the artists of various nations who had decided to converge on Paris in the same years.

Amedeo Modigliani
Gypsy with Her Child
1918
oil on canvas
42¼ × 26½ in.
(116 × 73 cm)
National Gallery,
Washington, D.C.

The exceptional control over form, achieved with an impeccable line of classical nobility, never detracts from the inward intensity of expression of Modigliani's figures, conveyed through little gestures, details of dress, and subtle but touching hints of personality. Modigliani's portraits are not frozen and insensitive idols, but people with unique and moving stories.

Right
Amedeo Modigliani
Red Nude
1917
oil on canvas
21¾ × 33½ in.
(60 × 92 cm)
Private collection, Milan

One of Modigliani's most intense nudes, it was exhibited in 1918 at Berthe Weill's gallery in Paris, where his friend Leopold Zborowski had organized the artist's first one-man show. Placed provocatively in the window facing onto the street, the painting was immediately confiscated by the police, who considered it indecent.

Amedeo Modigliani
Large Nude
1913-1914
oil on canvas
26½ × 42¼ in.
(73 × 116 cm)
Museum of Modern Art, New York

For a long time Modigliani's pictures of nude women were considered simplistically (and in vulgarly reductive fashion) "pornographic." In point of fact, they are among the few images in Western art that can truly be described as "erotic." Modigliani presents the outlines of the female body with the peerless refinement of a tradition of drawing rooted in Tuscan history, communicating a real and pulsating sensuality.

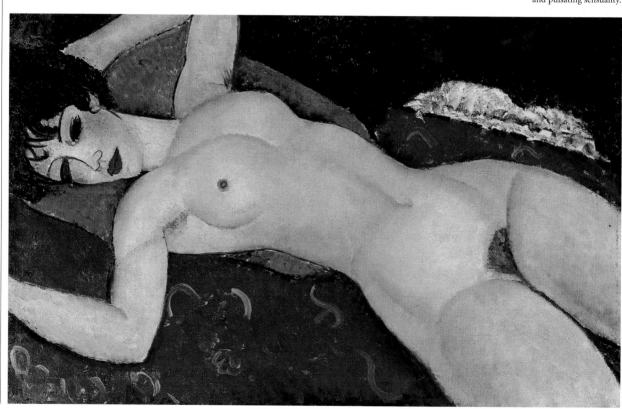

Piet Mondrian
Composition A
1919
oil on canvas
36 × 36¼ in.
(91.5 × 92 cm)
Galleria Nazionale
d'Arte Moderna, Rome

The painting, of
particular intensity and
richness, dates from tbe
period of collaboration
between Mondrian
and Theo van Doesburg.
The two Dutch artists
founded the magazine
De Stijl, "The Style,"
laying the theoretical
foundations for
geometric
and constructivist
abstractionism.

Piet Mondrian

Amersfoort, 1872-New York, 1944

The son of a strict Calvinist teacher (his name should actually be written Mondriaan), Piet was introduced to art by his uncle Frits, who painted agreeable landscapes in the Impressionist tradition. Mondrian's early activity, carried out chiefly in Amsterdam, comprised still lifes, landscapes, and academic studies in the late nineteenth-century mold. To earn a living, the young Mondrian made copies of old paintings in the Rijksmuseum and illustrations for books and treatises. Around 1901, deeply shocked by the spectacle of the bullfights he saw in

Spain, Mondrian underwent a sort of spiritual crisis which induced him to go and live by himself in the countryside, seeking a supreme order, a pure and concise set of rules. His landscapes were gradually stripped of their nineteenth-century Naturalism. Between 1907 and 1908 he came into contact with the Fauves and Munch through van Dongen, but his first experiments with a new style, exhibited at Amsterdam in 1909, met with violent criticism. Mondrian then moved to Paris, where he made a passionate study of Cubist decomposition, concentrating on the essentiality of the straight line. He painted his first canvases entitled simply *Composition*. In 1914 he went back to

the Netherlands and the outbreak of the First World War made it impossible for him to return to Paris for four years. In his enforced isolation, Mondrian moved away from Cubism: the paintings of these years consisted of a sequence of mathematical signs ("plus" and "minus") laid out on the surface of the canvas, with no depth. In 1917 Mondrian founded the movement De Stijl with the artist van Doesburg and in the same year painted his first pictures made up of blue, yellow, and red rectangles on a white ground, wholly divorced from any reference to reality. From 1920 onward Mondrian's work became one of the poles of the international debate over

Constructivism and the painter moved closer to the themes of the Bauhaus. After his lozenge-shaped pictures of the twenties, Mondrian began to insert more and more prominent elements, such as vertical double black lines. The Second World War induced him to leave Paris for London and then New York. Here, inspired by the soaring skyscrapers and the rhythms of jazz, Mondrian abandoned the continuous black line, replacing it by a series of small colored squares and rectangles. Mondrian died of pneumonia in 1944, just as the Allies were beginning to win the war, and it was to this prospect that he dedicated his last, unfinished masterpiece, *Victory Boogie Woogie*.

263

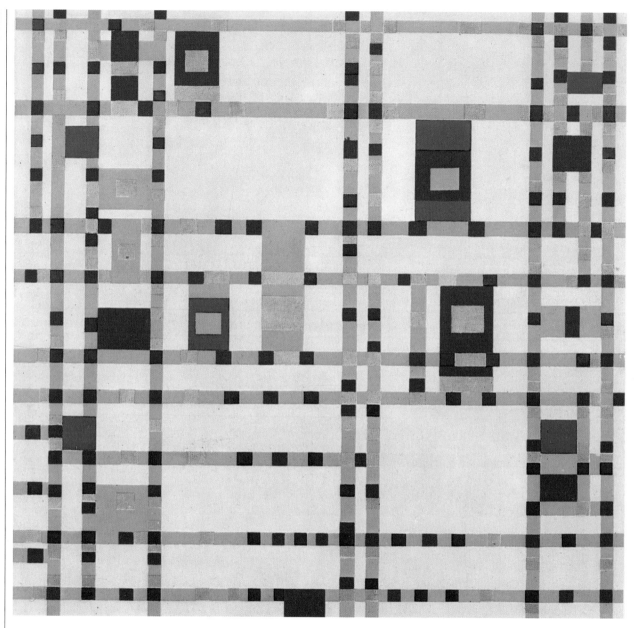

Piet Mondrian
Broadway Boogie Woogie
1942-1943
oil on canvas, 50 × 50 in.
(127 × 127 cm)
Museum of Modern Art,
New York

Only at the end of his
career did Mondrian
introduce a substantial
change into his
painting. Stimulated by
the vitality of New York,
where he had taken
refuge during the
Second World War, the
Dutch artist substituted
a succession of small
colored squares
and rectangles for his
previous straight black
lines. This imparted
a driving and joyful
rhythm to his pictures.

Claude Monet
Paris, 1840-Giverny, 1926

The youth of the painter who was destined to define the character and even the name of Impressionism was marked by a series of important encounters: first of all with the landscapist Eugène Bondin, from whom he imbibed a taste for painting the sea and water in general, and then, on his return to Paris in 1859, with Pissarro and the art of Courbet. After a first period devoted to landscape painting *en plein air*, Monet started to frequent Gleyre's studio, where he met his fellow students Renoir, Bazille, and Sisley. The friendship shared by these artists led to the birth of a movement of new ideas and passions. In the wake of the controversy aroused by Manet's *Déjeuner sur l'Herbe* in 1863, inspired by Renaissance art, Monet responded in 1865 with a painting of the same subject. This was followed by another entitled *Women in the Garden* (1866, Musée d'Orsay, Paris), in which the scheme of composition and above all the resplendent light and color invite us to "go out" of the museum and open ourselves to the delights of nature. Walks along the banks of the Seine prompted Monet to study the effects of light reflected on the water, making delicate use of colored shadows and combining complementary colors. Without resorting to a "manifesto" or theoretical declarations, Monet was laying the foundations for a new movement in art, Impressionism. His painting *Impression: Sunrise* (1872, Musée Marmottan, Paris) gave the name "Impressionists" to the artists who took part in the exhibition held in the studio of the photographer Félix Nadar in 1874. The location was no coincidence: the relationship between Monet's painting and photography is very important, if you consider the way light "impresses" the photographic plate. During the seventies and over the following decade Monet alternated scenes of Parisian life with increasingly deserted landscapes, continuing his research into the effects of color. The artist's relationship with nature, passionately experienced through the filter of color, became predominant when Monet decided to leave Paris for the country, moving to Giverny. Around 1890 Monet tried to organize his emotional reactions into groups of subjects, his famous "series," including those of Rouen Cathedral (1892-94), the banks of the Thames (1900), and the lily pond in his garden at Giverny. Monet painted this last group of canvases during the long years of his old age, from 1909 to his death in 1926.

Claude Monet
Women in the Garden
1866-1867
oil on canvas, 84¾ ×
100½ in. (205 × 255 cm)
Musée d'Orsay, Paris

The masterpiece of Monet's early career it marks the beginning of Impressionism. The controversy stirred by Manet's painting *Le Déjeuner sur l'Herbe* had given rise to a debate over the "museum" and "nature": he responded with freshness of color and light, clearing the way for a new conception of painting.

Claude Monet
The Promenade
1865
oil on canvas, 36½ ×
27¼ in. (93 × 68.9 cm)
National Gallery,
Washington, D.C.

This is a preliminary sketch for the group on the left of the *Déjeuner sur l'Herbe*. The man is the artist Frédéric Bazille, a fellow student of Monet's and one of the founders of Impressionism. Bazille's career was brought to a tragic end in 1870, when he was killed during the Franco-Prussian War.

Claude Monet
*The Terrace
at Sainte-Adresse*
1866
oil on canvas
35¾ × 51¼ in.
(90.5 × 130 cm)
Metropolitan Museum
of Art, New York

Thanks to this painting,
the summer resort
of Sainte-Adresse has
become one of the
landmarks in the history
of art. With all the
immediacy of the
"impression," Monet
shows us the carefully
tended flowers of this
terrace by the sea, while
steamers belch smoke
on the horizon. Once
again, however, the
freedom of composition
and color is
underpinned by an
artistic intelligence
of great refinement: the
whole painting, in fact,
is based on harmonies
of white, blue, and red,
the colors of the French
flag fluttering overhead.

Claude Monet
*Saint-Germain
l'Auxerrois*
1866
oil on canvas
32 × 39 in.
(81 × 99 cm)
Nationalgalerie, Berlin

The move from rural
landscapes to urban
views of Paris over
the course of the sixties
was a decisive stage
in the development
of Impressionism.
Previously, in fact, the
country scenes painted
en plein air by Monet
and his companions
(Renoir, Sisley, Bazille)
were only a slight
departure from a
tradition that had been
inaugurated by Corot
and the landscapists of
the Barbizon School.
Courageously shifting
his attention from the
countryside to Paris,
Monet maintained the
same freshness and
freedom in the handling
of light and color,
ushering in a new genre
that immediately
attracted other artists
and was to prove highly
successful over the
following years.

Luis de Morales
Badajoz, c. 1510-1586

His training must have taken place in Seville, following the Lombard currents imported into Spain during the first decades of the sixteenth century. In fact, his style is strongly influenced by Italian, and particularly Lombard, elements, as can be seen in the soft rendering of Leonardesque chiaroscuro, which suggests that the artist spent some time in Italy. Flemish art was also a crucial formative influence, leading him to accentuate the poignant expressions of the figures in his *Ecce Homo* and *Madonna and Child* paintings, thus anticipating in this mystic exaltation the Spanish art of the seventeenth century. He finds in Mannerism, expressed in tormented forms, in the arbitrary use of color, in livid tones, and black shadows, an effective means of communicating that mysticism that reveals him to be a fellow countryman of the great Spanish mystics. Summoned to court by Philip II, his stay there was short, perhaps because his popular style was not in keeping with the king's refined tastes. Despite the fact that he was acclaimed as one of the major artists of his day and called "*el divino*," because of the idealized mysticism of his works, Luis de Morales died in poverty. However, the enormous popularity of his oeuvre spread far and wide an iconography that was to have a great influence on seventeenth-century Spanish religious painting.

Luis de Morales
The Nazarene
1566
panel
Colegio del Patriarca, Valencia

In his maturity the artist devoted himself to half-length, deathly pale figures depicted with accentuated pathos, which gained him great popularity. Executed for Bishop Juan de Ribera, who greatly admired the artist, this painting, inspired by a work on a similar theme by Sebastiano del Piombo, is held by the Colegio del Patriarca, founded by Juan de Ribera in 1586, after he left the bishop's see of Badajoz.

267

Giorgio Morandi
Bologna, 1890-1964

One of the great figures in Italian painting in the twentieth century, Giorgio Morandi was a truly exceptional figure. He was a solitary painter, remote from any movement, who had little contact with any other artist. Morandi scarcely ever went anywhere other than Bologna and Grizzana, the tiny town in the Apennines where he spent his summers. Nevertheless, in his early work it is possible to pick out a thread that runs from his awareness of Cézanne's work through contacts with the Futurists and on to his approval of the Metaphysical painters. But from 1920 onwards his research centered on a handful of everyday subjects (by preference still lifes with bottles or landscapes) which he continuously reworked as he went deeper and deeper into his themes. In essence, Morandi's creative process did not need new subject matter. His was a completely inner intellectual journey which used patient contemplation to analyze the consistency, rhythm, surroundings, reflections, and delicate chromatic tones of objects. From the point of view of style, we should note how he moved on from his paintings of the Metaphysical period, typified by geometrical draughtsmanship and layers of shadow, to a progressive accumulation of forms. In his later works his brushwork was broader and thicker.

Giorgio Morandi
Still Life with a Brioche
1920
canvas
19½ × 20½ in.
(49.5 × 52 cm)
Kunstsammlung Nordrhein-Wesfalen, Düsseldorf

Angelo Morbelli
Alessandria, 1853-Milan, 1919

The recent critical revaluation of Morbelli, and the notable increase in the value of his works on the international art market, do justice to one of the most interesting Italian artists of the last two centuries. Without resorting to literary symbolism or paternalistic pieties, Morbelli set out to draw attention to the dramatic human and social problems of post-unification Italy. His training at the Brera Academy in Milan was influenced by late Romantic realism. He immediately started to paint pictures inspired by the themes of modern life and progress, such as the *Stazione Centrale* now in the Galleria d'Arte Moderna, Milan. Around 1890 Morbelli joined the group of Divisionists, adapting the technique to subjects intended to denounce injustice, with particular regard to the life of farm laborers and the loneliness and squalor of the charitable old people's home in Milan. Toward the end of his life, when the new style of the Futurists began to spread, Morbelli devoted himself chiefly to landscape painting, without abandoning the Divisionist technique. During the most intense period of his career, corresponding to the last decade of the century, Morbelli's work reached a level on a par with the finest examples of late nineteenth-century European art. Few other painters were able to interpret the themes of social deprivation, old age, and solitude with as much empathy and such freedom from rhetoric. The dusty light of his pictures, handled with great sensitivity, can be linked directly with Seurat's painting.

Angelo Morbelli
In the Rice Field
1898-1901
oil on canvas, 72 × 51¼ in.
(183 × 130 cm)
Museum of Fine Arts,
Boston

The Lombard painter devoted some of his finest works to the theme of the *mondine*, the young women who spent hours and hours in the water planting and harvesting rice. The precedent set by Millet is clearly discernible, but Morbelli dispenses with the aura of mysticism that made the scenes of the late Romantic French painter all too literary, even idealized. Morbelli was far more interested in social criticism of undeniably harsh working conditions.

269

Gustave Moreau
Paris, 1826-1898

With the encouragement of his family, and in particular his father Lonis Moreau, a Neoclassical architect, he decided on a career in art. In 1846 he was admitted to the Ecole des Beaux-Arts in Paris, but the decisive influence on his formation came from the journey he made to Italy. Between 1857 and 1859 he visited Rome, Florence, Milan, Venice, and Naples, collecting material for the future: drawings, watercolors, and copies of works from antiquity and by the primitives and Renaissance painters. In Rome he attended figure classes at Villa Medici, the seat of the Academy of France, explored churches and ancient ruins, and studied the works of Leonardo, Raphael, and Correggio. But the real revelation of his stay in Italy was the Venetian painter Carpaccio, who was little appreciated at the time. Moreau was fascinated by the grace, charm, and purity of his pictures and, above all, by their Venetian tonality. In order to study Carpaccio, he spent three months in Venice. He started to be successful in 1864, when he exhibited *Oedipus and the Sphinx* at the Salon. The powerful symbolism of the painting fascinated the emperor's cousin, Prince Napoleon,

who bought it. The following year the artist received the official seal of approval: one of his paintings shown at the Salon was acquired by the State. Yet the critics were perplexed by his work and his large canvases, for the most part ignored by dealers and collectors, did not meet with the public's approval. Moreau, greatly disturbed by the violent events of the Franco-Prussian War, decided to undergo treatment at the spa of Néris-les-Bains, which specialized in the cure of nervous disorders. When he recovered, he dedicated himself with new energy to his work and it was in these years that his style reached its peak: the figures are imbued with a strong symbolic charge, the naturalism is overwhelmed by the delirious fantasy of the whole, the chiaroscuro fades into golden shadows, and the representation is overlaid with a mesh of arabesques. Pictures like *Salome, Galatea, The Apparition,* and *The Unicorns* were destined to shape the taste of an entire generation, influencing the Decadent Movement. In his maturity the artist began to keep records of his works, in the form of tracings, drawings, and replicas in oil or watercolor, nursing the idea of turning his house into a museum, which is what he did in 1895.

Gustave Moreau
The Unicorns
c. 1885
oil on canvas
45¼ × 35½ in.
(115 × 90 cm)
Musée Moreau, Paris

Here history and myth are fused in a suggestive way: a pattern of arabesques is superimposed on the colored parts, filled with delicate shades, and the end result is a conscious and deliberately unfinished effect, lending an unusual transparency and freshness to the painting.

Gustave Moreau
The Apparition
1876
oil on canvas
56 × 40¼ in.
(142 × 103 cm)
Musée Moreau, Paris

A characteristic feature of his painting is the personal blend of biblical themes and elements drawn from mythology. Here, at the center of the composition, we see the decapitated head of the Baptist surrounded by a halo of light to signify that his thoughts and words will go on living after his death. The female figure on the left-hand side creates an atmosphere that is sensual and mystical.

Berthe Morisot

Bourges, 1841-Paris, 1895

A highly gifted and extremely sensitive painter, she was one of the most diligent and consistent participants in the group of Impressionists and their exhibitions. Entering Corot's studio along with her sister Edma in 1862, she served a long apprenticeship, working chiefly on landscapes painted directly from life. Eventually she started to show a few works at the Paris Salons. In 1868 she met Manet (she was later to marry his brother) and came into contact with the Impressionists. From that moment on Berthe Morisot's painting underwent a marked change; in addition to landscapes she began to depict domestic interiors, figures from everyday life, aspects of reality, and the typical activities of women. The quiet and subtle tone of Morisot's pictures brought a light and yet penetrating note into the work of the Impressionists. From 1875 up until her death, Morisot kept faith with the fundamental characteristics of Impressionism, while gradually inserting a greater dignity into her compositions.

Berthe Morisot
The Mirror
1876
oil on canvas
30 × 2½ in.
(76 × 54 cm)
Thyssen-Bornemisza
Collection, Madrid

Morisot was a painter of great importance within the Impressionist movement. In contrast to the joyful and animated work of Renoir and Degas the painter concentrated on moments of tenderness, silence, and intimacy. Many of her pictures represent domestic interiors, in which she repeatedly portrayed her sister and other relatives. Her refined technique and suffused intimacy anticipate the work of Vuillard and Bonnard.

271

Giovan Battista Moroni

Albino, Bergamo, 1520/24-Albino, 1575

Moroni was one of the greatest, albeit the shyest, portrait painters of the sixteenth century. Recent critical work has highlighted his abundant production of religious paintings and altarpieces which developed the ideas originated by Renaissance painters of the Brescia school. Nevertheless, the expressive power of his portraits is sufficient to classify Moroni as a specialist. After serving his apprenticeship with Moretto in Brescia, he spent nearly all his career in and around Bergamo, where he continued Lotto's tradition. The only deviance to this were two periods spent in Trent (1548 and 1551) when the Council of Trent was in session. On both occasions Moroni painted a number of works (including the *Altarpiece of the Doctors of the Church* for the church of Santa Maria Maggiore). He made contact with the Madruzzo family and with Titian. From the 1550s onwards, in fact, Moroni was often commissioned as an alternative portraitist to Titian. A whole stream of provincial lords and ladies took it in turns to sit for him. Heroism is not in their vocabulary, but they are all well grounded in everyday life. His religious paintings are rarer, but we should at least mention *The Last Supper* in the parish church at Romano in Lombardy.

Giovan Battista Moroni
The Gentleman in Pink
(Gian Gerolamo Grumelli)
1560, canvas
85 × 48½ in.
(216 × 123 cm)
Conti Morosini
Collection, Bergamo

Moroni's style was already mature when he painted this splendid picture which summarizes his qualities as a portrait painter. There is an intense truthfulness about the face of the sitter whose clothing and environment are littered with symbolic allusions. Moroni's sense of light and color can neatly be linked to the Bergamo tradition established by Lorenzo Lotto but perhaps even more to the Brescia school.

William Sidney Mount
Setauket, New York, 1807-1868

A champion of painting dedicated to scenes of daily life, Mount celebrated the values of rural America. Following apprenticeship in New York in a large workshop run by his older brother, Henry, a sign and ornament painter, Mount attended courses at the National Academy of Design beginning in 1826, the year it was founded. There he studied prints of works by great European masters. Having been among the academy's first students, in 1831 he became an associate member, and the next year a full member. When he returned to Long Island, Mount realized there was little correspondence between the models he had been studying and the life of his people. He therefore set about creating a language and subjects closer to his reality. By the close of the 1830s he had abandoned portraits to paint scenes of ordinary life. With careful craftsmanship he portrayed the reality of the world around him, the simple country folk and their habits, which he rendered with extreme naturalness. In their lively gestures and the realism of their expressions he captured something of the American character. He also became the first important American painter to present scenes from the daily lives of black Americans. Mount's works soon enjoyed great popularity with the public and critics alike, becoming widely known through reproductions as lithographs and engravings. In keeping with the artistic mood of the mid-nineteenth century, influenced by Emerson's transcendentalism, Mount believed that a work of art begins with the careful observation of nature. In 1843 he visited Thomas Cole at Catskill to study landscape painting; in Mount's opinion, painting in the open air is a necessary exercise, as important as the study of geometry and perspective. Whether painting figures outdoors or indoors, he constructed wide spaces, full of light, vigorously following vertical and horizontal lines, except for the occasional diagonal.

William Sidney Mount
Eel Spearing at Setauket
1845
oil on canvas
28½ × 36 in.
(72.4 × 91.5 cm)
New York State
Historical Association,
Cooperstown, New York

This painting was commissioned by a New York lawyer and presents an episode from that man's youth.

Edvard Munch
Löten, 1863-Ekely, 1944

The artist who gave voice to the cry of anguish of a humanity trapped in solitude was trained at the school of drawing in Oslo. His early works were still influenced by nineteenth-century Naturalism, but already revealed a desire to probe the intimate secrets of their subjects. The journeys he made to Paris (1885) and then again to France, as well as Germany and Italy, were fundamental. So, despite living in Norway, Munch was in constant contact with the contemporary avant-garde. Also inspired by the plays of his fellow countryman Ibsen, Munch embarked on a course of intense research in the closing decade of the century, venturing into the depths of the human psyche. Munch combined a light, continuous, and undulating line with an unreal, vivid, and forced color to produce unprecedented effects. Among his principal works it is worth mentioning, in addition to the celebrated *Scream* (1893), the unfinished *Frieze of Life* (begun in 1893). This includes the symbolic scene of *The Dance of Life*, dominated by brilliant colors and the disquieting reflection of the moon in the sea. His paintings were accompanied by a vast output of graphic work, part of it intended as illustrations of contemporary poems. In 1908 Munch suffered a serious nervous breakdown, from which he slowly recovered, though his painting never regained its previous expressive force.

Edvard Munch
Jealousy
1895
oil on canvas
26½ × 39¼ in.
(67 × 100 cm)
Historical Museum,
Bergen

The powerful tensions that ran through the painter's mind (eventually leading to the nervous breakdown that interrupted his career in 1908) were clearly apparent not only in his choice of subjects and technique, but also in some of his self-portraits. Here we are presented with the image of a deeply troubled man, racked by feelings of jealousy, offering a naked and moving glimpse of his inner being.

Edvard Munch
Red and White
1901
oil on canvas
36½ × 49 in.
(93 × 124.5 cm)
Munch Museum, Oslo

In Munch's painting, which was strongly molded by the artist's personal experience, we can discern a desire to create order and clarity: the white and red of the dresses worn by the two girls are laid on as compact and violent patches of color, in stark contrast.

Edvard Munch
The Scream
1893
tempera on panel
32¾ × 26 in.
(83.5 × 66 cm)
Nasjonalgalleriet, Oslo

A work symbolic of anguish and pain, it was described by Munch in the following words: "One evening I was walking along a path. On one side was the city and below me the fjord. The sun was setting, the clouds were tinged blood red. I felt a scream running through nature; I could almost hear it. I painted this picture, painting the clouds like real blood. The colors were screaming." Like van Gogh, Munch handled color with the force born out of desperation, laying it on in long and livid bands. The unbroken lines tighten like a noose around the figure's head, while his features are distorted to the point of paroxysm.

275

Bartolomé Esteban Murillo
Seville, 1618-1682

A leading figure in the "second generation" of Sevillian artists, Murillo is famous for his gentle, religious compositions that give an image of him that is endearing, but perhaps a little too sweet. In actual fact, the master's oeuvre and career are far richer and more complex. After training in his hometown, where he was noted for his precocious talent, Murillo established his own studio in 1639. A few years later he began to receive important commissions from the religious orders of the city. Unfortunately, many of his cycles of paintings have been dispersed and are now in museums throughout the world. His earliest works feature intense images of children playing, young beggars, and street urchins. While the influence of Ribera is evident, so is a taste for action, for genre scenes, and for descriptive detail. By 1650 the contrast between the essential paintings of Zurbarán and those of the younger, dynamic Murillo was already evident. In 1655 he introduced still greater freedom and monumentality into his work. Beautiful female saints, impassioned Virgins, and enchanting angels began to appear with increasing frequency. In 1660 he opened an academy of fine arts in Seville, and the activity of imitators and copyists led to a decline in his reputation for a certain period.

Bartolomé Esteban Murillo
The Pool of Bethesda
1671-1673
oil on canvas, 93¼ × 102¾ in. (237 × 261 cm)
National Gallery, London

This painting of great spatial breadth provides an excellent example of Murillo's familiarity with complex compositions.

Jean-Marc Nattier
Paris, 1685-1766

After training in the studio of Jean Raoux, a painter of mythological portraits, Nattier completed the works Raoux had left unfinished, an experience that was to prove decisive in his development. In 1710 he was commissioned by Louis XIV to make engravings of his drawings of Rubens's great cycle, The *Life of Marie de' Medici* in the Luxembourg Palace, and in 1715 he was admitted to the Academy as a history painter. Subsequently, however, he devoted himself solely to portrait painting, becoming the most famous exponent of the mythological genre established by Raoux. Having turned down the chance to stay at the Academy in Rome, an offer made by his godfather Jouvenet, in 1742 he became the official portrait painter to the court. He produced portraits of Louis XV, Queen Marie Leszczynski, and the king's daughters. The latter were portrayed innumerable times, depicted as nymphs, shepherd girls, or young goddesses, in a form of "posed" portraiture that preferred an unreal though measured elegance of attitude and pose to any kind of psychological interpretation. His portraits, the last record of a world still characterized by classical composure reminiscent of the art of Domenichino and Albani, have acquired emblematic value, becoming the symbols of a society, an environment, and a lifestyle marked by the taste for artificial grace and affected elegance.

Jean-Marc Nattier
Portrait of Madame Maria Zeffirina
1751
oil on canvas
27½ × 32¼ in.
(70 × 82 cm)
Uffizi, Florence

In this portrait the astonished expression, the rouged cheeks, and the coy gesture of stroking her lapdog all contribute to the sitter's doll-like appearance.

Kenneth Noland
Asheville, North Carolina, 1924

Noland belongs to the generation of American artists strongly affected by America's involvement in World War II. These artists arrived at the creation of geometric art by way of a precise intellectual operation, and their works do not show the sense of spiritual search common to the works of the first school of abstract expressionists. Noland moved to Washington in 1949 and taught painting, first at the Institute of Contemporary Art and then at the Catholic University, promoting the ideas of the so-called Washington color painters group, artists distinguished by their nongestural abstract art based on optical effects. Working directly on bare, unsized canvas, Noland used diluted solutions of a delicate luminosity to create combinations of gestural signs on fields of muted tints. This was the phase of his career in which Noland created his so-called circle paintings, concentric shapes like targets. In these paintings, circles of different colors achieve optical effects, hypnotically capturing the viewer inside the repeating circles in a skilled combination of clearly defined outlines and softly luminous surfaces. It is in fact due to the interaction of colors that Noland's circles take on animation and seem to expand or contract or extend outward to the viewer. Noland moved to New York in 1961 and began the series of V paintings in which the width of the color stripes, as well as the thrust and tension in the forms, leads to an entirely new dimension. The bands of color extend to the limits of the pictorial space, creating an interaction between the fulcrum and the dispersion within a lucid structural motif.

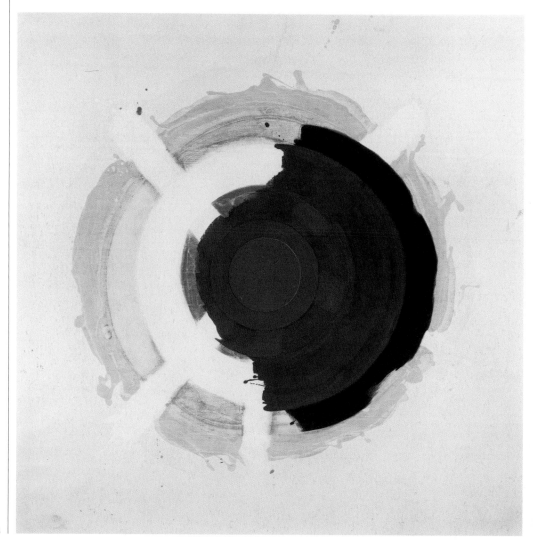

Kenneth Noland
Back and Front
1960
magna on canvas
74½ × 74½ in.
(183 × 183 cm)
Private collection

Emil Nolde

Nolde, 1867-Seebüll, 1956

The most unusual exponent of German Expressionism was actually called Emil Hansen: a perhaps too obviously Scandinavian surname that he replaced by the name of his hometown. He was an extraordinary self-taught artist, who operated outside schools and academies. He worked as a woodcarver supplementing his salary by selling postcards illustrated with droll "anthropomorphic" images of the Swiss mountains. On the proceeds he was able to spend time studying first in Munich and then in Paris (1899), eventually settling on painting as a career. From the outset, Nolde's pictures displayed the characteristics that were to distinguish his style throughout his life: simplified forms, imposing silhouettes, violent colors, and a magical and mystical feeling for nature. In 1906 he worked for a while with Schmidt-Rottluff, but though he was persuaded to tackle the Expressionist themes of Die Brücke and later on those of other German avant-garde movements, he maintained his independence. He gradually began accentuating the mystical, dramatic, and highly autobiographical character of his painting, a tendency that was reinforced by a serious illness in 1909. A long journey to the Far East (1914) resulted in a further change in the painter's style, with exotic elements being used to suggest a dynamic deformation of the human figure, with its features and attitudes exaggerated. In the twenties he became a well-known figure. But in 1927 he chose to retire to his house at Seebüll, almost on the border with Denmark, painting brightly colored pictures. He too was persecuted and denigrated by the Nazis and for a long time was practically forgotten, only to be rediscovered in the fifties.

Emil Nolde
*Flowering Garden,
Two Women*
1908
oil on canvas,
23½ × 27½ in.
(60 × 70 cm)
Erbengemeinschaft Lange,
Krefeld

Nolde had a great passion for flowers: all the houses he lived in were surrounded by luxuriant gardens, which he tended himself.

Georgia O'Keeffe

Sun Prairie, Wisconsin, 1887-Santa Fe, New Mexico, 1986

O'Keeffe was an intuitive artist, intensely subjective, and her abstract, almost hermetic work is both heavily indebted to symbolism and profoundly influenced by the photography of Stieglitz. In 1905 she enrolled in the Art Institute of Chicago; two years later she was in New York, studying at the Art Students League; in 1914 she began assiduously attending Stieglitz's gallery. The formal language she employed in the 1910s was already surprisingly innovative, already mature; what came later were repetitions, variations, and simplifications. Her originality as an artist is expressed in the series of *Still Lives* inspired by simple objects from daily life transformed into poetic visions through a skilled use of space and color. In 1917 her first one-woman show at 291 was the gallery's last exhibit. The next year, at thirty-one, she decided to live with the older Stieglitz, and they married in 1924. Their relationship was stimulating for their work, involving the contrasts and exchanges between painting and photography. O'Keeffe incorporated elements of the photographic vision in her art, taking details enlarged as though by the lens and bringing them into focus to reveal unexpected shapes and forms that she then daringly expanded to the far corners of her canvas. Simplified and reduced to their essence, her subjects project enormous formal and emotive density. Beginning in 1929 she spent her summers in New Mexico, moving there permanently in 1949, a few years after the death of Stieglitz. Her art became more mystical. The desert landscapes of the Southwest and the imposing mountain chains inspired grandiose views, while she continued to paint floral motifs. In presenting the infinite dimension of the desert, O'Keeffe moved toward extreme simplification, using a rigorous technique that sought the essence of reality without renouncing its objective existence. Starting in 1930, bones and skulls of animals appeared in her works in an isolated way; later they showed up in the vast Mexican desert. In 1997 a private museum dedicated entirely to O'Keeffe opened in Santa Fe. Its more than 120 works, including paintings, watercolors, pastels, drawings, and sculpture, offer a fitting tribute to a woman who dedicated fifty years of her life to that land.

Georgia O'Keeffe
Two Calla Lilies on Pink
1928
oil on canvas
40 × 30 in.
(101.6 × 76.2 cm)
Philadelphia Museum
of Art, Philadelphia

Rejecting all types of realism related to the European tradition of art, O'Keeffe took an object from nature, most often a flower, concentrated on a single detail, enlarged it, then located it on a flat canvas, simplified and rendered in transparent, antinaturalistic colors. In this close-up vision of two calla lilies, the intensity of the colors and the precision of the line concur to make an ordinary object sublime.

Johann Friedrich Overbeck

Lübeck, 1759-Rome, l569

Overbeck is the key figure in the group of the Nazarenes, an unusual attempt to create an artistic community that might appear naïve today, but should in fact be considered an important current in nineteenth-century artistic research. Overbeck was another of the painters who grew up in the years of the French Revolution, receiving an artistic education of the academic type, and who were then forced to seek new forms of expression in the first decade of the nineteenth century in order to deal with a radically changed world. The choice made by Overbeck (then a student at the Vienna Academy) was very different from the ones taken, during those same years, by Goya, Friedrich, and David: together with his friend Franz Pforr, Overbeck founded the *Lukasbrüderschaft*, or Brotherhood of St. Luke, which drew its inspiration directly from the religious confraternities of the Middle Ages. Driven by their strong leanings toward mysticism and Catholicism, Overbeck and Pforr moved to Rome in 1810 and settled in an abandoned monastery on the Pincio hill. They were joined by other German painters resident in Rome and set up a community on monastic lines. As a consequence of their long hair and absorbed demeanor, the members of this peculiar group came to be known as Nazarenes, a term that soon lost its originally derisory meaning. One characteristic theme of Overbeck's work is the harmony between the sunlit Humanism of Italy and the fascination of Gothic Germany, evoked by pictures of Goethe in the Roman countryside or of allegorical female figures. From the stylistic viewpoint, Overbeck and his companions looked back to the Italian art of the Quattrocento, in which they found not only a model of composition but also the religious attitude that was a goal shared by the whole of the group. Pforr's sudden and untimely death in 1812 left Overbeck in sole charge of the community: the painter deliberately adopted the style of fifteenth-century Umbrian and Tuscan frescoes, with sharply defined outlines and vivid colors. Overbeck's hand is also clearly recognizable in the group's joint undertakings, such as the *Scenes from the Life of Saint Joseph* in Palazzo Zuccari and the luminous frescoes depicting episodes from *Jerusalem*

Friedrich Overbeck
Italy and Germany
1812-1828
oil on canvas
37 ×41 in.
(94 × 104 cm)
Neue Pinakothek,
Munich

The very long time taken over this painting encompasses practically the entire history of the Nazarenes. The delicate embrace of the girls symbolizing the two nations can stand for the whole of the artist's cultural program.

Delivered in the Casino Massimo, begun in 1818 and not finished until 1830. The long time it took to represent the themes from Tasso's poem is a sign of the progressive difficulties encountered by the group of the Nazarenes, which in effect broke up after 1830, with the return of many artists to Germany and their dispersion amongst various cities. Overbeck's last masterpiece is a huge allegorical composition, the *Triumph of Religion in the Arts* (1840), now in Frankfurt and in a style that is an unmistakable homage to Raphael's frescoes in the Vatican.

Friedrich Overbeck
Odoerdo and Gildippe
1823
fresco
c. 118 × 82¾ in.
(c. 300 × 210 cm)
Casino Massimo, Rome

Michael Pacher
Bruneck, c. 1430-Salzburg, 1498

The most original and atypical figure in German painting in the second half of the fifteenth century was born in the Tyrol, a region on the periphery of the Empire that was also an important crossroads between the areas to the east and west, and north and south of the Alps. He was probably born at Bruneck in Val Pusteria and served his apprenticeship with an established Tyrolean artist before becoming independent and setting up his own workshop. Like many artists of his generation Pacher was both a sculptor and a painter, a twofold talent that found full expression in splendid, imposing hinged altarpieces with a sculptured scene in the central panel and painted scenes on the wing panels. In painting, Pacher is linked to the northern tradition as exemplified by Flemish art and that of the Rhineland. In fact, he is likely to have roamed as far afield as Flanders during his youthful *Wanderjahre*, the years that artists traditionally spent traveling to complete their training. He was, however, particularly aware of the radical changes taking place in the figurative arts, and soon also entered into contact with Italian art. He stayed in Padua around the year 1460, where he had the opportunity to admire works by Donatello, Andrea Mantegna, and Paolo Uccello. From then on he constantly followed the latest developments in Italy, and may have made other journeys as far as Florence and Urbino. This large range of stimuli produced an extraordinary effect. The northern elements blended with a typically Italian feeling for perspective and volume to create a style as unmistakable as it was isolated. Pacher won immediate fame and commissions to work outside the cramped confines of the Tyrol. The only one of his altarpieces that is still visible and practically intact was produced for the church of St. Wolfgang in the Austrian town of the same name. The massive altarpiece with hinged wings created for the parish church of Salzburg was to have measured fifty-six feet in height, but was left unfinished on his death. The work was dismembered in the Baroque era and now survives only in a very fragmentary form. In Pacher's paintings, his vigorous, dynamic style often gives way to calmer and more measured compositions, sustained by a coherent spatial framework and a balanced handling of form. No artist took up the legacy of this extraordinarily rich, creative career that fused heterogeneous elements into a convincing synthesis. It was not until the sixteenth century that Pacher's particular artistic "bilingualism" was taken up by Dürer and the artists of the Danube School.

Michael Pacher
Altarpiece of the Church Fathers, interior panels
c. 1482-1483
central panel
83½ × 78¾ in.
(212 × 200 cm)
wing panels
85 × 35¾ in. each
(216 × 91 cm)
Alte Pinakothek, Munich

Produced for the abbey church of the convent at Neustift near Brixen, this altarpiece was conceived as an imposing sculptural work but produced with solely pictorial means. The central panel is divided into four Gothic niches containing the fathers of the Church in different poses.

The canopies are decorated with marble columns in which small monochromatic painted statues are set. The architectural structures framing the figures are emphasized by the adoption of a single, low viewpoint. The harsh light penetrates from the right and helps to accentuate the monumental nature of the work, to enhance detail, and to create a subtly disquieting atmosphere that pervades the whole. The result is an unrivaled illusionistic synthesis of painting, sculpture, and architecture.

Palma the Elder

Jacopo Negretti
Serina, Bergamo, c. 1480-Venice, 1528

Palma was a typical exponent of a
group of painters from the mainland
Venetian territories. He represents the
easy-going strand in the rapid evolution
of Venetian painting. His nickname
"il Vecchio" (the Elder) was added to
distinguish him from his great-nephew
Jacopo Palma "il Giovane" (the
Younger), a prominent Venetian artist
of the late Renaissance. Although
originally from Bergamo, Palma moved
to Venice in 1510 where he
concentrated on two distinct types of
work: altarpieces for churches in Venice
and the Veneto region and, quite
separately, very marketable pieces
portraying seductive young women,
usually voluptuous blondes, sometimes
in mythological guise. The hallmarks of
his painting are diffused light, serenity,
richly luxurious colors, and an
atmosphere of calm splendor, reflecting
the influence of early Titian. The gentle
sensuality of these half-length portraits
of women (such as *The Girls Bathing*,
in the Kunsthistorisches Museum
in Vienna) is echoed in his religious
painting, which often includes sweet
female figures, for instance the *St.
Barbara Polyptych* (1522-1524, Venice,
Santa Maria Formosa) or *The Adoration
of the Magi* (Brera, Milan).

Palma the Elder

Sacra Conversazione
1521, wood panel
122 × 82 in. (310 × 208 cm)
Church of Santo Stefano,
Vicenza

Altarpieces by Palma the
Elder were hugely popular
in Venice and its mainland
territories. Their success
was more than justified by
the encompassing, luminous
beauty of the overall
composition combined
with the fascination of the
individual characters.
Although he incorporated
the most up-to-date trends
of the Venetian school (such
as the use of rich color that
owes a lot to Titian, the vast
and romantic landscapes,
and the wonderful play of
light on cloaks and armor),
he nevertheless revealed
his own distinctive style
in the smooth sensuality
of his women.

283

Giovan Paolo Panini
Piacenza, 1691-Rome, 1765

Panini was one of the most accomplished *vedutisti* (view-painters) of the eighteenth century. He came from a long tradition of Emilian view-painters and scenery-painters. In 1715 he moved to Rome where he first worked as a decorator painting counterfeit architecture in various palaces. He then found a fuller creative voice by painting scenes of holidays or special events. The spectacular backdrops he used for these works were the squares and buildings of Rome. The beauty of these monumental backgrounds, bathed in a clear light that seemed to exalt the very notion of the Eternal City, was so powerful that he had no need of a narrative pretext for them. Many of Panini's paintings are simply views animated by lively little figures. He had a considerable influence on Canaletto and the great Venetian view-painters of the eighteenth century.

Giovan Paolo Panini
The Piazza and Church of Santa Maria Maggiore
1744
canvas
104¼ 99½ in.
(265 × 253 cm)
Palazzo Quirinale, coffeehouse, Rome

Parmigianino

Francesco Mazzola
Parma, 1503-Casalmaggiore, 1540

Unnaturalistic, icy, and intellectual, Parmigianino is the stylistic opposite of Correggio. Their coexistence in the same town made Parma in the 1520s one of the chief centers of sixteenth-century art. Parmigianino's talent developed at a precocious age and he quickly rivaled Correggio, whom he admired, by putting himself forward as the exponent of Mannerism. When only 20 he produced his first major work, *Diana Bathing*, for the castle of Sanvitate at Fontanellato. In 1524 he went to Rome where he was deeply influenced by Michelangelo's and Raphael's works. This stay gave rise to a number of portraits and religious pictures heavily influenced by the Mannerists. After the Sack of Rome in 1527 he spent a few years in Bologna only to return to Parma in 1531. He then painted the frescoes in the church of the Madonna della Steccata showing an extremely refined and stylized form of Mannerism. His output in this period was marked by an unnatural lengthening of figures in snake-like poses. One example of this is his unfinished *Madonna with the Long Neck* in the Uffizi. In the last years of his short life, Parmigianino reputedly retired from painting to concentrate on alchemy.

Above
Parmigianino
Self-Portrait in a Convex Mirror
c. 1524, wood panel
diam. 9½ in. (24.4 cm)
Kunsthistorisches
Museum, Vienna

This famous painting was nothing less than a virtuoso tour-de-force. It simulated the way in which the face, hand, and the whole room are distorted when they are reflected in a convex mirror. Parmigianino took this picture to Rome to use it as a calling card that demonstrated his talent.

Parmigianino
Vision of St. Jerome
1526-1527, wood panel
135 × 58½ in.
(343 × 149 cm)
National Gallery,
London

Painted in Rome, the way in which the bodies are strongly contorted shows his own interpretation of Mannerism. For him this was a striking yet ambiguous way of impressing the viewer.

285

Joachim Patinir
Bouvignes or Dinant, c. 1485-
Antwerp, 1524

Dürer, who knew Patinir personally, described him as "*ein gut Landschaftmaier*," "a good landscape painter." The extraordinary depiction of immense vistas, distant horizons, incredible views of jagged rocks and stretches of water is the most exciting aspect of the oeuvre of Patinir, a leading exponent of the Antwerp School. Originally from Walloon Belgium, he probably trained under Gerard David in Bruges, and went to Antwerp in 1515. Previously he must have seen and admired the works of Bosch whose visionary style and skill in creating fantastic scenes by using naturalistic detail had a strong influence on him. Soon he enrolled in the Painters' Guild in Antwerp and made the acquaintance of the most important masters. He was a close friend of Quentin Metsys who became the guardian of his children after his death. Patinir asked Metsys to paint the figures in some of his works, since he was not very interested in this aspect and considered it irrelevant. Patinir's paintings, though boldly pioneering regarding the landscapes, in fact, contain mediocre figures that seem to be merely a pretext to paint immense panoramic scenes, in strong tones of blue and green. Patinir has left only four signed paintings; hence the chronology of his works is uncertain.

**Joachim Patinir
and Quentin Metsys**
*Temptation
of St. Anthony*
c. 1515
oil on wood, 61 × 68 in.
(155 × 173 cm)
Prado, Madrid

The figure of the tormented hermit, the three seductive girls, and the leering old woman are by Metsys.

Perugino

Pietro Vannucci
Città della Pieve, Perugia, c. 1450-
Fontignano, Perugia, 1524

Sought after by aristocratic and ecclesiastic patrons from all over Italy and capable of coordinating a huge output, Pietro Perugino created a real fashion for his elegant and slightly vague style. He deliberately shied away from exploring expression too deeply. He preferred dreamy poses wrapped in the sweetness of unified color. He probably studied under Verrocchio in Florence and soon became famous. In 1481 Pope Sixtus IV summoned him to Rome to decorate the walls of the Sistine chapel alongside Botticelli, and for the next two decades he was in great demand, with a busy studio producing gentle, pious, often sentimental religious works. Some of his most important work was produced around 1490 including *The Vision of St. Bernard* (Alte Pinakothek, Munich) and the *Deposition* (Galleria Palatina, Florence). After about 1505, he seems to have retired to Perugia, perhaps finding the atmosphere in Florence too competitive for his elegant but now repetitive art. But he maintained his prestigious links with the Duchy of Milan and the Gonzaga family. His most famous pupil was Raphael, whose famous serenity was perhaps derived from Perugino's art.

Perugino
Madonna Enthroned with Child and Two Saints
c. 1480
wood panel, diam. 58¼ in.
(148 cm)
Musée du Louvre, Paris

Perugino
Christ Giving the Keys to St. Peter
1450-1481
fresco
Sistine chapel, Vatican

This famous masterpiece marks the beginning of the central phase of Perugino's career. Pope Sixtus IV called him to Rome in 1481 along with Ghirlandaio and Botticelli. Perugino painted three large scenes on the side walls of the chapel. He was also the author of the composition on the back wall (later destroyed by Michelangelo to make way for his *Last Judgment*) and of a few portraits of some of the early popes at the top of the room. The composition shown here stands out for the importance of its symbolic meaning. It shows Christ investing the first pope (St. Peter), blessing his role as future pontiff, and underlining his authority as the Vicar of Christ. The scene is set in the place where the conclaves were held. From the compositional viewpoint, it contains a number of important new features including the wide-angled architectural and natural surrounds contained within a paved church square criss-crossed with lines to stress the perspective effect. The work's many borrowings from classical antiquity (the two triumphal arches) combine with the Renaissance model church with its central layout in the form of a Greek cross, then considered the ideal.

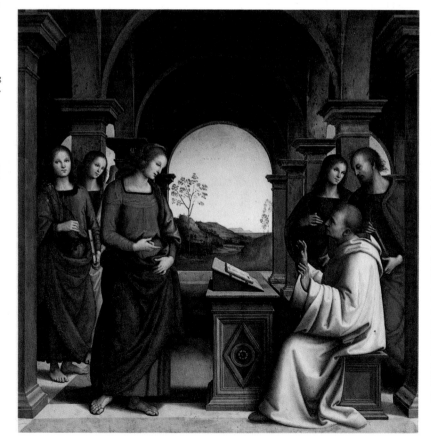

Perugino
The Vision of St. Bernard
wood panel
1488-1489
68 × 63 in.
(173 × 160 cm)
Alte Pinakothek, Munich

Originally painted for the Florentine church of Santo Spirito (for which he also designed the window on the front elevation) this is one of the painter's most heartfelt works. The nature of the mystic apparition justifies both the way the scene appears to be suspended in time and its contemplative tone. The severe, dark architecture of the bare pillars contrasts with the distant, serene view of the countryside. The saint's white cassock contrasts with the colored garb of the angels and the Virgin. Perugino's figure of the Virgin was used as a model by Raphael for his *The Betrothal of the Virgin* which is now in the Brera.

Giambattista Piazzetta

Venice, 1683-1754

Piazzetta shares with Sebastiano Ricci the merit of opening up new horizons for eighteenth-century Venetian painting, thus paving the way for the great decorative works of eighteenth-century European art. Unlike Ricci, Piazzetta painted mostly religious works and never executed frescoes, but his dynamic and dramatically intense altarpieces are to be regarded as cornerstones of international art. Considerable importance also attaches to his etchings and illustrations for books. The son of a wood carver, Piazzetta was to display throughout his long career a particular taste for well-rounded, sculptural figures outlined by light. From 1703 to 1705 he completed his training with an interesting stay in Bologna in the workshop of Giuseppe Maria Crespi. It is significant to note that Piazzetta drew inspiration in Bologna not from works by the Carracci family or Guido Reni, but from Guercino's early compositions and their strong chiaroscuro contrasts. On his return to Venice, he did not hesitate to tackle demanding altarpieces and increasingly important commissions for religious works. From the time of the canvases for the church of San Stae, he frequently found himself working alongside Sebastiano Ricci and the young Giambattista Tiepolo. The interplay of reciprocal influences, ideas, and cross references established among the three masters led gradually to a general lightening of the chromatic range. In his mature work, Piazzetta also opened up to "sunlight" and allowed light to flow freely into his canvases. After 1735, it was certainly through contact with Tiepolo that he produced a number of works on amorous themes for private collectors. In his old age, Piazzetta assumed a very important teaching role, initially with the numerous pupils that passed through his workshop and then as founder of the Accademia di Belle Arti.

Giambattista Piazzetta
Rebecca at the Well
c. 1740
oil on canvas
40¼ × 54 in.
(102 × 137 cm)
Pinacoteca di Brera,
Milan

This work dates from Piazzetta's late period, when his canvases were suffused with a clear light that indicates the influence of Tiepolo. The subject is taken from the Bible, but portrayed in charmingly secular fashion with narrative details precisely depicted around the beautiful, luminous central figure of the blonde girl.

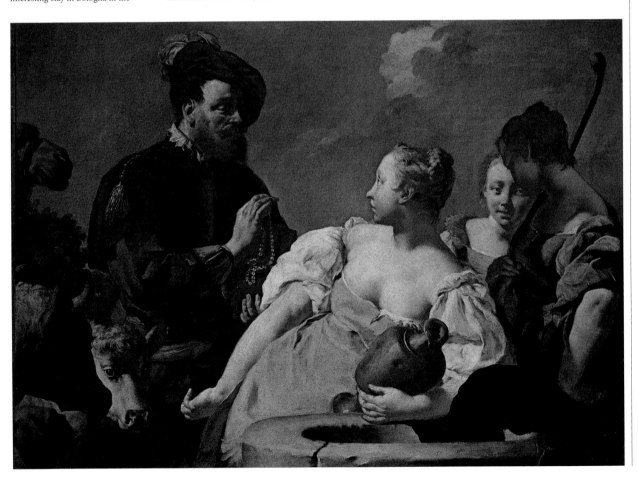

Francis Picabia
Paris, 1879-1953

A French painter of Cuban origin, he took up Dadaism after trying out the Fauvist and Cubist styles. In 1915 he left Paris for New York, where he had already spent six months in 1913, showing his celebrated picture *Udnie* at the Armory Show of modern art and establishing links with exponents of the avant-garde, including the photographer Alfred Stieglitz. His first one-man show of abstract watercolors was held at the gallery owned by Stieglitz. He also met Marcel Duchamp and Man Ray in New York and the three of them formed the nucleus of American Dada. Sharing with Duchamp a deep aversion to the myth of technological modernity,

he produced his cycle of large "machinist" pictures. Returning to Europe in 1918, the artist came into contact with Tristan Tzara, injecting new blood into the Dadaism of first Zurich and then Paris. These were the decisive years in which the Dada experience came to an end and its exponents were absorbed into the emerging Surrealist movement. Picabia joined the movement in 1924, the same year as Breton published the Surrealist manifesto, and displayed an extraordinary freedom of imagination in his series of "monsters" and "transparencies." After the Second World War, influenced by the poetics of nonrepresentational art, he devoted himself for a while to abstract painting and then went back to Surrealism.

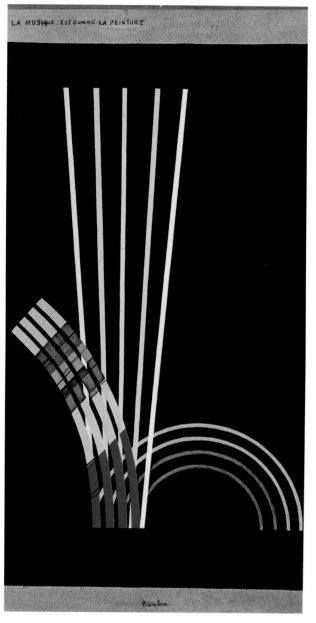

Francis Picabia
Dances at the Fountain
1913
oil on canvas
18¾ × 18¾ in.
(47.5 × 47.5 cm)
Philadelphia Museum
of Art, Philadelphia

Painted during the artist's phase of Orphic Cubism. Excluded from the Cubist exhibition at the Salon des Indépendants, it was included in the 1913 Armory Show in New York.

Francis Picabia
Music Is Like Painting
1917
oil on canvas
47¼ × 26½ in.
(120 × 67 cm)
Private collection

The break with traditional figurative language is evident in this painting, whose title is emblematic of the interest in music shared by all the artists

associated with the magazine *391*, which commenced publication at Barcelona in 1917.

Pablo Picasso
Malaga, 1881-Mougins, 1973

A key figure in twentieth-century art, Picasso displayed an impressive willingness to renew his own style, through experiments, avant-garde movements, and sensational proposals. The training he received in Spain gave the artist a perfect grasp of techniques of expression. In 1900 he began to spend time in Paris, which was to become his new home. After an initial revision of the themes and style of Impressionism, Picasso entered his "Blue Period" (1901-04), the first of the recurrent phases of reinterpretation of classical art that alternated with periods of the most daring experimentation throughout his career. The subjects and figures of the pathetic human comedy (harlequins, circus performers) also appeared in the subsequent "Pink Period" (1905-06), which touched on peaks of refined, aristocratic disenchantment. Now surrounded by an extensive network of literary and artistic friendships (Gertrude Stein, Matisse), he was profoundly influenced by Cézanne's pictures of *Bathers* and sober landscapes which he saw in 1907. With the *Demoiselles d'Avignon*, a seminal masterpiece of modern painting, Picasso commenced the rigorous breakdown of images into geometric solids, simplifying shapes and volumes by total abolition of the atmospheric effects of light and shade. The Bateau-Lavoir, the studio in Montmartre which Picasso shared with Braque, became the birthplace of the Cubist movement. In 1909, with the elimination of curved lines and the restriction of color to shades of gray alone, Picasso took Cubism to the level of an extreme, rarefied intellectual purity on the threshold of abstraction, only to partially return to recognizable objects in the later phase of "Synthetic Cubism." As a result of the First World War, he moved to Avignon. This was the stimulus for a new phase of classicism, in which an almost academic style of drawing was combined with the compact forms of Cubism. In the twenties and thirties Picasso became increasingly fascinated by sculpture. The outbreak of the Spanish Civil War forced Picasso to make radical choices: a militant opponent of Franco, he became director of the Prado Museum and, in 1937, painted *Guernica*. The bloody events of the war left a deep mark on Picasso's painting. Returning to Southern France, he started to devote particular attention to ceramics from 1947 on. By now a legend (partly as a result of his political activity), Picasso led an intense public life. His most profound research in the field of painting concentrated on the reinterpretation of celebrated masterpieces of the past and on his favorite theme of the relationship between the artist and his model.

Pablo Picasso
Family of Saltimbanques
1905
oil on canvas
87½ × 92¼ in.
(222 × 234 cm)
National Gallery,
Washington, D.C.

The academic training he received in Spain remained an indispensable foundation and term of comparison all through Picasso's extremely long career. During the "Blue Period" he demonstrated a control over form that was totally classical in nature, but applied to unconventional images and figures on the margins of society.

Pablo Picasso
Harlequin and His Friend
1901
oil on canvas, 28¾ × 23½
in. (73 × 60 cm)
Pushkin Museum,
Moscow

Picasso's "Blue Period"
dates to the first few years
of the twentieth century.
It was one of the great
poetic and artistic
adventures of the
emerging avant-garde
and the first true
demonstration of the
painter's quality. After
a thorough and shrewd
reexamination of the
whole course of the
Impressionist movement,
as well as the human
accents of the late Degas
(from whom Picasso took
the atmosphere of the
Absinthe Drinker) and the
graphic art of Toulouse-
Lautrec, he devoted a
series of paintings to the
world of acrobats and
strolling players.

Opposite
Pablo Picasso
Les Demoiselles d'Avignon
1907
oil on canvas
96 × 91¾ in.
(244 × 233 cm)
Museum of Modern Art,
New York

The painting that marks
a revolutionary turning
point in art was inspired
by the deep emotions
stirred by Cézanne's
posthumous exhibition.
Picasso definitively
undermined the
foundations of "beautiful
painting," composing a
group of figures from
which any hint of realism
has been eliminated.
Apart from using color,
the artist makes no
attempt to charm the
observer. Cézanne's
Bathers have become
prostitutes waiting for
clients.

Above
Pablo Picasso
Guernica
1937
tempera on canvas
139½ × 308 in.
(354 × 782 cm)
Museo de Arte Reina
Sofia, Madrid

This highly celebrated
picture, perhaps the
best-known work of art
of the twentieth century,
was painted during the
Spanish Civil War, in
which Picasso took the
Republican side. Intended
as the decoration for an
exhibition pavilion in
Paris, the work is based
on a real event that took
place during the war: the
bombing of the town
of Guernica. Drawing
on some elements of
Synthetic Cubism,
but adapted to the new
historical and artistic
situation, Picasso
composed a huge
allegory, crammed with
allusions and symbols.
Guernica immediately
became a model for a
whole generation.

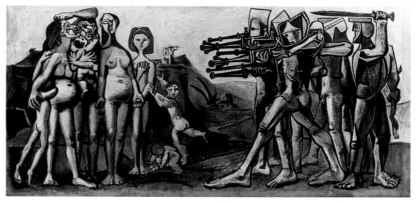

Pablo Picasso
Le déjeuner sur l'herbe
1960
oil on canvas
51¼ × 76¾ in.
(130 ×195 cm)
Musée Picasso, Paris

Once again Manet
serves as a point
of reference and
comparison: in fact the
painting takes a number
of elements (and not
just the title) from
Manet's masterpiece,
now in the Musée
d'Orsay.

Pablo Picasso
Massacre in Korea
1951
oil on canvas,
43¼ × 82¾ in.
(110 × 210 cm)
Musée Picasso, Paris

From the fifties onward, he
often tended to reinterpret
and reinvent important
paintings in the history
of art: his series devoted to
Velázquez's *Las Meninas* is
famous. As a protest against
the international crisis he
chose to repeat the scheme
of Manet's *The Execution
of Emperor Maximilian
of Mexico*.

Piero della Francesca

Sansepolcro, Arezzo, 1416/17-1492

Piero della Francesca occupies a pivotal position in fifteenth-century Italian and European art. A leading member of the second generation of Humanist painters, he fully reconciled the claims of art and geometry, the exquisitely calculated application of the rules of perspective and poetic expression. Piero's training took place in Florence, and there are records of him working alongside Domenico Veneziano in 1439 on a series of frescoes that has been almost completely lost. Apart from this early period, the painter worked in the "provinces" (Sansepolcro, Arezzo, Rimini, Ferrara, Urbino, and Perugia), not in Florence. Piero della Francesca thus appears also to have played a key role in spreading the concepts and rules of Humanist art in different parts of Italy. He preferred to live in his hometown, located along the road connecting eastern Tuscany, northern Umbria, and Montefeltro. During the 1440s Piero alternated periods of work at Sansepolcro (where he produced the *Baptism of Christ*, now in London, and the *Polyptych of the Misericordia*, Sansepolcro) with sojourns in other cities, including Rome. In Ferrara he came into contact with Leon Battista Alberti and possibly with the Flemish artist van der Weyden. In 1452 he started work on his major undertaking, the fresco cycle of the *Story of the True Cross* in the church of San Francesco, Arezzo. The variety of narrative situations, the monumentality of the figures, the flawless calculation of space, and the intensity of the expressions make this cycle one of the greatest works of European Renaissance art. Further examples of Piero della Francesca's mature style are provided by the monumental polyptych in Perugia (Galleria Nazionale dell'Umbria), ew works for Sansepolcro such as the *Resurrection of Christ* (Pinacoteca Comunale Sansepolcro), and the dismembered *Polyptych of St. Augustine*. During the 1460s Piero worked above all in Urbino at the court of Duke Federico da Montefeltro. In addition to a number of memorable masterpieces (the *Portraits of the Duke and Duchess of Urbino*, now in the Uffizi, and the two panels still in Urbino), this period was marked by numerous meetings with international artists and further studies on geometry, perspective, and algebra collected in important treatises. The last works produced in Urbino include the fine *Montefeltro Altarpiece* (now in the Pinacoteca di Brera, Milan). Halfway through the 1470s blindness forced Piero to abandon painting. He returned to Sansepolcro and devoted himself to mathematical studies and the completion of his treatises. By a strange coincidence, the artist who symbolizes the intellectual world of the fifteenth century died on October 12, 1492, the day on which the New World was discovered.

Piero della Francesca
*The Story of
the True Cross: Dream
of Constantine*
c. 1457-1458
fresco
129½ × 74¾ in.
(329 × 190 cm)
San Francesco, Arezzo

The decoration of the choir of the church of San Francesco in Arezzo dates from just over midway through the fifteenth century and constitutes a *de facto* dividing line between the pioneering stage of Humanism and the full application of the advances made in complex representation involving figures and architecture, nature and genius, light and movement. Piero developed and mastered new expressive techniques. In the Arezzo cycle, for example, he displays a masterly alternation of highly animated scenes and moments of stillness; dense groups of figures and more cadenced spaces, exteriors and interiors. One of the most thrilling moments is this very early nocturnal scene, a moonlit elegy in which the sense of mystery is enhanced by the glow of the few dim lights and the pointed tops of the tents disappearing in the gloom. The sleeping Constantine is granted a vision of the Cross, the emblem under which he will triumph in battle. An angel appears in the top left hand corner but the spectator's eye is drawn by the drowsy gaze of the page watching over the sleeping emperor, the reflections on the armor of the two soldiers silhouetted against the light, and the still, enchanted atmosphere.

Piero della Francesca
Montefeltro Altarpiece
1472–1474
tempera and oil
on wood
99 × 67¾ in.
(251 × 172 cm)
Pinacoteca di Brera,
Milan

This altarpiece was
painted for Duke
Federico da Montefeltro,
shown kneeling on the
right, and was originally
in the church of S.
Bernardino, Urbino. The
two aspects of the great
painter's personality are
evident in this work. On
the one hand, we have
the theorist of geometry
and author of
fundamental treatises
on perspective; on the
other, the creative artist
intent on forging an
ideal image. The scene
is set in a Renaissance
building, whose
proportions are
carefully calculated in
relation to the figures.
The light models the
volumes with still clarity
to give the group of
figures the elevated air
of a heavenly court
arrayed in accordance
with the canons of a
precise hierarchy.
An ostrich egg hangs by
a chain from the shell
decoration in the apse,
a celebrated detail in
which symbolic
meaning (alluding to
the birth of Christ and
the heraldic crest of the
Montefeltro house)
is combined with a
formidable rendering
of in-depth perspective.

Opposite
Piero della Francesca
Baptism of Christ
c. 1440
tempera and oil on
wood, 65¾ × 45¾ in.
(167 × 116 cm)
National Gallery,
London

297

Piero di Cosimo

Florence, 1461/62-1521

Piero di Cosimo's individuality makes him exceptional even in an age when artists had unprecedented freedom. According to Vasari's biography, he was a noted eccentric, living off hard-boiled eggs and hating the sound of church bells. He took his surname from the painter Cosimo Rosselli, whose pupil he had been and who he helped in decorating the Sistine chapel. Following this debut, Piero's career progressed slowly, but his style changed. He was influenced by Leonardo and by Luca Signorelli and Filippino Lippi. He excelled at painting animals with a sympathy rare in his age. The remarkable mythological scenes about early mankind he painted in the last decade of the fifteenth century were possibly based on Boccaccio's ideas. At the start of the sixteenth century Piero's style became even more eccentric.

Piero di Cosimo
Madonna and Child with Saints and Angels
1493, wood panel
80 × 77½ in.
(203 × 197 cm)
Museo dello Spedale degli Innocenti, Florence

Pietro da Cortona

Pietro Berrettini
Cortona, Arezzo, 1596-Rome, 1669

An eclectic artist, master architect of Baroque Rome, and imaginative painter, Pietro da Cortona provides the most brilliant and sumptuous examples of the most theatrical and rhetorical style of painting in seventeenth-century Europe. His abundant output of altarpieces, works for princely collectors, and vast cycles of frescoes, both religious and secular, always skillfully executed and never lacking in inspiration, make Pietro a fundamental point of stylistic reference. He also completes the trio of major artistic trends characterizing seventeenth-century art: the naturalism of Caravaggio, the academic classicism of Carracci and Reni, and the High Baroque of Bernini and Pietro da Cortona. Initially trained in Tuscany, he moved to Rome at the age of sixteen and immediately came into contact with Gianlorenzo Bernini. Both artists were noted by the Barberini pope, Urban VIII, who was to play an instrumental role in furthering their careers and who summoned them to work side by side in his palazzo. From the 1620s on, he began to receive commissions from aristocratic patrons, and he distinguished himself as a deft and inventive painter of frescoes. Taking as his starting point the noble classical approach of the Bolognese school, in his frequent choice of mythological or literary subjects, he added greater richness, color, and movement by including lively, dynamic elements. The culmination of this is the decoration of the banquet hall of Palazzo Barberini in Rome, a vast allegorical composition begun in 1633 and completed in 1639. This spectacular fresco with its wealth of symbolic figures and virtuoso foreshortening won Pietro the title of "prince" of the Accademia di San Luca. With his productive workshop, he obtained another prestigious commission in Florence, where he was called to decorate the reception rooms of Palazzo Pitti. In his last years in Rome, Pietro da Cortona continued to produce frescoes (for Palazzo Pamphili and the Chiesa Nuova), although the actual execution was by now largely left to his pupils. Among his architectural works, attention should be drawn to the delightful reconstruction of the church of Santa Maria della Pace, with a semicircular portico on the façade, which is framed by a suitably remodeled urban setting.

Pietro da Cortona
Madonna and Saints
1626-1628, oil on canvas
110¼ × 67 in.
(280 × 170 cm)
Museo dell'Accademia Etrusca, Cortona

This work is an example of the ostentatious richness of Baroque altarpieces. He depicts a profusion of gilded vestments, bright colors, smiles, and gestures of devotion. The painting contains a sophisticated and difficult dynastic "riddle." Produced for the Passerini family, it introduces the emblems of the chivalrous orders to which the family proudly belonged: the Knights of St. Stephen (whose cross appears on the cope of the pope St. Stephen), the Knights of Malta (symbolized by the figure of the patron saint, the Baptist, and the cloak bearing the cross in the center), and the Calatrava Order (with the figure of St. James the Great behind John the Baptist).

Pietro da Cortona
*The Triumph of Divine
Providence*
1633-1639
fresco
Palazzo Barberini, Rome

Pietro da Cortona's work
for the Barberini pope,
Urban VIII, marks the
climax of his career
and the period of closest
contact with Gianlorenzo
Bernini. The two masters
worked together on the
construction and
decoration of the
sumptuous palace of this
powerful family, which
now houses the Galleria
Nazionale d'Arte Antica.
Forty years after the
decoration of Palazzo
Farnese by Annibale
Carracci, Pietro da
Cortona puts forward a
new model of aristocratic
decoration. The calm and
sophisticated sequence of
classical subjects gives way
to violent and highly
animated, whirling
movement. The central
area is open to the sky
and great clouds support
groups of airborne figures
bathed in a gilded light
spreading downward
from above. Pietro da
Cortona takes up and
develops the foundations
laid over a century earlier
by Correggio in the
domes he painted in
Parma, and transforms
the fresco of the main
reception hall into an
extraordinarily rich
spectacle that astounds
the spectator and sweeps
him away in a whirl
of movement, in which all
sense of a focal point
is lost. The exuberance
of his imagination
oversteps all boundaries;
thus, alongside the
religious theme, ample
space is also found for
a celebration of the
Barberini family,
represented by the
heraldic emblem of three
bees with open wings.

Pinturicchio

Bernardino di Betto
Perugia, c 1454-Siena, 1513

A fascinating master of large-scale decoration, Pinturicchio produced some of the best ornamental ideas in Umbria and Rome during the whole Renaissance. He was still young when he joined Perugino's studio where he rose to be his assistant, learning Perugino's sweetness of style though not his subtle use of light. In this capacity, he worked initially on the *Life of St. Bernardino* (1473, Galleria Nazionale dell'Umbria, Perugia) and then on the prestigious project for the Sistine chapel (1481). After that Pinturicchio's own career took off and he continued to alternate between Perugia and Rome. These include frescoes in Santa Maria d'Aracoeli, Santa Maria del Popolo, and, most importantly, in the apartments of Pope Alexander VI in the Vatican (1492-1495). The work in Rome provides the proof of how up-to-date Pinturicchio was in his interpretation of mural decoration. He used the antique repertory with genius to stunning effect. Back in Umbria, Pinturicchio painted altarpieces and frescoes. But Pinturicchio's masterpiece remains the splendidly colorful frescoes that cover the walls of the Piccolomini Library in Siena cathedral (1505).

Pinturicchio
Annunciation
1501
fresco
Santa Maria Maggiore,
Baglioni chapel,
Spello (Perugia)

This enchanting scene has rightly become a symbol of the grace of Umbrian art at its best in the fifteenth century. Pinturicchio did not concentrate on the main figures in the scene. Even though they are pleasing to the eye, they do not possess much intensity. What he was really interested in was depicting a host of exuberant and fantastic descriptive details, especially elaborate architecture. He makes use of the very latest ideas. These translated naturally into his well-drafted and deep perspective. They can also be seen in the variety of classical references. To the right of the scene Pinturicchio included his own self-portrait in the form of a little picture on the wall.

Pisanello

Antonio Pisano
Verona (?) c. 1395-Mantua (?), 1455

Pisanello was one of the foremost
exponents of the courtly splendors
of the International Gothic style in
Italy, with a sometimes ironic,
sometimes romantic view of the world.
Because so many of his major works
have been lost, today we only have an
incomplete knowledge of this artist
who played a fundamental role in the
early part of the Quattrocento.
However, the few paintings we have are
supplemented by many excellent
drawings and his renowned medals.
The son of a Pisan merchant (hence his
nickname), the painter trained in the
Veneto, first in Verona and then in
Venice where he worked on frescoes
alongside Gentile da Fabriano (1418-
20). Pisanello then followed Gentile to
Florence in about 1423 and absorbed
the latest Gothic influences. In Verona
during the 1420s Pisanello's career took
off. He painted the *Madonna with a
Quail* (Museo di Castelvecchio) and
the *Annunciation* for the Brenzoni
Monument in San Fermo (c. 1426).
After Gentile da Fabriano's death
(1427), Pisanello was called to Rome to
complete the frescoes in St. John in the
Lateran, which were later destroyed
during the Baroque period. From the
1430s onwards, Pisanello was active in
courts of several princes. In the Palazzo
Ducale in Mantua he painted murals of
courtly scenes. In Ferrara he portrayed
people from the Este court (*Lionello
d'Este*, Bergamo, Accademia Carrara; an
unidentified *Princess*, Paris, Louvre). In
Rimini he produced medals for Novello
Malatesta. His most important work is
a fresco showing *St. George and the
Dragon* in the church of Sant'Anastasia
in Verona (1436-38). Following this
masterpiece, he concentrated mainly
on producing exquisitely elegant
commemorative medals for the rulers
of northern courts and for King
Alfonso of Aragon, to whose court in
Naples he moved in about 1450. After
the middle of the century, the triumph
of Renaissance classical art throughout
Italy led to a rapid decline in his fame
and after his death he was almost
forgotten.

Pisanello
Madonna with a Quail
1420-1422
wood panel
26¼ × 17 in.
(67 × 43.5 cm)
Museo di Castelvecchio,
Verona

Pisanello
St. George and the Princess of Trebizond
detail
1436-1438
fresco
Church of
Sant'Anastasia, Verona

The scene is divided into two contrasting parts. On one side a desolate and dragon-wasted land; on the other side, a Gothic city's fantastically ornate skyline forms the background to the main scene and St. George, watched by the princess, mounts his horse to set out against the monster. Pisanello studied each detail with extraordinary precision and was at pains to reproduce reality exactly, with the animals, the lords and ladies, even the macabre detail of the men hanging from the gallows. But the true magic of Pisanello's painting lies in his capacity to bring his characters to life through their inner spiritual frailty.

Camille Pissarro
Saint-Thomas, Danish West Indies,
1830-Paris, 1903

Settling in France in 1855, Pissarro kept faith throughout his career with the official definition of a painter of landscapes "from life," interested in direct representation of the visual phenomena that unfolded before his eyes. The initial influence of Corot and the Barbizon School gave way, around 1861, to a more up-to-date and stimulating interaction with Monet and Cézanne, with whom he took part in a historic exhibition at the Salon des Refusés in 1863. Pissarro declared that he wanted to eliminate black and dark shadows from his landscapes. For this reason he left Paris for the countryside, moving first to Pontoise and then to Louveciennes. After 1870, when cracks began to show in the solidarity of the Impressionist group, Pissarro saw himself as the custodian of the movement's original spirit.

Opposed to experimentation (apart from a brief dabble in Pointillism), the traditionalist Pissarro became an important point of reference for younger artists. The rural scenes of the sixties gradually gave way to urban views, culminating in his large pictures of boulevards, painted after his return to Paris in the last decade of the century. Pissarro's work at the end of his career remained consistent with that of his debut as he continued to apply the ideas of the Impressionists, using colors taken directly from life and vibrant light.

Camille Pissarro
Apple Picking
1888
oil on canvas,
23½ × 28¾ in.
(60 × 73 cm)
Museum of Fine Arts,
Dallas

Pissarro's paintings of figures deserve more attention than they have received. They are filled with poetry and feeling and are much more open to experimentation with new styles than are his better-known landscapes, which keep strictly to the tenets of Impressionism. In this work, perhaps rather naive in its dreamy idealization of country life, Pissarro adopts the technique of Pointillism.

Camille Pissarro
Factory near Pontoise
1873
oil on canvas, 18 × 21½
in. (45.7 × 54.6 cm)
Museum of Fine Arts,
Springfield

This painting gives a clear idea of the influence exercised by Pissarro on the younger artists who adhered to Impressionism.

Jackson Pollock

Cody, Wyoming, 1912-Springs, Long Island, New York, 1956

Youngest of five brothers, Pollock spent his adolescence in Arizona and California, seduced by the infinity of space in American landscapes. In 1925 he enrolled in the Manual Arts High School of Los Angeles, which he attended until 1929, when he left for New York. His teacher at the Art Students League was Thomas Hart Benton, the leading member of the American regionalist school, and Benton became a figure of great importance to Pollock's future, not only through his teaching but because of his friendship and assistance, becoming a kind of fatherly protector to Pollock. From 1938 to 1942 Pollock worked for the Federal Art Project, the organization set up by the federal government as part of Roosevelt's New Deal to offer public commissions to artists. Pollock's subjects were too private and his sense of scale was not suitable for the decorative needs of public buildings, and he enjoyed little success. The first important occasion in his career was the 1942 exhibit organized by John Graham at the McMillan Gallery in New York, and only one year later he came to the attention of the critics with his first one-man exhibition, held at Peggy Guggenheim's Art of This Century Gallery. He also became a member of Guggenheim's exclusive circle, signing a five-year contract. In 1945 Pollock married the painter Lee Krasner, and in 1946 they moved to East Hampton, New York, where he developed his dripping technique: in a sort of ritual dance he dripped paint directly onto a canvas spread on the floor until he had covered the entire surface with multiple layers of color. The result of this technique is a strongly homogeneous space, without borders or hierarchy, leaving the widest possible freedom for possible pictorial events across the surface of the canvas. In his last decade Pollock worked with violent, frenetic intensity. There was his large one-man show in 1948 at the Art of This Century Gallery in New York, he was at the Venice Biennale in 1950, he exhibited with de Kooning and Gorky, and he was at the Kunsthaus of Zurich in 1953. Consumed by alcoholism and plagued by creative blocks, Pollock lived in physical and moral decline until his death in a car accident, on August 11, 1956.

Jackson Pollock
Lavender Mist
1950
oil, enamel, aluminum on canvas, 87 × 118 in. (221 × 300 cm)
National Gallery of Art, Washington, D.C.

Silver aluminum paints, which first appeared in 1947, function much like other paints, but they guarantee a play of radiant tones. If the ambient light changes or if the viewer moves in front of the work, the silver tonalities shine and look paler or more luminous, or they become more static and opaque.

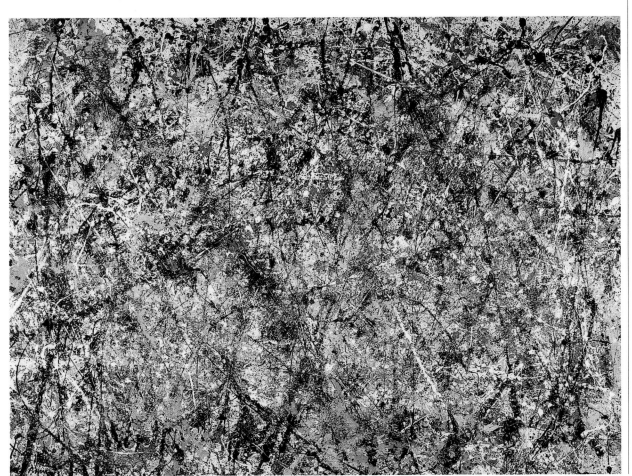

Pontormo

Jacopo Carucci Pontormo
Florence, 1494-Florence, 1557

The unhappy course of Pontormo's life was a decisive factor in the evolution of Mannerism in Florence, a style that was initially a "rebellion," polemically opposed to the elegant image inherited from the late fifteenth century. Later it gradually came to be a more "official" art, in which the relationship with Raphael and Michelangelo became almost an obsession. A central figure in Florentine painting in the early decades of the sixteenth century, Pontormo made insistent, almost relentless use of studio drawings of gestures and expressions. The subsequent application of color was deliberately cold and unnatural, and underscored the intellectual control of the compositions. Having trained in Florentine artistic circles in the early sixteenth century, surrounded by the echoes of Savonarola's sermons and the early works of Michelangelo, Pontormo started out, as a pupil of Andrea del Sarto, painting frescoes in the church of the Santissima Annunziata and in the cloisters of Santa Maria Novella. From the outset, his work was marked by an evident desire to fully depict the emotions of his figures, thus breaking with the tradition of less defined expression typical of Botticelli and Perugino. With this end in view, he did not hesitate to refer to new figurative models such as the prints of Dürer. Pontormo's career was rapid, filling the gap left in the Florentine school by the departure of Michelangelo and Raphael for Rome, and the return of the elderly Leonardo to Milan. Around 1520 he established himself as the most interesting Tuscan artist, and together with Rosso Fiorentino, was the leading figure in the emergence of Mannerism. He was invited by the Medici family to decorate their villa at Poggio a Caiano (1519-1521), and shortly afterwards executed the frescoed lunettes in the cloister of the Certosa del Galluzzo, which despite the rather poor state of preservation, still display an extraordinary creative power. Around 1525 he worked on the Capponi chapel in the church of Santa Felicita, Florence, painting the *Deposition* on the altar, the fresco of the *Annunciation* on the side wall, and three of the four *tondi* with the *Evangelists* on the vault, the fourth was executed by his promising pupil Bronzino. This phase of his career

came to an end in 1529, when the siege of Florence by the imperialist troops threw him into despair, leaving him beset by the feelings of unease that he had so far managed to keep largely under control. His strangeness turned into eccentricity, his melancholy into solipsism, and his difficulty in human relations into neurosis. An early example of the *artiste maudit*, Pontormo launched

himself into a massive undertaking, the decoration of the apse of the Basilica of San Lorenzo. His intention was to rival Michelangelo, but the results of years of toil, evidenced by the drawings that have survived, were disappointing. No trace of the frescoes remains.

Pontormo
Deposition
1525-1529
oil on wood
12¼ × 75½ in.
(313 × 192 cm)
Capponi chapel, Santa Felicita, Florence

One of the most disturbing works in all of Italian painting, this is the expression of innovative courage as well as of a growing sense of unease. The panel should more appropriately be called the *Bearing Christ to the Tomb* since it depicts a kind of funeral procession or, to be more precise, the moment in which the helpers raise the body of Christ to carry it toward the tomb. There is, however, no dynamic effect or sense of movement. The composition is frozen in a series of dramatic poses, a dense, concentric tangle of figures. The bright, unreal, enameled colors and the dazzling light accentuate the claustrophobic, stifling atmosphere of the painting. The incongruous little cloud to the left is the paradoxical evocation of a landscape that does not exist, of an evidently artificial atmosphere. The gap between the Florentine and Venetian schools at this time was extremely wide, as can be seen from a comparison with Titian's *Pesaro Altarpiece*.

Pordenone

Giovanni Antonio de' Sacchis
Pordenone, c. 1483-Ferrara, 1539

Named for the north Italian town where he was born, Pordenone is too often written off as a weird provincial rival to Titian. After training with an unknown master, Pordenone produced his first works in Friuli soon after 1510. These show the influence of Giorgione and Titian mingling with that of German woodcuts, especially Dürer's prints, and Mantegna's illusionism. During a trip to Rome he saw the work of Michelangelo and Raphael, which added solidity to his art. Later, he absorbed certain Mannerist influences. After painting illusionistic frescoes for the Malchiostro chapel in Treviso cathedral (a first for Venetian art) Pordenone began painting the frescoes on the inner façade and the main nave of Cremona cathedral (1520-1522) which show his gift for depicting bizarre groups of figures in melodramatic situations. This gift was confirmed in the doors he created for the Spilimbergo organ. After a brief period in Venice, in 1530 he went to work in Emilia. Bolstered by new stimuli learned from Correggio and Parmigianino, Pordenone tackled the Venetian art world again, becoming for a moment a real rival to Titian. He died in Ferrara, where he had gone to design tapestries for the Duke.

Pordenone
Crucifixion
1520-1522, fresco
Cathedral, Cremona

Located on the inner façade of the cathedral, this is the most impressive of the murals of the *Passion of Christ* that were the contribution of Pordenone to the large-scale decorative cycle painted by various artists in Cremona cathedral. The ample space offered by the Romanesque building allowed him to give free rein to his violent, dramatic, and highly charged theatrical vein.

The composition has the air of a painterly whirlwind and was much appreciated by the public. It was a fundamental departure from the traditional way that Calvary had previously been shown. The muggy, storm-laden atmosphere conjures up amazing effects of light. The three crosses are arranged in an asymmetrical fashion and are viewed from an angle. The crowd mills around uncomfortably and the dramatically foreshortened horses have an almost demonic look about them.

The entire composition focuses around the tall mercenary at the center. When he took over the job of painting the frescoes in the cathedral of Cremona from Romanino, he revolutionized the local school.

Nicolas Poussin
Les Andelys, 1594-Rome, 1665

Born into a noble family that had seen better days, against the wishes of his father, who wanted him to become a magistrate, Poussin became involved, at an early age, with the workshop of Quentin Varin, a modest Mannerist painter who was in Les Andelys from 1611 to 1612. This experience confirmed him in his vocation, and on Varin's departure, he ran away to Paris to begin a difficult period of training. In 1622 he met the Italian poet Giovan Battista Marino, who appreciated his painting and offered him protection and friendship. Although Poussin's fame was beginning to spread in Paris, where he received important commissions, he left the city for Rome in 1624. There he was reunited with Marino, who helped him secure the patronage of Cardinal Barberini, and

he continued his training through the study of Raphael and Roman sculpture, with an eye also on the Caravaggesque school and Bolognese classicism of Reni and Domenichino. In 1628 Poussin was commissioned by Cardinal Barberini to paint an altarpiece of the *Martyrdom of St. Erasmus* for an altar in St. Peter's, where Vouet and Valentin de Boulogne were also working. In 1630, having failed to secure an important commission for the church of San Luigi dei Francesi, he decided to abandon large-scale official works and devoted his energies to paintings on a smaller scale. He thus regained the favor of French collectors, who became his main admirers and patrons. Urged by friends to return to France, he hesitated until 1640, when the promptings became still more insistent and the promises of work more attractive. On his arrival in Paris, he was warmly

welcomed by Cardinal Richelieu and by Louis XIII himself, who appointed him "first painter to the king" and placed him in charge of all painting and decorative work for the royal residences. He soon found the obligations of this demanding life at court irksome and left Paris in 1642, and he took refuge in Rome. The deaths of Cardinal Richelieu at the end of the year and the king in the following year convinced Poussin that it would be better to remain in Rome, where he led a life devoted to work and enlivened only by visits from friends and French patrons. The last period of his career was marked by increased interest in the natural landscape. The Louvre series of *Four Seasons*, painted between 1660 and 1664 for the Duc de Richelieu, constitutes his artistic and spiritual testament.

Nicolas Poussin
Bacchanalian Revel Before a Herm of Pan
c. 1631-1633
oil on canvas, 39¼ × 56 in. (100 × 142.5 cm)
National Gallery, London

He drew inspiration from the *Bacchanals* painted by Titian in the Villa Aldobrandini in Rome. The composition is based on a diagonal line stretching from the tree trunk to the fallen nymph, a vertical line formed by the statue of Pan and the trees behind it, and a horizontal line linking the dancers in the foreground to the distant plain.

Nicolas Poussin
*Landscape with Orpheus
and Eurydice*
1648
oil on canvas
47¼ × 78¾ in.
(120 × 200 cm)
Musée du Louvre, Paris

The dramatic separation
of the two lovers of
Greek myth is depicted
in a Roman setting that
includes Castel
Sant'Angelo. This is
hardly surprising given
Poussin's view of
painting as primarily a
mental construct. In any
case, the discrepancy
regards the organization
of the canvas, but not
the depiction of the
individual elements,
where the artist never
loses contact with truth
and nature.

Nicolas Poussin
*Landscape with
Polyphemus*
1649
oil on canvas
59 × 78 in.
(150 × 198 cm)
Hermitage,
St. Petersburg

This is one of Poussin's
most important
landscapes, and indeed
contains no trace of the
dramatic Homeric
episode. The wholly
idyllic scene alludes to, if
anything, Virgil's bucolic
world and a sort of
primitive communion
between man and
nature.

Andrea Pozzo

Trent, 1642-Vienna, 1709

With the superb and highly imaginative use of perspective in works executed for the vast spaces of churches in Rome and Vienna, the Jesuit Andrea Pozzo marks a phase of scenographic development in Baroque art, understood in this case as a moving and convincing affirmation of belief in the Catholic faith and its heroes. Painter, architect, scenographer, and supplier of designs for sculptures and ornamentation, Father Pozzo was an extremely active, versatile artist of great importance in the development of Baroque religious art in the Catholic countries. He received his early training in northern Italy, and made journeys to study in Milan, Genoa, and Venice. Andrea Pozzo assimilated the best elements of Counter-Reformation figurative culture, and put his early training to good use during a long stay in Turin and Piedmont. In response to the requirements of the Jesuit Order, he produced a significant number of altarpieces, many for provincial towns, and successfully tried his hand at perspective frescoes in the church of San Francesco Saverio in Mondovì. He moved to Rome, where his career reached its climax with the work on the church of Jesus, including the astonishing polychromatic altar of precious materials, devoted to St. Ignatius. Andrea Pozzo thus took over the legacy of Bernini by continuing the idea of a "total work of art." His absolute masterpiece is the ceiling of the church of S. Ignazio, a memorable work of great importance for the future development of painting, especially in Austria and Germany, where Andrea Pozzo is a well-known figure. In 1703 he moved to Vienna, where he continued to work for the Jesuits (producing frescoes in the college of the Order and in the old university building, and restructuring the inside of the church), but also for the counts of Liechtenstein and for other patrons.

Andrea Pozzo
*The Glory of St. Ignatius
of Loyola*
1691-1694
frescoed ceiling
Church of Sant'Ignazio,
Rome

Enguerrand Quarton
Laon, c. 1415-Avignon, 1466

Active in the south of France—Aix, Arles, and Avignon—from 1444 to 1466, Enguerrand Quarton played a crucial role in the rebirth of Provencal art. While he is unquestionably the painter of the *Coronation of the Virgin* and the *Virgin of Mercy* (Musée Condé, Chantilly), the attribution to him of the *Avignon Pietà* is still uncertain. The characteristics peculiar to this artist include a rigorous composition based on a tripartite scheme, stylistic sobriety, and a monumental handling of figures, qualities that link him to the great Italian painters before him from Beato Angelico to Piero della Francesca. The stylized forms reduced to their essential volumes, the balanced handling of mass, and the violent light that emphasizes the facial bone structure reveal Quarton as a creative genius who was far ahead of his time and indeed anticipates the art of Cézanne.

Enguerrand Quarton
Avignon Pietà
c. 1450
oil on wood
64¼ × 85¾ in.
(163 × 218 cm)
Musée du Louvre, Paris

The isolated figures, each absorbed in their own sorrow, stand out against the gilded background of an imaginary Jerusalem in an atmosphere of restrained tragedy.

Mary, with the figure of the dead Christ stretched out on her knees, is flanked by St. John and Mary Magdalene. Kneeling in isolation on the left of the panel is the figure of a praying canon, whose white vestment echoes the different shades of the same color used for Mary's veil and the short loincloth covering Jesus.

Enguerrand Quarton
Coronation of the Virgin
1453-1454
oil on wood
72 × 86¾ in.
(183 × 220 cm)
Musée Municipal,
Villeneuve-lès-Avignon

The Carthusians of
Villeneuve-lès-Avignon
commissioned Quarton
to produce this splendid
work in 1453 to
decorate the altar of the
Trinity in their church.

Its scenographic layout
constitutes a singular
arrangement of the vast
Christian universe. The
space is divided into two
areas, heaven and earth,
connected by the figure
of Christ on the cross.
Earthly life is depicted
at the bottom, as though
forming a predella,
in scenes alluding to
Hell and Purgatory.
The work is dominated
by the depiction of
heavenly life. Groups of

red angels are arranged
in two parallel rows
against a gold ground
with groups of the elect
and the blessed
on either side also
participating in the
divine event taking place
in the center, where the
great figures of the
Trinity are grouped
around Our Lady.

Raphael Santi
Urbino, 1483-Rome, 1520

Having studied under his father, Giovanni Santi, a painter at the court of the Montefeltro family, Raphael, from an early age, assimilated the serene spirit of the art of Urbino. On his father's death in 1494, the eleven-year-old Raphael needed to find somewhere to complete his apprenticeship, and during his studies he soon came into direct contact with Pietro Perugino, the most celebrated artist at the time. His early period ended in 1504 when, after painting the *Betrothal of the Virgin* (now in Milan), he moved to Florence to study the works of Leonardo and Michelangelo. His style developed and matured; he was now a full-fledged independent artist. In 1508 Pope Julius II summoned him to Rome to work on the decoration of the papal apartments. He thus began the series known as the "Raphael Rooms," a project initiated in 1508 and concluded after the artist's death, one of the most astounding art works in the world. The first room was once the pope's private library, divided into four sections: theology, philosophy, poetry, and law. These branches of learning are alluded to in the vast compositions that decorate the walls, with scenes of impressive breadth and serene poise. The nobility of antiquity, the power of Michelangelo, the color of the Venetian artists, and, above all, a new dramatic energy characterize the style of the thirty-year-old Raphael, at the time of the Stanza di Eliodoro, the second to be executed in the Vatican, begun in 1511 and finished in 1514, the year after the death of Julius II. This room, whose general tone is undoubtedly more intense and violent compared to the previous one, clearly expresses the political purpose of the pope, who is conspicuously present in the first two scenes. In 1514, for Leo X, Raphael began work on the room known as the Stanza dell'Incendio after the theme of the main fresco, the only one executed personally by Raphael. The depiction of the fire that had broken out in medieval Rome became an opportunity for a spectacular evocation of the gestures, customs, and figures of the past. For almost a century the fresco would remain a source of inspiration for Mannerist painters. Raphael's activity in Rome was intense, and his intellectual role extended to other fields: architecture, the study of

archeology, the conservation of the cultural heritage, and the organization of increasingly complex decorations. He often left the manual execution of the works to his pupils, and concentrated on creating extraordinary drawings. He continued, however, to paint unforgettable

masterpieces that were to become new and original chapters in the history of art. In the last few years of his life, he took particular interest in architecture and archeology. His tribute to antiquity is clear in the decorative work in the Vatican, which accompanied the constant extension

of the palaces designed by Bramante. Raphael died on April 17, 1520, at the age of only thirty-seven. His last work was the magnificent unfinished *Transfiguration* in the Pinacoteca Vaticana.

Opposite
Raphael
Sistine Madonna
1512-1513
oil on canvas
104½ × 77¾ in.
(265 × 196 cm)
Gemäldegalerie,
Dresden

The title of this work is taken from its original location in the Church of San Sisto in Piacenza. The enchanting figure of the Virgin Mary, who seems to be advancing toward us, appears from open drapes on a bank of clouds. The face of the Virgin resembles that of Raphael's mistress, Margherita Luti, who became famous as the "Fornarina," the daughter of a Sienese baker who had a shop in the Santa Dorotea neighborhood of the city.

Raphael
Madonna of the Chair
1513
oil on wood
diam. 28 in. (71 cm)
Galleria Palatina,
Palazzo Pitti, Florence

If it were possible to look at the *Madonna of the Chair* as an "ordinary" painting, it would be easy to see it as a remarkable synthesis of the *Mona Lisa* and the *Doni Tondo*. Such an exercise, however, is impossible, for the simple reason that it is not we who are looking at the Madonna, it is she who is looking at us, drawing us gently into a whirl of feelings and smiles, a spiral of caresses and glances that has no equal in the whole history of art.

Raphael
Alba Madonna
c. 1509
oil on wood transferred to canvas
diam. 37¾ in. (96 cm)
National Gallery of Art, Washington, D.C.

This Virgin with her reassuring smile and moving beauty is the first in a remarkable series of variations on the most celebrated theme in the history of painting. One after the other, Raphael's paintings of Madonnas form a gallery of delicate, tender, subtle charms and smiles; they also display his exceptional ability to develop poses, groups, landscapes, and light in increasingly complex ways.

Raphael
The Miracle of Bolsena
1512
fresco, base 260 in.
(660 cm)
Stanza di Eliodoro, Palazzi
Vaticani, Vatican

Raphael
The Deliverance of St. Peter
1512-1513

fresco, base 260 in.
(660 cm)
Stanza di Eliodoro, Palazzi
Vaticani, Vatican

Julius II died in 1513.
This extraordinary fresco
of *The Deliverance of
St. Peter* is very probably a
reference to the death of
the pope.

Raphael
School of Athens
1510
fresco, base 303 in.
(770 cm)
Stanza della Segnatura,
Palazzi Vaticani, Vatican

Robert Rauschenberg

Port Arthur, Texas, 1925

Rauschenberg shares with Johns the idea of the relationship between a painting and an object. In his so-called combine paintings, the painting is recognized as an object that is itself composed of other objects, all with the aim of translating daily life to the canvas. In the works of Johns, although painting is taken as the means used for creating the pictorial, it maintains its supremacy; Rauschenberg, on the other hand, considers painting as a work of art complete to itself and on the same plane as other objects. Rauschenberg's constant objective is current events: the works of Ingres, integrated with photographs of contemporary events, introduce the past in the daily, in the definition of a reality joined to the present. Rauschenberg began studying painting in 1946, attending the Kansas City Art Institute; in 1948 he went to Paris and studied at the Académie Julian. Then he went to North Carolina's Black Mountain College, where, in keeping with the teaching of Josef Albers, he created his monochrome paintings, from the White Paintings (1951) to the Black Paintings (1951–52) to the Red Paintings (1953). As early as 1953, however, he joined to his monochromes his first combine paintings, the assemblages of objects, photographs, and painting that would constitute his principle production.

Halfway between avant-garde and kitsch, his combinations set off an inventive process in continuous evolution, in the conviction that only in this dynamic dimension can art preserve its vitality. In 1958 Leo Castelli gave Rauschenberg his first one-man show in his New York gallery. During the 1960s, at the height of his experimentations in combine paintings and trying to overcome the fixity of the canvas, Rauschenberg abandoned the two-dimensional sphere to introduce materials picked up in the street, such as the wheels or doors of cars, constructing a mobile urban landscape in continuous transformation.

Robert Rauschenberg
Untitled
1955
combine painting,
15½ × 20¾ in.
(39.4 × 52.7 cm)
Jasper Johns Collection,
New York

Man Ray
Philadelphia, 1890-Paris, 1976

An American painter, photographer, and filmmaker, he was convinced of the absolute prominence of the image and its significance over the technique used to produce it, assigning complete equality to all means of expression. He met Picabia and Duchamp in New York in 1915 and together they founded the American Dada movement. When he moved to Paris in 1921, Duchamp introduced him to the Dadaists there, who involved him in their activities. While Duchamp with his ready-mades turned any chosen object into a work of art, Man Ray intervened to modify the object, taking away its natural function. Famous are his *Gift* (1921), an iron with a row of tacks fixed onto its bottom, and *Object to Be Destroyed* (1923), a metronome with a photograph of the eye of the woman he loved and hated attached to its pendulum. His irreverent research led him to try out new techniques in the realm of photography. Working directly on the film, without a camera, Man Ray produced abstract images in black and white. He called these pictures, made by placing objects directly on light-sensitive paper and exposing them, "rayographs." In 1922 he published a collection of twelve rayographs, entitled *Les Champs Délicieux* and with an introduction by Tzara. He brought a similar freedom of imagination to the language of film: irrationality, automatism, absence of plot, psychological and dream sequences devoid of apparent logic.
In 1926 he made the short film *Anémic Cinéma* in collaboration with Marcel Duchamp. In the thirties he went back to the construction of enigmatic objects, often repeating them several times as he considered the act of making them more important than the idea itself. From 1940 to 1951 he lived in the United States and then returned to Paris, where he remained until his death.

Man Ray
Good Weather
1939
oil on canvas
112 × 108 in.
(284.5 × 274.3 cm)
Private collection

The painting, which remained in the possession of his wife Juliet until her death, was sold at Sotheby's in London in 1994. In the foreground we see two mysterious and threatening figures: an androgynous mannequin, whose head is a lantern lit by a candle, is opening a door with a trickle of blood running from its keyhole. On each side of the mannequin, two gigantic forks are outlined against the backdrop of a breached wall, under a limpid sky. On the other side of the door, itself anthropomorphic in appearance, the second mannequin stands in front of a building. Through its glass walls we can see an easel and a man and woman embracing, while two wild beasts are locked in combat on the roof. With this work, painted on the eve of the Second World War, Man Ray took his leave of Paris and returned to the United States.

319

Rembrandt Harmenszoon van Rijn

Leyden, 1606-Amsterdam, 1669

A miller's son who grew up with a lower-middle-class, provincial background, Rembrandt determinedly pursued his vocation for painting, and was prepared to follow a difficult and arduous path when he was young to reach artistic heights. Though he never left Holland and only traveled the short distance between Leyden and Amsterdam, he measured himself against international painters. A truly versatile artist, he tackled the most varied themes, subjects, and formats with remarkable energy and originality. A highly skilled draftsman, Rembrandt is also one of the greatest engravers in history and specialized in etchings. His prodigious oeuvre follows a human and individual course and the long series of self-portraits, executed over a period of forty years, provides the most direct, moving, emotional testimony of his life. After learning the rudiments of his art in Leyden, the young Rembrandt went to Amsterdam. He trained with the Italianate master Pieter Lastman and learned the style and composition of great classical painting. He made the decision to devote himself mainly to historical subjects and compete with the Italian models. In fact, following the example of artists like Titian,

Raphael, and Leonardo, he decided to sign his paintings with his first name only. On his return to Leyden, he collaborated with Jan Lievens, and for several years the two young painters worked side by side, often exchanging roles and painting similar subjects. Because of his commissions, Rembrandt painted what the Leyden customers preferred: small works on biblical and literary subjects, executed with finesse and precision down to the tiniest detail. Noted by intellectuals and art dealers, Rembrandt was urged to leave the provincial environment of Leyden and work in the capital, Amsterdam. The riveting *Anatomy Lesson of Dr. Tulp* (1632, Mauritshuis, The Hague), Rembrandt's first major public commission in Amsterdam, marked his passage from youth to maturity. Promoted by a competent art dealer, Rembrandt soon became known as an impassioned portraitist. His fame constantly increased, and so did his wealth, which he mostly used to amass a confused though impressive collection of art works and natural curiosities. Rembrandt married Saskia van Ulyenburch and their early years together were the happiest of his life. He was then engaged in painting a series of canvases depicting the *Passion of Christ* for the stadtholder Frederick Henry of Orange. During the 1630s Rembrandt abandoned the meticulous style of his early works and turned to

monumental compositions, similar to those by Italian Renaissance masters, but characterized by a highly individual play of light and shadow, and color. In 1642, the painter's career reached its height with the execution of the imposing group portrait known as *The Night Watch* (Rijksmuseum, Amsterdam). However, in the same year, the death of Saskia marked the beginning of a ruinous series of personal misfortunes, which led Rembrandt through endless legal wrangles to complete bankruptcy and the auction of all his possessions. Rembrandt's decline was also linked to the changing tastes of the Dutch public, which was little inclined to accept the artist's late works, that appeared to be merely sketched and unfinished because of their free brushwork and thickly applied paint. Rembrandt did not receive further public commissions until his last years, and these included the historical painting *The Conspiracy of the Batavians*. Rembrandt's style toward the end of his life is similar to the late manner of Titian. He painted outstanding masterpieces like the *Prodigal Son* and *The Jewish Bride* that are intensely human and have a depth of feeling that becomes almost unbearable. The death of his beloved son Titus, in 1668, was the final blow in an exemplary, unique life.

Rembrandt Harmenszoon van Rijn

The Night Watch
1642
oil on canvas
41¼ ×172½ in.
(359 × 438 cm)
Rijksmuseum, Amsterdam

The title of Rembrandt's most famous masterpiece, a landmark in the history of art, is not a true description of the scene, which does not take place at night, but in broad daylight, and depicts a festive parade rather than a watch. The protagonist is Captain Frans

Banning Cocq, at the center of the composition, who is inviting his extremely elegant lieutenant, Willem van Ruytemburg, to line up the company for the parade. The painting was destined to decorate the meeting room of the Amsterdam civic militia, and was in the tradition of group portraits of the companies that defended the city, a genre in which Frans Hals excelled. Compared with Hals's already very animated scenes, Rembrandt renders this painting

even more dynamic and full of action. Twenty-eight adults and three children are moving confusedly in this scene. The striking contrasts of light and color, the individual portrayal of all the various characters, and the total mastery of this complicated composition set this painting at the height of Rembrandt's career. This large work also contains some disturbing and unusual details, like the little fair-haired girl on the left, with a chicken tied to her belt, running

away in fear, and the face of Rembrandt himself between the standard bearer and the helmeted man to the right of him. Because the painter was short, only the top part of his face is visible, but this is enough to recognize his unmistakable features that were made famous by his many self-portraits.

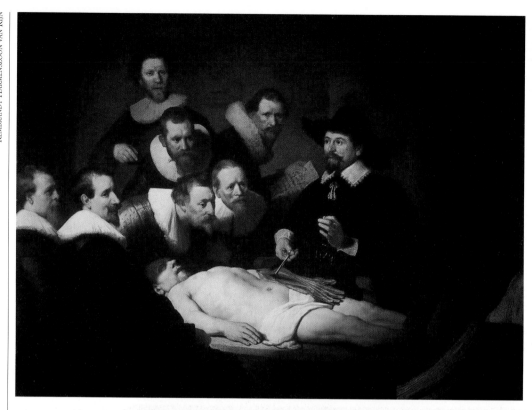

Rembrandt Harmenszoon van Rijn
The Anatomy Lesson of Dr. Tulp
1632
oil on canvas
66¾ × 85 in.
(169.5 × 216 cm)
Mauritshuis, The Hague

This masterpiece marks a turning point in Rembrandt's career; in fact it is the painting that gained the twenty-six-year-old artist entry into the artistic circles of Amsterdam, which resulted in his consequent departure from Leyden. The work, originally painted for the seat of the surgeons' guild in Amsterdam, depicts a lesson given by Dr. Tulp, one of the most celebrated physicians in Holland. The seven men gathered around the dissecting table are not doctors but town councilors (their names are on the piece of paper one of them is holding). Their expressions are a mix of scientific interest and repulsion. Dr. Tulp is dissecting the left arm of the corpse, exposing the tendons; his left hand is miming the contractions and movements of the fingers. The anatomical precision indicates Rembrandt's direct observation; he was interested in movement and had a knowledge of the human body equal to Leonardo's.

Rembrandt Harmenszoon van Rijn
The Blinding of Samson
1636
oil on wood, 93 × 119 in. (236 × 302 cm)
Städelsches Kunstinstitut, Frankfurt

The artist gave this to the celebrated scholar Costantijn Huygens, as a sign of his esteem and gratitude for the support he had received at the court of The Hague. Huygens was a connoisseur and admirer of Italian art, and for this reason Rembrandt is inspired by the dynamism and diagonal light of Caravaggio. This religious painting depicts Samson captured and blinded by the Philistines. In the background, the traitress Delilah is seen holding the cut hair of the hero.

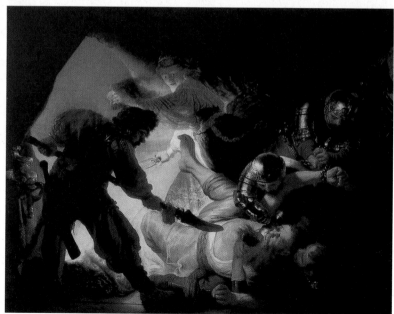

**Rembrandt
Harmenszoon van Rijn**
*The Syndics of the Cloth
Guild*
1662
oil on canvas
75¼ × 109¾ in.
(191 × 279 cm)
Rijksmuseum,
Amsterdam

In 1662, as a sign of his
return to favor with the
patrons of Amsterdam,
Rembrandt was
commissioned to paint a
group portrait (the last
one had been *The Night
Watch*, twenty years
earlier). The syndics of
the cloth guild are
depicted around a table
looking through a book
of samples. The group,
which the painter
studied at length in
drawings and sketches,
is rendered extremely
dynamic by the free,
broad handling typical
of Rembrandt's last
years.

**Rembrandt
Harmenszoon van Rijn**
*The Conspiracy of the
Batavians*
1661
oil on canvas
77¼ × 121¾ in.
(196 × 309 cm)
Nationalmuseum,
Stockholm

Like the portrait of the
group of syndics of the
cloth guild, this marks
Rembrandt's return to
large, important works for
public commissions. The
painting depicts the
conspiracy of Guido Civile
who led the Batavians of
Holland against the
Roman invaders, and it
was executed for the town
hall in Amsterdam (now
the Royal Palace). This is
only the central portion of
a much larger
composition, which was
seriously damaged and has
long since been forgotten.

Frederic Remington

Canton, New York, 1861-Ridgefield, Connecticut, 1909

Painter and sculptor of exceptionally popular success, Frederic Remington was the bard of the West. Many directors of western movies proudly acknowledge having drawn inspiration from his works; John Ford himself cites a Remington painting in a famous sequence in *Stagecoach*, one of the masterpieces of the genre. Remington had a solid classical education, including art studies at Yale, and although he made only one trip to Europe, late in life and in a hurried manner, he kept up to date on Old World artistic trends. Such considerations are indispensable to any understanding of Remington's special style, apparently so inspired by immediate, even "photographic"

experience, but in reality the result of thorough skills and a great deal of preparation. Although he was born on the East Coast and spent his childhood there, Remington felt the call of the frontier and made his first trip west, to Montana, in 1881, at the age of twenty. The next year he began contributing to the leading periodicals of the day, such as *Harper's Weekly* and *Century Illustrated Magazine*. He soon developed a singular style, with images of striking visual impact using primarily pale colors. Over the course of the next decade he alternated trips to the West—during which he made sketches from life to later work into paintings and sculptures—with activity as a popular writer and illustrator of books. His fame received a further boost in 1901 when nationally popular periodicals began printing full-color, double-page

reproductions of his paintings. Remington was and is acclaimed as the witness to an adventure shared by all Americans, as Theodore Roosevelt acknowledged in a commemorative speech given a year after the artist's death. Although praised by the public and critics, who enthusiastically ranked him among the greatest of all American artists, Remington felt a growing melancholy during the last years of his life. Just before his fortieth birthday, he lamented, "My West passed out of existence so long ago as to make it merely a dream." Only eight years later he died of appendicitis.

Frederic Remington
Dismounted: The Fourth Troopers Moving the Led Horses
1890
oil on canvas, 34 × 48¾ in. (86.5 × 124 cm)
Sterling and Francine Clark Art Institute, Williamstown, Massachusetts

Remington reached the heights of his celebrity with dramatic action-packed scenes that today seem like painted photographs, while the canvases with only a few, solitary figures have more of a sense of melancholy for a world on the verge of ending.

Guido Reni
Bologna, 1575-1642

Pupil and follower of Annibale Carracci, model student of the Carracci Academy, expert in classical art and Raphael, Guido Reni is an outstanding master of seventeenth-century European art. For nearly three centuries, his pure, adamantine style, perfectly poised between formal precision and expressive density, was regarded as an absolute model. In the twentieth century, however, Reni's alleged "coldness" led to his being considered boring and monotonous. A more balanced critical view now prevails, and Guido Reni is again seen as one of the most intense figures in seventeenth-century European painting. After training in Bologna, he moved to Rome around the year 1600. This marked the beginning of a truly

exciting decade. Reni went from Annibale Carracci's Farnese Gallery to the chapels with canvases by Caravaggio, seeking a stylistic point of contact between the two apparently very different approaches. The resulting works of great interest demonstrated Guido Reni's critical acumen and artistic talent, and brought him to the attention of collectors and patrons. On the death of Annibale Carracci (1609), Guido Reni became the leading exponent of classicism and of the Bolognese school in Rome. The fresco of *The Dawn* in Palazzo Rospigliosi constitutes the ideal continuation of Annibale Carracci's work for the Farnese family and a solemn token of the painter's love for classical art. The great altarpieces painted for churches in Bologna, most of which are now exhibited in the city's Pinacoteca

Nazionale, mark the apotheosis of a style of painting based on ideas, formal control of the emotions, and perfect balance between all the elements (light, color, expression, draftsmanship, and composition). Until the 1630s, Guido Reni remained faithful to a rich stylistic model full of color and energy. Then, in the last few years of his life, his painting became attenuated and evanescent, and he used a limited range of almost transparent colors, in which beauty and melancholy are mingled.

Guido Reni
Atalanta and Hippomenes
1622-1625
oil on canvas, 81 × 117 in. (206 × 297 cm)
Galleria Nazionale di Capodimonte, Naples

The subject lends itself to a dynamic interpretation, but Reni instead chooses to adopt a sophisticated stylistic device in which the gleaming bodies of the two adversaries are set in contrasting poses against the blue-brown background of earth and sky. The scene depicts the race between the quick-footed and invincible Atalanta and the wily Hippomenes.

325

Pierre-Auguste Renoir
Limoges, 1841-Cagnes-sur-Mer, 1919

Born into a family of craftsmen, his entry into the art world was a difficult one, comparable to that of an apprentice in the Renaissance. Before starting to paint on canvas, in fact, the young Renoir was obliged to work as a decorator of porcelain and textiles. Entering the Ecole des Beaux-Arts in 1862, he became a fellow student of Monet and Sisley at the teaching studio run by Marc-Gabriel Gleyre. The suffocating academicism of the Ecole, contrasting strongly with the realism professed by Courbet and developments in landscape painting *en plein air*, induced Renoir and his companions to lighten their palettes and take their inspiration directly from reality, not only where the subjects were concerned but also (and no less importantly) in their choice of colors and tones. His family origins and lifestyle led Renoir to paint the locations and figures typical of Sunday outings by the Parisian *petite bourgeoisie*: open-air dances, meeting places, boat trips, and the parks along the Seine. During the sixties Renoir experimented successfully with the use of colored shadows, which proved particularly effective in landscapes. At the memorable exhibition held at Nadar's studio in 1874, Renoir showed *La Loge* (*The Theater Box*, Courtauld

Institute, London), demonstrating his exceptional talent as a portraitist, especially of young women and children. His way of painting faces is highly characteristic, using brilliant light to accentuate the eyes and lips and leaving the rest of the features almost neutral. Among his Parisian paintings, the *Moulin de la Galette* (1876, Musée d'Orsay, Paris) has rightly become a symbol of *joie de vivre*. The year 1881 marked a significant turning point in Renoir's career. A long journey through Central and Southern Italy brought him into contact with the classical painting of the Renaissance and Hellenistic art, impelling him to produce more carefully considered compositions. Thus the spontaneous and delightful images of nature as it appears to the eye gave way to sweeping compositions of volumes (especially women's bodies, increasingly often nude and of ample, almost Rubensian, proportions), in a color that was still very luminous but less brilliant and light in tone. In his old age a progressive form of arthritis confined him to a wheelchair: in order to paint, Renoir was obliged to tie the brushes to his fingers. Even under these conditions, he went on painting to the end, courageously producing paeans to youth and the beauty of women set in the dazzling light of the Côte d'Azur.

Pierre-Auguste Renoir
Dance at the Moulin de la Galette
1876
oil on canvas
51¼ × 69 in.
(130 × 175 cm)
Musée d'Orsay, Paris

A favorite hangout of the lower middle-class, the Moulin de la Galette was the most typical of the Sunday rendezvous spots in nineteenth-century Paris. For Renoir, who came from a humble family, the outdoor dancing, tables laden with refreshments, and summer dresses worn by the girls were a genuine delight. Renoir joyfully immersed himself in the buzz of voices, rustle of clothing, and laughter, presenting an image of carefree happiness. The picture, one of the most famous of all Impressionist works, was painted at perhaps the most original and important stage of Renoir's career, when he developed the interests he shared with other artists in the group (subjects drawn from daily life, colored shadows, painting in the open air) into an independent style characterized by its unmistakable brushwork rich and dense in color.

Pierre-Auguste Renoir
The Pont Neuf, Paris
1872
oil on canvas
29½ × 36½ in.
(75 × 93 cm)
National Gallery,
Washington, D.C.

Renoir painted relatively
few urban views of
Paris, usually preferring
people to landscapes.
When he did paint
the city, he chose well-
known landmarks,
flooded with light
and animated by the
movement of people
and vehicles.

Pierre-Auguste Renoir
*The Luncheon of the
Boating Party at Bougival*
1880-1881
oil on canvas, 51¼ × 69
in. (130 × 175 cm)
Philips Collection,
Washington, D.C.

The fact that he painted
pictures of similar
subjects over a span of
several decades makes it
possible to gain a clear
idea of the evolution
of his style. From the
*Dance at the Moulin
de la Galette*, there was a
gradual shift to more
rounded and solid forms,
in softer, less vivid colors.

Ilya Repin

Cugujev, 1844-Kuokkala, 1930

Repin is the most interesting and representative of the Russian painters of the nineteenth century. The meaty and vital realism of his pictures may appear in line with movements in Central and Southern Europe, but at home his work was initially seen as subversive, or at any rate very bold. In fact it is necessary to consider the vast gap in culture and technique that separated the paintings of Repin and the other nineteenth-century "Wanderers" (*Peredvizhniki* in Russian) from a tradition that still harked back to Byzantine art. Dissatisfied with the teaching in the academies, and above all irritated with the insistence on non-Russian themes, Repin gathered a group of artists around himself and became the leading figure in a cooperative on the Abramtsevo estate that later came to be known as the Society of Wandering Exhibitions. This group, flanked by writers like Tolstoy and composers like Mussorgsky, found a generous patron in Pavel Tret'jakov, who organized many exhibitions and eventually created a museum in Moscow dedicated to Russian art. In reality, Repin only occasionally took part in meetings of the "Wanderers."
He made important journeys to Italy and France, especially during the crucial 1870s, and always kept in close touch with developments in European painting. For his subjects Repin chose scenes from Russian history, social themes and figures and activities drawn from modern life. It should be remembered that the tsar had only freed the serfs in 1861. Appointed professor at the St. Petersburg Academy, Repin had a decisive influence on the shift in Russian painting toward a popular and straightforward realism. After the avant-garde phase in the second decade of the twentieth century, his style was adopted as an "academic" model for official and propaganda painting, which was quite the contrary of Repin's intentions.

Ilya Repin
Boatmen at the Ford
1872
oil on canvas
24½ × 38¼ in.
(62 × 97cm)
Tret'jakov Gallery, Moscow

This type of painting, in which the heaviness of the figures' labor seems almost to distort their features but not to affect their inner dignity, provided a precise point of reference for the development of Socialist Realism. This was true not only in Russia but also, in varying forms, in a number of twentieth-century schools of painting in other countries that were also characterized by socialist or Communist ideals, up to the Mexican mural painters and the movements that followed the Second World War.

Joshua Reynolds
Plympton Earl, Devonshire, 1723-
London, 1792

A major exponent of the great period of English portrait painting, Joshua Reynolds began his training in 1740 at the London studio of the fashionable portraitist Thomas Hudson, but, at the same time, he also took a considerable interest in the work of Hogarth and Ramsay. His journey to Italy, begun in 1749 with his friend Commodore Keppel, had a decisive effect on his development. During his stay in Rome from 1750 to 1753, interrupted by brief visits to major Italian cities such as Florence, Bologna, and Venice, Reynolds was particularly attracted by classical statuary and by sixteenth-century painting, especially that of Raphael and Michelangelo, although his fierce parody of the *School of Athens*, the fresco by Raphael in the Stanze Vaticane, might suggest a desire to distance himself from the solemn decoration that characterizes sixteenth-century art. Although he rejected the title of academician, he did in fact nurture sincere admiration for classical art, both ancient and modern. This is evident in the portrait of his friend Commodore Keppel (1753, National Maritime Museum, Greenwich), inspired by the Apollo del Belvedere, where he evolves a highly personal style that shows his debt to the great Venetian artists of the sixteenth century, from Titian to Paolo Veronese, and to seventeenth-century Flemish and Dutch painting, from Rembrandt to Rubens and van Dyck. In 1753 he settled in London, where he stayed for the rest of his life, except for a brief journey to Belgium and Holland in 1781, which confirmed his lively interest in the dramatic possibilities of color and in the momentary, impetuous gesture, characteristics he had admired in the paintings of Rubens. Around 1774, his unquestioned fame as a portrait painter began to be overshadowed by the rising star Thomas Gainsborough.

Opposite
Joshua Reynolds
*Colonel George K.H.
Coussmaker, Grenadier
Guards*
1782
oil on canvas
93¾ × 57½ in.
(238.1 × 145.4 cm)
Metropolitan Museum
of Art, New York

Against the background
of a typically English
landscape, the
aristocratic figure of the
colonel is captured in
a pose of studied
nonchalance, in which
the line of the body is
repeated in the trunk
of the tree and the
extended neck of the
horse, thus underlining
the noble bearing of the
figure.

Joshua Reynolds
Master Hare
c. 1788-1789
oil on canvas
30½ × 25 in.
(77 × 64 cm)
Musée du Louvre, Paris

This is one of the most
refined examples
of child portraiture, a
genre in which Reynolds
was an unrivaled master.
The informal
atmosphere, the fantasy
and lightness of touch,
and the skillful use of
light make this portrait
an extremely fine
example of Reynolds's
great freedom
of interpretation.

Jusepe de Ribera

Lo Spagnoletto
Játiva, 1591-Naples, 1652

Ribera acts as a link between Spanish painting and the Neapolitan school, and is one of the most interesting and original interpreters of the Caravaggesque style. The painter's once frequently used nickname "lo Spagnoletto" has now fallen almost completely into disuse. He was active mostly in Italy, but many paintings were for Spanish patrons. A particularly important role was played in terms of Ribera's career by the Duke of Osuna, the Spanish viceroy of Naples, who summoned the painter and introduced him to Neapolitan painting, but commissioned important canvases for his hometown in Andalusia. Taking Caravaggio's realism as his starting point, he developed a figurative model that was taken still further to become a violent expressionism marked by intense religious pathos, and a great interest in unusual physical traits and the psychological characterization of his figures. After initial training in Valencia, Ribera moved to Italy and by 1615 he was a key member of the brilliant colony of Spanish painters in Rome's via Margutta. His earliest works were characterized by the influence of Caravaggio together with classical art. He moved shortly afterward to Naples, where he found the perfect cultural environment to develop his study of pictorial expression. With the unfailing support of the viceroy and the Spanish nobles, he devoted himself totally to his art. He also produced works for the many Neapolitan churches, and became the model for the development of local religious painting throughout the first half of the seventeenth century. The arrival of Velázquez in Naples, in 1630, encouraged Ribera to adopt a less harsh form of chiaroscuro and pay greater attention to color. This marked the beginning of a period in which he gradually used a range of lighter tones and a combination of bright colors. Despite being forced by a serious illness to paint slowly he managed to overcome his physical difficulties to produce a last group of masterpieces.

Jusepe de Ribera
Drunken Silenus
1626
oil on canvas
72¾ × 90¼ in.
(185 × 229 cm)
Galleria Nazionale di Capodimonte, Naples

This painting plays a key role in his career, showing the development of elements drawn from Caravaggio in the direction of an accentuated expressionism pushed to the limits of caricature.

Sebastiano Ricci
*The Punishment
of Cupid*
1706-1707
canvas
Palazzo Marucelli-Fenzi,
Florence

This is a splendid
example of the work
Ricci produced during
his Florentine period. It
incorporated references
to Luca Giordano but
brought to them a
completely new richness
and innovation.

Sebastiano Ricci

Belluno, 1659-Venice, 1734

Ricci was an exuberant personality,
internationally renowned and an
archetypal "traveling" painter. After
training in the Veneto, he spent some
time in Emilia. This proved crucial
to his development as his style was
influenced by the local classicism,
deepened when Ricci made a trip to
Rome, where Annibale Carraci's frescoes
in Palazzo Farnese deeply moved him.
After a brief trip to Vienna, Ricci went
back to Venice in 1708, where his art
changed. His *Altarpiece of St. George the
Great* was a deliberate homage to Paolo
Veronese and inaugurated a totally new
era in eighteenth-century Venetian
painting, trying to revive the glories of
its Renaissance. Compared to his earlier
works, his art was now remarkably free
in composition and brushwork. This
new style of painting was an immediate
success. By 1711 he had joined his
nephew Marco Ricci in London where
he remained for five years, working for
many great noblemen. After a brief
stop-over in Paris (enough to gain him
admittance to the Académie Royale),
he went back to work in Venice where
he produced canvases for collectors
and altarpieces. At the end of his career
he painted the *Assumption* in the
Karlskirche in Vienna for the Emperor
Charles VI.

333

Hyacinthe Rigaud
Perpignan, 1659-Paris, 1743

Rigaud was a shrewd observer of the Parisian aristocracy orbiting around the court of the Sun King and his work provides singular documentation of this world. Having completed his artistic apprenticeship in Montpellier and Lyons, in 1681 Rigaud moved to Paris, where he was admitted to the Royal Academy of Art three years later with the help of his protector Charles Lebrun. Influenced by the Flemish tradition, he modeled his portraits on those of van Dyck. Noticed by the king's brother, who commissioned a portrait of himself and one of his son, Rigaud was appointed court painter in 1688. He painted two portraits of Louis XIV, in 1694 and 1701, creating an image of the king that has become established in the collective memory. In the *Portrait of Louis XIV* in the Louvre, the pomp of the drapery and the bright range of colors offer a distinct image of regality. As court painter, Rigaud was a resounding success, and his list of clients expanded to include all the European courts. In order to cope with the ever increasing flow of commissions, he employed assistants and divided his workshop on a specialized basis, Sevin de la Pennaye being responsible for clothing, Monnoyer for inserts with flowers, Charles Parrocel for battles, and François Desportes for landscapes and animals.

Hyacinthe Rigaud
Portrait of Louis XIV
1701
oil on canvas
109¾ × 74¾ in.
(279 × 190 cm)
Musée du Louvre, Paris

In 1701 Louis XIV ordered his official court painter to paint a portrait intended as a gift for Philip V of Spain. He then decided, however, that he would keep the work, a pompous and rhetorical painting exemplifying the parade portraits of the *Grand Siècle*. The sumptuous materials and hangings, the royal cloak of ermine and the royal insignia all feature in this official portrayal of the Sun King, the subject of which plays a secondary role with respect to the royal attributes. The dais, the throne, the classical column, and the theatrical hangings all contribute to the grandiose effect of the scene.

James Rosenquist
Grand Forks, North Dakota, 1933

To James Rosenquist, painting means bringing into play his subjectivity. The result is a conspicuous group of spectacle-paintings, puzzles whose meaning is never open to an unequivocal interpretation. Arriving in New York in 1955, he began painting large-scale images that reflect a vision of reality by way of fragments. Such is the case with the Times Square installations he made for the Artkraft Strauss Sign Corporation, in which the parts are juxtaposed in an incongruous way, creating contradictory spatial effects: the first levels project toward the spectator, others move backward, following an absolutely unpredictable focusing. A surprising example of his gigantic works is *F-111*, fifty-one panels (for a total of about eighty-five feet, or twenty-six meters) exhibited at the Leo Castelli Gallery in New York in 1965. The images present a cross-contamination of themes related to war with others drawn from consumer society: a cake, a bomber, a girl under a hair dryer, a frogman whose helmet gives off air bubbles. Over the course of the 1960s and 1970s Rosenquist participated in many important exhibitions, such as Six Painters and the Object at the Guggenheim in 1963, the São Paulo Biennale in 1967, the joint exhibit American Pop Art at the Whitney, and the 1978 Venice Biennale.

James Rosenquist
Joan Crawford Says: "..."
1964
oil on canvas
95¼ × 77 in.
(242 × 196 cm)
Ludwig Museum, Cologne

Dante Gabriel Rossetti

London, 1828-Birchington-on-Sea, 1882

The son of an Italian political exile, he was a painter, a poet, and the translator of Dante's *Vita Nuova*. He was also one of the founders of the Pre-Raphaelite Brotherhood, a movement that was descended from the German Nazarenes and adopted their program of a return to the stylistic simplicity, purity, and feeling for nature typical of pre-Renaissance art. Rossetti, together with Holman Hunt and John Everett Millais, took his inspiration from the Middle Ages and set out to create a truthful and deep-felt kind of painting. He started by illustrating literary texts, such as Goethe's *Faust* and Poe's *The Raven*, showing a preference for drawing as a free and immediate technique. Between 1848 and 1850 he painted two oils with religious subjects, *The Girlhood of Mary* and *Ecce Ancilla Domini*, both now in the Tate Britain, London. Critics took offence at the domestic setting, analytical representation, and painstaking detail, considered inappropriate to a sacred scene. Queen Victoria even asked to view them in private so that she could judge their provocative character for herself. In 1853 cracks started to appear in the Brotherhood: Rossetti's medievalism clashed with Hunt's analytical realism and Millais's Victorian taste. After 1860 the movement entered a second phase, distinguished by its smooth and flowing lines defined as "soft edge." Rossetti now shifted his attention from the Middle Ages to the art of the High Renaissance and, in particular, the great portraits of the sixteenth century. His art found its most significant expression in female figures, angelic girls or perverse creatures, women of an imposing, distant beauty, imbued with an inaccessible fascination. Rossetti's woman was half goddess and half *femme fatale*, on the one hand an idealized figure derived from Dante and Stil Novo poetry and on the other a sensual source of evil. In his maturity, the artist's favorite model was Jane Burden, the wife of his friend William Morris, a languid creature with an enigmatic face for whom he nursed an exclusive passion right up until his death.

Dante Gabriel Rossetti
Ecce Ancilla Domini
1850, oil on canvas
28¾ × 17 in.
(72 × 43 cm)
Tate Britain, London

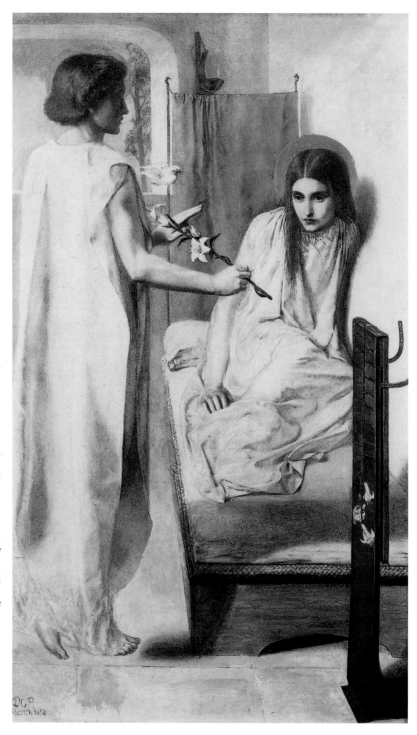

Rosso Fiorentino

Giovan Battista di Jacopo
Florence, 1495-Fontainebleau,
Paris, 1540

Rosso Fiorentino was the principal artist connected with the first and more adventurous period of Florentine Mannerism. He trained, along with Pontormo, in Andrea del Sarto's studio and made his debut working with them on the frescoes in the small Voti cloisters in SS. Annunziata. The tormented story of his *Assumption* (1513-1517), which he deliberately damaged, demonstrated early on that Rosso would become a controversial and polemical painter. His characters often had odd, almost diabolic, physiognomies ("with a cruel and desperate air" according to Vasari) which left his patrons a little perplexed. His *Deposition* in Volterra (1521) is a good example of the violent and disconcertingly aggressive way he deformed figures as well as colors. Developments in his style happened astonishingly fast. Within the space of a few years during which he continued to produce major works, his style moved away from its Florentine background to absorb the latest of Michelangelo's work. Rosso's art from this period is comparable to Parmigiano. After the Sack of Rome (1527), he started to travel. His style fluctuated wildly, sometimes intense, even demonic, sometimes more elegant and sweet, more in keeping with the official nature of his commissions. In 1530 he moved to Paris and was commissioned by Francis I to decorate an imposing gallery in his chateau at Fontainebleau (1532-1537). This, along with Primaticcio's work in the chateau, formed the basis of the highly influential Mannerist School of Fontainebleau, which dominated French taste for three generations.

Rosso Fiorentino
Madonna and Child with Four Saints
1518
wood panel
67¾ × 55½ in.
(172 × 141 cm)
Uffizi, Florence

A neurotic, even deformed stylization that at times verges on the grotesque is the most immediate characteristic of his paintings, and can be glimpsed already in this picture. Most notably, the restlessness of the whole work contradicts a High Renaissance ideal: that of serene majesty. This accentuates the expressive dynamism of his compositions, whose colors and tones seem burnt or lividly overstated. The almost infernal aspect of some of the characters has given rise to a number of sometimes wild hypotheses about the painter's far-from-happy psychology (he committed suicide).

337

Mark Rothko

Dvinsk, Latvia, 1903–New York, 1970

As a leading exponent of color field abstraction, Mark Rothko is located at the opposite end of American abstract art from the world of action painting. Among the first abstract painters to appear at the beginning of the 1940s, Rothko distinguished himself by the intensely personal style of his work and by its powerfully spiritual content. At the age of ten, together with his mother, he emigrated to the United States; in 1924 he enrolled at the Art Students League, where he studied under Max Weber, whose influence is legible in his first, still figurative, oil paintings. In the early *Subway* series, Rothko developed the theme of loneliness in contemporary society with images that composed, according to Rothko himself, a *tableau vivant* of human incommunicability. He then found a rich source of inspiration in primitive myths and rites, which he presented in Freudian interpretations in paintings of a surrealist matrix. Rothko's talent as an expressionist painter flourished after his 1945 exhibit at Peggy Guggenheim's Art of This Century Gallery. Exploiting the geometric symmetry of the rectangle, Rothko creates images of a disarming simplicity, luminous panes of color that seem monumental to the eye of the viewer, who becomes entirely engulfed in the light and color given off by the surface of the canvas. Rothko worked on several important public commissions between the end of the 1950s and the early 1960s, including murals for a restaurant in New York and for Harvard University, but serious depression and heart problems threw a shadow over his last works. The paintings he made for the Menil family chapel in Houston can be considered his poetic testament; these are chromatically austere, composed of dark tones that create a transcendent quality evoking a sense of mysterious emotional depth. On February 25, 1970, Rothko committed suicide in his studio.

Mark Rothko
Number 14, 1960
1960
oil on canvas
114½ × 105½ in.
(290.8 × 268.6 cm)
Museum of Modern Art,
San Francisco

In the eyes of the viewer, Rothko's simple images take on a monumental quality, not only because of the large size of the canvases but most of all because of the absence of a central focal point.

Georges Rouault

Paris, 1871-1958

Born in a cellar in Paris during the "bloody week" of massacres when the Commune was suppressed, Rouault's work seems to be imbued with an anarchic pessimism. He received his training from Gustave Moreau, along with Henri Matisse, which led him briefly to adopt the style of the Fauves. His early experience as a restorer of stained-glass windows lies at the origin of some of the peculiar features of his painting, such as the nocturnal luminosity of the backgrounds or the use of black lines in an expressionistic and tonal manner, as a color that compresses and flattens the others, conditioning their chromatic scale. From Moreau he derived the evocative and symbolic use of colors in pictures like *The Mirror* of 1906. His meeting with the Catholic philosopher J. Maritain in 1911 had a decisive influence on him, with the result that Rouault became the greatest painter of sacred art of the twentieth century. After 1930 the artist's dramatic tension attained a greater formal equilibrium, as can be seen in pictures like *The Old King* (1936), *Tiberias* (1947), and *Dusk* (1952).

Georges Rouault
Duo
c. 1948
oil on paper mounted
on panel
25¼ × 16½ in.
(64 × 42 cm)
Private collection

The emblematic figure of the clown, which appears constantly throughout Rouault's work, represents the modern artist in exile, his rootless and derisory condition. In the years from 1943 to 1948, Rouault extended this identification to all human beings, representing his clowns in groups of two or three.

Henri Rousseau,

called Le Douanier
Laval, 1844–Paris, 1910

Rousseau is a truly unique figure in
the panorama of art at the turn of the
century. For a long time artists, critics,
and the public were divided into two
distinct camps: was his simple and
primitive painting really a naïve form
of expression, or was its apparent
simplicity the fruit of a calculated
choice? A petty official in the Paris
customs office (whence his nickname
of *Le Douanier*), he started to paint
at the age of forty, producing still lifes
and landscapes in which the
representation of reality relied on
the exact reproduction of individual
details, ignoring the spatial relations
of perspective. Self-taught, he
obtained permission to copy works in
the Louvre and other museums in
1884 and exhibited his first pictures
at the Salon des Indépendants in 1886.
Initially his works were ridiculed
by the critics, but his style was soon
recognized as original and modern
and his paintings aroused the interest
of Impressionists, Symbolists, and
even Picasso, who in 1908 held a
banquet in his studio in Rousseau's
honor. The support of intellectuals
and artists like Apollinaire, Gauguin,
and Picasso made him a famous
painter, a rallying point for the avant-
garde and, perhaps involuntarily, for
those opposed to it.

Henri Rousseau
The Snake Charmer
1907
oil on canvas
65 × 70¾ in.
(165 × 180 cm)
Musée d'Orsay, Paris

The painting recalls an
engraving by Gauguin
shown at the Salon
d'Automne in 1906.
Here the exotic
landscape is inserted
in a complex structure,
illuminated by a cold
light that is reflected
in the water. The figures
are flat and motionless
silhouettes, immersed
in a monumentality that
has no depth, while the
landscape is that of
a fantastic and unreal
forest.

Henri Rousseau
The Exotic Jungle
1909
oil on canvas
55¼ × 50¾ in.
(140.5 × 129 cm)
National Gallery,
Washington, D.C.

The painting belongs
to the series of exotic
landscapes that became
almost virtuoso
exercises between 1908
and 1910.

Peter Paul Rubens
Siegen, 1577-Antwerp, 1640

Born in Germany, where his father—a wealthy man from Antwerp who had embraced the Calvinist religion—had gone into exile, Rubens acquired the first rudiments of art in Cologne, but his real training took place in Antwerp. In 1598, at the age of nineteen, he joined the Guild of St. Luke, the corporation of painters in Antwerp. Two years later he left for Italy. For a gifted painter like Rubens, going to Venice and Rome in the year 1600 marked a decisive turning point in his career. During the early years, Rubens studied art history voraciously. He followed the traditional method of copying the old masters to learn their style, and Holbein, Lucas van Leyden, and Dürer were the inevitable points of reference for a northern artist, but in Italy he added Raphael, Michelangelo, Correggio, Tintoretto,

Leonardo, and, most important of all, the great Titian. Rubens also studied classical antiquities. He was extremely interested in Caravaggio's work and became one of the first to admire him. He entered the service of the Duke of Mantua and stayed in Italy until 1608, making frequent trips from Genoa to Rome. His Italian journey was marked by memorable works, including a group of altarpieces that allow us to follow the different stages in the development of an individual style, based on figures that fill the space and the use of rich colors, in which he was clearly influenced by the Venetian school. In 1608, his mother died and Rubens hastily left Italy to return to Antwerp. He very soon became the leading painter in the country and this was confirmed by the grandiose works executed for the cathedral. The triptych of the *Descent from the Cross*, one of the most moving works in religious Baroque painting, is the

synthesis of all his early training, but also the key turning point that led to the rapid development of his career. After his marriage to the beautiful Isabella Brandt, Rubens extended his fine house in Antwerp by converting it into an Italianate palace and studio, with a garden containing elegant pavilions. Thanks to the patronage of the grand dukes of the Netherlands, Rubens's commissions increased and he extended his workshop to over a hundred assistants. Rubens's atelier was the largest "mine" of Baroque art; all the most famous Flemish artists went through the experience of working there. During the second decade of the seventeenth century, he was living permanently in Antwerp, but he sent works to patrons who were increasingly high-ranking. Then, from 1620 on, he traveled to the great European capitals. In Paris he executed the spectacular series of canvases for Marie de' Medici and Henry IV,

twenty-one vast compositions now in the Louvre. Then he visited Holland, Madrid, and London between 1627 and 1630. During this period, Europe was being devastated by the Thirty Years' War, and Rubens drew up a well-thought-out peace plan. He was now one of the most famous men in Europe. After the death of Isabella Brandt, he married Hélène Fourment and painted several delightful portraits of her. Rubens became very wealthy as the result of his highly successful career.

Peter Paul Rubens
Juno and Argos
1610-1611
oil on canvas
98 × 116½ in.
(249 × 296 cm)
Wallraf-Richartz
Museum, Cologne

Rubens's great feeling for narrative and his extremely sensual style achieve full expression in his highly imaginative and spectacular secular paintings. Here the artist takes as his starting point an episode from Ovid's *Metamorphoses* (Jupiter's love for the nymph Io) and sumptuously depicts the macabre, pathetic subject of the killing of the mythical herdsman Argos, who has one hundred eyes so that he can keep good watch over the herd in his keeping. After he has been decapitated by the wily Mercury, Juno commemorates the faithful Argos by symbolically placing his eyes in the peacock's tail.

Peter Paul Rubens
Self-Portrait with Isabella Brandt Under a Honeysuckle Bower
1609-1610
oil on canvas
70 × 56¼ in.
(178 × 143 cm)
Alte Pinakothek, Munich

Self-satisfied and confident, this is how Rubens paints himself with his first wife, Isabella Brandt, in this superb canvas celebrating their marriage. With his left hand resting on the hilt of his sword, Rubens appears as a refined gentleman in his early prime. He looks impeccably genteel and wealthy enough to be able to afford the extravagance of the gaudy orange stockings enveloping his shapely calves. A work by an obviously successful man, charmingly accompanied by a woman of enviable beauty, Rubens's self-portrait can be compared with similar pictures by other leading seventeenth-century painters, including, first and foremost, Rembrandt.

Opposite
Peter Paul Rubens
The Rape of the Daughters of Leucippus
c. 1618
oil on wood
87½ × 82¼ in.
(222 × 209 cm)
Alte Pinakothek, Munich

This episode, drawn from Theocritus, represents the abduction of the girls by Castor and Pollux. Rubens presents the enormous group composed of the girls, the divine twins, the horses, and the cupids as a single quivering unit. The result is one of the great examples of the pictorial representation of mythological subjects, interpreted not in terms of intellectual elegance but as a sensual wave of forms and colors.

Peter Paul Rubens
The Straw Hat
1630
oil on wood
31 × 21½ in.
(79 × 55 cm)
National Gallery,
London

The traditional title of this magnificent work, certainly one of the most intriguing seventeenth-century portraits, does not correspond to the subject. The hat the young girl is wearing is certainly not made of straw, and the mistake may be the result of a copying error or a misunderstanding of the French title (*Chapeau de poil* has become *Chapeau de paille*). Quite apart from this, the portrait palpitates with the feeling emanating from the girl's expression, and it is animated by the shadow cast by the brim of the hat, and the contrast between the light blue of the ground and the warm, hazy red of the sleeves. Titian's influence can be seen in the extraordinary immediacy of this figure full of warmth and life. The girl is probably Suzanne Fourment, the sister of Rubens's second wife.

Peter Paul Rubens
Hélène Fourment in Her Wedding Gown
1630-1631
oil on wood
64½ × 53¾ in.
(163.6 × 136.5 cm)
Alte Pinakothek,
Munich

Isabella Brandt left Rubens a widower when he was nearly fifty and he began to court a distant relative of his first wife. She was a fair-haired, shapely girl, perhaps not as intelligent as Isabella, but certainly very pretty and very attractive to a sensual man like Rubens. In 1630, sixteen-year-old Hélène married Rubens, who was then fifty-three. This was an injection of youth and vitality for Rubens during the last ten years of his life and work. The portrait of Hélène in her wedding gown exudes tenderness and cheerfulness. The girl, with her rosy cheeks and blond bangs, looks happy but almost intimidated, and she is leaning slightly toward the left, as though she is trying to be self-possessed and not finding it easy.

Juan Sánchez Cotán
Orgaz, 1561-Granada, 1627

Highly individual and extremely interesting both as an artist and as a human being, Sánchez Cotán is one of the first and greatest still-life painters. It is due to his work that the *bodegónes* genre (the term used for still life in Spanish art) rapidly reached a height perhaps only attained by Goya and, in the twentieth century, by Picasso. Trained in the artistic circles of Toledo, but steeped above all in the pure, intense, mystical spirituality of the late sixteenth century, Sánchez Cotán nearly always painted the same subject: a few pieces of fruit or vegetables inside a "box."

Juan Sánchez Cotán
Still Life with Fruit and Vegetables
c. 1602-1603
oil on canvas
27¼ × 38 in. (69.5 × 96.5 cm)
José Luis Várez Fisa
Collection, Madrid

This is one of the "metaphysical" heights reached by the painter, who here sets "silent" fruit and vegetables against his habitual black ground.

Juan Sánchez Cotán
Still Life
1602
oil on canvas
26¾ × 35 in.
(68 × 89 cm)
Prado, Madrid

This is one of the painter's richest and most complex compositions, with an unusual variety of objects, and perhaps this is why he signed it right in the center. The cardoon reappears, but it is lying on its side in an unusual position so as to describe a sweeping upward curve that embraces the other items.

John Singer Sargent
Florence, 1856-London, 1925

One of the greatest and most acclaimed portraitists of all time, closely tied to the ambience, mood, and ideals of the novelist Henry James, Sargent was fond of defining himself as "an American born in Italy, educated in France, who looks like a German, speaks like an Englishman, and paints like a Spaniard." Son of an American doctor living in Florence, after early academic training in Italy (between Florence and Rome), Sargent completed his studies in Paris, studying the masterpieces of Velázquez and Frans Hals. He developed a rapid style, full of color, with strong brushstrokes and a dramatic sense of the physical presence of his figures. At twenty he began exhibiting his works at the Salon and made his first short trip to the United States. This trip was followed by several others to many different nations, from Mediterranean Africa to Holland. Although he continued to send works to Paris and showed a notable stylistic affinity with Manet, Sargent kept his distance from the Impressionists to specialize in portraiture. His fresh-faced children and girls and seductive femmes fatales enjoyed enormous success, up to the "scandalous" *Portrait of Madame X* (*Madame Gautreau*) at the Salon of 1884. Faced with the hostile reaction of public and critics (comparable to the response awakened a few years earlier by Manet's *Olympia*), Sargent left Paris and settled in London, soon becoming the favorite high-society portraitist. In 1888 he went to Boston, where he received the commission for large mural paintings for the city library, soon joined by requests and commissions of the highest prestige. With the passing of years Sargent came to prefer working in watercolors, and from 1907 on he refused to paint any more portraits. His style and subject changed radically: during World War I the British government sent him to the front lines in France to paint images of the conditions of the wounded and the soldiers in the trenches.

Opposite
John Singer Sargent
*The Daughters of
Edward Darley Boit*
1882
oil on canvas
87 × 87 in.
(221 × 221 cm)
Museum of Fine Arts,
Boston

The central period
of Sargent's career was
clearly dominated
by portraits. In 1887,
not long after Sargent
painted this
masterpiece, Henry
James (who found this
work "astonishing")
exalted his friend's
qualities as a portraitist:
"There is no greater
work of art than a great
portrait—a truth to be
constantly taken to
heart by a painter
holding in his hands the
weapon that Mr. Sargent
wields. The gift that he
possesses he possesses
completely."

John Singer Sargent
*Mrs. Fiske Warren with
Her Daughter Rachel*
1903
oil on canvas
60 × 40½ in.
(152.4 × 102.6 cm)
Museum of Fine Arts,
Boston

For American high
society, sitting for a
Sargent portrait became
a singular social
achievement. But then,
it is difficult to resist the
fascination of his
portraits; while there
may be something of the
artificial about them,
there is no doubting
their power. The artist's
brush fills in clothes and
background details with
a skillful rapidity,
slowing its headlong
rush only to achieve the
definition of faces.

347

Egon Schiele
Tulln, 1890-Vienna, 1918

Schiele's meteoric life and career has often been seen as a dramatic metaphor of the *finis Austriae*, the end of an era and an empire that had long played a dominant role in history. Initially linked to that of Klimt, Schiele's dramatic and graphic style quickly developed into almost the antithesis of the blazing colors and aesthetic elegance of the founder of the school. Influenced by his friendship with Kokoschka and his ties with the international Expressionist movements Schiele turned his attention to the harrowing conflicts of existence: his stupefied and terrified figures are surrounded by empty space, filled with doubts and anxieties. This tension, which led Schiele to look back to the themes, distortions, and suggestions of Gothic art, was conveyed chiefly through the harsh and dramatic force of his drawing. In the troubled years of the war Schiele experienced a glimmer of serenity, through the marriage to his beloved Edith Harms. His young wife became the recurrent, almost obsessive subject of the painter's canvases and watercolors. The violence of the war and his wife's illness reopened the conflict between life and death, which was again to characterize the last works of the painter's short life. Egon and Edith died in 1918, one shortly after the other. They were buried in the same tomb, mourned by the world of culture which, deafened by the roar of the guns, had been unable to hear Schiele's penetrating voice and could now only pay him posthumous tribute.

Egon Schiele
Death of the Maiden
1915
oil on canvas, 59 × 70¾ in. (150 × 180 cm)
Österreichische Galerie, Vienna

Love and death are interwoven in all of his work, but in 1915 this contrast took on a new significance: the painter married Edith Harms before being enrolled in the imperial army.

Karl Schmidt-Rottluff
Rottluf, 1884-Berlin, 1976

An important and versatile exponent of Expressionism, he was one of the youngest of the original members of the Die Brücke group. After training as an architect (which left him with a preference for robust and well-defined volumes), he founded the movement together with Kirchner and Heckel (Dresden, 1905). Schmidt-Rottluff's paintings are distinguished by their synthetic forms, with blocks of color that are reminiscent of van Gogh and related to the style of Nolde. In 1911 the painter (who also produced prints and sculptures) moved to Berlin and his art, consisting chiefly of landscapes and portraits, became even more brutal, almost naïf. On the outbreak

of the First World War he enlisted. His experience of fighting imparted a new, religious quality to his work and, over the following years, he painted almost mystical images of rural life. Schmidt–Rottluff too was placed on the Nazi list of "degenerate artists."

Karl Schmidt-Rottluff
*Fall Landscape
in Oldenburg*
1907
oil on canvas,
29½ × 38¼ in.
(75 × 97 cm)
Thyssen-Bornemisza
Collection, Madrid

The picture belongs to a highly characteristic phase in the artist's development and throws light on his fundamental influences. Moving with Heckel to Dangast, a village on the North Sea coast, Schmidt-Rottluff painted numerous

landscapes between 1907 and 1911, experimenting with the expressive qualities of free brushwork and the mixture of colors and producing results that recall the work of van Gogh. Later on, he would partly abandon this approach to dedicate greater attention to the outlines of forms.

Johann Heinrich Schönfeld
Biberach an der Riss, 1609-Augsburg, 1683

Like his fellow countrymen Liss and Loth, Schönfeld is a German painter who spent very important periods of his working life in Italy. In addition to the unquestionable attraction of Rome and the other Italian cities, one should not forget the tragic consequences of the devastating Thirty Years' War, which constituted a very concrete obstacle to the development of painting and the art market in Germany. It is significant that shortly after the war came to an end with the Treaty of Westphalia in 1648, Schönfeld returned to Germany, where he was very successful both with collectors and in terms of commissions for religious works. His work as a highly regarded engraver also contributed to his fame throughout the seventeenth century. Having completed his artistic training in southern Germany, he settled in Rome in 1633. It should be noted that the popularity of Caravaggio and his followers had by then declined. They had been replaced by the classicism of the French masters, the triumphant Baroque of Bernini and Pietro da Cortona, and the small paintings of everyday subjects produced by the northern *Bamboccianti* and the members of the *Schildersbent*, the association of Dutch painters in Rome founded by Cornelis van Poelemburgh. In this context, Schönfeld became a leading artist thanks to his exquisite workmanship and the unusual compositional device of causing his figures to recede toward the background. This success was repeated during his long and important stay of over a decade in Naples, where he moved in 1638. In Naples he apparently took little interest in Ribera's full-bodied and occasionally brutal realism. If anything, he was attracted by Bernardo Cavallino's success in producing scintillating, dynamic effects capable of illuminating generally brownish, somber settings. He gained considerable experience in the composition of very large, theatrical canvases, suitable for representing the triumph of ruling houses.

Johann Heinrich Schönfeld
Hippomenes and Atalanta
1650-1660
oil on canvas
48½ × 79 in.
(123 × 200.5 cm)
Brukenthal National Museum, Sibiu, Romania

It is interesting to compare this work with Guido Reni's historic interpretation of the same subject, with which Schönfeld was probably familiar. While the classical Bolognese master focuses on a monumental depiction of the two nudes, Schönfeld prefers to distance the viewer and give a narrative representation of the episode including the running track, the arrival, and the spectators. The paint, applied lightly with the tip of the brush and almost transparent in some parts, seems to foreshadow certain eighteenth-century effects.

Martin Schongauer

Colmar, c. 1450-Breisach, 1491

Martin Schongauer is an outstanding figure in the artistic culture of his day, and not only in Germany. He was born in Alsace into a family of artists and goldsmiths, and this family environment certainly played a crucial part in determining his vocation. He was trained in the artistic tradition of the Netherlands. He saw Rogier van der Weyden's *St. Columba Altarpiece* during a visit to Cologne, and made a journey to Burgundy after his studies at the University of Leipzig. These experiences led him to forge a style that combines outstanding sensitivity and a balanced perspective handling of space and figure. He thus abandoned the vigorous late-Gothic style in favor of classical serenity, and produced essential compositions focusing primarily on the human and poetic element. In addition to numerous panels, he also painted a fresco of the *Last Judgment* for the church of Breisach during his maturity. For all his importance as a painter, however, Schongauer's renown derives above all from his parallel work as an engraver. He succeeded in realizing all the potential of this means of expression, and made a decisive contribution to the development of graphic art throughout Europe. He employed his virtuoso craftsmanship and extraordinary manual dexterity to produce works where dynamic, broken lines convey a strong impression of solidity and a marked, three-dimensional effect. His engravings enjoyed wide circulation from the very outset, and provided a repertoire of motifs and models from which many contemporary artists drew inspiration, including Michelangelo. Albrecht Dürer, the artist who was to raise the technique of engraving to one of its heights in the history of art, also acknowledged his debt to his older colleague, and set off on a journey to Alsace in 1492. By the time he arrived at Colmar, however, Schongauer had unfortunately already died.

Martin Schongauer
Holy Family
1475-1480
oil on wood, 10¼ × 6¾ in. (26 × 17 cm)
Kunsthistorisches Museum, Vienna

The extreme formal simplification reduces the setting to a few elements. All the attention is focused on the Holy Family and the everyday objects that gleam in the half-light. This unadorned domestic work is pervaded by a silent force and the intense presence of the divine.

Sebastiano del Piombo

Sebastiano Luciani
Venice, c. 1485-Rome, 1547

Sebastiano was a fascinating and important figure in the art worlds of two capitals (Venice and Rome). He was in contact with all the major artists of the first half of the sixteenth century, including Giorgione, with whom he probably trained, Titian, Raphael, and Michelangelo, and his own personal and robustly attractive style grew from them. He produced his first works in about 1510 (an organ screen now in the Gallerie dell'Accademia and the altarpiece in San Giovanni Crisostomo). These proved to be masterpieces of Venetian painting in its moment of transition between Giorgione's soft harmony and Titian's dynamic style. It was presumably Titian's meteoric rise that made Sebastiano leave for Rome in 1510 where he had been invited to work alongside Raphael on the Farnesina frescoes. He soon reconciled Venetian color with the creative research undertaken by painters of the Roman school, and particularly by Michelangelo with whom Sebastiano became firm friends—reputedly after quarrelling with Raphael. Thanks to his *Pietà* which is now in Viterbo and the paintings for the Borgherini chapel in San Pietro in Montorio, by about 1516 Sebastiano had become the artist who put Michelangelo's ideas into pictorial form. Michelangelo even provided the drawings for his huge altarpiece of *The Resurrection of Lazarus* (1519, National Gallery, London) that was painted to compete with Raphael's *Transfiguration*. After Raphael's death, Sebastiano became the most important painter in Rome, as is shown by the numerous official portraits he produced for the court of Pope Clement VII. Sebastiano remained in Rome even after the Sack (1527) and in 1531 was rewarded with the post of "officio del Piombo" (Keeper of the Seals) hence his nickname, a highly paid ecclesiastic sinecure. After this his output of paintings fell off.

Sebastiano del Piombo
Portrait of a Young Woman Called "Dorotea"
1513
wood panel
30¾ × 24 in.
(78 × 61 cm)
Staatliche Museen Preussischer Kulturbesitz, Berlin

This is a superb example of Sebastiano's Venetian training combining with the monumentalism he was learning in Rome. With extreme sensitivity he depicts the dying light of the countryside at sunset, showing it spilling into the foreground until it is lost in the fluffy fur. On the other hand, the way he structures the strong and sculpted physical presence of the young girl already reflects the figurative influence of Rome derived from Raphael and Michelangelo, to both of whom Sebastiano was soon to be compared.

Giovanni Segantini

Arco, 1858-Schafberg, Maloja, 1899

In a century that abounded in artists who led "romantic" lives, the story of Segantini's development and career provides one of the most typical examples. His restless character was apparent from his early youth and found its first outlet during the years he studied at the Brera Academy in Milan. Here he acquired the style of the Lombard naturalism of the second half of the nineteenth century, but was unable to find a place for himself in the art world. Segantini could not bear city life and, with the help of the painter and writer Vittore Grubicy, moved to the provinces in 1881. In the hills of Brianza he painted his first scenes of peasant life and a number of landscapes. The limpid panoramas he glimpsed from the heights of the Grison

mountains persuaded him to adopt the Divisionist technique, which conferred an unusual, diffuse luminosity on his pictures. Around 1890 his views of the Alps and images of life in the fields began to turn into allegories of a moral or symbolic character, imbued with a strong sense of religious mysticism. His style, made up of sinuous lines and elegant figures, had features in common with Art Nouveau. He increasingly withdrew into a solitary meditation, seeking moral purity and clear horizons in the high mountains, right up to his final work, the *Triptych of the Alps*, left unfinished and now in the museum devoted to the painter at Saint-Moritz. Segantini represented the apprehensions of the late nineteenth century, that sense of a rejection of progress which made the passage between the two centuries a particularly difficult threshold to cross.

Giovanni Segantini
Love at the Fountain of Life
1896
oil on canvas
27¼ × 39½ in.
(69 × 100 cm)
Galleria d'Arte
Moderna, Milan

The artist himself described this painting as representing "the playful and carefree love of the female and the pensive love of the male, bound together by the natural impulse of youth and springtime. An angel, a mystic and suspicious angel, spreads his great wing over the mysterious fountain of life. The water flows from the living rock, both symbols of eternity."

Georges Seurat
Paris, 1859-1891

The cultivated, refined, and intellectual product of a good family, Seurat shot through the history of art like a blazing but unfortunately short-lived meteor: death took him at the age of thirty-two, cutting short a process of technical and aesthetic evolution that had only just begun. Seurat painted only a few pictures, in part because of the extreme slowness of the technique he adopted, the huge scale of the paintings themselves, and the lengthy and well-documented preparation he carried out. Initially influenced by Millet's sweeping scenes of mystical realism, Seurat then embarked on an intense scientific investigation of the physics of light and color, comparing his results with those of photography and researchers into the phenomena of perception. With *La Grande Jatte* (1886), Seurat produced a seminal masterpiece. The color is handled in a totally new way, broken down into an infinite series of tiny points, each one separate and detached. Called Pointillism, this technique enhanced the effect of light and shade and provided the model for a "scientific art" based on a thorough grasp of the principles of optics. His subsequent paintings continued this approach, applying it to performances in the street and circus, but the process was interrupted by his dramatically early death.

Georges Seurat
Sunday Afternoon on the Island of La Grande Jatte
1884-1886
oil on canvas
79¼ × 120 in.
(201 × 305 cm)
Art Institute, Chicago

Completed at the end of a long succession of drawings, sketches, studies, and trials, this large picture is a key work in the history of painting. The subject and the diffuse luminosity may be reminiscent of Impressionism, but the technique and the balanced rhythm of the composition are in complete contrast to the efforts to capture the moment made by Monet and his colleagues. Seurat has created a stately, carefully considered scene, turning on the frozen monumentality of the figures. The sacred immobility of their attitudes has suggested a comparison with the fifteenth-century images of Piero della Francesca. The paint is laid on the canvas in a myriad of little touches, tiny points that form an almost imperceptible passage between light and shade.

Ben Shahn

Kovno, Lithuania, 1898-
New York, 1969

Shahn is one of the most famous artists of the social realism movement of the 1930s. Born in Lithuania, he arrived in New York in 1906 and began working as an apprentice lithographer in 1913. From 1919 to 1922 he studied at the National Academy of Design and was in Europe from 1924 to 1925, going back in 1927 to 1929. In Europe he encountered the works of the expressionist painters George Grosz and Otto Dix. The dramatic realism of their expressive language, incisive and essential, and their subjects related to urban and political realities had a deep influence on Shahn's later work. Back in New York, Shahn dedicated himself to social and political themes, using a graphic style and a caustic point of view to deal with themes of social protest, such as government mistreatment of innocent victims. The series of works he dedicated to the Sacco and Vanzetti trial (1931-1932) became famous for its dramatic intensity. His later works, inspired by deep human compassion and not weighed by propaganda, are intense and almost surreal presentations of the loneliness of humans and the conditions of poverty and abandonment found at the lower levels of society, among poor immigrants and the displaced. In 1933 Shahn worked with the Mexican painter Diego Rivera on the mural entitled *Man at the Crossroads* for the RCA Building, part of Rockefeller Center in New York, which was destroyed before being completed because it included a portrait of Lenin. He later worked on murals for the Federal Art Project. A photographer of great talent, Shahn worked for the Farm Security Administration from 1935 to 1938, taking photographs of impoverished areas in Ohio and the surrounding states to document the effects of the Depression on the lower levels of rural America.

Ben Shahn
Study for the mural painting in the Jersey Homesteads
c. 1936
tempera on panel
19½ × 27½ in.
(49.6 × 69.9 cm)
Private collection

This is a preparatory study for a mural commissioned by the federal administration for the Jersey Homesteads, a workers' community in New Jersey (now Roosevelt, New Jersey).
The experience of working alongside the Mexican muralist Diego Rivera marked Shahn's formative years, and in this work he indicates that he has developed his own expressive language. To the upper left are the bodies of Sacco and Vanzetti in their coffins.

Charles Sheeler

Philadelphia, 1883-New York, 1965

The principal interpreter of precisionism, Sheeler arrived at painting by way of photography, an experience that proved decisive to his later style. After three years of study at a school of industrial art and applied design, he enrolled in the Pennsylvania Academy of Fine Arts in 1903, completing his studies among the students of William Merritt Chase. For the next several years he traveled, visiting London, Holland, Spain, and finally, in 1908, Italy, where his most important stop was the Tuscan city of Arezzo, where he was struck by the frescoes of Piero della Francesca, a painter skilled at the construction of

elaborate architecture in works illuminated by a crystalline light, aspects later found in the mature works of Sheeler. Sheeler completed his artistic training with a trip to Paris, where he encountered the most advanced European art movements, chief among these the works of Cézanne and Matisse. He returned to America in time to exhibit six works in the 1913 Armory Show; in 1916 he participated in the *Forum Exhibition*, directed by Stieglitz and Henri; and the works he displayed in the 1917 Independents show make it clear that he had assimilated the leading currents of modernism. He moved to New York in 1919, and to make a living added photography to his activity as a painter, contributing

to *Vogue* and *Vanity Fair*. The next year he confirmed his decision to use urban landscapes as the subject for his paintings and photographs. Factories, skyscrapers, and architectural details became the protagonists of what could be defined as his metaphysical realism. In presenting his views of New York, Sheeler followed the route taken by the photographers and painters of the opening decade of the century. However, comparison of Sheeler's work to that of Max Weber, for example, reveals that while the most daring of Weber's paintings led to Cubism, Sheeler went further, testing the possibilities hinted at by Man Ray of painting that is both photographic and surreal.

Charles Sheeler
American Landscape
1930
oil on canvas, 24 × 31 in.
(61 × 78.8 cm)
Museum of Modern Art,
New York

Painter, photographer, and architect, he achieved a daring synthesis between the synthetic phase of Cubism and the photography of Stieglitz; in his works, geometric, well-defined volumes and clean surfaces characterize the landscape of provincial America.

Paul Signac
Paris, 1863-1935

A student of architecture, Signac commenced his career as an artist like so many other dilettantes, painting on the banks of the Seine. Invited to show his work at the Salon des Indépendants in 1884, he quickly became one of the most prominent figures of the new generation. In 1886 he adopted the Pointillist technique developed by Seurat, enthusiastically embarking on research into the division of color and producing theoretical writings of some value. This analysis translated into a style of painting in which Seurat's "point" was transformed into a small spot or stroke of color, similar to that used by the Italian Macchiaioli. Around 1890, prompted by a powerful desire to travel, he explored the coasts of the Mediterranean, from the Côte d'Azur to Venice and Constantinople: according to contemporary calculations, this entailed passage on no less than thirty-two different boats. Signac was responsible for the "discovery" of Saint-Tropez as a tourist resort. Beaches, sand dunes, seascapes, and sailboats became his favorite subjects. His meeting with van Gogh in 1889, Seurat's premature death in 1891, and his substantial independence of the Parisian art world led Signac to develop a style of his own, known as Neo-Impressionism. In doing so, Signac left a profound mark on French and Belgian painting; in 1904 the young Matisse asked to come and study with him at Saint-Tropez. In his later years, after the emergence of Cubism, Signac's brushstrokes grew broader, rectangular, and more detached from one another with the result that they no longer allowed the reconstruction of the form through the optical superimposition of the colors.

Paul Signac
*The Large Pine,
Saint-Tropez*
1909
oil on canvas
28¼ × 36¼ in.
(72 × 92 cm)
Pushkin Museum,
Moscow

His evolution in the early years of the twentieth century was influenced by his relationship with the Fauves.

357

David Alfaro Siqueiros
Cihuahua, 1898-Cuernavaca, 1974

Along with Rivera and Orozco, Siqueiros made up the trio of great Mexican mural painters who set out to revive the grandeur and function of the cycles of frescoes of the past, usually with a strong element of political and social criticism. Trained at the San Carlos Academy of Fine Arts, Mexico City, Siqueiros gave his enthusiastic support to the Mexican revolution, joining Carranza's army. Sent to Paris as a military attaché in 1919, he was able to bring his style up to date. He also met his fellow countryman Diego Rivera and returned to Mexico with him in 1922 to launch a movement of monumental and heroic painting. The redemption of the Mexican people, along the lines of Marxist-Leninist ideology, was illustrated through a revival of Mayan and Aztec art. During the thirties the painter underwent a series of strong personal and artistic experiences in Spain and the United States. Siqueiros's epic realism, often rendered dramatic by the gulf between social aspirations and everyday life, maintained its lofty declamatory tone even after the Second World War, not only in his large-scale murals but also in paintings on canvas. This resulted in a definitive break with Rivera, who in Siqueiros's eyes was guilty of having at least partly abandoned ideology for a "non-committed" stylistic research.

David Alfaro Siqueiros
*Self-Portrait
or The Great Colonel*
1945
synthetic lacquer on masonite, 36 × 47¾ in. (91.5 × 121.6 cm)
Museo Nacional de Arte, Mexico City

In the midst of the Mexican revolution, the painter presents himself as the demiurge of reconstruction.

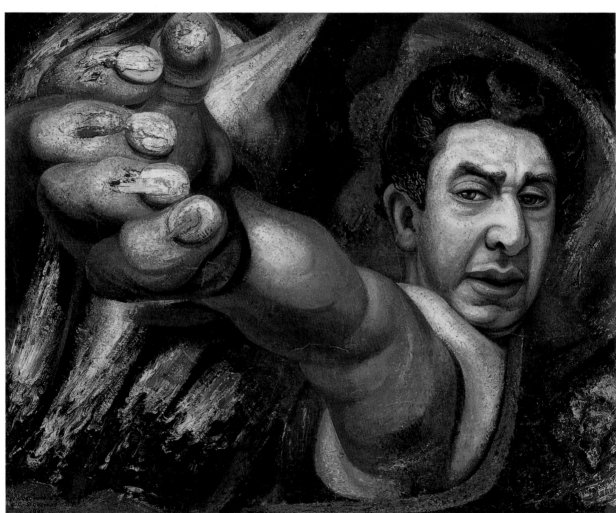

Mario Sironi
Sassari, 1885-Milan, 1961

Sironi's long career straddled a number of decades and covered many of the important moments in Italian twentieth-century art. The fact that Sironi went along with certain facets of Fascist-approved art has in the past made art critics question his worth. Today, however, it is generally agreed that Sironi was one of the most interesting figures of our century. The painter's beginnings were stormy. After studying engineering at Rome University, in 1910 Sironi made his first, rather unhappy, attempts at painting in Giacomo Balla's studio. He became both Balla's pupil and his friend. Despite this, Sironi became dissatisfied and anxious with what he was doing, so he gave up art and moved to Milan. It was there that in 1914 he made contact with the Futurists and started painting again. Compared to Boccioni's brilliant and lively vein, Sironi's colors were always somber and dark. He tended to underline the heavy volumes of the objects he painted. Nevertheless, his participation in the Futurist movement was a strongly personal statement which was an indicator of things to come. During the First World War Sironi also used *collage* to block out forms in rigorously succinct blocks which brought him very close to Metaphysical painting. From 1919

onwards he concentrated on subjects connected with the urban landscape, becoming the artistic spokesman for human and social unrest after the end of the First World War. The industrial suburbs, which were perhaps Sironi's best known and most original subject, were dominated by gloomy buildings that loomed disproportionately large. This gave a sense of drama about to unfold in places where the human figure seemed irrelevant. For Sironi existential anguish could be resolved by recourse to the *Valori Plastici* (Plastic Values) he shared with Carrà. Sironi was naturally attracted toward order and reason. He did not limit himself to transmitting this through his painting but also worked on construction projects and alongside architects, set designers, and decorators. Sironi made his name through traditional genres such as frescoes, mosaics, or monumental low reliefs. His painting was dominated by studies of nudes, mountainous landscapes, and cityscapes. They were all marked however, by his dark colors and the sense of monumentality that inspired all of his work. As he grew older, his painting tended to contain more fragments, memories, archeological quotations, and recollections of classical antiquity, sometimes placed in sequence, sometimes just a random collection. This type of subject dominated Sironi's later output.

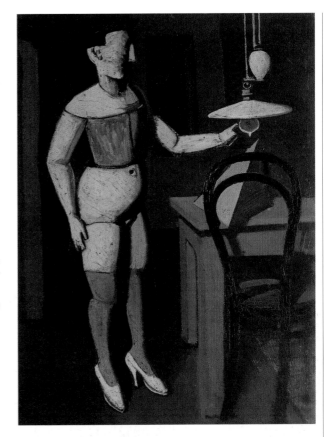

Mario Sironi
The Suburbs
1920
oil on canvas
23½ × 30¼ in.
(60 × 77cm)
Private collection,
Venice

The silent, ghostly city suburbs that Sironi painted in the years after the First World War provide a tense and obsessive image of a victorious nation going through serious economic and social difficulties. The high, somber walls have no exits. The square blocks of the industrial buildings and the total absence of life create an inhuman environment.

Above
Mario Sironi
The Lamp
1919
oil on canvas
30¾ × 22 in.
(78 × 56 cm)
Pinacoteca di Brera,
Milan

This is an extremely interesting work from Sironi's Metaphysical period. It draws on the theme of the tailor's dummy so dear to de Chirico. The scene seems set in an immobile fantasy world where Sironi remains chained to the shadows of reality and becomes the disturbing subject of his own picture.

he received his training in England,

Alfred Sisley

Paris, 1839-Moret-sur-Loing, 1899

Though his parents were British, Sisley was born in Paris where his father ran a commercial business. However, he received his training in England, where he made a particular study of Gainsborough's cold tones and brushwork and the landscapes of Constable and Turner. Returning to France in 1862, he developed an intelligent blend of the figurative culture he had absorbed in London and the French tradition of Corot and the Barbizon School. His friendship with Monet, Renoir, and Pissarro soon led him to experiment with color. Together with Monet, he decided to paint in the open air. For a while, Monet and Sisley painted the same views and compared the results. Sisley soon showed a preference for a range of cold colors, in which greens and blues dominated: an expression of his great intellectual control, which never allowed him to abandon himself to pure contemplation of the landscape. In 1871, after his father's death, Sisley went to live in the countryside and led a very secluded existence in which he was forced to move frequently because of financial problems. In general, the sobriety of Sisley's palette and his unusually autumnal and subdued vision of the region around Paris served as a valuable counterbalance to the sometimes overly pretty painting of his French colleagues. Yet this also partly explains his relative obscurity and lack of success on the market. In 1882 he settled permanently at Moret. The small town surrounded by greenery and its Gothic church became Sisley's favorite subject toward the close of his life, almost as a belated response to the series of views his friend Monet had devoted to Rouen Cathedral.

Alfred Sisley
Road at Hampton Court
detail, 1874, oil on
canvas, 21½ × 15 in.
(55 × 38 cm)
Neue Pinakothek,
Munich

Though he lived and worked mostly in France, Sisley never lost contact with England and it was there that he painted some of his most successful pictures.

361

John Sloan
Lock Haven, Pennsylvania, 1871-
Hanover, New Hampshire, 1951

Painter, illustrator, and etcher, John
Sloan was one of the members of the
Eight, the group also known as the New
York realists. He moved to Philadelphia
in 1876 and enrolled in the Pennsylvania
Academy of Fine Arts, where he studied
under Thomas Anshutz; he stayed there
until 1894. During this period he
became a skilled draftsman and began
a career as illustrator for several of the
city's most famous dailies, primarily
the *Philadelphia Inquirer* and the
Philadelphia Press. The rapid, essential
style of his early works showed the
influence of art nouveau and the

decorative style of Japanese painting.
In 1892 he met Robert Henri, who
encouraged him to become an artist,
inviting him to attend the evening
meetings he held in his studio. Sloan
moved to New York in 1904 and
dedicated himself to painting; in that
same year he exhibited his works at
the National Arts Club in New York.
Between 1905 and 1907 he began
painting urban subjects, streets, squares,
and views of New York, while also
working on etchings. In 1908 he
exhibited along with the other members
of the Eight; the next year he joined the
socialist party—running for office in the
1910 and 1915 elections—and worked
for several socialist newspapers, such as
The Masses, where he served as director

from 1912 to 1916. Sloan exhibited in
the famous Armory Show in 1913; in
those years he diversified his subjects,
beginning to paint nudes and
landscapes. In 1916 he began teaching
painting at the Art Students League,
where he remained for twenty-five
years. Among his students were
Alexander Calder, John Graham,
Reginald Marsh, Adolph Gottlieb,
and Barnett Newman. He collected his
teachings in the book *Gist of Art*,
published in 1913. In that same year he
was commissioned to make a mural for
the Bronxville post office. A year after
Sloan's death, Lloyd Goodrich organized
a large retrospective with more than
two hundred works at the Whitney
Museum of American Art.

John Sloan
*Sunday, Women Drying
Their Hair*
1912
oil on canvas
26 × 32 in.
(66.1 × 81.3 cm)
Addison Museum of
American Art, Phillips
Academy, Andover,
Massachusetts

Francesco Solimena

Canale di Serino, 1657- Barra,
Naples, 1747

A long-lived and brilliant painter of
European renown, Solimena was the
leading painter of southern Italy from
the end of the seventeenth to the mid-
eighteenth century. Solimena was
trained in the workshop of his father, a
fairly good painter of the Neapolitan
school, and made his debut in the
intense atmosphere of seventeenth-
century Neapolitan art. The first frescoes
executed independently (for the chapel
of St. Anne in the church of Gesù
Nuovo in Naples in 1677) display a
careful study of Baroque decoration
and an early taste for rich, dynamic,
monumental compositions. In the 1680s,
he received important commissions for
work in Neapolitan churches and
established himself as one of the leading
painters of the local school. With their
spectacular impact and expressive
tension, the frescoes in the sacristy of S.
Paolo Maggiore constitute an authentic
masterpiece. The vigor of his contrasts
was partially attenuated during a stay
in Rome shortly before the year 1700.
Contact with artists connected with the
Accademia di San Luca and the French
Academy at Villa Medici led him to
address mythological subjects with
a restraint drawn from classicism.
In Naples, he was for many years the
unchallenged leader, a role confirmed
by the frescoes executed at an advanced
age: *Expulsion of Heliodorus from the
Temple* on the broad secondary façade
of the Gesù Nuovo. His style was a source
of inspiration not only for painters but
also for those working in the decorative
arts, such as goldsmiths, silversmiths,
and the creators of the figurines used in
Neapolitan Christmas crèches.

Francesco Solimena
*St. Bonaventura Receives
the Banner of the Holy
Sepulchre from the Virgin*
1710
oil on canvas, 94½ × 51¼
in. (240 × 130 cm)
Cathedral, Aversa (Caserta)

His religious works are
a triumphant spectacle
of striking poses, gestures,
and colors. He uses taut
sculptural modeling based
on a strong contrast of
light and shadow to stage
magnificent Baroque
scenes.

Bartholomäus Spranger

Antwerp, 1546-Prague, 1611

A master who epitomizes the trends of late European Mannerism, Spranger was a typically dynamic figure on the artistic scene at the court of Rudolf II of Hapsburg. The emperor moved his court from Vienna to Prague, thus initiating a period in which imaginative collections were built up and sophisticated works were commissioned. Spranger began his training in Antwerp, a city that was already influenced by High Renaissance Italian art and, in 1565, he set off on a journey to Italy. After becoming acquainted with the Mannerist Fontainebleau School, he went to Milan, Parma, and finally Rome. He thus assimilated the new trends in Lombard art, became familiar with the work of Correggio and Parmigiano, received prestigious commissions from the Farnese family, and became so established in Roman Mannerist circles that he was appointed painter to the pope in 1570. However, he executed few religious works and showed a decided preference for mythological and literary themes. This marked the beginning of his official career. Spranger evolved a sophisticated, elegant style in which intellectuals could have the satisfaction of recognizing various artistic and cultural allusions, but he also succeeded in expressing a kind of cold sensuality, as provocative as it is apparently detached. In the service of Emperor Rudolf II, he worked first in Vienna and then, from 1581, in Prague, a city which also drew Arcimboldo, Joseph Heintz, Hans van Aachen, as well as Milanese goldsmiths and engravers. The works the emperor most admired were those in which Spranger, on the pretext of depicting classical myths, portrayed voluptuous female nudes. Engravings of his works made them widely known and they soon became very famous in various European countries, thus contributing to the international dimension of the Mannerist style.

Bartholomäus Spranger
Venus and Vulcan
c. 1610
oil on canvas
55 × 37½ in.
(140 × 95 cm)
Kunsthistorisches
Museum, Vienna

A typical example of the transformation of Mannerism from an "avant-garde" movement to "official" art, this is one of the painter's masterpieces. The overt sensuality, evidently to satisfy Emperor Rudolf II's taste for curvaceous figures, is displayed in a controlled, formally perfect composition, which is the result of a refined selection of cultural and artistic influences.

Jan Steen

Leyden, 1626-1679

A painter of great originality and narrative force, Steen is one of the major exponents of seventeenth-century Dutch art. His favorite subjects were scenes from daily life, observed with a certain disenchanted, amused irony. Unlike most of his fellow artists, Steen did not have permanent residence in one city, but moved frequently, thus detaching himself from the local schools. His prolific output was the result of his confident rapid execution. Thanks to his varied training, Steen succeeds in conferring a solid monumentality and compositional complexity on his genre subjects, and in developing his own individual style. Though he was born in the same city as Rembrandt, Steen completed his apprenticeship in Utrecht and Haarlem, where he acquired a fair knowledge of Italian painting, and admired the free manner of Frans Hals and the picturesque subjects painted by Adriaen van Ostade. In 1648, he married the daughter of the landscapist Jan van Goyen, and acquired from his father-in-law a taste for refined, atmospheric, light effects. In 1649, he moved to The Hague, but his earnings from painting were meager, so he moved to Delft (Vermeer's city), where he divided his time between painting and running a brewery. After further travels, and particularly a long, profitable stay in Haarlem, Steen spent the last years of his life in his hometown. During his career, Steen painted the same scenes several times, but with variations. His very enjoyable canvases sometimes have a tone of underplayed realism, amused detachment, or critical moralism.

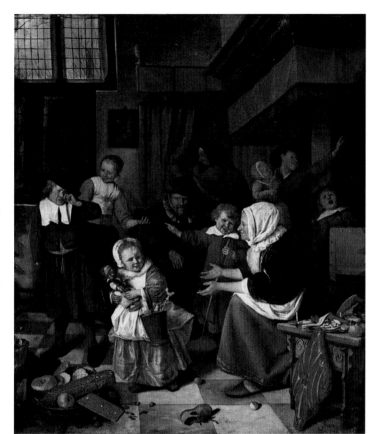

Jan Steen
The Feast of St. Nicholas
c. 1660
oil on canvas
32¼ × 27¾ in.
(82 × 70.5 cm)
Rijksmuseum,
Amsterdam

Steen is an observant painter of children. The day of Santa Claus, in northern Europe, is when gifts are exchanged; it is the tender moment that brings together grandparents and grandchildren. At the center of the painting a little girl is happily hugging her new doll. Baroque painting rarely has scenes of such smiling tenderness. By contrast, on the left a boy is crying desperately; he has been naughty and has not received any presents, and his little brother points this out to his grandmother. The old woman's amused expression makes one think that soon an unexpected gift will appear for her punished grandchild.

Jan Steen
The Cheerful Family
1668
oil on canvas
43½ × 5½ in.
(110.5 × 141 cm)
Rijksmuseum,
Amsterdam

The real title of this work should be the Dutch proverb written on the piece of paper, top right: "As the old people play, so the young people sing," which alludes to the example adults should set children. The family in this picture is certainly no model of order and discipline; confusion reigns and is increased by the general uproar.

Sebastian Stosskopf
Strasbourg, 1597-Idstein, 1657

A painter working on the "borderline," as befits an artist born in Alsace, Stosskopf is one of the most mysterious and fascinating specialists in Baroque still life. He trained in the Rhineland and Flanders, but a series of parallels can be drawn with other painters of the period, including Georg Flegel and Jan Davidszoon de Heem. At the same time, Stosskopf's work remains totally original. With his almost maniacal passion for precision, Stosskopf often verges on trompe-l'oeil. All his works explore the inner nature of things. The objects appear as though metaphysically transfixed, immobile, and yet precarious, threatened by the possibility of imminent disaster. Fragile, precious, and defenseless, Stosskopf's rare paintings are like a moment of silence in the often deafening concert of Baroque art.

Sebastian Stosskopf
Still Life with Basket of Glass Objects
1644
oil on canvas
20½ × 24½ in.
(52 × 62 cm)
Musée des Beaux-Arts, Strasbourg

Reserved for an elite group of patrons, some of Stosskopf's works depict precious collections of sophisticated objects. The crystal glasses in the straw basket are all different and do not form a single set but a small, select collection, depicted with astonishing imitative skill. One of the glasses is broken, however, and the slivers of crystal, now completely useless, introduce the poignant theme of the fleeting nature of beauty.

Bernardo Strozzi
Genoa, 1581-Venice, 1644

Strozzi was a Capuchin friar who led a tumultuous life. He was also the most important exponent of the rich vein of Genoese art in the seventeenth century. The Ligurian school was molded through its contacts first with the great Flemish master Rubens, which led to him using rich, thick colors applied with wide brushstrokes, and later with Van Dyck, whose refined elegance added its own influence. Strozzi's interpretation of these trends was highly original and combined with his thorough knowledge of other currents in art, from the Lombard school to the diffusion of Caravaggio's style. After producing a splendid series of frescoes, altarpieces, and paintings for private collectors in Genoa, Strozzi moved to Venice in 1630 after a serious disagreement with his Capuchin order. His paintings were an immediate success in Venice, partly because Palma the Younger had recently died and there was a lack of native painters. From then on, Strozzi could be considered one of the most important painters in seventeenth-century Venice. Apart from religious paintings, he was also much admired for the fleshy but lively portraits he painted.

Bernardo Strozzi
The Cook
c. 1620, canvas, 69¼ × 72¾ in. (176 × 185 cm)
Palazzo Rossi Gallery, Genoa

The scene as a whole can be considered a masterpiece of Italian genre painting.

Gilbert Stuart

North Kingstown, Rhode Island, 1755-
Boston, 1828

Celebrated for his portraits of George
Washington, Stuart was the leading
American portraitist at the end of the
century. He studied with the Scottish
painter Cosmo Alexander, first in
Newport, then in South Carolina, and
finally in Scotland, returning to
America in 1772. With the approach
of the Revolution, commissions for
portraits diminished to the point that
Stuart, in 1775, decided to go to
London, where he entered the studio
of Benjamin West. Although he
worked and lived with West from 1777
to 1782, Stuart did not adopt his style.
Instead he was influenced by the
pictorial manner of such English
portraitists as Thomas Gainsborough
and Joshua Reynolds; his technique
was based on the sumptuous style and
the compositional layouts typical of
those painters. Blending
compositional majesty with a lively,
natural technique, his portraits
emanate both immediacy and eternity,
freshness and vigor. With an observer's
sharp eye, Stuart was able to capture
personality traits in a few swift strokes,
and rarely presented more than a head
or bust. Following exhibits of his
works at the Royal Academy in 1777,
1779, and 1782, Stuart acquired
considerable fame and received many
commissions, despite strong
competition from English painters. An
artist with no business sense, he was
so deeply in debt that he was forced to
take refuge in Dublin in 1787, where,
however, he continued to paint with
success. He returned to America in
1793, living first in New York and then
in Philadelphia, where he made his
first portrait from life of Washington.
In 1796 Stuart made a second portrait
of Washington, which became very
famous. There is yet a third type,
known as the Lansdowne type because
the original was painted for Lord
Lansdowne. Other portraits of the
president were painted from memory.
Although his fame is tied primarily
to his portraits of Washington, Stuart
painted the portraits of five other
presidents and those of leading
citizens and national and local heroes.
This portrait work increased his
stature in Philadelphia, Washington,
and Boston, where he moved in 1805.
In Boston he gradually abandoned the
grandeur and vivid colors derived
from the English school of portraiture
that marks his previous work.

Pierre Subleyras

Saint-Gilles-du Sard, 1699-
Rome, 1749

Subleyras trained in Paris in the workshop of Jean-Pierre Rivalz, a painter of lower-class scenes. In 1727 he won the Prix de Rome for his *Bronze Serpent* (Fontainebleau), and the following year he moved to Italy. A protégé of Cardinal Valenti, in 1740 he was admitted to the Accademia di S. Luca and in 1743 he obtained the commission for the *Mass of St. Basil*, one of the altarpieces in the basilica of St. Peter's, where he worked together with Vouet, Poussin, and Valentin, thus becoming one of the public painters of eighteenth-century Rome. Subleyras worked in large and small formats with notable results. He painted fine portraits, such as *Benedict XIV* (Museum, Chantilly) and the *Abbess Battistina Vernasca* (Musée Fabre, Montpellier), as well as magnificent altarpieces such as the *Crucifixion* (Brera, Milan) and the *Miracle of St. Benedict* in the church of Santa Francesca Romana in Rome, revealing hidden talent as a colorist. His last works display an almost Jansenist rigor in the spare lines of the composition and the limited range of color, reminiscent of that of Philippe de Champaigne.

Pierre Subleyras
The Marriage of St. Catherine de' Ricci
c. 1740-1745
oil on canvas
Private collection, Rome

The skillful distribution of light and shadow heightens the center of the picture, where the mystical union is celebrated, while an enigmatic, isolated figure to the right draws the viewer's attention.

Opposite
Gilbert Stuart
The Skater
1782, oil on canvas, 96½ × 58 in. (245.3 × 147.6 cm)
National Gallery of Art, Washington, D.C.

Left
Pierre Subleyras
Mass of St. Basil
1743
oil on canvas
52½ × 31½ in.
(133.5 × 80 cm)
Hermitage,
St. Petersburg

This is the magnificent
model for the altarpiece
executed for the church
of Santa Maria degli
Angeli in Rome. Perhaps
his masterpiece of
religious painting,
it is no coincidence that
Subleyras placed it
at the center of

The Painter's Studio
reproduced below.
He draws from and
develops a number
of different sources,
achieving a work of high
nobility and great
composure. The starting
points are the Holy
Conversations of
sixteenth-century
Venetian painting
(such as Titian's *Pesaro
Altarpiece* in the Basilica
dei Frari in Venice, or
the Madonna and Saints
of Paolo Veronese).
The scene is dominated
by a controlled sense of
composition, beginning

with the monumental
architecture in the
background.
The two fluted columns
give a sense of rhythm
to the space and create
an atmosphere
of high solemnity.
The figures are arranged
along a clear diagonal
axis, but, despite the
rigid control, the scene
remains lively. Once
again Subleyras unfurls
his memorable whites
in the center
of the canvas, creating
the bright luminosity
that is his most
distinctive feature.

Pierre Subleyras
The Painter's Studio
c. 1747-1749
oil on canvas
Academy of Fine Arts,
Vienna

Having reached the end
of his career, Subleyras
effectively and
evocatively remembers
his oeuvre. Taking the
form of a self-portrait in
his studio, the painting

becomes a summary of
the artist's works and
also, through the
presence of classical
statuettes, of his sources
and influences. This
work belongs to an
important line of
seventeenth- and
eighteenth-century
painting, which extends
from the allegories of
Jan Bruegel and Rubens
to the museum images

of early neoclassicism,
such as Zoffany's
Tribuna of the Uffizi.
The artist's poetic
sensibility can be seen in
details such as the
figures with their backs
to us, which may even
remind us of Vermeer's
Allegory of Painting.
Particularly touching is
the small figure of the
fair-haired boy intent (it
seems) on drawing.

Gerard Ter Borch

Zwolle, 1617-Deventer, 1681

Portraitist and refined painter of domestic interiors, Ter Borch has many of the stylistic and poetic characteristics of seventeenth-century Dutch art. He moved to Amsterdam when he was just fifteen, and first studied with a local painter, but soon, attracted by the echoes of Italian painting that reached him from Utrecht and Haarlem, and stimulated by Rembrandt's monumental manner, he began to travel. From 1635 to 1642, he studied abroad, and came in contact with all the major European schools and great masters. He went first to London where he met van Dyck, then to Rome and Spain. On his return to Amsterdam, he immersed himself in local painting and became acquainted with Rembrandt's use of light effects and, later, with the early works of Vermeer; they must have struck up a friendship since he was best man at Vermeer's wedding. In 1654 he moved to Deventer, where he quietly spent the rest of his life. As well as portraits, executed above all during his second stay in Amsterdam, Ter Borch painted peaceful, delicate domestic scenes, which display great finesse of execution and a very effective feeling for calm depiction, which is not limited to virtuosity for its own sake (as sometimes happens in Dou's works), and deliberately does not venture into psychological analysis in the manner of Vermeer, but remains within the sphere of precise, sympathetic representation.

Gerard Ter Borch
The Guitar Lesson
c. 1660
oil on canvas
26½ × 22¾ in.
(67.6 × 57.8 cm)
National Gallery,
London

The remarkable characterization of the figures reflects Ter Borch's consummate skill as a portraitist. The scene is reminiscent of the interiors of Vermeer, an artist with whom Ter Borch was definitely in direct personal and professional contact.

Gerard Ter Borch
Interior with Figures
c. 1650
oil on canvas
28 × 8¾ in.
(71 × 73 cm)
Rijksmuseum,
Amsterdam

Also entitled *The Father's Admonishment*, this is one of Ter Borch's favorite subjects and he painted it frequently. A typical feature is the silvery reflections of the girl's silk gown that gleams softly in the serene, dim light of the domestic interior.

Hendrick Terbrugghen
Deventer, 1588-Utrecht, 1629

The major exponent of the Utrecht school, Terbrugghen played a decisive role in the history of Dutch painting by leading the transition from the late sixteenth-century Mannerist tradition to the Caravaggesque style, which was spreading throughout Europe. It is important to remember that the city of Utrecht, the episcopal center of Holland, had remained mostly Catholic, in a country that had almost entirely converted to Calvinism. For this reason Terbrugghen and his colleagues (like van Honthorst) frequently painted traditional religious subjects, which were far rarer in the rest of Holland. During the years of his training with Abraham Bloemaert, the young Terbrugghen made a close study of Renaissance prints by Dürer and Lucas van Leyden, thus acquiring a taste for distinctive expressions, unusual physical types, and strongly marked features. In 1604 he moved to Rome where he made the personal acquaintance of Caravaggio. Terbrugghen spent ten years in Italy and during this time he mastered the technique of painting large canvases, with strong contrasts of light and shadow, and great dramatic intensity. The subjects, light effects, and compositions are directly influenced by Caravaggio, but the painter adds his personal interest in physiognomy and his characters reappear in various contexts in different pictures.
On his return to Utrecht in 1614, Terbrugghen became the driving force in the local school of painting and he encouraged all the young artists to spend a period of study in Italy. He himself returned there in 1620, and found a new artistic climate in which the paler and more luminous tones of the Bolognese school predominated. Terbrugghen's painting also became lighter, and he began to paint genre scenes and to give a more realistic and picturesque rendering of religious subjects.

Hendrick Terbrugghen
Calling of St. Matthew
c. 1616
oil on canvas
41¾ × 50½ in.
(106 × 128 cm)
Museum of Fine Arts,
Budapest

This is one of the painter's favorite subjects, inspired by the famous canvas by Caravaggio in the church of S. Luigi dei Francesi in Rome, though his compositions constantly vary.

Giambattista Tiepolo
Venice, 1696-Madrid, 1770

Eighteenth-century European art is dominated by the figure of Tiepolo, who set the tone for the great late Baroque decoration of stately palaces throughout Europe, both through his numerous spectacular works and through those of his many followers. His sumptuous and fascinating large-scale frescoes are the best-known aspect of his activities, so much so that there is a risk of regarding him primarily as a great decorative artist. On the contrary, Tiepolo was a versatile master capable of tackling a whole range of different subjects, techniques, and formats. His eclectic approach is based on an inimitable blend of wild fantasy and minute realism. In every composition, even the most extravagant and whimsical, Tiepolo always includes naturalistic details. A pupil of Gregorio Lazzarini, he completed all his training and the early stages of his career in Venice. In 1719 he married Cecilia Guardi, the sister of the painters Giovanni Antonio and Francesco. This period marked his debut as a promising painter of religious scenes for Venetian churches, and in 1722 he was engaged in the collective task of decorating S. Stae. Encouraged by Piazzetta, the young Tiepolo began to create effects of diffused lighting and bold, melodramatic gestures, and developed a remarkable talent for the decoration of palatial interiors. A spectacular demonstration of this is provided by the series of frescoes in the archbishop's palace in Udine (1726), a splendidly rich and varied cycle of works that gave Tiepolo a leading role not only in the Venetian school, but in European Rococo art. Tiepolo was inspired by Venetian sixteenth-century art and worked on commission both for important Venetian churches and for nobles in different regions. His works include the important frescoes executed in Milan (Archinto, Dugnani, and Clerici) during the 1730s. He was very competently assisted by Girolamo Mengozzi Colonna, a specialist in *quadrature*, illusionistic architectural settings that Tiepolo filled with narrative scenes. The climax of his consistent talent as a painter of religious scenes and secular allegories came in Venice in the early 1740s with his almost simultaneous work for the Scuola del Carmine and frescoes for Palazzo Labia. Though collectors and patrons throughout Europe were competing for his services, he accepted the proposals of the prince-bishop of Würzburg, who offered him the opportunity to fresco the staircase and the most imposing area of the Residenz, the masterpiece of Balthasar Neumann. In 1750 he left for Germany, where he was to stay for three years, accompanied by his son Giandomenico. On his return to the Veneto, he painted decorations for many villas before leaving again in 1762 for Madrid. He painted his last great secular compositions in the palace of the Spanish kings, but was exposed to competition from Mengs and Neoclassicism. His last years (he died in 1770) were filled with bitterness at his sudden loss of favor.

Previous page
Giambattista Tiepolo
Maecenas Presents the Arts to Augustus
1744, oil on canvas
23¼ × 35 in.
(69.5 × 89 cm)
Hermitage, St. Petersburg

Below
Giambattista Tiepolo
Hannibal Recognizes the Head of His Brother Hasdrubal, 1725-1730
canvas, 150¾ × 71¾ in.
(383 × 182 cm)
Kunsthistorisches Museum, Vienna

Giambattista Tiepolo
Rachel Concealing the Idols
c. 1726
fresco
157 × 196¾ in.
(400 × 500 cm)
Gallery of the Archbishop's Palace, Udine

Giandomenico Tiepolo
Venice, 1727-1804

Giambattista Tiepolo had many children, two of whom (Giandomenico and Lorenzo) followed in their father's footsteps, first as his assistants and then embarking on their own careers to pursue their respective inclinations. Lorenzo distinguished himself as a portraitist and engraver, but without ever completely abandoning his father's sphere. On the other hand, Giandomenico took advantage of the training received in his youth, the journeys undertaken with his father, and the work carried out alongside him to forge an unmistakable style of his own that was to make him one of the most interesting painters in the second half of the eighteenth century. The stages of Giandomenico's early career are sign-posted by his father's great works in Venice, Würzburg, Vicenza, Stra, and Madrid. Giandomenico soon established himself as his father's principal and most faithful assistant. He acquired a perfect mastery of fresco technique and executed a splendid *Stations of the Cross* in the Venetian church of San Polo, which was a superb tribute to the style of Giambattista. Very soon, however, Giandomenico was to strike out on an expressive path of his own linked to themes of everyday life, viewed with a hint of irony but also with a sincere spirit of involvement. Excellent examples of this are furnished by the frescoes in the guest wing of Villa Valmarana in Vicenza. He followed Giambattista to Madrid in 1762 and experienced first hand the sudden demise of Tiepolesque art, since its popularity with the court was supplanted by the Neoclassicism of Mengs. The years in Spain were, however, very important for the contact between Giandomenico and the young Goya, who was influenced by the Venetian's particular and highly effective way of interpreting reality. On his father's death in 1770, Giandomenico returned to Italy and executed important decorative projects in Brescia, Genoa, and Venice. In later years the decadence of Venice led Giandomenico to withdraw to Zianigo in the country, where the moving cycle of frescoes on the walls of the family villa display lightness of touch, but also the melancholy of a highly aware and disenchanted artist.

Giandomenico Tiepolo
The Offering of Fruit to a Lunar Divinity; Peasant Family at Table
1757
frescoes
Villa Valmarana ai Nani, Vicenza

The fresco shown above is from the "Chinese room" in the guest wing of Villa Valmarana, one of the most interesting parts of the building. The taste for chinoiserie spread throughout eighteenth-century Europe with very striking results. Attempts to imitate the celebrated and extremely expensive porcelain led in the various courts to an almost obsessive fascination with the Orient. Pagodas were erected in aristocratic gardens from England to Prussia, the rooms and façades of princely residences were decorated with "Chinese" motifs, and fashions supposedly deriving from Cathay were imitated even in food. Giandomenico Tiepolo illustrated a less sumptuous China for this family of the provincial nobility, but the elegance of the frescoes in the "Chinese room" in the guest wing of Villa Valmarana is unequaled by the Chinese-style decorations found anywhere else in Europe. Against pale, luminous backgrounds, Giandomenico Tiepolo painted groups of figures and single trees to conjure up human situations and landscapes with very simple means in precisely the same way as the art of the Far East.

Tintoretto

Jacopo Robusti
Venice, 1519-1594

Tintoretto was the last grand figure of Venetian Renaissance art. After his death, art in the Republic shrank to repetitive copies, chiefly of him. Tintoretto claimed to have been a pupil of Titian but Bordone was a more likely master. No work can be ascribed to him before 1545, although he was already his own master. He burst onto the Venetian art scene with his spectacular *The Miracle of St. Mark* (1548, Accademia, Venice). He was hailed as a rival to Titian, and claimed to unite "the color of Titian with the drawing of Michelangelo," although in fact he was not much like either, being much more melodramatic in his art. Tintoretto certainly retained a Venetian love of color and light, but added grandiose gestures, muscular bodies, and amazing viewpoints in the fashion of the Mannerists. During the 1550s Tintoretto produced both mythological and religious scenes marked by fluid brushwork and very contorted poses. He was never daunted by tasks of colossal proportions and in 1564 started decorating the huge Scuola di San Rocco. In many respects, this work contains the story of his own development. From grandiloquent and crowded scenes, he moved on to intensely moving compositions until he reached the final, astoundingly visionary images in the rooms on the ground floor. Assisted by his own studio, which included his daughter Marietta, Tintoretto produced dozens of altarpieces for Venetian churches. From 1575 onward, he was also engaged in redecorating the Palazzo del Doge which he left off at the unfinished canvas of *Paradiso* in the Sala del Maggior Consiglio. By this time Titian and Veronese had died and Tintoretto was also old. His last works, including *The Last Supper* in San Giorgio Maggiore, were markedly mystical, showing almost disembodied spirits scaring through the air. He had a great influence on El Greco.

Tintoretto
The Miracle of the Slave
1548
canvas
163¾ × 214¼ in.
(416 × 544 cm)
Gallerie dell'Accademia, Venice

Pietro Aretino, Titian's literary friend, was among the many who greeted this huge canvas with much enthusiasm. It had been painted as part of the decorative program in the Scuola di San Marco (a religious fraternity, not a school). With it, aged 30, he established his place as the leading artist of the new generation. But his work started some heated debate, with Titian reputedly being shocked. The grandiose tone of the scene, its exaggerated foreshortening, the discrepancy between the detailed immediate naturalism and the unreal atmosphere of the miracle, were unprecedented in Venetian art, although the rich colors and the noble Renaissance architecture in the background were typically Venetian. Even though he claimed to stick to his twin reference points of Michelangelo and Titian, by now Tintoretto was in the process of discovering his own unmistakable, creative style.

Tintoretto
Christ Before Pilate
1565-1567
canvas
202¾ × 149½ in.
(515 × 380 cm)
Scuola di San Rocco,
Sala dell'Albergo, Venice.

Tintoretto was not above resorting to distinctly dubious tricks to get the better of his competitors. He won the vital commission for decorating the Sala dell'Albergo, the start of work in the Scuola di San Rocco which was to last for 23 years, by sneaking into the room and painting his specimen work complete and in situ the night before, while his rivals could show only rough sketches. The brethren were of course dazzled by his finished work and awarded him the contract. The walls of the vast room are covered in huge canvases showing the Passion. The scenes were arranged in a free order, reflecting his own artistic aims as much as the Scuola's. Sincere and intense devotion was coupled with Tintoretto's desire to push innovation and his own talent to their limits. In this picture the figure of Christ appears luminously frail and almost disembodiedly spiritual against the opulently gleaming marble pillars flanking Pilate's throne.

Titian

Tiziano Vecellio
Pieve di Cadore, Belluno, c. 1490-
Venice, 1576

Indisputably the greatest painter
of the Venetian school, Titian's long
life can be seen as an endless train
of successes and honors. In reality he
is the supreme example of an artist
constantly researching and
inexhaustibly renewing his art. Titian's
career covers almost a century of
Renaissance art, starting at its High
Renaissance zenith and ending in its
dramatic dissolution in his last works.
Titian was originally Bellini's pupil but
moved to Giorgione's studio, becoming
his collaborator on the Fondaco dei
Tedeschi and completing some
canvases like *The Sleeping Venus*. By the
time he had started work on the
Assumption of the Frari in 1516, he was
recognized as the greatest painter in
Venice and Giovanni Bellini's successor
as the Republic's official painter. This
was chiefly thanks to his richness
of color and the dynamism of his
compositions. In 1518 he began
painting a series of brilliant
mythological works for Alfonso d'Este,
Duke of Ferrara. This marked the
beginning of his paintings for such
courts. Titian's fame as a painter was
mainly due to the immense vitality of
his portraits. In the 1530s, perhaps due
to his wife's death, Titian's colors
became more subdued and his style
less dramatic. Around 1540 he became
aware of new developments in
Mannerism. Partly because of this,
partly for family reasons (he was trying
to get his son Pomponio a church post)
he traveled to Rome in 1545-1546,
where he had a famous argument with
Michelangelo. The two great masters
had utterly opposing visions of art:
Michelangelo put drawing at the center
of his art, Titian opted mainly for color
but he had long ago assimilated
Michelangelo's monumental forms.
After two trips to Germany in the train
of Emperor Charles V, from 1551
Titian's oeuvre divides into two.
On the one hand he produced his last,
terrifying altarpieces (*The Martyrdom
of St. Lawrence*, church of the Gesuiti;
Pietà, now in the Accademia). On the
other, he painted his *Poesie* for Philip II
of Spain, mythological scenes which
seem tragic mirrors of the human
condition. Gradually his colors became
darker, thicker, and heavier and he
seemed not to finish his works. In his
last works he no longer used brushes to
apply paint, but rubbed it on directly
with his fingers.

Titian
*The Madonna and Child
Enthroned with Saints
and the Pesaro Family
(The Pesaro Altarpiece)*
1522-1526
canvas, 188¼ × 105½ in.
(478 × 268 cm)
Santa Maria Gloriosa
dei Frari, Venice

In contrast to the
traditional layout, Titian
has moved his Madonna
over to the right. Titian's
assured use of classical
architecture—with the
two great pillars soaring
past the human figures
and even clouds into
the blue heavens—is
combined with the
vividness with which he
painted the Pesaro
family in all their
different generations,
joining heaven and
earth in his art. For
centuries *The Pesaro
Altarpiece* was the
archetype for Venetian
altarpieces, from
Veronese to Sebastiano
Ricci.

Titian
Assumption
1516-1518
wood panel
271¾ × 141¾ in.
(690 × 360 cm)
Santa Maria Gloriosa
dei Frari, Venice

The enormous altarpiece is sited over the high altar in the Franciscan church in the Gothic style. It marks the start of Titian's dominance of Venetian art, combining the dynamic vigor of the Roman High Renaissance with a Venetian love of rich colors. The Virgin soars up to God the Father in heaven amid a blaze of gold. When finished, it was the largest altarpiece ever painted in the city, and the first designed to be seen from a single viewpoint. Ordinary people were enthusiastic; those who had commissioned it were puzzled by the rough appearance of the Apostles. Fellow painters reacted hostilely, for they were not yet ready for his radically new way of painting, so different from Bellini's or Giorgone's gentler art. Within a short time, however, the painting became a tonchstone for the whole Venetian school.

Titian
Violante
c. 1515
oil on wood
25½ × 20 in.
64.5 × 51 cm)
Kunsthistorisches
Museum, Vienna

Mark Tobey

Centerville, Wisconsin, 1890-
Basel, Switzerland, 1976

An independent figure in the panorama
of American art in the 1940s, Tobey
can be seen as an early forerunner of
abstract expressionism. Although his
vision of art, permeated with Eastern
mysticism (he converted to the Bahai
faith in 1918), is too personal for him
to be fitted within any of the usual
classifications of art, his most important
contributions led in the direction
of abstract expressionism. After studies
at the Art Institute of Chicago, Tobey
moved to New York, where he worked
as a fashion illustrator for magazines.
He then moved to Seattle, where he
taught in an art school. He traveled
widely: to Paris in 1925, to the Middle
East in 1926. In 1934 he made a long
trip to China and Japan, where he spent
a month in a Zen monastery and was
greatly influenced by contact with the
painter Deng Kui, who taught him the
art of Chinese calligraphy. He returned
to Seattle, where he painted and taught,
finally settling in Basel in 1960. In
keeping with Zen principles, Tobey
elaborated a style of painting in which
the automatic-gestural component
assumes cognitive values as a form
of meditation on reality. The quest for
authentic artistic expression led him to
an investigation of the value of the sign.
Beginning with the famous work
Broadway (1936), his painting includes
his so-called white writing, in which
white or light calligraphic symbols
appear across an abstract field. This
white writing became Tobey's stylistic
trait, particularly during the postwar
period when the figurative references
that until then were noticeable in
his works began to dissolve into an
essentially symbolic art that belongs
to the realm of nonrepresentational art.

Mark Tobey
Ghost Town
1965
oil on canvas, 81¾ × 52¾
in. (207.8 × 134 cm)
Michael Rosenfeld
Gallery, New York

Tobey developed a method
of calligraphic painting
that he repeats across the
entire surface of the canvas.
Far from being deserted,
this imaginary city is
populated by enigmatic
signs, vertiginous spirals,
and symbols.

Henri de Toulouse-Lautrec

Albi, 1864-Malromé, 1901

Born into one of the oldest aristocratic families in France and inclined by family tradition to the noble pursuits of hunting and riding as well as to an amateur dalliance with drawing, Toulouse-Lautrec was afflicted by a series of infirmities from childhood. Aggravated by falls from his horse, his physical handicap stunted his growth and shaped his destiny. Leaving the provinces and his prospects of leading the life of a gentleman, Toulouse-Lautrec moved to Paris, where he took academic courses in painting but was drawn to the work of the Impressionists, sharing their taste for the representation of reality and

fondness for Oriental prints. He grew particularly close to Degas, who was then concentrating on his ballerinas and laundresses, painted with sympathy and none of the distortion of caricature. Over the same period as van Gogh, Toulouse-Lautrec too found his own way to go beyond Impressionism, studying and developing the instruments of line, graphics, and simplification of expression. The scion of the noble Toulouse-Lautrec family found his inspiration in popular, even disreputable settings: cafés–chantants, brothels, squalid dancehalls, and suburban circuses. In the last decade of the nineteenth century, thanks to technical improvements in color printing, Toulouse–Lautrec produced

paintings, drawings, lithographs, and advertising posters: different means of expression, often combined to their mutual advantage, in an art of great freedom that did not hold back from ticklish subjects and displayed an unprecedented aggressiveness. Over his all too short career, Toulouse-Lautrec laid the foundations for important developments in art: on one hand, with his abandonment of Impressionism, he became a source of inspiration for the Expressionists; on the other, the skillful fusion of images, words, and color in his prolific output of posters and illustrations made Toulouse-Lautrec the originator of a new genre, that of advertising and commercial art.

**Henri
de Toulouse-Lautrec**
*Dance at the
Moulin Rouge*
1890
oil on canvas
45½ × 59 in.
(115.5 × 150 cm)
Private collection,
Philadelphia

Only a few years had
gone by since Renoir
painted his pictures
of dances at the Moulin
de la Galette and other
petit bourgeois haunts in

Paris, yet Toulouse-
Lautrec's interpretation
is quite different.
Instead of the typical
joie de vivre of the
Impressionists,
we perceive a sense
of strain, uncertainty,
and the unspoken.

**Henri
de Toulouse-Lautrec**
*The Salon on Rue
des Moulins*
1894
pastel
52½ × 45¼ in.
(132.5 × 115.5 cm)
Musée Toulouse-
Lautrec, Albi

Thanks to Toulouse-
Lautrec, the red divan in
the *maison close*, or
brothel, on Rue des
Moulins in Paris has
become one of the most
characteristic locations

of late nineteenth-
century painting. It is
easy to imagine some of
the scenes from the
great French novels of
that time in this setting.
In the room, brightly-lit
and furnished with an
ostentatious and
somewhat kitsch luxury,
several prostitutes are
waiting for their clients.
Without the slightest
hint of caricature
or cartoon, Toulouse-
Lautrec portrays a
group of real and living
women. The picture

seems to offer us
fleeting glimpses of
their personal histories,
as the painter captures
with great refinement
their expressions of
embarrassment,
indolence, boredom,
and fatigue.

John Trumbull

Lebanon, Connecticut, 1756-
New York, 1843

Inspired by the paintings of
contemporary history by Benjamin
West and John Singleton Copley,
Trumbull dedicated his career to
painting the heroes and events of the
American Revolution, in which he
took part as an aide to Washington
and a cartographer. After studies at
Harvard, he resigned his commission
in 1778 and in 1780 was in London,
attending the school held by West.
In 1785 he became the first American
ambassador to Paris, where he met
Jacques-Louis David, although the
great French painter had no influence
on his style. Following a diplomatic
career, Trumbull divided his time
between London and New York while
dedicating himself to painting, making

many portraits and several history
paintings. After the end of the War
of 1812 he obtained the important
commission of painting four of the
eight commemorative paintings for
the U.S. Capitol rotunda, but these
works fell short of expectations. An
artist of central importance to the
visual culture of early nineteenth-
century America, Trumbull became
president of the American Academy
of Fine Arts in 1878 and went on to
direct that institution for nine years,
making cultural decisions based on
the model of Old World academies,
such as giving absolute priority to the
study of classical masters, considered
an exercise essential for the proper
formation and training of American
artists. In 1831, by which time he was
famous in America, he gave fifty-five
of his works to Yale University in New
Haven in exchange for an annuity.

John Trumbull
Philip Church
1784
oil on canvas, 18 × 13¾
in. (45.4 × 35 cm)
Fine Arts Museums,
San Francisco

John Trumbull
*The Declaration of
Independence, July 4, 1776*
1787-1820
oil on canvas, 21 × 31 in.
(53.7 × 79 cm)
Yale University Art
Gallery, New Haven,
Connecticut

The "Philadelphia
meeting room" is
decorated with a colorful
arrangement of flags.

Cosmè Tura

Ferrara, c 1430-1495

Tura was the first, most original, and best-known artist of the Ferrara school, introducing to the Este city a strange and totally original style. In Padua in the 1450s, the young Tura came into contact with Squarcione's circle and Mantegna who was at the beginning of his own career. These encounters produced the sculptural quality of his often tortuous art. On his return to Ferrara, Tura became court painter to the d'Este family and never left the city again. He was also in charge of decorating the Este residences which included frescoes in the salone dei Mesi in Palazzo Schifanoia.

Cosmè Tura
Virgin Enthroned
1474, wood panel
94 × 40 in.
(239 × 102 cm)
National Gallery, London

This was the central part of the *Roverella Altarpiece*. He had to paint the scene in a steep vertical format. To suit this he invented an unusual throne with steps, decorated with Hebrew inscriptions and crowned by a richly carved summit.

Cosmè Tura
Spring
c. 1460, wood panel
19 × 13 in. (48 × 33 cm)
National Gallery, London

The title traditionally given to this painting has nothing to do with the identity of the mysterious and fascinating figure seated on a throne decorated with sharp-edged copper dolphins. The picture probably shows one of the Muses painted to decorate the Este study at Belfiore.

Joseph Mallord William Turner

London, 1775-1851

Gifted with a precocious and brilliant talent, Turner was able to find a highly unusual balance between his natural inspiration and a thorough and complete course of studies. Admitted to the Royal Academy of Arts at the age of only fourteen, Turner assiduously attended the courses of engraving, watercolor, topography, and finally painting, showing a distinct preference for the landscape. In spite of the pedantry and long-windedness of the lessons, the young Turner acquired an unexceptionable stock of technical skills. He studied and admired the great painters of the past and found the stimuli he needed to go beyond the imitation of nature and seek a freer and more personal means of expression. A very important factor in this process was the journey he made to Switzerland in 1803. Among its snowy peaks Turner experienced the feeling of the sublime, overwhelmed by the huge mountains and the extreme weather phenomena. During his early maturity Turner sought to reconcile the lessons of the past (in particular, the much admired Claude Lorrain, but also the seventeenth-century Dutch landscapists) with his desire to experiment. Characteristic of this period are the themes of some of his landscapes, inspired by episodes from ancient history. In 1819 Turner's life and career reached a turning point: his first visit to Italy took him to Venice, where he was enthralled by the play of light on water, stone, sky, and clouds. Although he admired the luminous skies of Rome and Naples, Turner nursed a special affection for Venice. He returned there several times, depicting radically different aspects of the city than those caught by Canaletto. In particular, the buildings reflected in the water are only vaguely recognizable, their outlines blurred in the light. Late in his career, Turner accentuated his research into the effects of mist and steam, eventually producing the first painting of a moving train.

Previous pages
William Turner
Snowstorm in Val d'Aosta
detail
1818
oil on canvas
36 × 48¼ in.
(91.5 × 122.5 cm)
Art Institute, Chicago

A journey through
the Alps made a deep
impression on William
Turner.

He was struck by
the swirling of wind
and snow, the unusual
light, and the
uniformity of color
under the falling snow
rather than by the
majesty of the
mountains. He turned
sharply away from the
analytical precision
of Constable in order
to convey sentiments
and emotions.

William Turner
*Stevedores Unloading
Coal by the Light
of the Full Moon*
1835
oil on canvas
36¼ × 48½ in.
(92 × 123 cm)
National Gallery,
Washington, D.C.

The world of ports, cargo
ships, mysterious
nighttime activities
on the dockside or, by

contrast, the perils
of navigation, deeply
attracted Turner.
The element of water
still plays the leading
role in an adventure
of light in which things
and people are magically
caught up. Here we have
another example
of the poetic effect of
moonlight, a theme
that runs right through
the art of the nineteenth
century.

Paolo Uccello

Paolo di Dono
Florence, 1397-1475

Like Masaccio and Beato Angelico, Uccello made his debut in Florence in the 1420s in artistic circles dominated by Gentile da Fabriano but also open to the Humanist innovations of Brunelleschi, Donatello, and Lorenzo Ghiberti. He was fascinated with the exact, geometric, and almost cerebral component of perspective. In 1425, after his first Florentine works, frescoes with *Episodes from Genesis* in the Green Cloister of Santa Maria Novella, he spent some years in Venice, involved in important works in St. Mark's, including cartoons for mosaics and drawings of geometric solids for the inlaid marble floor. After visits to Padua and Bologna, he returned to Florence,

where he painted the *Sir John Hawkwood* in the cathedral, in 1436, followed by the frescoes around the clock face, and cartoons for the stained-glass windows. In this period he also executed the frescoes in San Miniato al Monte and Prato Cathedral, and above all the *Scenes from the Life of Noah*, in Santa Maria Novella, with their bizarre systems of perspective. His most celebrated work remains the decoration of a room in the Palazzo Medici with three panels showing scenes from the *Battle of San Romano*. Around 1465 he was summoned by Federico da Montefeltro to Urbino, where he produced a *Profanation of the Host*, the predella of the altarpiece by Justus of Ghent. However, his style seemed outmoded in comparison to masters of the new generation like Botticelli. He died in poverty at nearly eighty.

Paolo Uccello
St. George and the Dragon
c. 1455
tempera on canvas
22½ × 28¼ in.
(57 × 73 cm)
National Gallery, London

This delightful interpretation of the subject has a deliberately fairy-tale and paradoxical air. Suffice it to mention

the long leash on which the princess holds the bizarre dragon and the fragility of the slender lance used by the Christian hero. Even in this appealing scene, Paolo Uccello explores the possibilities of perspective and arranges the vegetation in depth on a regular grid plan.

Valentin de Boulogne
Coulommiers, 1591-Rome, 1632

Born into a family of Italian artists, after his apprenticeship in France, he moved to Rome in 1613 where he met Simon Vouet and was attracted by the Caravaggesque painting that was still in vogue. He entered the Bemtvögel circle under the nickname "Innamorato" and painted works that, though their subjects—for example, *The Cheat*, now in Dresden—are reminiscent of the carefree climate of the Dutch circle, depart from this to anticipate the composed, tragic quality of Louis Le Nain's figures. As a tavern habitué, even when he tackles biblical and religious themes, he is always concerned with depicting everyday reality in its most humble aspects. In Rome the artist enjoyed the protection of such illustrious patrons as the Barberini family, who were reputedly francophiles. Thanks to the support of Cardinal Francesco Barberini, nephew of Pope Urban VIII, de Boulogne was commissioned to work alongside Vouet, Poussin, and Subleyras in the basilica of St Peter's. He died tragically in Rome in the summer of 1632.

Valentin de Boulogne
Martyrdom of Saints Processus and Martinian
1629
oil on canvas
119 × 75½ in.
(302 × 192 cm)
Pinacoteca Vaticana,
Rome

Painted for the basilica of St. Peter's, it was placed on an altar as a pendant to Poussin's *Martyrdom of St. Erasmus*, executed during the same period. The late influence of Poussin's classicism can still be discerned alongside the newly acquired Caravaggesque style in this work by Valentin, despite the conflicts and quarrels between the two artists.

Hugo van der Goes

Ghent, c. 1440-Roode Clooster,
Brussels, 1482

Hugo van der Goes occupies a special
position on the artistic scene of the
time, as his career as a painter was
interwoven with an intensely religious
and tormented life. He was active in
Ghent from 1467 on, when he joined
the painters' guild. He received
numerous commissions from the city
and was also called upon for decorative
work, though the bulk of his output was
of a religious nature. Around the year
1475 his deep faith led him to enter the
Augustinian monastery at Roode
Clooster as a lay brother. Though he
was to remain there until his death, this
secluded life did not prevent him from
working. Indeed, his fame drew many
important people to the monastery,
and the painter was granted special
privileges enabling him to entertain
his illustrious guests. The monastery's
records give details of the artist's
increasingly severe emotional problems
and deep depression. While it is not
certain that his personal life had any
direct influence on his artistic concepts,
van der Goes did develop a tense and
anguished style. Through his individual
interpretation of tradition, he gradually
came to subvert the canons of the
sophisticated realism that was then
widespread. His mature works thus
show the predominance of a
discontinuous, artificial treatment of
space that emphasizes the dichotomy
between reality and the painted image.

Hugo van der Goes
Fall of Man
c. 1473-1475
oil on wood
12¾ × 8¾ in.
(32.3 × 21.9 cm)
Kunsthistorisches
Museum, Vienna

This small panel forms
part of a diptych together
with a *Lamentation*.
Van Eyck's influence is
still evident in the precise
handling of detail and
minute depiction of the
flowers and plants. The
scene depicts the moment
of disobedience to the
divine injunction not
to pick the fruit of the
Tree of Good and Evil.
Nothing disturbs the
calm of this almost
idyllic image.

Jan van der Heyden
The Martelaarsgraft in Amsterdam
c. 1670
oil on wood
17¼ × 22¾ in.
(44 × 57.5 cm)
Rijksmuseum, Amsterdam

Landcsape is one of the most popular genres in seventeenth-century Dutch art. Van der Heyden's interpretation of it is lucid, precise, and as objective as possible. Hence the painter was far-removed from the evocative "Romanticism" of van Ruisdael and from the generic views of the countryside or sea. On the contrary, he wants the viewpoint to be precisely recognizable and the place depicted to be compared with reality. To obtain this effect he pioneered the use of a scientific instrument called the camera obscura, which allowed him to observe the landscape through a lens that cast the image onto a flat surface.

Jan van der Heyden
Gorinchem, 1637-Amsterdam, 1712

A typical exponent of Dutch painting in the second half of the seventeenth century, van der Heyden trained with the still-life painter Job Berckheyde. Though he was not interested in the flowers and sumptuously laid tables painted by the master, van der Heyden acquired from this experience a taste for great pictorial precision and the accurate representation of objective reality. A great traveler, van der Heyden visited Cologne, Brussels, and London, but his favorite subject is without doubt Amsterdam, with its canals and imposing buildings, monuments and simple houses. Van der Heyden can be considered a forerunner of vedutism, both in his original approach to the image and in his use of technical and scientific instruments in order to reproduce his urban contexts with accuracy. In fact, his paintings are nearly always townscapes, depicted with a taste for documentation, so much so that he can be considered a very important precedent for van Wittel. During his last years, around 1700, the painter also painted still lifes and landscapes, but without ever equaling the limpidity of his views of Amsterdam.

Jan van der Heyden
The New Town Hall in Amsterdam
after 1652
oil on canvas
28¾ × 33¾ in.
(73 × 86 cm)
Musée du Louvre, Paris

Erected by Jacob van Campen to replace the earlier building that was destroyed by fire, the imposing Town Hall in Dam Square in the center of Amsterdam marks the swing toward classicism in architecture and more generally in Dutch taste in the second half of the seventeenth century. Van der Heyden depicted the building several times from different angles, and he was evidently fascinated by the precision of the forms, by the smooth surfaces, by the studied elegance of relations and proportions, but also by the play of light and shadow on the octagonal tower.

Rogier van der Weyden
Tournai, c. 1399-Brussels, 1464

This artist, whose real name is Rogier de la Pasture, was born in Tournai, the son of a master cutler. He received his early training, influenced by the elegant Franco-Flemish style, in this bustling city, then under the rule of France. His most significant experience as a youth was his apprenticeship in Robert Campin's flourishing workshop. Given Campin's numerous public commitments, it is likely that from the late 1420s on, Rogier obtained a large degree of independence within the workshop, as did other pupils, and produced some works on his own account. It was not until 1432, however, that he became an independent master, and in 1435 he moved to Brussels, where he was appointed official city painter. His first major commission was some panels for the Town Hall, a large-scale work that has unfortunately been lost. Evidence of the artist's increasing wealth is provided not only by his numerous commissions, but also by the fact that he did a great deal of charity work, thus benefitting his town. His style derives from the work of his two most illustrious contemporaries, Jan van Eyck and Robert Campin. Rogier admired the former's extraordinary technique and meticulous rendering of detail, and learned from the latter how to handle volume and space. The artist reworked these models by using a dynamic language and his realism acquired a human aspect that conveyed a vast range of emotions tempered by a calm dignity.

Rogier van der Weyden
Deposition
c. 1430-1435
oil on wood
86¾ × 103¼ in.
(220 × 262 cm)
Prado, Madrid

The sculptural life-size figures stand out against the shallow space of a gilded niche. The gestures and poses create a continuous rhythm and heighten the grief of the individual figures, culminating in the parallel placement of the deathly pale bodies of Christ and the Virgin.

393

Anthony van Dyck
Antwerp, 1599-London, 1641

A great specialist in Baroque portraiture, van Dyck is one of the most refined painters of the early seventeenth century. A real child prodigy, he began painting at a very early age as a pupil of the famous Antwerp artist Hendrick van Balen, but in 1615, when he was only sixteen, he opened his own independent workshop. The great Rubens soon noted the young man's talent and his already evident success with local collectors. As soon as he became a member of the painters' guild, van Dyck joined Rubens's studio not as a pupil, but as the master's assistant. Rubens and van Dyck worked together, side by side, on some works, then the older master began to realize that the young artist might become a dangerous rival and he encouraged him to specialize in portraiture. However, van Dyck also continued painting mythological subjects, altarpieces, and religious and literary works all his life. From 1620 on, his fame as a portraitist quickly spread throughout Europe. In 1621, after a brief journey to England, van Dyck moved to Italy and chose to settle in Genoa; he was to stay there until the end of 1626. During his long and prolific Italian period, van Dyck also visited Venice, Rome, and Palermo for study purposes, but his base remained Genoa, which had a flourishing colony of Flemish painters and maintained close links with Rubens's workshop. Van Dyck's direct observation of Titian's works was to be pivotal in his development, and he clearly drew inspiration from him. During the years he spent in Genoa, van Dyck painted the portraits of members of the Genoese aristocracy. Decrepit old men and tender children, young noblewomen and haughty noblemen, all sat before the easel of the master, who usually painted the face and hands from life, and completed the elaborate garments and details of the setting in his studio. Van Dyck worked at a dizzying pace and consequently earned a great deal of money. When he returned to Antwerp (he was still very young, only twenty-six) he set himself up as Rubens's rival and encroached on the master's terrain. He painted several monumental and very successful altarpieces that were evidently influenced by Titian, and, in 1628, he became court painter to Archduchess Isabella. In 1632, despite his successful career in his homeland, he decided to move to England, and he sold the Castle of Steen to Rubens; it was to be the great master's "garden of love" during the last years of his life. In London, van Dyck was soon chosen as court painter to Charles I. Surrounded by a large group of pupils, during the years spent in England, van Dyck painted hundreds of pictures, nearly all of them portraits. Except for two visits to the continent (Antwerp in 1634, Paris in the last year of his life), van Dyck permanently settled in England and was knighted.

Anthony van Dyck
Self-Portrait
1621-1622
oil on canvas
32 × 27¼ in.
(81 × 69.5 cm)
Alte Pinakothek,
Munich

Van Dyck, a strikingly good-looking young man with a brilliant, precocious talent, often painted his own portrait. They are all very fresh works, executed with rapid, almost casual brushstrokes, in which a smiling youth at the outset of his career looks on the world with confidence and a feeling of eager participation.

Opposite
Anthony van Dyck
The Lomellini Family
1625
oil on canvas
104¼ × 97¾ in.
(265 × 248 cm)
National Gallery of
Scotland, Edinburgh

A canvas of pivotal importance in the history of family portraiture, this large composition portrays the members of the noble Genoese family at a time of danger. The city runs the risk of being attacked and besieged and the inhabitants are preparing for war. Hence the head of the family, on the extreme left, is dressed from head to foot in armor, ready to play his role as defender of civic liberty. He is seen on the threshold of his home, since he has to leave his family to occupy himself with state affairs. His brother, armed with a sword, is turning toward the interior of the house; it is his duty to protect his sister-in-law and her children. The matronly, self-possessed mother represents stability. Seated in the center of the composition, she is the pivot of the painting and of the Lomellini family. The two children are close to their mother: while the daughter seems to realize her father is about to leave, and observes him with a worried expression on her face, her younger brother has only a vague idea of the danger and looks questioningly at his elder sister. The portrait thus becomes a masterly emotional and psychological work.

Anthony van Dyck
*James Stuart, Duke
of Richmond and Lennox*
after 1632
oil on canvas
85 × 50¼ in.
(215.9 × 127.6 cm)
Metropolitan Museum
of Art, New York

Van Dyck's numerous
English paintings are
among the most
important in the history
of aristocratic
portraiture. They also
laid the foundations for
the future development
of the English school of
painting. In order to
meet the overwhelming
demand, van Dyck
employed assistants, and
the works executed in
London are not always
entirely painted by him.
In contrast, this large
canvas, an extraordinary
masterpiece, is all his
own work. The slim
figure of the young
nobleman, dressed in an
extremely elegant suit
with delicate touches
of light blue, is
enhanced by the thin
greyhound.

Jan van Eyck

Maaseik, c. 1390-Bruges, 1441

The training of this great innovator in Flemish painting was firmly rooted in tradition, and his early works were in the field of illumination. His paintings also display a sophisticated technique and a passion for minute detail that are typical of illuminated manuscripts. He worked from 1422 to 1424 at the court of John of Bavaria in The Hague, and his entire career is connected with officialdom in Flanders. In 1425 he was appointed court painter to Philip the Good, duke of Burgundy, a position he held until the end of his life. The relations between the painter and the Burgundian court extended far beyond. He won the duke's confidence and also served him as confidant and diplomat. At Lille, and later at Bruges, he developed a personal style based on an extraordinarily detailed rendering of reality.

Jan van Eyck
Madonna with Chancellor Nicolas Rolin
c. 1435
panel, 26 × 24½
(66 × 62 cm)
Musée du Louvre, Paris

This work was commissioned by the powerful counselor to the Duke of Burgundy, Nicolas Rolin, kneeling in the presence of the Virgin. The spectator's eye is drawn, however, toward the open loggia and a landscape bathed in clear light. The Gothic buildings of the city can be discerned together with the limpid waters of a river that stretches toward the mountains, as though trying to encompass the variety of the world in a single image.

Jan and Hubert van Eyck
*Polyptych of the
Adoration of the Lamb,*
exterior panels
1425-1432
oil on wood
147¾ × 102½ in. each
(375 × 260 cm)
Cathedral of St. Bavon,
Ghent

This imposing
polyptych is regarded
as Jan van Eyck's
masterpiece. It was
commissioned for the
old church of St. John
by Jodocus Vijd and his
wife, and begun by Jan's
brother Hubert.
On his death in 1426, it
was completed by the
more famous Jan.
The altarpiece
constitutes an unrivaled

synthesis of a material
universe pervaded by
profound symbolic
meaning. The exterior
panels are bathed
in a hushed, subdued
atmosphere dominated
by the gray of the
monochromatic figures
and shades of ocher and
brown. The figures,
including the two
donors shown kneeling
in the outer panels,
express sincere devotion
and generate a
continuous rhythm that
rises from the lower
section to culminate in
the figures of the
prophets and sibyls
surmounting the
altarpiece.

Jan and Hubert van Eyck
*Polyptych of the
Adoration of the Lamb*
interior panels
1425-1432
oil on wood
central panel
147¾ × 102½ in.
(375 × 260 cm)
side panels
147¾ × 51½ in.
(375 × 130 cm)
Cathedral of St. Bavon,
Ghent

While the exterior panels
are very subdued, the
open polyptych emanates
great spiritual power.
In the lower section, the
central panel of which
shows the altar with the
Mystic Lamb, the scene
takes place in a vast
and luxuriant garden

traversed by processions
of figures depicted with
extraordinary realism.
This acutely observed
space apparently
extending to infinity
is juxtaposed to the
monumental figures
in the upper section,
dominated by the highly
stylized God the Father,
in a frontal position,
enthroned in the center.
The artist's exceptional
virtuoso work
culminates in the
striking figure of Adam,
who emerges from the
darkness of a niche, his
remorse evident in the
lines that furrow his
forehead and the
throbbing veins at his
temples and in his neck.

398

Vincent van Gogh

Groot Zundert, 1853-
Auvers-sur-Oise, 1890

The son of a Protestant pastor, he studied theology as a child and then, in 1869, went to work for the art dealers Goupil and Co., first in The Hague, then at the London branch, and finally in Paris until 1876, when he was fired. In 1878, after repeated but vain attempts to fit into the world of work, in which he was hampered by his inability to accept the rules of society, he decided to go to Belgium to do missionary work. The following year, however, he was dismissed by the religious authorities for his literal interpretation of Christian teaching. Yet it was here, among the miners of the Borinage region, that he discovered his vocation for painting. In the faces of those men, ravaged by the pain and toil of their lives spent in the harsh conditions of the coal mines, he recognized the living image of Christ's suffering and everything that he saw automatically became part of his artistic imagery. His early work, with its marked social content, is clearly derived from the Realism of the second half of the nineteenth century, and in particular Daumier's ability to accentuate expression to the point of distorting reality.

In February 1886 he was called back to Paris by his brother Theo. At that time debate was raging over the future course of Impressionism, but van Gogh became only partially involved. In 1888 he moved to Arles, in the South of France, where he was dazzled by the light of the Mediterranean and his style was enriched with new colors, transferred onto canvas in separate brushstrokes laden with paint. Gauguin came to stay with him in Arles, but the friendship between the two painters lasted only a few dramatic months. Tormented by recurrent bouts of anxiety and fits of self-destructive violence van Gogh left Arles the following year and admitted himself for treatment at the mental hospital in Saint-Rémy. His work grew feverish and passionate: into every subject, and not just his numerous self-portraits, he poured all the drama of his complex existential crisis. In May 1890 he left Saint-Rémy for Auvers-sur-Oise, where he was a guest of Doctor Gachet. Here, after a short period in which he seemed to be recovering, he started to suffer from increasingly frequent attacks of madness.

These found expression in a visionary style of painting of unprecedented violence. In July of the same year in a field of ripe wheat flooded with sunlight, the artist shot himself.

Vincent van Gogh
The Bridge at Langlois
1888
oil on canvas
19½ × 25¼ in.
(49.5 × 64 cm)
Wallraf-Richartz
Museum, Cologne

This is one of several
pictures van Gogh
painted of a drawbridge,
in a technique that is
already remote from
the earlier Parisian
paintings: the very clear-
cut divisions of the
space and the stylized
brushstrokes are
reminiscent of Japanese
prints.

Vincent van Gogh
The Artist's Room in Arles
1888
oil on canvas
28¼ × 35½ in.
(72 × 90 cm)
Rijksmuseum Vincent
van Gogh, Amsterdam

Based on three pairs of
complementary colors,
red-green, yellow-violet,
and blue-orange, this
was a painting very
dear to the artist, who
thought that it
represented the highest
expression of his
pictorial language.
He wrote: "It seems to
me that the technique
is simpler and more
energetic. No more
dotting, no more
hatching, nothing, just
uniform colors in
harmony."

Vincent van Gogh
The Night Café
1888
oil on canvas
27½ ×35 in.
(70 × 89 cm)
Yale University Art
Gallery, New Haven

A haunt of vagabonds
and failed artists looking
for solace, the interior
of this café is dominated
by the looming presence
of a billiard table.
Behind it the owner
of the café dressed in
white, constitutes a sort
of visual pause in the
midst of the vivid and
exaggerated tones of the
rest of the picture.

Above
Vincent van Gogh
Portrait of Joseph Roulin
1888
oil on canvas
32 × 25¾ in.
(81.2 × 65.3 cm)
Museum of Fine Arts,
Boston

This is the first and
largest of six portraits
of Roulin the postman,
painted in Arles between
July 1888 and April
1889. The man, with
his high forehead, small
gray eyes, and thick
beard, embodies the
Provençal type: a person
with a dignified
appearance, wise, and
with a good heart.

Above
Vincent van Gogh
La Berceuse
1888-1889
oil on canvas, 36½ × 28¾
in. (92.7 × 72.8 cm)
Museum of Fine Arts,
Boston

There are five versions of
the portrait of Madame
Roulin, all with the same
pattern of wallpaper
in the background.

Vincent van Gogh
*Haystacks near a
Farmbouse*
1888
oil on canvas
28¾ × 36½ in.
(73 × 92.5 cm)
Rijksmuseum Kröller-
Müller, Otterlo

The series of wheat fields
and other farm scenes was
painted during van Gogh's
stay at Arles, where he had
moved from Paris.

Gerard van Honthorst
Utrecht, 1590–1656

Van Honthorst and Terbrugghen synthesize the development of Dutch painting that followed Italian models. Van Honthorst lived longer than his colleague, hence he witnessed the decline of Caravaggism and the subsequent revival of classicizing themes in the Netherlands. After his early training with the Mannerist master Abraham Bloemaert, in Utrecht, van Honthorst moved to Rome in 1610 and remained in Italy for ten years. During this period of intense study and work, he mastered the Caravaggesque style, to which he added echoes of Guido Reni's classicism. Van Honthorst specialized in the execution of evocative night scenes, with tones that were sometimes delicately poetic and sometimes dramatic, which earned him the nickname in Italy of "Gerardo delle notti," by which he is still known today. On his return to Utrecht he alternated vast canvases on religious subjects with genre scenes, always influenced by the great Italian masters. After the death of Terbrugghen in 1629, and as a result of Rembrandt's increasing popularity, the Utrecht school began to lose favor with the Dutch patrons. Van Honthorst, however, continued to enjoy great personal success and ended his career as court painter to stadtholder Frederick Henry of Orange, in The Hague.

Gerard van Honthorst
Adoration of the Shepherds
1622
oil on canvas
64½ × 74¾ in.
(164 × 190 cm)
Wallraf-Richartz Museum, Cologne

Like his colleague Terbrugghen, he sought to convey a sense of delicate poetry in his works, through scenes of touching, pleasant lyricism. The Nativity is one of the painter's favorite themes.

Following page
Gerard van Honthorst
Christ Before the High Priest
c. 1618
oil on canvas
107 × 72 in.
(272 × 183 cm)
National Gallery, London

A specialist in night scenes, van Honthorst frequently uses the emotional device of a candle as the source of light, illuminating the composition from within. In the seventeenth century this idea became very popular with collectors, and many painters often copied it; consequently this poetic solution became a mere expression of bravura. This is not the case with van Honthorst, who uses the wavering, unsteady light as an unusual and effective way of sensitively rendering psychological insights.

Jan van Scorel

Schoorl, Alkmaar, 1495-Utrecht, 1562

Scorel's name comes from the Dutch town where he was born. He served his apprenticeship in the nearby town of Alkmaar, a small center for the arts with a reputation for highly realistic painting. Van Scorel completed his training with visits to Amsterdam and Utrecht (1517-1519), where he studied the painting of Mabuse. Before finally settling in Haarlem, he set off on a long journey through Europe.

He traveled for four years, getting as far as Palestine. He also visited Nuremberg (where he met Dürer), Venice, and, most important, Rome. In the Eternal City, where his visit coincided with the pontificate of his countryman Hadrian VI of Utrecht, van Scorel was strongly influenced by the motifs of Raphael and Michelangelo, and was appointed keeper of Vatican antiquities. When he returned to Holland, van Scorel harvested the fruit of his many cultural experiences, introducing

a new kind of painting that owed almost nothing to the Flemish tradition, being clearly influenced by the "new" Mannerism. In this regard, it is also interesting to note how Venetian influences (Giorgione and Titian) began to replace the fantastic scenes painted by Patinir and Bosch. Among pupils of note trained by van Scorel in Haarlem are Maarten van Heemskerck, whose precocious talent irritated his teacher.

Jan van Scorel
Magdalene
c. 1528
oil on wood
26½ × 30 in.
(67 × 76.5 cm)
Rijksmuseum,
Amsterdam

Gaspar van Wittel
Amersfoort, 1653-Rome, 1736

Founder of the veduta genre, which was to be enormously successful in the eighteenth century, van Wittel moved to Italy in 1675 at the very young age of twenty-two, and virtually divided his whole career between Rome and Naples. However, he assimilated the typically northern taste for objective, precise, clear landscapes, as opposed to the "ideal landscapes" of the Bolognese and French artists active in Rome. His concern for natural and architectural truth can be seen to derive from the success of van der Heyden's views of Amsterdam, but van Wittel developed and extended this in a direction that his predecessors could never have foreseen. Fascinated by the Mediterranean sunshine, drawn by the ancient monuments, enraptured by the relation between nature and architecture in central and southern Italy, van Wittel exploited his great scenographic skill to create images that are truly monumental in range and scope. Gaspar van Wittel's technique is based, first and foremost,

on extremely accurate drawings from life, and then on a blend of faithful realism and narrative elements, through the introduction of figures, animals, and means of transport. Working at the turn of the century, van Wittel assimilated the tastes of the new traveling public who wanted to buy impressive souvenirs of their Grand Tour in Italy. Thus he painted outstanding views of the great cities of art (Florence, Venice, and, above all, Rome, an inexhaustible source of monumental and picturesque vistas), destined to be the model for the eighteenth-century *vedutisti*, beginning with Canaletto, who did his training in Rome. The son of van Wittel, whose name was Italianized to Vanvitelli, was to become one of the greatest architects of the eighteenth century. Van Wittel was active particularly in Naples and Campania, and designed the impressive Royal Palace at Caserta.

Gaspar van Wittel
View of Florence from Via Bolognese
c. 1695
oil on canvas
18 × 29½ in.
(46 × 75 cm)
Duke of Devonshire collection, Chatsworth

Van Wittel succeeded in unforgettably capturing the major sights of the Grand Tour, the cultural journey that was to become indispensable for every young European aristocrat at the turn of the eighteenth century. In Italy, one of the musts was a "room with a view" in Florence. The blend of nature and monuments, geographical context, and city created by van Wittel contributed toward spreading a knowledge of Italian cities of art.

Diego Velázquez
Seville, 1599-Madrid, 1660

Encouraged to paint since his childhood, Velázquez entered the workshop of Herrera the Elder at the age of ten. One year later, as proof of his precocious talent, he was apprenticed to Francisco Pacheco, a very influential figure in the cultural circles of Seville, known as a painter, art theoretician, and man of letters. Velázquez owed Pacheco not only his artistic training but also his taste for classical culture, and even his wife. In 1618, already regarded as an independent painter, although he was only nineteen years of age, he married

Juana Pacheco, the daughter of his mentor. His first works are mainly *bodegónes*, that is, genre scenes of everyday life with still-life studies (for example, *Old Woman Frying Eggs* or *The Water Seller of Seville*), or religious subjects interpreted in a "naturalistic," contemporary manner. Caravaggio was a decisive influence, and his compositional layout of scenes and powerful interplay of light and shade were elements taken over directly by Velázquez. This immediate and intelligent reference to Caravaggio indicates the painter's precise orientation toward Italian art. The main turning point in his career came

in 1623, when the conde-duque de Olivares, the powerful prime minister at the court of Philip IV, summoned his fellow Sevillian to Madrid to become the king's official painter. He worked mainly as a portraitist and was thus obliged to take into consideration Titian's sixteenth-century portraits. His initial Caravaggesque naturalism was thus enriched by a new monumental dimension that enabled him to tackle vast scenes of a historical or literary nature with great confidence and perfect chromatic intuition. He made his inevitable first visit to Italy between 1629 and 1631, and his contact with the great examples of Renaissance art made

his painting technique still more varied and flexible. On his return to Madrid, where he was now firmly established as official painter to the Spanish court, he began to produce a large number of works for the royal residences, and a whole series of individual and group portraits of court figures, including not only the king and the princes, but also the dwarfs and jesters. A painting like *Las Meniñas* is sufficient in itself to epitomize an entire century and define the master's style. The work, carried out above all for Philip IV and his family, explains why so many of Velázquez's paintings have remained in Madrid and are now housed in the

Prado. His second visit to Italy was made between 1649 and 1651. The most famous result of this, the portrait of Pope Innocent X, has remained in its original location, the Galleria Doria Pamphili in Rome. During these years, he carried out a kind of wonderful and intense rereading of his own output and, going further back, of the links between the painting of the sixteenth and seventeenth centuries. Following the example of Titian, and exactly as Rembrandt was doing in the same period, Velázquez started to paint with large, separate brushstrokes, thickly laden with material and charged with expressive intensity. With his absolute freedom of style, he is rightly indicated as an artist of pivotal importance in the history of art. Rediscovered by the French painters of the nineteenth century, and in particular by Manet, he also constitutes a precise point of reference for Picasso and the movements of modern art.

Previous page
Diego Velázquez
Surrender of Breda
1633-1635
oil on canvas
120¾ × 144½ in.
(307 × 367 cm)
Prado, Madrid

This absolute masterpiece of historical painting commemorates an episode in the war between Spain and Holland in 1625. The defeated Justin of Nassau symbolically consigns the key of the fortress of Breda to the victor, Ambrogio Spinola. Against the background of a desolate landscape marked by the smoke of fires, the two generals meet in an atmosphere of calm and mutual respect. They have both dismounted and there is no sense of rhetoric. Velázquez accentuates the human element in this episode. Memorable gestures are thus absent in the ranks of soldiers and there is nothing to distinguish the victor from the vanquished. For soldiers, war is a dirty, fatiguing business with little room for heroics. The scene is given a very theatrical setting with the soldiers on the left and the large horse dominating the right-hand side. The two groups are symmetrically juxtaposed to leave the center of action free for the meeting of the two generals, who are moved slightly out of the foreground. At this point, with splendid pictorial inventiveness, Velázquez inserts the mobile "screen" of lances raised high in silhouette to separate the proscenium from the backdrop, where the landscape fades away into the distance bathed in a pale light.

Diego Velázquez
The Rokeby Venus
1650
oil on canvas, 48¼ × 69¾ in. (122.5 × 177 cm)
National Gallery, London

Throughout his life, Velázquez cultivated his own great independent talent, though he constantly admired the Italian art of the sixteenth and seventeenth centuries. Like the other great masters of his time he studied the great paintings of the High Renaissance and the innovations of Caravaggio. In this splendid female nude, he pays extraordinary homage to Titian.

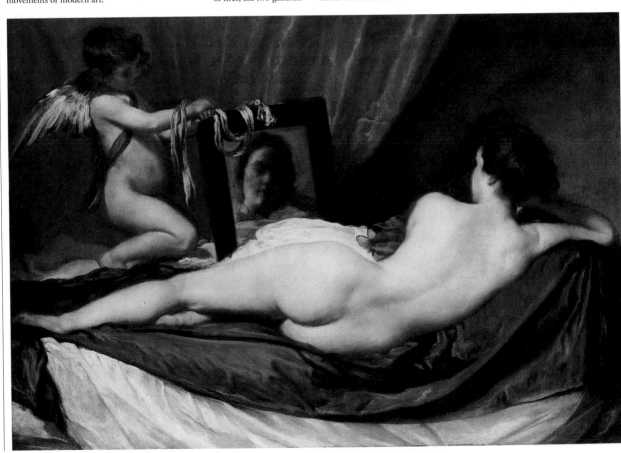

Jan Vermeer

Delft, 1632-1675

Vermeer's works disappeared for a long time and were completely lost in the prodigious output of Dutch painting. His name only re-emerged in the nineteenth century, and he gradually became established as one of the most precious and best-loved painters of all time. Vermeer's fame rests on a few small, or very small, works, but in a century and a school of painting that produced so many charming pictures of daily life Vermeer captures the magic, the deep and intimately human aspect of everyday tasks. A painter of the soul, of peace, and of light, Vermeer was the son of an innkeeper. His father was a member of the painters' guild, an essential requirement if one was to practice the profession of art dealer. From his childhood on, Vermeer saw countless paintings pass through his father's shop. They may not all have been top quality, but they certainly provided an effective range of styles, fashions, and trends. On his father's death in 1632, Vermeer inherited his business and became an innkeeper and art dealer. He had a preference for Italian painting or at least works that were influenced by Caravaggio. He also began to paint, in the artistic climate influenced by Carel Fabritus. Vermeer's early works, which already displayed extremely fine brushwork, were religious (in mainly Calvinist Holland, he was probably Catholic, or became a convert after his marriage) and mythological scenes. His contact with various artists of the period, including Gerard Ter Borch, led him, from 1656 on, to abandon the elevated subjects of his early works and tackle more ordinary themes, to which he brought a new creative vein. He painted consummate masterpieces, the result of a painstaking and highly refined technique, in which the echoes of fifteenth-century Flemish painting, especially in the use of light and the importance given to the minutest detail, blend with an awareness of the tendencies in the art of his day. Vermeer led a brief and uneventful life (he died when he was only forty-three), though he had no less than thirteen children. He was dean of the Delft painters' guild, made brief trips into the environs of the city and, in the end, had contracted so many debts that his widow had to sell his paintings to pay back the baker. He had no public commissions, and only sporadic and indirect links with other

countries. Very few of his works can be dated with certainty, and their chronological order is very difficult to determine. His was a simple, modest life, but he established important friendships, particularly with Anthony van Leeuwenhoek, the great Delft scientist who invented the microscope. This may be an interesting key to understanding the miracle of Vermeer's painting, which lies in the revelation of the secret life hidden in little things that light unveils to those who have eyes, a heart, and patience.

Jan Vermeer
Allegory of Painting
c. 1675
oil on canvas
47¼ × 39¼ in.
(120 × 100 cm)
Kunsthistorisches Museum, Vienna

Painted toward the end of Vermeer's brief career, this magnificent painting almost has the significance of a spiritual testament. This is a self-portrait of the painter, seen from behind, sitting at his easel, but, at the same time, he takes the viewer's standpoint and has folded back the heavy curtain on the left to be able to see the interior of the studio. In the sharp clarity of the bright room, a young woman is posing in classical attire like an ancient Muse. All is peace, beauty, contemplation that becomes action. A large map of Holland decorates the back wall.

Opposite
Jan Vermeer
The Milkmaid
c. 1658
oil on canvas
17¾ × 16¼ in.
(45.4 × 41 cm)
Rijksmuseum,
Amsterdam

Held by the great
museum in Amsterdam,
the fundamental "temple"
of the Dutch painting
of the "golden age," *The
Milkmaid* and *The Letter*
almost form a diptych,
since they have in
common a similar
composition, the
customary light entering
from the left, the vigorous
beauty of a lower-class
girl and a young lady.
The Milkmaid gives an
extraordinary rendering
of many different
surfaces, ranging from
the basket of bread to the
mousetrap on the floor,
the hanging woven basket
and the polished metal.
Despite the exceptional
beauty of the still life, the
picture concentrates on
the girl's robust beauty.

Jan Vermeer
The Letter
c. 1663
oil on canvas, 18¼ × 15¼
in. (46.5 × 39 cm)
Rijksmuseum,
Amsterdam

Silence, concentration,
and an almost
metaphysical purity
of the image create a
rarefied atmosphere,
heightened by the fact
that every element is
perfectly set in an ideal
pattern of volumes, voids,
and colors. It is yet again
a masterpiece of evocative
poetry, in which even
someone's absence is felt;
we sense the distance
between the person who
wrote the letter and the
girl who is now reading
it. The empty chair and
the map allude to
someone who is not there,
whose presence is evoked
by the piece of paper.

411

Paolo Veronese
Paolo Caliari
Verona, 1528-Venice, 1588

After completing his apprenticeship in the workshop of the painter Antonio Badile, in 1551 Veronese painted the *Giustiniani Altarpiece* for the church of San Francesco della Vigna, thus making his entrance on the scene of Venetian painting, of which he was soon to become a much-admired exponent. Veronese had an exceptional capacity to give a living, realistic atmosphere to even the most complicated allegories. Through the palpable charm of his figures, the subjects acquire great expressive power. His success was marked by a constant increase in commissions in a wide range of fields: altarpieces, works for private collectors, large official allegories, and frescoes in villas, like the unforgettable cycle decorating the walls of the Palladian Villa Barbaro in Maser. His profane compositions, rich in captivating, often seductively sensual figures dressed in sumptuous garments, were very successful on the art market, and he produced many copies of certain subjects, like the *Finding of Moses*, or variations on the theme of the loves of Venus. One of his favorite subjects was the so-called "Suppers," enormous canvases in which biblical episodes (like the *Last Supper* or the *Marriage at Cana*) turn into spectacular society feasts in sixteenth-century dress. A vein of subtle, aristocratic melancholy runs through Veronese's late paintings, creating an intense interpretation of the mysteries of Christianity in his late religious works. After his death in 1588, he was buried in his favorite church of San Sebastiano.

Paolo Veronese
Christ in the House of Levi
1573, oil on canvas
218½ × 515¾ in.
(555 × 1310 cm)
Gallerie dell'Accademia,
Venice

This canvas was originally a *Last Supper*, destined for the refectory in the Monastery of San Zanipolo. Veronese set his scenes within regular frames of Palladian-style architecture. In his *Last Supper*, in addition to Christ and the Apostles, the room is crowded with figures completely unconcerned about the biblical episode.

Alvise Vivarini
Venice, 1442/53-1503/05

Antonio's son and for many years assistant to his uncle Bartolomeo, Alvise understood the need to update the family tradition by taking into account the new ideas introduced by Giovanni Bellini and Antonello da Messina. This is amply demonstrated in the *Sacra Conversazione* in the Accademia in Venice (1480). The graphic clarity and steady light of the Vivarini studio is combined with a monumental and perspective vision that gives a unified concept of space. The success of Alvise's artistic repositioning is proved by the numerous Virgins in the Bellini mold that he turned out as well as the number of altarpieces that still remain in Venice (although two of particular interest are now in the Staatliche Museen Preussischer Kulturbesitz in Berlin). There are also a lot of interesting virile portraits which reveal his great admiration for Antonello. Toward the end of his career Alvise produced a work of great commitment, the *St. Ambrose Altarpiece* for the church of the Frari.

Alvise Vivarini
Sacra Conversazione
1480
wood panel
69 × 77 in.
(175 × 196 cm)
Gallerie dell'Accademia, Venice

Maurice de Vlaminck

Paris, 1876-Rueil la Gadelière, 1958

Of Flemish origin, Vlaminck took up painting as a result of the strong impression made on him by van Gogh's pictures, seen at an exhibition in Paris in 1901. A friend of Derain and Matisse, he was the most radical exponent of the Fauvist movement. He painted landscapes, still lifes, and portraits in a systematically aggressive manner, making arbitrary use of pure colors squeezed directly from the tube onto the canvas. On the breakup of the Fauves in 1907, Vlaminck was inspired to return to the painting of Cézanne by Picasso, with whom he worked in the famous Bateau-Lavoir studio in Montmartre. From the twenties onward his landscapes and still lifes lost the emotional charge of earlier years and showed a more calculated and geometric approach to composition.

Maurice de Vlaminck
The Gardens at Chatou
1904
oil on canvas
32 × 39¾ in.
(81 × 101 cm)
Art Institute, Chicago

Strong colors, combined to form violent contrasts, characterize this picture. Its title is a reminder of his collaboration with Derain, in the so-called school of Chatou, named after Derain's birthplace where the artists used to go to paint.

Maurice de Vlaminck
The Olive Trees
1905
oil on canvas
21 × 25½ in.
(53.5 × 65 cm)
Thyssen-Bornemisza Collection, Madrid

In a manner that is clearly influenced by van Gogh, Vlaminck transfers the violence of his own feelings onto the canvas, using arbitrary colors squeezed directly from the tube.

Simon Vouet
Paris, 1590-1649

Having made his name as a portraitist
when he was very young—it is said that
he followed a French lady to London
to paint her portrait when he was only
fifteen—Vouet moved to Italy in 1613.
He went first to Venice where he became
acquainted with the painting of Titian,
Veronese, and Tintoretto, and was
impressed, above all, by the great
compositions in the Doges' Palace, then
to Rome where he frequented the circle
of the Dutch Caravaggists. He received
major commissions in several Roman
churches from Pope Urban VIII. In
1624, he painted the canvases of *The
Temptation of St. Francis* and *The
Investiture of the Saint* for the church
of San Lorenzo in Lucina, examples of
a compositional style rich in theatrical
effects, in which Caravaggesque
influences blend with the Baroque.
That same year Vouet was elected
president of the Accademia di San Luca
and, in 1627, now a famous artist, he
returned to France where Louis XIII
appointed him "first painter to the king"
and gave him an apartment in the
Louvre and an annual stipend. Having
set up a studio frequented by the
greatest artists of the day, Vouet devoted
himself to the decoration of Parisian
churches and palaces, in which Baroque
eloquence was tempered by Poussin-
style classicism.

Simon Vouet
Crucifixion
1622
oil on canvas
147¾ × 88½ in.
(375 × 225 cm)
Church of Jesus, Genoa

This painting, executed in
Rome, was sent to Genoa
in 1622, where Vouet had
spent a year in the service
of Paolo Orsini and the
Doria family. His stay in
Genoa, and above all his
contact with Orazio
Gentileschi, who was
also in the city in 1621,
encouraged Vouet
gradually to abandon the
Caravaggism of his early
manner for a Baroque
style that is light,
vigorous, and
chromatically
extraordinarily refined.

Edouard Vuillard

Cuiseaux, 1868-La Baule, 1940

After initial academic training, his style developed rapidly under the influence of a series of important encounters. He became one of the principal figures in the debate over the course to be taken by art after Impressionism. Through Emile Bernard and Paul Sérusier he came into contact with the Nabis, forming a lasting friendship with Bonnard. Together they argued that the successor to Impressionism should not be Symbolism but a refined and highly sensitive style known as Intimism. The use of areas of flat color gradually gave way to a revival of the traditional values of perspective. His favorite subjects were tranquil scenes of family life, often set in rooms lit by electric light. Like his friend Bonnard, he also tried his hand at large-scale works and decorative panels in which it is possible to clearly follow the development of his style, from the time of his membership of the Nabis, influenced by Japanese prints, to his later manner in which forms and colors were represented in serene compositions.

Edouard Vuillard
Café in the Bois de Boulogne
c. 1898
oil on cardboard
19 × 20 in.
(48 × 51 cm)
Musée des Beaux-Arts et d'Archeologie, Besançon

EDOUARD VUILLARD

Andy Warhol

Pittsburgh, 1928-New York, 1987

Together with Roy Lichtenstein, Andy Warhol is without doubt the most original artist within the sphere of the new approach to mass media. Turning his attention to the degradation of meaning and the consumption of the images made for mass consumption, he brought a new set of values to art. In 1949, after earning a diploma in Pittsburgh, he moved to New York and began a successful career as a commercial illustrator for magazines like *The New Yorker* and *Harper's Bazaar*. In 1952 he had his first one-man show, at the Hugo Gallery in New York, with fifteen drawings inspired by stories by Truman Capote. Warhol was among the first artists to make systematic use of industrial and typographical inks. In fact he abandoned painting in oil in 1962 and adopted instead the technique of silkscreening, the application of photographic images to silk, which offered him a range of unnaturally bright colors with potent visual impact. Works dating to these years include his first series images, silkscreen images on canvas of photographs of stars like Elvis Presley or Marilyn Monroe and, later, such symbolic figures as John and Jackie Kennedy or celebrated art masterpieces, such as the *Mona Lisa*, and even car crashes or other grim images from the news. These are reproduced like motifs in series, in some cases row upon row. In giving visibility to any mass-consumption image, no matter how banal, including nationally advertised popular brands and the most photographed people in the world, Warhol uses—or mimicks—the linguistic and communication modalities of mass culture. To do so he follows two procedures: the first is the isolation and dilation of the image, such as the portraits of Hollywood stars; the second is the serial repetition of the subject, such as the rows of bottles of Coca-Cola or cans of Campbell's Soup.

Andy Warhol
210 Coca-Cola Bottles
1962
silkscreen, acrylic, and pencil on canvas
82½ × 105
(209.5 × 266.5 cm)
Thomas Ammann
Fine Arts, Zurich

A mass-advertised product, Coca-Cola is part of the popular imagination. Warhol appropriates this icon-object of American civilization and turns it into a work of art for the use and consumption of the public at large.

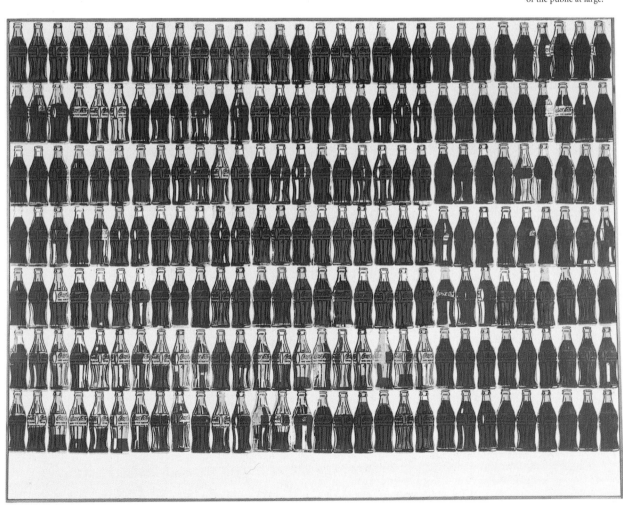

Andy Warhol
*Big Torn Campbell's
Soup Can*
1962
acrylic on canvas
72 × 54 in.
(183 × 137 cm)
Kunsthaus, Zurich

Warhol takes a typical
example of mass
consumption, a
Campbell's Soup can,
and uses it as a
representative of
American society,
dominated by a mass
culture that sucks in
everything with
sovereign indifference.
To make an object more
visible Warhol either
repeats it in series or, as
in this case, isolates and
dilates it.

Jean Antoine Watteau
Valenciennes, 1684-Paris, 1721

The greatest French artist of the early eighteenth century, he chose the intimacy of genre scenes, the witty improvisation of the Commedia dell'Arte, and the frivolous or pathetic idyll of *fêtes galantes*, in open contrast with the rhetorical and pompously classical style of the Academy. In the *Querelle des anciens et des modernes*, which raged at the beginning of the century in France, he immediately showed himself to be anti-Academy. He frequented the workshop of Pierre and Jean Mariette, collectors and printers, representatives of a trend that opposed the official taste of the court and the Academy, preferring the most free and open currents of French and Flemish-Dutch painting. In opposition to the classical style of Poussin he favored the wide, free rein of the imagination, whose fullest expression was in the theater—not in classical theater, but in the contemporary genres of comédies-ballets and *Comédie Italienne*, performances of which resumed after the death of Louis XIV in 1715. This type of theater, populated by comedians, clowns, and masks, constituted the main theme of his work. A fundamental experience in his development was his stay with Claude Audran, the keeper of the Luxembourg Palace, the home of the great Rubens cycle of the *Life of Marie de' Medici*. This contact with the work of the Flemish master was to prove decisive from a thematic and formal standpoint. His style became more free and immediate, his painting ductile and rapid, the tones delicate and bright, and the figures fluid and light. While it is impossible to order his works chronologically, it is possible—from a thematic point of view—to identify two main lines: theater scenes and *fêtes galantes*, imaginary gatherings of ladies and gentlemen evoked in a sweetly nostalgic atmosphere and in a swift, ductile manner that combines the warm colors of Rubens with the iridescent tones of the Venetian school. It was precisely as a painter of *fêtes galantes* that he was received into the Academy. Almost the whole of Watteau's output was executed in the last six years of his life, between 1717, the date of *Embarkation for Cythera*, and 1721, the date of *Gersaint's Shop Sign*, a eulogy of modern painting and of its most illustrious predecessors (from Rubens to van Dyck), considered to be his artistic testament.

Jean Antoine Watteau
Réunion Champêtre
1717-1718
oil on canvas
23½ × 29½ in.
(60 × 75 cm)
Gemäldegalerie, Dresden

In a natural setting, Watteau arranges single groups like frames in a collage. Unlike in classical composition, there are no main characters and no hierarchy of figures. The imaginative, rhythmic composition and the magical atmosphere make Watteau resemble a brilliant theater director.

Benjamin West
Pennsylvania, 1738-London, 1820

An American who came at an early age to Europe, West established a new kind of history painting featuring contemporary subjects. After his stay in Italy, from 1760 to 1763, during which he came into contact with Winckelmann's circle, he settled in London, where he first set up as a portrait painter. He subsequently devoted himself to subjects of ancient history, winning the favor of the court and of George III, who commissioned a series of religious paintings, never completed, on themes from the Old and New Testaments, conveniently modified to suit Protestant requirements. He then began to evolve a new form of modern history painting, with figures in contemporary dress treated in classical and Baroque style. *The Death of General Wolfe* and *Penn's Treaty with the Indians* are typical examples of this new genre, in which the real and the ideal are combined in a rather confused way, after the classical manner, in particular that of Poussin. On the death of Reynolds in 1792, he was nominated the second president of the Royal Academy (founded in 1768). His later works are more individual in style, and are also interesting due to the clear influence of the romantic theories of Edmund Burke and his meditation on the concept of the "sublime."

Benjamin West
Portrait of Colonel Guy Johnson
c. 1775
oil on canvas, 80 × 54¼ in.
(203 × 138 cm)
National Gallery of Art,
Washington, D.C.

West's preference for neoclassical canons is evident in his portrait of the British Colonel Guy Johnson, the officer in charge of problems regarding the American Indians. In the shade behind him is an Indian chief, his helper during the war missions. The focal point of the composition, the figure of the Indian, acts as a link between the colonel and the scene in the background, an Indian camp at the foot of a waterfall, visible on the left.

James McNeill Whistler

Lowell, Massachusetts, 1834-
London, 1903

Despite dandyism, involvement in
literary debates, an international
identity, and a vague and unresolved
"Oedipus complex" with Europe,
James Abbott McNeill Whistler
remains an emblematic figure of
American art and society at the end of
the nineteenth century. He is a painter
of extraordinary technical talents and
of definite importance, but more for
European painting (in particular
English) than for the North American
school, from which he always
maintained his distance. After early
training at home, and with the
unusual sideline of time spent
learning engraving as a navy
cartographer, Whistler moved to Paris
in 1855, immediately coming in
contact with such realist painters
as Gustave Courbet and Henri Fantin-
Latour. In 1859 he went to London,
where he spent much of his life
importing and promoting an English
version of Impressionism. So complete
was Whistler's insertion in the artistic
scene of London that in 1886 he was
made president of the Society of
British Artists. Thanks to him the
period of the Pre-Raphaelites came to
an end, replaced by his more seductive
and rarefied images of Victorian high
society. It was a world of refined
conventions and formalities beneath
which far different emotions were held
in check, but only barely. Whistler
was aware of the subtle line that runs
between an accurate portrait and an
overly highbrow image. He made the
gradual movement to sophisticated
symbolism, the fruit of his careful
"aesthetic" selection of subjects.

James McNeill Whistler
Symphony in White No. 1
1862
oil on canvas, 84½ × 42½
in. (215 × 108 cm)
National Gallery of Art,
Washington, D.C.

"As music is the poetry
of sound, so is painting
the poetry of sight."
Whistler liked to give his
works titles from the
world of music, adding
an indication of the
dominant color tone.
For this painting, he used
his lover Joanna
Hiffernan as model.

James McNeill Whistler
Nocturne in Blue and Gold: The Old Bridge at Battersea
1872-1875
oil on canvas
26¾ × 19¾
(68 × 50 cm)
Tate Gallery, London

A splendid landscapist, Whistler made sage use of many elements from nineteenth-century European painting. As in his portraits, in his landscapes he prefers titles that declare the primary tonalities of the work. His London views are clearly related to Turner, from whom Whistler adopted the hazy effect, the mistiness that wraps around all the shapes in the painting. At the end of the nineteenth century panoramas of the Thames rivaled those of the Seine: Monet, for example, painted many views of the Houses of Parliament and Westminster. With his refined, almost decadent technique, Whistler can be taken as a bridge between the late romantic period and the "mental" landscapes of the avant-gardes.

Konrad Witz

Rottweil am Neckar, c. 1400-
Geneva or Basel, c. 1445/46

Konrad Witz was one of the great
innovators in painting north of the
Alps, and moved sharply away from
the languid overtones and lyricism
of the previous generation of German
painters. Born in a small town in
Swabia he became a member of the
Basel guild of painters in 1434 and
was granted citizenship the following
year. In the cosmopolitan atmosphere
of the city, where a council was being
held to resolve the religious schism,
Witz established himself as an original
personality with a vigorous talent and
a down-to-earth vision of life. Despite
the influence of works by
contemporary Flemish masters,
the powerful physicality of his figures
reveals a knowledge of Burgundian
sculpture and Claus Sluter in
particular. His two most important
works are the *Heilspiegel Altarpiece*,
produced for the choir of the Abbey
of St. Leonard in Basel, and the *St.
Peter Altarpiece*, produced for Geneva
Cathedral. The first is a monumental
work inspired by the devotional book
Speculum Humanae Salvationis, where
scenes drawn from the Old Testament
prefigure events in the New. The
altarpiece was dismembered during
the spate of iconoclasm in 1529 and
is incomplete today.

Konrad Witz
*Augustus and the
Tiburtine Sibyl,* panel
from the *Heilspiegel
Altarpiece*
c. 1435
panel
40 × 32 in.
(101.5 × 81.5 cm)
Musée des Beaux-Arts,
Dijon

The two gesticulating
figures are captured in
poses that are slightly
awkward and comical
but highly expressive.

Konrad Witz
Sabobai and Benaiah
panel from the
Heilspiegel Altarpiece
c. 1435
panel, 40 × 32 in.
(101.5 × 81.5 cm)
Kunstmuseum, Basel

The two knights
carrying water to King
David of Israel from the
well at Bethlehem are
portrayed in an abstract
space against a
background of gold
brocade. The sculptural
quality of the figures is
emphasized by the light
and by Witz's deft
handling of reflections
and shadows on the
gleaming armor. He
dwells on details such
as the crystal pommel of
the sword and the visor
to create an image that
is simple yet impressive.

Konrad Witz
Esther before Ahasuerus
panel from the
Heilspiegel Altarpiece
c. 1435, panel
33½ × 31¼ in.
(85 × 79.5 cm)
Kunstmuseum, Basel

The significance of this
scene is expressed not so
much through the faces
and poses of the figures
as through the
extraordinary rhythm of
the rumpled folds of their
garments. The authority
of King Ahasuerus, who
has chosen a young
woman of lowly birth as
his bride, is symbolized
by the spread of his royal
mantle over the ground
in contrast to the timid
folds of the woman's
simple dress.

Konrad Witz
Presentation of Cardinal de Mies to the Virgin
panel from the *St. Peter Altarpiece*
1443-1444
panel, 52 × 60¾ in.
(132 × 154 cm)
Musée d'Art et
d'Histoire, Geneva

Cardinal François de Mies, who commissioned the *St. Peter Altarpiece*, is depicted as being presented to the Virgin. The solemnity of the moment is conveyed by the geometric rhythms of the monumental figures. While the Virgin seated on a massive marble throne is shown in all her majesty, once again the relationship between the two main figures is symbolized by the interplay of the rumpled folds of their garments.

Konrad Witz
Miraculous Draft of Fishes
panel from the *St. Peter Altarpiece*
1443-1444, panel, 52 × 59½ in. (132 × 151 cm)
Musée d'Art et
d'Histoire, Geneva

The miraculous event is set against the sweeping and easily recognizable backdrop of Lake Geneva, a landscape with which the painter was very familiar. The countryside stretching away to the horizon is interspersed with details that are reflected in the water, or that slope toward the mountains in the background, where the glaciers of Mont Blanc are visible. His observation of natural features is not confined to an analytic representation of reality, but dwells on the vast expanse of nature stretching to infinity.

Grant Wood
Anamosa, Iowa, 1892-
Cedar Rapids, Iowa, 1942

Grant Wood was born in the Midwest, lived his life there, and described that region of the United States in his works. He is one of the most famous members of the regionalist movement, the group of artists whose works present a visual record of American reality in all its many aspects, including the daily life of small towns on the seemingly endless expanses of the West and Midwest. The style used in these works is primarily realistic, with touches of nostalgia, for in fact it was usually directed at the past, eager to present in the most explicit and objective way an authentic version of the nation's traditions. Wood is the author of *American Gothic* (1930), one of the most famous works in American painting, an icon of American culture that represents, more than any other image, the spirit and essence of an epoch. Wood began his career as an artist by enrolling, in 1910, in the Minneapolis School of Design and Handicraft and Normal Art, where he studied under Ernest Batchelder, an advocate of the English Arts and Crafts movement. Later he entered Iowa State University and then the Art Institute of Chicago. During the 1920s he traveled overseas, studying at the Académie Julian in Paris in 1923. During the Great Depression, in 1934, he was appointed state director for Iowa of the Public Works of Art Project and began teaching art at the University of Iowa. His artistic production can be divided into two periods: until 1928 he painted views and landscapes and several portraits in a style not unlike that of French Impressionism; in 1928, following a trip to Munich during which he encountered the late Gothic and Renaissance styles of northern Europe, his way of painting changed. His style became more realistic, more attentive to detail, also more austere and meticulous, its surfaces smooth and its focus clear. *American Gothic* represents the culmination of this evolution. Despite their austerity, Wood's representations of the realities of rural America are not without touches of humor and satire, aspects that make his images seem even more accurate as views of American life in the years of the Depression.

Grant Wood
American Gothic
1930
oil on composition board, 29¼ × 24½ in. (74.3 × 62.4 cm)
Art Institute of Chicago

Some images achieve a special kind of synthesis, a felicitous combination of form and meaning that adds enormously to their evocative power. Such an image is *American Gothic*, which presents the rural society of Iowa at a time when it was struggling to exalt its traditional and puritan moral virtues in the face of new ideas arriving from the industrial, urbanized areas of America. For regionalist painters like Wood, art was a means of keeping the memory of the past vividly alive, a past that was seen as preferable to new ideas, a past that needed to be defended against threats of modernity, against the rise of a new political, social, and economic system. He recalls the virtues of a certain time by way of the subtly satirical presentation of two farmers, father and daughter, presented in front of their farmhouse, the heart of their world. She is absorbed; he gazes out at the viewer with a grimly proud expression, holding before him his pitchfork, the tool of his trade. The models are Wood's sister Nan and his dentist.

Joseph Wright
Wright of Derby
Derby, 1734-1797

Tradition and modernity, admiration for the art of Caravaggio and, at the same time, an interest in scientific and technical discoveries, intertwine and merge in the painting of Joseph Wright, which was in many ways atypical of English eighteenth-century art. Despite his training in London in the studio of the portrait painter Thomas Hudson, Wright was actually more attracted, from the beginning, by compositions with artificial lighting, in the manner of the Dutch Caravaggists, from van Honthorst to Terbrugghen. Hence his journey to Italy, in 1773, was decisive, bringing to a conclusion a line of research begun around 1750, documented by his many candlelit pictures and illustrations of scientific experiments and industrial subjects. His frequent visits to factories and foundries stemmed from his need to draw from life scenes in which artificial lighting is employed. The results are paintings that record the dawn of the Industrial Revolution and reflect the well-known interest in technology of the British. In the last twenty years of his career, he painted classical themes and subjects drawn from Shakespeare, as well as landscapes of his native Derbyshire.

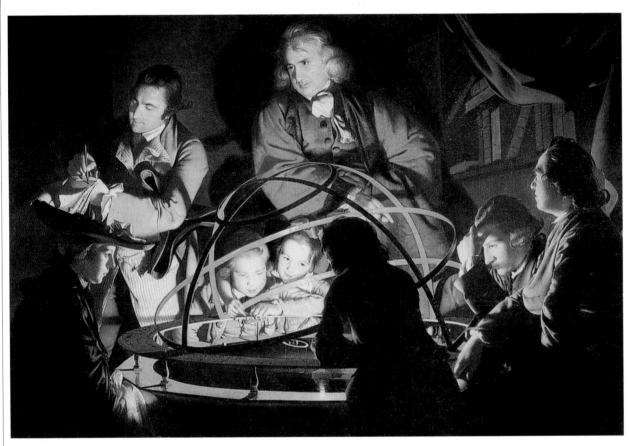

Joseph Wright
A Philosopher Gives a Lesson with a Mechanical Planetarium
1766
oil on canvas
58 × 80 in.
(147.3 × 203.2 cm)
Derby Museum and Art Gallery, Derby

Exhibited at the Society of Artists in 1768 together with the *Experiment with an Air Pump*, the painting shows a group gathered around a planetarium with a lamp in place of the sun. The canvas is animated by an intense play of light and shadow that highlights the faces of the figures, completely absorbed in the philosopher's lesson, creating a self-contained scene that totally excludes the spectator.

Johann Zoffany

Frankfurt, 1733-London, 1810

German by birth, Zoffany trained in the workshop of Marteen Speer, one of the leading exponents of Bavarian Rococo. From 1750 to 1753 he worked in Rome, where he met the portrait painter Anton Raphael Mengs. In 1760 he moved to London, where he changed his surname from Zauffely to Zoffany. Here he found himself in an artistic context in which the main demand was for portraits and conversation pieces. His meeting with the famous actor David Garrick marked a turning point, for it led to the commission of a portrait and a series of theater scenes that, by following a tradition established by Hogarth, brought him immediate success. His great gift for capturing a likeness and his attention to detail constitute the main distinctive features of his pictorial language. He painted numerous portraits of the royal family and in 1772 was nominated as a member of the Royal Academy by George III. In the same year he visited Florence, where he remained until 1778 to paint *The Tribuna of the Uffizi*, commissioned by Queen Charlotte. On his return to London in 1779, he found that tastes had changed and that his fame had been overshadowed by the rising stars of English painting, Reynolds and Gainsborough.

Johann Zoffany
The Tribuna of the Uffizi
1772-1778
oil on canvas
48½ × 61 in.
(123.5 × 155 cm)
Royal Collections,
Windsor Castle

In the famous octagonal Buontalenti Room, classical sculptures on high pedestals are arranged in a disorderly manner, observed by a crowd of ordinary spectators, museum staff, and art lovers. On the red velvet walls it is possible to make out paintings by Pontormo (*Charity*), Reni (*Suicide of Cleopatra*), Raphael (*Madonna of the Chair*, *Madonna del Cardellino*, and *Saint John the Baptist*), Rubens (*Consequences of War*), Pietro da Cortona, Titian, and Hals, "paintings within the painting" of exceptional documentary value.

Francisco de Zurbarán

Fuente de Cantos, 1598-Madrid, 1664

An artist of great appeal, the painter of images that have a penetrating spiritual impact, Zurbarán can even be compared with Rembrandt as regards the highly significant course of his life. An early beginning in the provinces and a successful career with a great many commissions, some of considerable official importance, were followed, from the middle of the century on, by a swift decline due to changes in taste, and then death in poverty and obscurity. From his youth on, Zurbarán belonged to the flourishing Seville school, first as a pupil of Pedro Diaz de Villaneuva and then, from 1617, as an independent painter. An immensely prolific artist, Zurbarán had a workshop in Llerena but sent most of his works to Seville, where he built up a well-deserved reputation. His own specific style became evident as early as 1620: austere spiritual images with sequences of friars, saints, and Holy Virgins captured in significant gestures and concentrated expressions. The young painter's fame grew with the delivery of the twenty-one canvases for the monastery of St. Pablo in Seville. This group of works, now partially dispersed, constitutes an anthology of sculptural figures, of dramatic and determined champions of the faith. In his narrative pictures with various characters, Zurbarán always shunned dynamic compositions in favor of static scenes, in which spiritual intensity and deep emotion outweigh action and interlinking events. In 1629, the city corporation invited Zurbarán to move to Seville, where he received an uninterrupted flow of commissions from various monastic orders, interested in a style of painting that was simultaneously evocative and dramatic, where the inner conflict of the figures and the strength of their faith emerged with great impact. While religious paintings thus remained his favorite, some innovations appeared after 1633, when he painted the *Still Life* now in Pasadena, a rare and striking example of genre painting that is almost metaphysical. In 1634, he moved to Madrid at Velázquez's invitation. There he worked for the court on paintings with secular themes for the royal palace of Buen Retiro. This experience ended quite soon: after a few months he returned to Seville to resume his customary production of religious works. Typical paintings are the captivating images of saintly girls or young women, dressed in sumptuous garments, appearing surprised before the spectator. Around 1650, however, the ascetic spirituality expressed by Zurbarán began to lose ground to the warmer religious images produced by Murillo. He looked for new markets elsewhere, including the colonies in Latin America. Exhausted, Zurbarán moved to Madrid in 1658. He died, alone and forgotten, in 1664.

Francisco de Zurbarán
St. Casilda
c. 1640, oil on canvas
72¼ × 35½ in.
(184 × 90 cm)
Thyssen-Bornemisza
Collection, Madrid

This saint was the
daughter of the governor
of Toledo during the
Moorish domination,
who disobeyed her
Saracen father and took
food to the Arabs'
Christian prisoners.
Surprised by the guards,
she saw the loaves she
was carrying in her skirt
turn miraculously into
flowers.

Below
Francisco de Zurbarán
St. Margaret
c. 1640
oil on canvas
72¼ × 35 ½ in.
(184 × 90 cm)
National Gallery,
London

The series of paintings
of female saints
constitute perhaps
the most captivating
part of Zurbarán's
oeuvre.
Unfortunately, these
groups of paintings
have been dispersed
over the years and
we no longer have the

impression of a mystical
procession of
enchanting inhabitants
of paradise, lining the
aisles of churches or
the corridors of
convents, all of identical
format and often similar
in their features.
St. Margaret is depicted
in traveling clothes,
with a large hat and
striking embroidered
bag. Zurbarán has
conferred a subtle
melancholy upon this
motionless pilgrim,
who possesses a natural
elegance, and he
captures her evocative
gaze and frozen gesture.

Opposite
Francisco de Zurbarán
*Apparition of St. Peter to
St. Peter Nolasco*
1629
oil on canvas
70½ × 87¾ in.
(179 × 223 cm)
Prado, Madrid

A striking combination
of tangible realism and
mystical vision, this
is one of the most

dramatic works in the
whole of seventeenth-
century art. Imbued
with the intense
devotion of Spanish
Catholicism, and based
on the relationship
between two static,
sculptural figures
modeled by the light,
this work is one of
the best examples
of Zurbarán's powers
of concentration.

Through his use of light
and plastic intensity, the
painter succeeds in
making us almost forget
the figure of St. Peter
Nolasco and places the
viewer in the saint's
position of ecstatic and
terrible contemplation
of St. Peter nailed
upside-down to the
cross.

Photographic Credits

Archivio Mondadori Electa, Milan,
courtesy of the Ministero
per i Beni e le Attività Culturali
© Biblioteca Ambrosiana, Milan
© Photo RMN, Paris

We wish to thank the photo archives of
Italian and foreign, public and private
institutions, which have kindly provided
the material for the illustrations
in this volume.

Holders of rights to any unidentified
photograph sources should contact the
publisher.

© G. Balla, J.-M. Basquiat,
M. Beckmann, G. Boldini, P. Bonnard,
G. Braque, S. Davis, G. de Chirico,
W. De Kooning, R. Delaunay,
S. Delaunay, P. Delvaux, M. Denis,
F. Depero, A. Derain, J. Dine,
M. Duchamp, R. Dufy, J. Ensor,
M. Ernst, L. Feininger, N. Gončarova,
G. Grosz, J. Johns, V. Kandinskij, P. Klee,
F. Kline, O. Kokoschka, M. Larionov,
F. Léger, R. Lichtenstein, R. Magritte,
J. Miró, C. Monet, G. Morandi,
E. Munch, K. Noland, G. O'Keeffe,
F. Picabia, J. Pollock, R. Rauschenberg,
M. Ray, P.-A. Renoir/R. Guino,
J. Rosenquist, M. Rothko, G. Rouault,
K. Schmidt-Rottluff, B. Shahn, P. Signac,
D.A. Siqueiros, M. Sironi,
M. de Vlaminck, E. Vuillard, A. Warhol,
G. Wood by SIAE 2005
© Fundación Gala-Salvador Dalí
by SIAE 2005
© Succession Henri Matisse by SIAE 2005
© Succession Pablo Picasso by SIAE 2005

This volume was printed and bound in Spain
by Artes Gráficas Toledo, SAU, in the year 2005